NORTH AMERICA IN QUESTION

Regional Integration in an Era of Economic Turbulence

Can North America survive as a region in light of the political turbulence provoked by the global economic crisis? Or have regional integration and collaboration reached a plateau beyond which disintegration is likely? In *North America in Question*, leading analysts from Canada, the United States, and Mexico provide theoretically innovative and rich empirical reflections on current challenges sweeping the continent and on the faltering political support for North American regionalism.

This collection begins by reviewing the recent trajectories and events that have undermined North America's trilateral relationship, and then addresses concerns that go beyond NAFTA and economic issues, including labour, immigration, energy, the environment, quality of citizenship, borders, women's and civil society struggles, and democratic deficits. Although demonstrating that many informal dimensions of North American integration continue to flourish, the contributors assess whether the future will hold greater economic instability, security crises, and emerging bilateral relationships.

(Studies in Comparative Political Economy and Public Policy)

JEFFREY AYRES is a professor and chair of the Department of Political Science at Saint Michael's College.

LAURA MACDONALD is a professor in the Department of Political Science at Carleton University.

Studies in Comparative Political Economy and Public Policy

Editors: MICHAEL HOWLETT, DAVID LAYCOCK (Simon Fraser University), and STEPHEN MCBRIDE (McMaster University)

Studies in Comparative Political Economy and Public Policy is designed to showcase innovative approaches to political economy and public policy from a comparative perspective. While originating in Canada, the series will provide attractive offerings to a wide international audience, featuring studies with local, subnational, cross-national, and international empirical bases and theoretical frameworks.

Editorial Advisory Board

Jeffrey Ayres, St Michael's College, Vermont
Neil Bradford, University of Western Ontario
Janine Brodie, University of Alberta
William Carroll, University of Victoria
William Coleman, McMaster University
Rodney Haddow, University of Toronto
Jane Jenson, Université de Montréal
Laura Macdonald, Carleton University
Riane Mahon, Carleton University
Michael Mintrom, University of Auckland
Grace Skogstad, University of Toronto
Leah Vosko, York University
Kent Weaver, Brookings Institution
Linda White, University of Toronto
Robert Young, University of Western Ontario

For a list of books published in the series, see page 407.

North America in Question

Regional Integration in an Era of Economic Turbulence

EDITED BY JEFFREY AYRES AND
LAURA MACDONALD

UNIVERSITY OF TORONTO PRESS
Toronto Buffalo London

© University of Toronto Press 2012
Toronto Buffalo London
www.utppublishing.com
Printed in Canada

ISBN 978-1-4426-4214-0 (cloth)
ISBN 978-1-4426-1114-6 (paper)

Library and Archives Canada Cataloguing in Publication

North America in question : regional integration in an era of economic turbulence / edited by Jeffrey Ayres and Laura Macdonald.

(Studies in comparative political economy and public policy)
Includes bibliographical references and index.
ISBN 978-1-4426-4214-0 (bound). – ISBN 978-1-4426-1114-6 (pbk.)

1. North America – Economic integration.   2. North America – Economic conditions – 21st century.   3. North America – Economic conditions – 21st century – Regional disparities.   4. North America – Politics and government – 21st century.   5. North America – Social conditions – 21st century.   6. Global Financial Crisis, 2008–2009.   7. Economic forecasting – North America.   I. Ayres, Jeffrey McKelvey   II. Macdonald, Laura, 1960–   III. Series: Studies in comparative political economy and public policy

HC95.N62 2012   330.97'0054   C2012-904484-9

This book has been published with the help of a grant from the Canadian Federation for the Humanities and Social Sciences, through the Awards to Scholarly Publications Program, using funds provided by the Social Sciences and Humanities Research Council of Canada.

University of Toronto Press acknowledges the financial assistance to its publishing program of the Canada Council for the Arts and the Ontario Arts Council.

  Canada Council   Conseil des Arts   ONTARIO ARTS COUNCIL
for the Arts   du Canada   CONSEIL DES ARTS DE L'ONTARIO

University of Toronto Press acknowledges the financial support of the Government of Canada through the Canada Book Fund for its publishing activities.

Contents

Contributors

James P. Allan, Department of Political Science, Wittenberg University, U.S.A.

Jeffrey Ayres, Department of Political Science, Saint Michael's College, U.S.A.

Brian Bow, Department of Political Science, Dalhousie University, Canada

Janine Brodie, Department of Political Science, University of Alberta, Canada

Jorge Cadena-Roa, Centro de Investigaciones Interdisciplinarias en Ciencias y Humanidades, Universidad Nacional Autónoma de México, Mexico

Stephen Clarkson, Department of Political Science, University of Toronto, Canada

Neil Craik, School of Environment, Enterprise and Development, University of Waterloo, Canada

Christina Gabriel, Department of Political Science, Carleton University, Canada

Randall Germain, Department of Political Science, Carleton University, Canada

Emily Gilbert, Department of Geography and Canadian Studies, University of Toronto, Canada

Stephanie R. Golob, Department of Political Science, Baruch College–CUNY, U.S.A.

Teresa Healy, Canadian Labour Congress, Canada

Rosalba Icaza, Institute of Social Studies, Erasmus University, Netherlands

Laura Macdonald, Department of Political Science, Carleton University, Canada

Debora L. VanNijnatten, Department of Political Science and North American Studies, Wilfrid Laurier University, Canada

Richard Vengroff, Department of Political Science, Kennesaw State University, U.S.A.

Acknowledgments

All of the authors in this volume have made important contributions over the years to ongoing discussions over the uncertain future of North America. There have been countless workshops and conferences in Canada, the United States, and Mexico in which most of us have kept alive dialogue about the evolving North American relationship, a largely trilateral arrangement that has taken on multiple economic, political, social, and cultural dimensions since the creation of the North American Free Trade Agreement (NAFTA) in 1994. The idea for a book that would respond specifically to growing concerns over the future of North America in the midst of what has become referred to as the 'Great Recession' first emerged in February 2009 out of discussions during two panels titled 'The Past and Future of North American Integration,' organized for the meeting of the International Studies Association in New York City. Later that summer, the editors of this volume approached Daniel Quinlan of the University of Toronto Press with the idea for a book that would reflect on the future of North America. We are grateful to Daniel for being such an early enthusiast of the project and for helping us secure a contract in advance from his Publications Committee.

We began this project in earnest, then, in the summer of 2009 by developing a set of theoretical and empirical 'contributor themes' questioning the future of North American integration. We then invited leading scholars in Canada, the United States, and Mexico who had been actively working around North American issues to contribute original chapters to the project. We wish to acknowledge the financial support of the Canadian Embassy in Washington, D.C., which awarded us a Canada Conference Grant to support a two-day workshop hosted by

Richard Vengroff, then Dean of the College of Humanities and Social Sciences at Kennesaw State University, and held at the Consulate General of Canada in Atlanta. This grant allowed us to invite all of the contributors (all but three were able to attend) to the 'North America in Question' workshop, to present chapter drafts and to engage in collaborative discussions on how to strengthen the book's theoretical and empirical coherence. This workshop was essential to producing the final manuscript, and we thank Dean Vengroff and many of his colleagues at Kennesaw State as well as officials at the Canadian Consulate in Atlanta, all of whom were wonderful hosts for this event. We also appreciate the thoughtful discussant commentary provided at that workshop by David Biette, Director of the Canada Institute, Woodrow Wilson International Center for Scholars, and by Michele Zebich-Knos, Professor of Political Science and Director, International Policy Management Program, from Kennesaw State University. Mr Kim Butler, then Director General, North America Relations, of Canada's Department of Foreign Affairs and International Trade, also provided useful reflections during the workshop on the North American agenda.

The editors also wish to acknowledge separately support they received for research on this project. Jeffrey Ayres benefited from a spring 2010 semester sabbatical from his teaching and administrative duties as Chair of the Department of Political Science at Saint Michael's College, and also from a Research Grant from the Canadian Embassy as well as a Faculty Development grant from St Michael's College. Laura Macdonald benefited from a sabbatical leave from the Department of Political Science at Carleton University in 2010–11, and thanks the Social Sciences and Humanities Research Council of Canada for its financial support. She also thanks Blayne Haggart for his research assistance. Finally, we gratefully acknowledge that this book has been published with the help of a grant from the Canadian Federation for the Humanities and Social Sciences, through the Awards to Scholarly Publications Program, using funds provided by the Social Sciences and Humanities Research Council of Canada.

NORTH AMERICA IN QUESTION

Regional Integration in an Era of Economic Turbulence

Introduction: North America in Question

JEFFREY AYRES AND LAURA MACDONALD

Recent discussions of the North American region have had an air of scepticism, uncertainty, resignation, and even gloom. The idea that North America – viewed herein as Canada, the United States, and Mexico – is evolving toward a more deeply integrated region is unravelling. Strong and politically threatening lobbies have emerged to oppose the North American project, and North America appears to lack a broad constituency for pursuing new forms of cooperation. Whether through a continuation of top-down trilateralism or through a revamped continentalism from below through cross-border civil society engagement, North American trilateral engagement is at its lowest level since the early 1990s. Furthermore, the North American Free Trade Agreement (NAFTA), once heralded by governments and economists in Canada, the United States, and Mexico as the key to the economic prosperity of the region, appears to have run its course. NAFTA seems to have failed to put the region on a higher-growth path; meanwhile, China, India, and Brazil are experiencing higher growth rates while experimenting with elements of state capitalism that wilfully ignore NAFTA's neoliberal orthodoxy. The global financial crisis, born in the United States, has hit the region hard, with profound implications for the future of continental economic integration and more broadly for what limited sense of regional community may have existed. Mexico, which was supposed to be the main beneficiary of NAFTA, has been struggling through a crisis characterized by severe economic, political, and security challenges. The United States appears increasingly unsure of itself: sharply divided politically, beset by a dysfunctional political system and by a public uncharacteristically lacking confidence in their nation's economic future and global leadership. Meanwhile, although Canada appears less destabilized by the economic crisis, the recent Conservative victory confirms the leadership of a party and prime minister with no interest in deepening the trilateral relationship.

Additionally, the mechanisms for political governance of the region remain in doubt. NAFTA created very few regional institutions, and most of those that exist have little relevance (see Clarkson 2008; Ayres and Macdonald 2006). The labour and environmental side agreements, which attracted some attention and excitement in the mid-1990s as potential mechanisms for civil society engagement, have largely been deemed inconsequential. In 2005, after the 9/11 terrorist attacks on the United States had reshaped continental relationships and threatened cross-border trading relationships, the three governments created the Security and Prosperity Partnership of North America (SPP) as a means of extending the benefits of continental integration after most elements of the NAFTA agreement had been implemented. The SPP's proponents had hoped to deepen regional integration on the basis of broad-based regulatory harmonization achieved through bureaucratic negotiations designed to bypass the various political obstacles and protectionist impulses of the legislative arenas. But at some point during 2009, the three governments pulled the plug on the SPP, without any fanfare or public announcement, leaving the annual North American Leadership Summit (NALS) as the only remaining process for continuing trilateral discussions. And even the future of that initiative appears in doubt: the meeting planned for Canada in the summer of 2010 was postponed until the spring of 2011 and then postponed again (Robertson 2011, 43).* As a result of the SPP's demise, the framework for political governance of North America for possibly managing problems of cross-border concern has been left in doubt, and pressures to abandon the trilateral model have grown stronger. This was captured recently in the title of a 2009 *Economist* article, 'Canada and NAFTA: No Mariachis Please' (2009), and more dramatically illustrated by the move by Canada and the United States to exclude Mexico beginning in February 2011 from so-called Perimeter Security and Economic Competitiveness discussions.[1]

In this context, North America faces an existential dilemma: Does it exist at all as a meaningful political entity, economic region, cultural idea, or community in the midst of continued global economic turbulence and changing and unpredictable political realignments? Clearly,

---

* A sixth summit was held in Washington, D.C., in April 2012.

with hindsight, even before the global financial crisis erupted in late 2008, questions were being raised about the substance and future of the North American region. One of the most important recent academic evaluations of North America, by Stephen Clarkson, is titled provocatively *Does North America Exist?*, and questions whether North America 'exists in any way similar to the EU, with its increasing political, economic, sociological, and cultural integration' (2008, 15). A 2007 collection edited by Isabel Studer and Carol Wise titled *Requiem or Revival?* also suggests further uncertainty. Although the book's subtitle, *The Promise of North American Integration*, appears somewhat optimistic about the prospects for deeper integration, many of the book's contributors highlight the limitations of NAFTA and the obstacles to deeper integration and strengthening of a sense of community across the continent. A more recent volume, *Contentious Politics in North America: National Protest and Transnational Collaboration under Continental Integration* (Ayres and Macdonald 2009), highlights the long and still evolving opposition to integration undertaken by continental civil society groups. While earlier civil society mobilizations and cross-border exchanges sought to develop a more coherent social democratic and environmentally sustainable alternative to NAFTA, more recent protests have included right-wing, xenophobic impulses condemning any efforts at cross-border cooperation. Finally, Robert Pastor's most recent effort, *The North American Idea: A Vision of a Continental Future* (Pastor 2011), seems the most optimistic in its efforts both to define North America and to argue for its existence as a strategic foundation for continued U.S. leadership into the twenty-first century.

This book brings together leading analysts from the three North American countries to reflect on the region's immediate challenges, which include the recent financial crisis and broader and continued global economic instability, which have only intensified the political and economic challenges across the region. One of our central preoccupations is whether North American integration has reached a plateau, and we consider whether continued integration is inevitable or whether a disintegration of the project of a deeper North American community is more likely. The contributors to this volume consider the impact that the current financial instability, deep and prolonged economic recession, mounting political uncertainty, and mushrooming cross-border problems across the three states are having on the North American project. Will the current impulses away from trilateralism and towards bilateralism further destabilize the North American region? In the face of rising protectionist pressures and nationalist passions, can a more transparent and inclusive form of regional governance be developed to respond to the burgeoning array of transborder problems involving drugs, migrants, a deteriorating environment, energy concerns, terrorist threats, and economic decline? What about the perceived democratic deficit across the region? And finally, could the inclusion of a wider array of civil society stakeholders inject future discussions on North America with a greater sense of legitimacy and wider public acceptance?

In addition to providing a timely appraisal of current economic uncertainty and its impact on the various dimensions of North American integration, we hope to develop a fresh theoretical approach to understanding North American issues. Three conceptual perspectives are considered variously throughout the book to help readers understand the recent evolution of the North American region as well as evaluate trends towards convergence or divergence. First, we invite interpretations from the 'new regionalism' school, which (among other things) emphasizes developments in the broader global economic environment, a concern for the diversity of actors involved in integration processes, and an interest in the informal or illicit dimensions to continental integration that are often overlooked in mainstream integration theory. Second, we consider insights from the literature on the 'democratic deficit' and the potential democratizing impact on regional governance if a wider array of stakeholders were to participate in the continent's civil society. Finally, we are interested in ideational aspects of North America, encouraging more consideration of the role played by ideas, norms, and identities on the construction (or destruction) of a North American community.

Overall, we argue, North America in its multiple dimensions does exist and will continue to exist. Despite the challenges the region faces, high levels of economic integration persist, and this creates shared problems that require some degree of conscious cooperation and public governance. Nevertheless, the prevailing economic model on which economic integration in North America was based, one that – arguably, more than in any other world region – assumed that free trade and liberalized markets would deliver higher standards of living for all residents, has been subjected to fundamental criticism. Moreover, the political model of shallow governance (Ayres and Macdonald 2006), characterized by limited regional institutions, entrenched state sovereignty, and lack of democratic participation by citizens in defining the future of the region, has also failed, as witnessed by the demise of the SPP. The so-called bicycle theory of multilateral trade liberalization (Bergsten and Cline 1982, 71) posits that multilateral trade talks must move forward towards higher levels of liberalization or else they will collapse. If the same is true of regional integration, then the North American project is in deep trouble.[2]

Impact of the Global Financial Crisis on the North American Model

The financial crisis has had a dramatic impact on the economies of the three North American states in the short term. It has also raised important questions about the future of the economic model on which North American integration was based. While both Canada and the United States are facing economic problems not seen for decades, the economic crisis hit much harder in Mexico, which was already facing significant economic challenges. In 2008, economic growth was sluggish: only 0.4% in Canada, 0.4% in the United States, and 1.3% in Mexico. For 2009, IMF figures showed a decline of 2.5% in the Canadian GDP, a decline of 2.7% in the United States, and a dismal decline of 6.1% in Mexico. Moreover, the U.S. recovery has been anemic and is still uncertain, with a 2.8% GDP growth rate in 2010 and 2.7% predicted for 2011. The Canadian economy has seen somewhat more respectable growth levels – 3.1% in 2010 and 2.8% predicted for 2011 – but its recovery still depends on what happens to the U.S. economy. The Mexican economy has, quite surprisingly, bounced back, with robust levels of 5.5% growth in 2010 and a predicted 4.6% for 2011, but its economic future is also tied to the U.S. economy and its continued recovery will depend on the impact of its security crisis (see the Cadena-Roa chapter in this volume; see also Table I.1).

Even though Canada, and to a lesser extent Mexico, had maintained significant autonomy from the U.S. financial system, both countries' economies have been affected seriously in the medium term by the downturn and the still sluggish economic growth of their major trading partner, the United States. Mexico has also been hard hit by the recession's impact on migrants' remittances. U.S. border control policies have done little to reduce the flow of migrants; the recession, on the other hand, seems to have reduced migration at least temporarily. Mexico's statistical agency, INEGI, reports that migration declined by over 50% between August 2007 and August 2008, from 455,000 to 204,000 (Lit-

Table I.1. Gross domestic product, annual percentage change, selected years (constant prices, domestic currency)

	1990	1994	1995	2000	2001	2002	2003	2004	2005	2006	2007	2008	2009	2010	2011e
							Annual percentage change								
Canada	0.2	4.8	2.8	5.2	1.8	2.9	1.9	3.1	3.0	2.9	2.5	0.4	−2.5	3.1	2.8
Mexico	5.1	4.4	−6.2	6.6	−0.2	0.8	1.7	4.0	3.2	5.1	3.3	1.3	−6.1	5.5	4.6
United States	1.9	4.1	2.5	4.1	1.1	1.8	2.5	3.6	3.1	2.7	2.1	0.4	−2.7	2.8	2.7

e = IMF estimate

Source: International Monetary Fund, World Economic Outlook Database, April 2011, http://www.imf.org/external/pubs/ft/weo/2011/01/weodata/index.aspx, accessed 31 May 2011.

tlefield 2009). In 2009, remittances declined by a record 15.7%; in 2010, they remained level; they are expected to recover gradually, depending on the fate of the U.S. economy (CBS News, 2010; Harrup, 2011). The exact size of remittances is difficult to calculate; that said, they represent a significant element of Mexico's gross domestic product (GDP), and a decline in remittances has serious implications for the country's economy. While neoliberal leaders currently remain in place in Canada and Mexico, the economic crisis brought about a dramatic shift in U.S. leadership and continues to destabilize political alignments in that country. The election of Barack Obama, who during his election campaign called for a renegotiation of NAFTA,[3] signalled general disenchantment with free trade in the political system of the region's hegemon, as well as rising protectionist pressures and a temporary revival of Keynesianism. All three countries adopted stimulus packages and deficit spending to counter the recession, yet these policies have increasingly been questioned as government deficits have soared. U.S. border control policies in the wake of 9/11 have been perceived by Canadian businesses and governments as unfair restrictions on Canada's access to the U.S. economy – access that NAFTA was designed to guarantee. The same can be said of the more recent 'Buy American' provision of the 2009 American Recovery and Reinvestment Act adopted by the Obama administration to counter the threat to American jobs.

Most concerning for advocates of greater integration is the prospect that the effects of the economic crisis will not be limited to the short to medium term and that we may be seeing a long-term structural evolution of the North American economy, one that will affect intraregional trade. NAFTA was undertaken as part of an economic strategy that envisioned ever higher levels of integrated cross-border production based on the 'just in time' principle. A just-in-time production strategy is designed around the idea that instead of stockpiling large quantities of finished goods and spare parts, producers contract suppliers to provide needed parts within hours when required. This strategy often depended on rapid transportation across the Canada–U.S. and U.S–Mexico land borders. After the adoption of the Canada–US Free Trade Agreement (CUSFTA) and NAFTA, we saw a dramatic increase in cross-border trade and investment levels and in intrafirm trade. Intraregional trade rose some 200% in the first years after NAFTA was implemented, which was much higher than the rise in trade with the rest of the world.

However, the recent crises in the automobile and steel sectors, which were perhaps the most integrated industries in this North American economy, have called into question this model of North American economic development. These problems are not just related to the 2008 crisis, although they were certainly aggravated by it. A 2007 Conference Board of Canada briefing report stated that U.S. border controls meant that Canadian exporters had changed their approach to trade since 9/11, adopting less efficient practices of stockpiling goods in warehouses – practices that had prevailed before just-in-time was adopted: 'These responses may indicate an erosion of some of the advantages of greater U.S. market access gained under the free trade agreement and its successor, [NAFTA]. This, in turn, could make it less attractive to buy Canadian inputs or locate production in Canada, ultimately diminishing Canadian living standards' (Goldfarb 2007 [June], 2). A 2008 Conference Board report, authored by Danielle Goldfarb and Doris Chu, argues that a rapid increase in Canadian firms' integration into global and regional supply chains that occurred in the 1990s reached a plateau after 2000, largely reflecting decreased Canada–U.S. trade in inputs. This report notes that the post-9/11 security environment is not to blame for the slowdown in trade volumes; instead, it targets remaining non-tariff barriers, such as regulatory differences among Canada, the United States, and Mexico (Chu and Goldfarb 2008). Another factor may be increased competition from China and other emerging markets (Goldfarb 2009).

Mexico faces particularly serious problems in the current environment. In recent years, Mexico has been one of the slowest-growing countries in the Latin America region, in contrast to countries such as Brazil, Chile, and Argentina, which registered high levels of growth through the 1990s and early 2000s. The low-value-added economic model adopted by Mexico after the debt crisis, designed to attract industry to the *maquiladora* region based on its low wage levels, was strongly challenged by China's entry into the WTO in 2001. Mexico's failure to diversify its economy into more high-value-added sectors has resulted in low growth levels and persistent high levels of poverty. The crisis in peasant agriculture after the Salinas government's rapid and unilateral liberalization of agriculture prior to NAFTA has devastated rural areas and fuelled high levels of migration. Mexico's competitiveness has also been adversely affected by the drug cartels' relocation of drug transshipments from Colombia to Mexican territory. This development has led to high levels of drug-related violence that have driven away investment, particularly in the border areas that were earlier benefiting from the NAFTA strategy.

Overall, levels of intraregional trade appear to be declining significantly in the North American region – more so than in another other world regions (see Table I.2).

Cross-border travel has also declined dramatically post-9/11. U.S. residents' cross-border travel to Canada declined from 38,743,000 crossings in 2000 to 17,784,000 in 2008. (Canadian crossings remained more or less stable.) U.S. residents' cross-border travel to Mexico declined over the same period, from 94,140,000 to 73,987,000.[4] The future of North American integration thus appears unclear. These patterns have been magnified by the economic crisis, deflationary pressures, and the threat of a double-dip recession; presumably, interactions among the three countries will increase again once economic recovery occurs, but it is not clear whether they will return to pre-crisis levels.

The economic crisis has exacerbated a trend that was already prominent in the North American region – the move away from trilateral relations towards 'double bilateralism,' with discussions and relations largely taking place within two dyads: Canada–U.S. on the one hand, and U.S.–Mexico on the other (see the chapter by Golob in this volume). This tendency became particularly apparent with the agreement between Obama and Harper on 4 February 2011 to move forward on a 'Shared Vision for Perimeter Security and Economic Competitiveness.' The declaration of the agreement, which referred directly to the objective of economic recovery after the recession, involves bilateral cooperation in four areas: 'addressing threats early; trade facilitation, economic growth and jobs; integrated cross-border law enforcement; and critical infrastructure and cyber security.'[5] The use of the term 'perimeter' is striking, since this term was used and then rejected in the post-9/11 context because of its connotations of a surrender of sovereignty by member-states. As well, this agreement clearly excludes Mexico, in what the title of an article by Duncan Wood calls 'Mexico's latest, greatest rejection' (2011, 1). The consolidation of a double-bilateral North America with the United States at the centre appears to have been confirmed by this recent development, even though the outcome of the perimeter talks remains unclear.

Theories of Regionalism – Where Does North America Fit?

One objective of this volume is to evaluate the usefulness of dominant theories of regionalism to explain the North American case. The North American pattern of a rapid increase in levels of integration followed

Table I.2. North American (NAFTA) intra- and inter-regional merchandise trade ($US current)

	2000		2004		2005		2008		2009	
	$US millions	%	$US millions	%	$US millions	%	$US millions	%	$US millions	%
Intra-NAFTA exports	680,438	55.5	739,094	56	824,478	55.9	1,013,216	49.8	767,507	47.9
NAFTA exports to world	544,482	44.5	580,523	44	651,286	44.1	1,022,419	50.2	834,886	52.1
Total	1,224,920	100.0	1,319,617	100.0	1,475,764	100.0	2,035,635	100.0	1,602,393	100.0
Intra-NAFTA imports	670,810	39.8	717,750	35.7	790,881	34.6	967,688	33.2	716,970	32.9
NAFTA imports from world	1,015,978	60.2	1,293,920	64.3	1,492,476	65.4	1,943,261	66.8	1,459,745	67.1
Total	1,686,788	100	2,011,670	100.0	2,283,357	100.0	2,910,949	100.0	2,176,715	100.0

Source: Calculated from World Trade Organization Statistics Database, http://stat.wto.org/Home/WSDBHome.aspx?Language=E, accessed 31 May 2011.

by stagnation and (at least short-term) decline is not easily explained using dominant theories, based on the European model, that predict inevitable and irreversible progress towards ever higher levels of integration. The most influential theories of regionalism – functionalism and neofunctionalism – emerged in the context of postwar integration in Europe. Functionalism, associated with advocates of European integration like David Mitrany, was highly technocratic, predicting that the promotion of increased cooperation in technical 'low politics' areas by enlightened, rational elites would gradually and inevitably lead to higher levels of integration. In reaction to the apolitical character of this approach, neofunctionalist theorists like Haas placed greater emphasis on the role of non-governmental actors, who would, they believed, gradually gain an interest in greater cross-border cooperation and push for higher levels of integration. They believed that the formation of a regional bloc, and the ensuing rapid expansion of trade and investment linkages, would generate problems that would lead to higher levels of institutionalization and cooperation. New transnational institutions would address technical problems, and once progress was made in a specific area, a spillover process would automatically generate cooperation in ever more areas (O'Brien 1995, 696). Neofunctionalists also emphasized the important role played by supranational institutions, which would promote higher levels of cooperation and to which states would eventually cede elements of their sovereignty.

The authors of the integration project in North America explicitly rejected the European model of integration advocated by the functionalists and neofunctionalists. The United States in particular, but also Mexico and Canada, jealously protected state sovereignty and were sceptical of international institutions. As a result, North America has few institutions, and those that exist are extremely weak. Moreover, a prominent feature of North American integration has been the opposition it has generated from non-state actors other than business, in contrast to the pro-integrationist role that neofunctionalists expected civil society to play (see Ayres and Macdonald 2009). And, as discussed in this volume, the process of integration has not been automatic. Theories of North American regionalism thus must remain open to the role of contingency and agency in the evolution of continental relationships.

We suggest in this volume that alternative theoretical models and conceptual approaches provide more insight into the dynamics of regionalism in the North American context. Theories of the new regionalism emerged in the 1990s in response to a new wave of regional integration schemes, including CUSFTA and NAFTA, but also including new regional blocs in Asia, Africa, and the Americas. While dominant European approaches focused primarily on intraregional dynamics as instigating and promoting integration, the theorists of the new regionalism placed significant emphasis on the role of the broader global economy. In North America, such international factors as the growth of regionalism in Europe, the decline of U.S. international hegemony, and the rise of U.S. protectionism, as well as the general process of globalization, played an important role in the decision of North American state actors to pursue a regionalist strategy. As well, we argue, the global financial crisis and the resulting continued economic uncertainty are playing an important role in the current crisis of the regional project, as well as in the rise of other important global competitors, such as China.

Another important contribution of the new regionalism approach is its promotion of a more pluralistic understanding of the nature of regionalism and of the actors involved in the process. In contrast to the rather statist orientation of much of the European literature, theorists of the new regionalism emphasize the importance of non-state actors (see, for example, Söderbaum 2007). As we will explore in this volume, both business and non-business civil society actors are playing an important role in the evolution of the North American region. Business leaders were important advocates of CUSFTA and NAFTA and during the SPP were taken on board as official advisers to the heads of state. The leaders even created a North American Competitiveness Council (NACC), composed of representatives of big business in the three countries, to advise them on how to increase the competitiveness of the North American region.

Non-business civil society actors were, on the other hand, extremely critical of what they viewed as the secretive and exclusionary model of decision making adopted by both NAFTA and the SPP. Although it failed to derail CUSFTA and NAFTA, civil society opposition did provoke President Clinton to adopt side agreements on labour and the environment in an attempt to satisfy important constituencies of the Democratic Party. The anticipation of civil society opposition also played an important role in shaping the SPP. Fearing popular opposition to more ambitious integration projects, the SPP's architects adopted a low-profile model of bureaucratic cooperation and consultation across borders that would, they hoped, result in regulatory convergence without requiring parliamentary or congressional approval. Nonetheless, the SPP generated significant public scepticism and opposition. True to its below-the-radar style, the SPP was quietly dropped by the three North American governments, without public announcement or consultation. Civil society leaders have claimed victory in its demise. Clearly, both business and non-business civil society actors have played an important role in the evolution of the North American region. The focus of the 'new regionalism' on the role of diverse actors also encompasses, to some extent, a greater emphasis on the role of agency in the construction of new regions.

Finally, in addition to recognizing the diversity of the actors involved in the integration process, theorists of the new regionalism tend to adopt a more holistic and pluralistic understanding of regionalization itself. Mainstream integration theories tend to focus on the more obvious elements of regionalization that are explicit objectives of the architects of integration (such as new regional institutions or increased trade and investment flows); by contrast, theories of the new regionalism emphasize unintended or even unwanted dimensions of integration. These may include 'illicit' activities such as the trade in drugs or weapons, undocumented migration, and the widespread devastation of small-scale Mexican farmers, who are unable to compete with subsidized U.S. agricultural exports. As we will see in this volume, perhaps because the initial objectives of North American integration were so limited (essentially just an increase in economic linkages, with little attention to the social and political dimensions of integration), the unintended consequences are many, and the mechanisms to deal with these problems in a cooperative fashion are extremely limited. These unintended or informal elements of the regionalization process may have important consequences for the formal dimensions.

As well, theories of the new regionalism, which often focus on regions in the global South, pay more attention to the development implications of these regional arrangements. The case of North America – the first region in the economic world to include both a developing country (Mexico) and two of the world's wealthiest countries (Canada and the United States) – has potentially important lessons for other developing countries. Mexico's failure to achieve significantly improved living standards despite its access to these two affluent markets, and its accelerating crisis of political security, have presented significant challenges to the North American integration project and may help explain the region's weak level of cohesion and legitimacy. Again, many unintended consequences of integration – including changing immigration flows across the U.S.–Mexican border, continental labour market restructuring, the fate of women's rights, and pressures to privatize Mexico's energy resources – are relevant to this developmental focus.

Ideas Matter: Restructuring North American Politics

While theories of the new regionalism provide significant insights into the political economy of regionalization in the context of globalization, other important perspectives can be drawn from constructivist approaches. Mainstream integration theories tend to take interests as givens and to view ideas as epiphenomenal. Constructivists do not deny the importance of interests, but they also contend that there is no such thing as a 'real' interest independent from the discursive context in which that interest emerges (Diez and Wiener 2004, 86). Moreover, what is critical is how political actors perceive and interpret the idea of a region and notions of 'regionness': all regions are socially constructed and hence politically contested (Hurrell 1995, 38–9). In recent years, constructivist approaches have become increasingly influential in the study of the European Union (Diez and Wiener 2004, 9; Rosamond 2001). Also, as Larner and Walters note, while some of the 'new regionalists' have begun to engage with constructivism and have placed greater attention on the 'inventedness' of regions, most 'remain wedded to the notion that regions, the objects of "new regionalism," exist prior to discourses about them' (2002, 393).

In the context of North America, most of the early literature relied heavily on interest-based approaches. Both neoliberal advocates of integration and neo-Marxist critics tended to approach the birth and evolution of the North American region as the outcome of the pursuit of rational self-interest by state and business actors. More recently, however, and particularly since 9/11, some authors have emphasized the importance of processes of identity construction. The 'idea' of North America has certainly been debated and constructed in a multitude of continental civil society venues, from social activist groups on the U.S.–Mexican border, to labour and environmental groups engaged in cross-border collaboration, to academic circles. Civil society networks, the proliferation of conferences post-NAFTA, and the rapid cross-border diffusion of information via the Internet have encouraged a process of learning about the 'continental other' – a process that has challenged the elite-driven conception of North America as a model of trade and investment liberalization in what socially has otherwise been a vacuum. Conferences about 'inventing' or 'envisioning' North

America have been held in major research universities across Canada, the United States, and Mexico, including Duke University, Carleton University, and the Universidad Nacional Autónoma de México, where academics with little previous contact have grappled with visions of an emergent North American community.

Thus, we feel that ideational or constructivist accounts are particularly useful in explaining the recent stalling of the seemingly intractable integration process. Emily Gilbert (2005) argues that ever since the 9/11 attacks, a discourse of inevitability has surrounded discussions of North American integration. This language of inevitability, she argues, 'harnesses facts and figures, institutions, and practices in such a way as to legitimate particular kinds of neoliberal proposals in the name of national sovereignty while, at the same time, limiting the options that can be placed on the table for discussion. It is this fatalism that has infused the proposals with their greatest potency' (2005, 204). Despite this apparent inevitability of integration, she argues, a Foucauldian perspective emphasizes the potential to contest dominant discourses: 'Discourse transmits and produces power; it reinforces it, but also undermines and exposes it, renders it fragile and makes it possible to thwart it' (Foucault 1980, cited in ibid., 216). As she comments, the rise of protectionism in the United States and 'generally lukewarm interest in the proposals [for deeper integration] also indicate that the inevitability of deeper North American economic integration is shaky at best' (ibid., 216).

Stephanie Golob (2002) presents another constructivist reading of Canada–U.S. border politics after 9/11 in the North American context. As she argues, constructivist accounts help account for a variety of state behaviours that might otherwise be viewed as unlikely or irrational: 'States ... delineate and judge their options for international action based upon criteria that may advance symbolic or identity-inscribed values as opposed to material interests' (2002, 8). She notes that constructivist scholars view state identity as consisting of both 'a subjective self-schema, or the story one tells to oneself about what makes the self unique, and an inter-subjective assessment of the meaning of the self and its role in a society of states based upon how one is viewed by others.' The project of North American integration, and its discourse of inevitability, has thus been troubled by ambivalence among the participating states regarding 'mutual identification,' based on the historical asymmetry of the region and historical sensitivities over sovereignty.

Thus a teleological version of 'the story of "North America" is punctuated by the intrusion of ideological and identity-inscribed borders erected by the two national governments and defended via foreign policy rhetoric, ostensibly to protect "the nation" from the neighbor's designs on its sovereignty, security, and identity' (ibid., 2002). If successful region-building projects are based on a process of gradual identification of all participating states as 'us' and identification of outsiders as 'them,' the architects of North American regionalism have failed woefully. If this is true even for the Canada–U.S. relationship discussed in this article by Golob, it is even more applicable to the U.S.–Mexican relationship, which gradually has been submerged below a protectionist and xenophobic tide in American public opinion.[6] Subjective identification between Canadians and Mexicans remains very weak, and Mexicans' normally rather benign view of Canada has been aggravated by Canada's 2009 decision to impose a visa requirement on Mexican visitors. The disappearance or demise of the SPP, despite official state support from the three member-states (until the election of Obama), and despite support from the corporate sector in all three countries, and the newer push by Canada and the United States towards exclusive northern border perimeter discussions, is a sign of the contingency of regional projects. This collection contributes to our understanding of the role that identity construction and the social construction of interests perform in processes of regional integration or disintegration.

Citizenship and the North American Democratic Deficit

Another important contribution this collection makes is that the authors consider the implications of recent events for democracy and citizenship in the North American region. As previously noted, civil society actors have done much to shape the debate over North American integration since the divisive debates and negotiations over the Canada–U.S. Free Trade Agreement in the mid-1980s. Since that time, much of the ongoing debate – including some of the previous discussion – over continental integration has revolved around the socio-economic costs and benefits of strengthening relations among Canada, the United States, and Mexico. Accelerated losses of manufacturing jobs, increased conflicts over drugs and illegal immigration, devastated small farmers, unequal distribution of productivity gains – these are but some of the ongoing concerns that have motivated civil society groups across the continent to engage in frequent acts of protest and transnational collaboration (see Ayres and Macdonald 2009). However, North American integration and its limited governance structures can also be criticized on normative grounds, and found to suffer from democratic deficits that arguably have further compromised the project of building a North American community.

The question of North America's future cannot be disentangled from concerns over democracy and citizenship, and this volume discusses democratic deficits – in terms of both institutions and actors – as they relate to the trends and turbulence afflicting the region. Our concern lies with the evidence that anti-democratic outcomes seem to be evolving from attempts to deepen North American integration – particularly through the failed SPP and the Canada–U.S. perimeter security talks – attempts that do not invite a close examination by elected representatives or wider public scrutiny. Ironically, the death of the SPP and its rebranding in the NALS process seemed at first to create higher-level diplomatic leadership trilateralism with even less opportunity for citizen input; where some imperfect institutionalization and some guarantee that governments were working on a North American 'agenda' emerged from the SPP, the rebranding of the SPP through the NALS further entrenched a continental democratic deficit. However, the new Canada–U.S. perimeter discussions depart from the trilateral model and simultaneously hint at more bureaucratic openness to civil society consultation (see Ayres and Macdonald in this volume).

The literature on global governance and democratic deficits has become voluminous and has been applied to defects in a wide variety of regional and global institutions (Held 1995; Nye 2001; Scholte 2002; Glenn 2008; Steffek, Kissling, and Nanz 2008). While it has been used perhaps more frequently to support the concerns of Eurosceptics, who are critical of the pace and direction of European integration, the concept of a democratic deficit more generally can be understood as 'the perceived loss of control over their own political destinies experienced by many citizens in an age of rapid globalization' (Tanguay 2009, 223). Applied more generally to global governance, the concept of a democratic deficit directs attention to the failure of representation in these institutions, as Van Rooy argues, 'either in their own governance, or in the cumulative failures of their member governments or shareholders' (Van Rooy 2004, 128). Scholte (2002) highlights characteristics – the lack of control, consultation, global representation, and central oversight – that contribute to this sense, while Van Rooy describes democratic deficits in terms of citizens' perceptions of whether they have 'much say in what goes on globally' (Van Rooy 2004, 129). Thus, critics of the democratic deficit in global governance point to the need for both input and output legitimacy (Scharpf 1999), where the problem-solving effectiveness of international institutions is matched by processes of decision making that become more democratic by enhancing participation, accountability, and transparency for civil society actors (Bexell, Tallberg, and Uhlin 2008).

Throughout the 1990s, proponents of North American integration looked positively on the NAFTA agreement's output legitimacy, commenting favourably on the increase in cross-border trade flows and investment across the region. However, critics have consistently condemned North American input legitimacy, noting the toothless and ineffective record of NAFTA's labour and environmental side agreements as well as the elitist, non-transparent, and exclusionary character of the SPP process (Ackelson and Kastner 2006; Anderson and Sands 2007). Ayres and Macdonald (2006) have previously described the 'shallow governance' in place in the North American region that has both failed to address adequately civil society concerns about representation and accountability and failed to respond usefully to the growing number of trans-sovereign problems challenging the continent's three partners. In fact, North America's limited efforts at governance have betrayed a preference for an older, top-down stakeholder model, eschewing moves in other forums of global and regional governance over the years towards a 'new multilateralism' (O'Brien et al. 2000), one that evolves from the bottom up, that encourages more participation from a wide variety of civil society groups, and whose agenda increasingly is open to more social issues.

If the widely shared concerns over the legitimacy and democratic character of North American governance (as well as the criticisms over some negative socio-economic outcomes) have contributed to a long-running pattern of civil society protest, these actors themselves, interestingly enough, have come under less scrutiny than is perhaps warranted for their own democratic credentials. While we are intrigued by the literature suggesting that the democratic character of global governance can be enhanced by the increased participation of civil society actors (McGrew 2002; Scholte 2005; Bexel, Tallberg and Uhlin 2008), we understand that in the North American context, as elsewhere, the diversity of actors around such debates can reflect a complex and sometimes bewildering array of democratic and progressive or reactionary and regressive perspectives (Ahrne 1998; Söderbaum 2007). Again, Scholte's caution on the global governance–civil society nexus warrants highlighting for its applicability to today's protests against North American integration, where groups on the political left and right have mobilized in often contradictory campaigns. While in the past, social activist groups across Canadian, American, and Mexican civil society have more often than not aligned on the left of the political spectrum, right-wing populist, anti-immigrant, and xenophobic groups more recently have played a highly public role in campaigning against the SPP in the United States, raising fears about a potential loss of U.S. sovereignty that have attracted significant state and national political attention (Bow and Santa Cruz 2009).

In short, we believe that discussions about the future of the North American region, as well as the potential for renewing efforts towards transnational collaboration in response to the continent's mounting trans-sovereign problems, demand that we pay more attention to the 'legitimacy game' (Van Rooy 2004). The current lack of clarity regarding the future of North America seems partly rooted in the questionable democratic credentials of the shallow governance structures developed as well as in the elitist character of the actors that are involved most heavily in promoting the trajectory of North American integration. How can the rules of 'representivity,' expertise, and moral authority – rules that, Van Rooy argues, help confer greater legitimacy on civil society activists engaging with global and regional governance – be considered in future discussions of the North American region? How might we envision a new model for civil society engagement in debates about the future of North America? And what model might we adopt that responds to the concerns of citizenship and democracy across the region by promoting a broader model of citizen engagement? Has North America in fact reached a plateau, beyond which efforts to respond creatively and transnationally to problems of mutual concern across the continent will be ill fated unless we move beyond a neoliberal elitist model and consider the ideas and voices of multiple stakeholders – what in the literature is oftentimes referred to as conferring legitimacy on 'discursive representation'? (Keck 2004, 45). While the democratic credentials of the SPP were found wanting, the remaining NALS again seems a poor substitute for engaged trilateralism, in that it neither addresses North American problems nor considers the democratic legitimacy of any remaining North American project. Again, while the new Canada–U.S. perimeter discussion working groups – the Beyond the Border Working Group and the Regulatory Cooperation Council – have made overtures to consult with a wider array of civil society groups than was the case with the SPP, it is far too early to judge whether these initiatives are ameliorating more than a decade's worth of a deficit of democracy in North American governance.

Plan of the Book

This book assesses the current state of North America as a meaningful political entity, economic arrangement, and cultural idea in the midst of slowly unfolding and still unpredictable global economic instability and changing and unpredictable political alignments. This simultaneous confluence of political and economic challenges raises a number of interesting and important questions about the future of the North American trilateral relationship. Part I of the book, 'North America and Political-Economic Turbulence,' presents several perspectives on the financial turbulence that has struck the region and its impact on North American governance. Chapter 1 by Randall Germain with Abdulghany Mohamed examines the trajectory of the financial crisis across North America, reviewing the cause of the crisis and its 'asymmetrical impact' on the countries of the region. Germain argues that the crisis will lead to a diminished form of institutionalized governance and to a reassertion of American influence as a result of increased informal forms of economic integration. In Chapter 2, Brian Bow presents a constructivist perspective on the responses to the recent economic crisis in the North American region, arguing that the fact that the crisis has led to diminished regional integration was neither inevitable nor automatic. In fact, as his review of earlier economic crises in the North American region since the early 1980s shows, these crises have most often served as catalysts for advances in regional integration. Drawing from the literature on the role of ideas in shaping economic policy, he argues that the implications of an economic crisis on the prospects for further regional integration depend on how the crisis itself is diagnosed by powerful actors, what kinds of solutions are seen to be available, and whether regional coordination is seen to contribute to those solutions.

Chapter 3 by Stephen Clarkson focuses on the institutions of continental governance in North America (or lack of them). Clarkson argues that the idea of an integrated North American entity that is more than the sum of its Mexican, Canadian, and American parts, along the lines of the European Union, had already failed before the recent crisis, and that this crisis is further contributing to the region's disintegration. He contends that this situation is a result of numerous factors: the creation of deliberately weak continental institutions at the time of NAFTA; the fact that some North American economic sectors (such as agriculture and steel) demonstrated real continental economic integration but did not develop significant transborder governance; and the fact that since 9/11, U.S.-dominated bilateralism has predominated in matters of military defence and border security. The final chapter in this section, by Jorge Cadena-Roa, focuses specifically on the political security crisis in Mexico, assessing its implications for North American regionalism. Ongoing wars between drug gangs (engaged in cross-border trade in narcotics) and the Mexican state's 'war on drugs' have together resulted in a dramatic increase in violence in recent years, particularly in the Mexico–U.S. border region. The United States has responded with increased military and police assistance, but not with trilateral mechanisms for addressing Mexico's problems. The result is likely to be an increase in bilateral mechanisms such as the U.S.-backed Mérida Initiative.

Part II of the book, 'North American Problems without North American Governance,' turns its attention away from the regional dimensions of the crisis towards the implications for specific sectors or policy areas. In Chapter 5, Teresa Healy, a senior researcher for the Canadian Labour Congress, reviews how the concept of 'community' has been mobilized by elite, state- and business-led actors promoting a form of North American community from above and has been contested by workers and their organizations, who are experiencing 'communities in crisis.' She discusses opposition 'from below' to both NAFTA and the SPP and presents research findings on the impact of the economic crisis on Canadian workers, focusing specifically on workers in Oshawa, Ontario, one of the main sites of automobile production in Canada. In Chapter 6, Debora VanNijnatten and Neil Craik discuss the regulation and governance of energy and environmental policies in the region. They argue that in these policy areas there may be more support for regional cooperation than in other areas, partly because of the urgency of the threat of global climate change. VanNijnatten and Craik identify three trends in North American governance in the areas of environment and energy: the rejection of supranational institutions in favour of transgovernmental networks; the growing significance of subnational governments, with a resulting governance structure that is multilevel and overlapping; and a move towards 'bundled' governance structures that link various environmental issue areas or cross-cutting issues –

such as trade and environment, and energy and environment – within a single cooperative framework.

In Chapter 7, Emily Gilbert focuses on issues related to border control and security, an area in which there has been a dramatic increase in attention on the part of all three countries since 9/11. Gilbert argues that we have seen in recent years the emergence in North America of two competing narratives: enforcement of national territorial borders *and* deepening of North American integration. Also following a constructivist approach, Gilbert's chapter examines North American borders through three frames: (1) transnational border agreements; (2) security policies and practices at the border; and (3) mobility and migration. In her view, the international financial crisis has made it patently clear that greater security cooperation has not ensured economic openness. While some degree of harmonization of policies has occurred, this has not resulted in new institutions of regional governance or in common understandings of citizenship and rights. The final chapter in this section, by Christina Gabriel, focuses more specifically on migration and mobility. Gabriel reviews some of the dimensions of mobility within the North American region, underlining the 'continental dissonances' that distort policy making in this controversial policy area. In particular, NAFTA promoted the mobility of highly skilled workers but failed to incorporate mechanisms for the movement of low-skill workers. Mexican workers are disproportionately affected by this, and as a result, large numbers of them exist as 'precarious residents' in both the United States and (to a much lesser extent) Canada, with extremely weak citizenship rights. According to Gabriel, the recent financial crisis has only aggravated this situation as well as the already marginal status of low-skill Mexican migrants.

In Part III of the book, 'Democratic Deficits, New Actors, and Responses to the Crisis,' the contributors examine some of the ongoing challenges facing the region. In Chapter 9, Stephanie Golob discusses how recent events have confirmed an underlying tendency of the North American region – its 'double-bilateral' nature. Instead of developing gradually more robust trilateral institutions and modes of behaviour, the North American region has increasingly taken the shape of two parallel relationships, between the United States and Canada on the one hand and between the United States and Mexico on the other. Golob's chapter reviews the development of the double-bilateral track, from the negotiation of NAFTA through to the SPP and its demise. She concludes somewhat optimistically by projecting the possibility of the formation of a 'triple-bilateralist' future for North America, based on the development of a Canada–Mexico dyad, driven from below by civil society and business actors.

In Chapter 10, Richard Vengroff and James P. Allan evaluate the role of subnational actors – that is, states and provinces, which are often overlooked in discussions of North American governance. They argue that increasingly, while the process of North American regionalization seems to be faltering at the level of nation-states, at the subnational level, relations appear to be flourishing. Allan and Vengroff's chapter examines the impact of the financial crisis on the paradiplomatic activities of Canadian provinces and U.S. states. They argue that a 'new regionalism' approach is helping us move beyond the state-centrism of traditional regionalism theories. Chapter 11 introduces a gender and post-colonial perspective. The author, Rosalba Icaza, analyses NAFTA and the SPP from the perspective of working-class and indigenous women, based on research in Mexico City and Chiapas, the southern-most state of Mexico and site of the *Zapatista* rebellion. Based on this research, she questions the idea that the SPP has failed and empha-sizes the persistence of the SPP framework in the ongoing dynamics of regional and bilateral (Mexico–U.S.) governance. Icaza also reflects on working-class and indigenous women's perspectives that might help challenge assumptions about both North American regionalism specifi-cally, and the more general concept of 'region' more generally.

Jeffrey Ayres and Laura Macdonald raise issues in Chapter 12 related to the 'democratic deficit' of North American integration, and look at the role played by civil society opposition to the SPP initiative. They argue that the SPP's supposedly depoliticized institutional architec-ture created a fundamental inequity between the form of representa-tion offered to elite-level business, and the lack of consultation or only very limited forms of consultation that non-elite civil society might have had access to. They suggest that even if North American integra-tion may continue under a different guise – and possibly, with the turn towards Canada–U.S. perimeter discussions, it has done so – the failure to devise a successful legitimacy strategy undermined the success of the SPP initiative and points to fundamental problems with the entire integration process. Finally, Janine Brodie in this volume's conclusion ties together many of the threads of analysis developed by the book's contributors. Prompted by these multiple analyses, she raises some broader questions about the form and future of the 'new regionalism': Is institutional 'thickness' and input legitimacy necessary for successful region building? What is the relationship between input and output legitimacy in transnational governance? Drawing upon the 'short life and times of the SPP,' she concludes that the new regionalism is far more fluid and experimental than our theories perhaps concede and that even failed or abandoned experiments in transnational governance leave indelible imprints on political geographies. Her chapter concludes with some reflections on possible scenarios for the future of North American regionalism.

Notes

1 'Beyond the Border: A Shared Vision for Perimeter Security and Economic Competitiveness,' http://www.borderactionplan-plandactionfrontalier.gc.ca/psec-scep/declaration-declaration.aspx?lang=eng.
2 Of course the European Union has gone through periods of progress, followed by phases during which regional integration stalled. The EU, however, possesses strong regional institutions that can maintain the regional ideal even while political progress is stalled and then revive it when more propitious circumstances emerge. Europe also possesses a stronger sense of itself as a region, and regional identity is much more deeply engrained there than in North America.
3 Obama appeared to turn away from this stance after assuming office, but he is unlikely to support a renewed push for the type of integration promoted under NAFTA and the SPP.
4 Americans' travel to Canada was undoubtedly affected by the rise of the Canadian dollar in addition to new travel restrictions.
5 http://www.borderactionplan-plandactionfrontalier.gc.ca/psec-scep/index.aspx?lang=eng.
6 For other references to the usefulness of constructivist explanations of North American regionalism, see Duina 2006; Spitz 2009; Mace 2007; and Capling and Nossal 2009.

References

Ackelson, Jason, and Justin Kastner. 2006. 'The Security and Prosperity Partnership of North America,' *American Review of Canadian Studies*: 207–32.

Ahrne, Göran. 1998. 'Civil Society and Uncivil Organizations.' In *Real Civil Societies: Dilemmas of Institutionalization*. Edited by Jeffrey Alexander. London: Sage.

Anderson, Greg, and Chris Sands. 2007. *Negotiating North America: The Security and Prosperity Partnership*. Washington: Hudson Institute. http://www. hudson.org/files/pdf_upload/HudsonNegotiatingNorthAmericaadvance-proof2.pdf. Accessed November 1, 2011.

Ayres, Jeffrey. 1998. *Defying Conventional Wisdom: Political Movements and Popular Contention against North American Free Trade*. Toronto: University of Toronto Press.

Ayres, Jeffrey, and Laura Macdonald. 2006. 'Deep Integration and Shallow Governance: The Limits to Civil Society Engagement across North America.' *Policy and Society* 25, no. 3: 23–42.

– eds. 2009. *Contentious Politics in North America: National Protest and Transnational Collaboration under Continental Integration*. Basingstoke: Palgrave Macmillan.

Bergsten, C. Fred, and William R. Cline. 1982. *Trade Policy in the 1980s*. Washington: Institute for International Economics.

Bexell, Magdalena, Jonas Tallberg, and Anders Uhlin. 2008. 'Democracy in Global Governance: The Promise and Pitfalls of Transnational Actors.' Paper presented at the Annual Conference of *Millennium Journal of International Studies*, 'Interrogating Democracy in International Relations,' London, 25–6 October.

Bow, Brian, and Arturo Santa Cruz. 2009. 'A Certain Idea of America: Identity Politics and North American Integration.' Paper presented at the Annual Meeting of the American Political Science Association, Toronto.

'Canada and NAFTA: No Mariachis Please.' 2009. *The Economist*. 12 February.

Capling, Ann, and Kim Richard Nossal. 2009. 'The Contradictions of Regionalism in North America.' *Review of International Studies* 35, no. 1: 145–65.

CBS News. 2010. 'Mexico Sees Record Drop in Remittances.' 27 January. http://www.cbsnews.com. Accessed 14 June 2011.

Chu, Doris, and Danielle Goldfarb. 2008. 'Stuck in Neutral: Canada's Engagement in Regional and Global Supply Chains.' Conference Board of Canada. http://www.conferenceboard.ca/documents.aspx?did=2550. Accessed 1 November 2011.

Clarkson, Stephen. 2008. *Does North America Exist? Governing the Continent after NAFTA and 9/11*. Toronto: University of Toronto Press.

Diez, Thomas, and Antje Wiener. 2004. *European Integration Theory*. Oxford: Oxford University Press..

Duina, Francesco. 2006. *The Social Construction of Free Trade: The European Union, NAFTA, and MERCOSUR*. Princeton: Princeton University Press.

Gilbert, Emily. 2005. 'Inevitability of Integration? Neoliberal Discourse and the Proposals for a New North American Economic Space after September 11.' *Annals of the Association of American Geographers* 95, no. 1: 202–22.

Glenn, John. 2008. 'Global Governance and the Democratic Deficit: Stifling the Voice of the South.' *Third World Quarterly* 29, no. 2: 217–38.

Goldfarb, Danielle. 2007. 'Reaching a Tipping Point: Effects of Post-9/11 Border Security on Canada's Trade and Investment.' http://www.conferenceboard.ca/documents.aspx?did=2028. Accessed 1 November 2011.

Goldfarb, presentation, Carleton University, 15 January 2009.

Golob, Stephanie R. 2002. 'North America beyond NAFTA? Sovereignty, Identity, and Security in Canada–U.S. Relations.' *Canadian–American Public Policy* 52: 1–44.

Haggart, Blayne. 2011. 'North American Integration: Politics, Economics, Culture and Copyright Law.' PhD diss., Carleton University, Department of Political Science.

Harrup, Anthony. 2011. 'Mexico's March Remittances Up 4.8% on Year.' *MarketWatch*. 2 May. http://www.marketwatch.com. Accessed 14 June 2011.

Held, David. 1995. *Democracy and the Global Order: From the Modern State to Cosmopolitan Governance*. Cambridge: Polity.

Hettne, Bjorn. 2005. 'Beyond the "New" Regionalism.' *New Political Economy* 10, no. 4: 543–71.

– 1997. 'Europe in a World of Regions.' In *A New Europe in the Changing Global System*. Edited by Richard Falk and Tamás Szentes. Tokyo, New York, and Paris: United Nations University Press. 16–40.

Hurrell, Andrew. 1995. *Regionalism in World Politics: Regional Integration and World Order*. Oxford: Oxford University Press.

Keck, Margaret. 2004. 'Governance Regimes and the Politics of Discursive Representation.' In *Transnational Activism in Asia: Problems of Power and Democracy*. Edited by Nicola Piper and Anders Uhlin. London: Routledge.

Larner, Wendy, and William Walters. 2002. 'The Political Rationality of "New Regionalism": Toward a Genealogy of the Region.' *Theory and Society* 31: 391–432.

Littlefield, Edward W. 2009. 'Immigration Matters: Bolstering Mexico with Immigration and Economic Reforms,' Council on Hemispheric Affairs, accessed at http://www.coha.org/immigration-matters-bolstering-mexico-with-immigration-and-economic-reforms. Accessed 1 November 2011.

Mace, Gordon, ed. 2007. *Regionalism and the State: NAFTA and Foreign Policy Convergence*. Aldershot: Ashgate.

Marchand, Marianne, Morten Bøås, and Timothy Shaw. 1999. 'The Political Economy of New Regionalisms.' *Third World Quarterly* 20, no. 5: 897–910.

McGrew, Anthony. 2002. 'Transnational Democracy: Theories and Prospects.' In *Democratic Theory Today: Challenges for the 21st Century*. Edited by April Carter and Geoffrey Stokes. Cambridge: Polity.

Mittelman, James H. 1996. 'Rethinking the "New Regionalism" in the Context of Globalization.' *Global Governance* 2: 189–213.

Nye, Joseph, Jr. 2001. 'Globalization's Democratic Deficit: How to Make International Institutions More Accountable.' *Foreign Affairs*, July–August.

O'Brien, Robert. 1995. 'North American Integration and International Relations Theory.' *Canadian Journal of Political Science/Revue canadienne de science politique* 37, no. 4: 693–724.

O'Brien, Robert, et al. 2000. *Contesting Global Governance: Multilateral Economic Institutions and Global Social Movements.* Cambridge: Cambridge University Press.

Pastor, Robert. 2011. *The North American Idea: A Vision of a Continental Future.* New York: Oxford University Press.

Robertson, Colin. 2011. 'Embracing the Americas, Starting with Mexico.' *Policy Options*, May, 40–4.

Rosamond, Ben. 2001. 'Discourses of Globalization and European Identities.' In *The Social Construction of Europe.* Edited by Thomas Christiansen, Knud Erik Jørgensen, and Antje Wiener. London and Thousand Oaks: Sage. 158–73.

Scharpf, Fritz. 1999. *Governing in Europe: Effective and Democratic?* Oxford: Oxford University Press.

Scholte, Jan Aart. 2005. 'Civil Society and Democratically Accountable Global Governance.' In *Global Governance and Public Accountability.* Edited by David Held and Mathias Koenig-Achibugi. London: Blackwell.

– 2002. 'Civil Society and Democracy in Global Governance.' *Global Governance* 8: 281–304.

Söderbaum, Fredrik. 2007. 'Regionalisation and Civil Society: The Case of Southern Africa.' *New Political Economy* 12, no. 3: 319–37.

Spitz, Laura. 2009. 'The Evolving Architecture of North American Integration.' *University of Colorado Law Review* 80, no. 735: 101–57.

Steffek, Jens, Claudia Kissling, and Patrizia Nanz, eds. 2008. *Civil Society Participation in European and Global Governance: A Cure for the Democratic Deficit?* Basingstoke: Palgrave Macmillan.

Studer, Isabel, and Carol Wise, eds. 2007. *Requiem or Revival? The Promise of North American Integration.* Washington: Brookings Institution Press.

Tanguay, Brian A. 2009. 'Reforming Representative Democracy: Taming the "Democratic Deficit."' In *Canadian Politics,* 5th ed. Edited by James Bickerton and Alain G. Gagnon. Toronto: University of Toronto Press. 221–48.

Van Rooy, Alison. 2004. *The Global Legitimacy Game: Civil Society, Globalization, and Protest.* Basingstoke: Palgrave Macmillan.

Wise, Carol. 2007. 'No Turning Back: Trade Integration and the New Development Mandate.' In *Requiem or Revival? The Promise of North American Integration*. Edited by Isabel Studer and Carol Wise. Washington: Brookings Institution Press. 1–27.

Wood, Duncan. 2011. 'Perimeter Security in North America: Mexico's Latest, Greatest Rejection and the Emergence of a Two-Speed Region,' Center for Strategic and International Studies, accessed at http://csis.org/blog/perimeter-security-north-america-mexicos-latest-greates-rejection-and-emergence-two-speed-region. Accessed 1 November 2011.

Zepeda, Eduardo, Timothy Wise, and Kevin Gallagher. 2009. 'Rethinking Trade Policy for Development: Lessons from Mexico Under NAFTA.' Washington: Carnegie Endowment for International Peace (December). http://www.carnegieendowment.org/files/nafta_trade_development.pdf. Accessed 21 December 2009.

PART I

North America and Political-Economic Turbulence

1 Global Economic Crisis and Regionalism in North America: Region-ness in Question?[1]

RANDALL GERMAIN, WITH ABDULGHANY MOHAMED

The global economic crisis that erupted in October 2008 affected the major regions of the world unevenly. Emerging giants in Asia such as India and China were only briefly touched, while economies throughout Latin America suffered recession but in a mild form. Trade and industrial production in Europe, on the other hand, which had slowed considerably over the first half of 2008, experienced a sudden plunge during the six months after Lehman Brothers went bust. And North America, arguably the heartland of the global economy, suffered a ferocious economic collapse that by some measures has been its worst period of economic performance since the Great Depression.[2] This chapter examines the contours of this crisis, which continued to affect the three economies of the region throughout 2010.

The focus in this chapter is twofold. First, I explore how the crisis – which was and continues to be a global event – has interacted with some long-standing trajectories in North America's regional development, most importantly but not only associated with NAFTA. Here I am especially concerned with whether and how the response to the crisis has consolidated or undermined a sense of *region-ness*, defined in the first instance as a region-specific policy horizon for official decision makers, together with a coherent ensemble of region-wide institutions. I ask, in other words, whether and to what extent the effects of the crisis have pushed North America closer together as a region or pulled it further apart (also see Bow, this volume). Second, I explore the extent to which the crisis has accentuated the peculiar asymmetrical balance of North America when considered as a region. Of primary importance here is the vulnerability of regional integration to political developments in the United States that embrace protectionism and that encourage the regulatory thickening of borders (see the introduction to this volume).

My main argument is twofold. First, the longer-term future for formalized regionalism in North America will be further constrained by a diminished institutional capacity and a reduced regional policy horizon. The *region-ness* of North America will become, I believe, even more hollowed out than at present, and importantly, it will be accompanied by a reassertion of American influence via the steady increase in informal economic integration among Canada, Mexico, and the United States. Second, this does not however mean that regionalism in North America has reached a plateau. The regional identity of North America, I argue, is overwhelmingly economic in nature, and the economic crisis is exacerbating this by pushing the United States more towards an America-first set of economic policies that will tilt the region even further towards the American orbit. This shift is most clearly associated with a 'beyond NAFTA' form of regionalism, evident in the American (and to a certain extent also Canadian) responses to the financial crisis. Critically, these responses do not work through existing regional 'institutions,' but instead accentuate the provision of assistance to national economies at the expense of *region-ness*. This stands in stark contrast to Europe, where the European Commission and indeed major European governments such as France and Germany have channelled their responses to the global economic crisis at least in part through regional institutions. The result in North America will be tighter economic integration alongside weakened regional institutions. In this scenario, the Canadian and Mexican economies will become even more dependent on economic growth in the United States than at present, while the ability of American decision makers to shape the economic environment in North America will strengthen. I argue that this is a form of informal regional integration that goes 'beyond' NAFTA.

Regionalism and NAFTA: Preliminary Considerations

The conceptual debate about regionalism has established that the phenomenon is about more than simply geographical proximity and economic integration (Katzenstein 1996; Hettne 1999; Hveem 1999; 2000; Marchand, Bøås, and Shaw 1999; Schulz, Soderbaum, and Ojendal 2001; see also the introduction to this volume and chapters by Clarkson and Bow). My view of regionalism is that it must have at its core a certain level of *region-ness* that is multidimensional and that embraces both ideational and material processes and arrangements. I prefer here to consider these arrangements as being composed of two key attributes: the policy horizon of decision makers, and the depth and robustness of regional institutions. This view transcends the narrow equating of regionalism with free trade agreements (e.g., Bhagwati 1992; Sampson and Woolcock 2003), although such agreements can certainly be an intrinsic part of regionalism.

In the context of North America, regionalism has most often been associated with the two free trade agreements (CUSFTA and NAFTA) signed over the past twenty-five years. Of course it was NAFTA that crystallized the 'North American' dimension of *region-ness*, but at the core of NAFTA's *region-ness* is a weak and hollowed-out institutional capacity to further the process of integration. Compared to previous regional developments, NAFTA was established with only a minimal level of common institutional arrangements. Some have described this as an 'institutional deficiency' (Appendini and Bislev 1999); others have maintained that it makes the NAFTA model unsustainable (Mace and Bélanger 1999; Bélanger 2007). In addition, strong national cultural traditions have contributed to the limited development of a regional policy horizon for senior government officials, except in certain areas of technocratic expertise such as energy and environmental protection (see chapter by VanNijnatten this volume). Instead, what has imposed itself on the regional entity that is North America is an asymmetrical policy horizon for decision makers characterized by a form of economic integration that is uniquely vulnerable to political developments in the United States. This vulnerability has become more significant as a result of the global financial crisis and the various national responses to it.

The Global Economic Crisis and 'North America'

The crisis that struck North America in the autumn of 2008 was led by weaknesses in the organization of finance – weaknesses that had been simmering since the summer of 2007, when global credit markets began to tighten and liquidity problems emerged across banking systems worldwide. Note well, however, that this was not the first financial crisis to face North America. In 1994, as a new administration was taking office in Mexico, a massive wave of capital outflows occurred that resulted in a significant peso devaluation in December of that year. Swap lines that had been established earlier in the year between the

Banco de México, the Federal Reserve Board ('the Fed'), and the Bank of Canada proved unable to contain the crisis, and the Clinton administration had to orchestrate a support fund for Mexico that was funded primarily through the U.S. Treasury (Cameron and Aggarwal 1996; Pastor 2001). What emerged from this crisis was the realization that NAFTA did not have the capacity to prevent or resolve such crises.

NAFTA was unable to respond positively to the peso crisis for two important reasons, above and beyond the fact that it was virtually brand new. At one level, like many trade agreements, it was not set up to pool resources in the event of a severe economic disruption. NAFTA established rules, along with procedures to deal with breaches of those rules; it was not designed to deploy significant resources to support signatories in the event of a crisis. This is not unique to NAFTA: APEC and the EU also focus on rules and procedures rather than pooled resources, although the EU is beginning to develop such pooled resources through the European Central Bank. Equally important, NAFTA works entirely through governments because it is a product of interstate bargaining. Sovereignty is firmly protected and is wielded only by its three signatories, which means that in the event of a crisis, each government must either look to its own resources or work to convince other signatories to come to its aid. This is what happened during the peso crisis, and this reinforced the individual policy horizons of officials in all three countries.

The 'Great Freeze'

The global financial crisis, which has been identified elsewhere as the 'Great Freeze' (Germain 2010), began to unfold publicly in September 2007, when Northern Rock, the fifth-biggest mortgage lender in the United Kingdom, had to be given government help to prevent a run on its deposits from spreading to other High Street banks. The crisis then proceeded in fits and starts for the rest of 2007 as credit markets in the United States and Europe became increasingly constricted on the back of growing uncertainty over subprime-linked securities. Ominously, the pace of problems picked up in early 2008. First, Countrywide Financial, one of the most aggressive non-bank subprime mortgage providers, ran into difficulty and had to be guided towards a rescue by Bank of America. Then, much more spectacularly, Bear Stearns – one of the so-called bulge-bracket Wall Street investment banks – became insolvent and was rescued by JPMorgan Chase (albeit with the help of the Fed, which underwrote a good chunk of the bailout's costs). The first half of 2008 ended with the failure in July of Indymac Bank, a large California-based mortgage provider, which was taken over by the Federal Deposit Insurance Corporation (FDIC). Still, at that point in the year, Indymac Bank was only the fifth U.S. financial institution to close its doors.[3]

It was the spectacular failure of Lehman Brothers on 15 September that opened the floodgates. In the space of a single week, a storied Wall Street firm with roots stretching back to the American Civil War filed for bankruptcy protection, Merrill Lynch was rescued by Bank of America, and the giant insurance firm AIG was effectively nationalized by the U.S. government. It was at this point that the U.S. financial system fully entered the financial maelstrom. Beginning in mid-September, almost every aspect of credit throughout the economies of many countries went from being merely difficult to actually being imperiled. Mortgage financing became more difficult to arrange. Commercial credit became more expensive even as central banks lowered interest rates in a coordinated fashion. Interbank lending slowed to a trickle. Corporate bond markets shrank. Merger and acquisition activities as well as initial public offerings (IPOs) stalled. Trade finance availability plummeted. In sector after sector, the normal organization and operation of credit markets quite simply seized up.[4] That is why I can refer to this train of events as the Great Freeze.

Given the interconnectedness of the global financial system, these effects of the Great Freeze were instantly transmitted to Europe. The British, Irish, Dutch, Belgian, German, and Icelandic governments were all required to act decisively before September ended. In Britain, Bradford and Bingley (a building society) was nationalized to avoid insolvency and the government had to organize a shotgun merger between HBoS (Halifax–Bank of Scotland) and LloydsTSB to forestall the failure of the former. In Belgium and the Netherlands, two giant banking concerns – Fortis and Dexia, each with liabilities substantially outstripping the GDP of its home country – were saved from the brink by concerted intergovernmental action. Iceland and Ireland were particularly hard hit, with the three largest banks in each country requiring government action to guarantee their retail deposits (along with the rest of the banking system). This action, which soon spilled over to guaranteeing interbank lending throughout the banking system (a move picked up by other EU governments), resulted eventually in the whole or partial nationalization of the biggest Icelandic and Irish banks. It was only such full-scale rescues that saved their banking and financial systems from complete collapse. Germany faced its second bank failure in late September 2008 when Hypo Real Estate Bank required a government-backed rescue. By the end of October 2008, almost every major European government had stepped in to support and/or nationalize significant sections of its banking system; this included injecting hundreds of billions of dollars into vulnerable banks to recapitalize them. And as these countries did so, their central banks – together with the Fed and the Bank of Canada, among others – were cutting interest rates and pumping extra liquidity into their financial systems in order to forestall a complete implosion of credit markets.[5]

Bank rescues and failures in the United States and Europe had an immediate impact both on the world's accumulated stock of wealth and on its real economy. Losses in stock markets worldwide during 2008 totalled between 30 and 70% of market value across all developed and emerging market economies. This loss of wealth was further reflected across a wide range of value-generating activities: the value of hedge fund assets plummeted by 25% between September 2008 and April 2009; many individual firms saw their levels of capitalization almost wiped out; bankruptcies skyrocketed (corporate as well as personal); and of course, house prices fell significantly across many crisis-stricken countries.[6] Such dramatic declines in global stocks of wealth fed through to the real economy. By the end of the third quarter of 2009, year-on-year industrial production had fallen by nearly 6% in America, 19% in Japan, 17% in Germany, and 11% in the United Kingdom.[7] Such declines were replicated in eastern and central Europe – including Russia – as well as in many parts of South and East Asia and in Latin America. Of the world's largest or fastest-growing economies, only China and India were spared.[8]

The collapse in industrial production was accompanied by significant disruptions to international trade. Between the last quarter of 2008 and the first quarter of 2009, the combination of loss of wealth and contraction of credit produced a stunning drop in economic activity – and especially in international trade – among almost all of the leading trading nations of the world. From North America to Europe and Asia, export and import levels plummeted between 15 and 50%. Overall, world trade contracted by 9% in 2009 – the first contraction since 1982 and only the second since 1945.[9] Indeed, global GDP is estimated to have shrunk by about 1.5% during 2009. By most accounts, at a global level the Great Freeze was the most significant economic 'event' since the Great Depression.

North America and the Great Freeze

The Great Freeze affected the three North American economies asymmetrically. In the United States, although the economy had been in recession since December 2007, it worsened significantly after September 2008, when growth plummeted and unemployment spiked. U.S. GDP (gross domestic product, the broadest measure of total economic activity in a country) grew 2% in 2007 and just over 1% in 2008, then declined by nearly 3% in 2009. During this time, the U.S. unemployment rate shot up from an average of 4.6% in 2007 to 5.8% in 2008 to nearly 10% at the end of 2009.[10] More than 7 million jobs have been lost since the recession began in 2007 (*ERP* 2010, 5; ILO Bulletin of Labour Statistics 2009, 123).[11] Despite emerging officially from recession in mid-2009, GDP growth in the United States has remained sluggish, with unemployment hovering around 9% well into 2011.

There are several reasons why the United States was uniquely vulnerable to economic disruption as a result of the Great Freeze. Economic growth during the Bush years depended heavily on consumer spending and housing growth, both of which were fuelled by excessive credit growth. As credit markets tightened, this retail consumer spending eased, and when the subprime crisis hit, housing starts plummeted. Worse, house prices had been falling since early 2006, further constricting consumers' access to easy credit. The finance-led growth of the American economy also generated international vulnerabilities in terms of growing trade and current account deficits; this were exacerbated by growing government deficits connected to the wars in Iraq and Afghanistan. The repeal of the Glass–Steagall Act in the final year of the Clinton administration also played a part in this economic disruption. By allowing banks and other non-bank financial institutions to compete across a wider array of financial markets (including subprime), the repeal of this act made the American economy even more finance-dependent and thus vulnerable to disruptions in the organization of credit.[12]

In tandem with severe contractions in industrial production, GDP, and employment, government finances in the United States have been adversely affected. The budget deficit, already steep, hit 10% of GDP in 2009 and was only slightly lower, closer to 9%, in 2010, still exceeding more than $1 trillion for the second year in a row. The ratio of public debt to GDP, which stood at about 50% not more than five years ago, has shot up and now stands to peak at 100% by 2015.[13] This deficit and the growing aggregate debt load of the United States is associated in part with the normal operations of welfare stabilizing payments; in part with the large fiscal stimulus package passed by the government in 2009; in part with the continued growth in health care and social security costs; and in part with the ongoing costs associated with fighting the global 'war on terror.' And part of it, of course, is directly linked to efforts by the Bush and Obama administrations to combat financial collapse. Between the initiatives designed to combat financial collapse and the stimulus actions alone, the U.S. federal deficit hit $459 billion in 2008 and $1.4 trillion in 2009 and will hit nearly $1.6 trillion in 2010 (ERP 2010).

Canada, by contrast, entered the crisis with relatively strong macroeconomic fundamentals and a stable and sound financial system. Still, it was hit by spillover effects of the Great Freeze due to its reliance on global trade and its particularly close trade and financial ties to the United States (Duttagupta and Barrera 2010). The price of energy – a major Canadian export – plummeted between September 2008 and March 2009; furthermore, its principal export partner went into the equivalent of economic shock. Indeed, over the final quarter of 2009, Canada ran a small trade *deficit* for the first time in a decade. Even foreign direct investment (FDI) into Canada declined significantly over this period, by over 65% from 2007 levels. The result was a recession, albeit much milder than the one experienced in the United States, with a decline of GDP of about 0.5% in 2009 (Canada's State of Trade and Investment Update 2009) and a rise in unemployment from just over 6% in 2008 to nearly 9% in 2009 (ILO Bulletin of Labour Statistics 2009, 119).

Public finances in Canada, however, were well positioned to respond to the Great Freeze. Canada had been running budgetary surpluses since 1995, and its overall external debt was the lowest among G7 industrialized countries, at just under 30% of GDP in 2009. Canada, along with other major governments, responded to the financial collapse by pumping relatively large (by Canadian standards) amounts of liquidity into the financial system and by loosening monetary policy. Eventually, the new Conservative government also undertook corrective fiscal actions.[14] An economic action plan eventually called for some $30 billion of stimulus spending, which together with automatic welfare stabilizers ushered in a deficit of about $50 billion for 2009 (with a similar amount projected for 2010). Even with this deficit, however, Canada's federal debt will only hit about 65% of GDP in 2012 before beginning to fall. Overall, the Great Freeze has had a relatively mild impact on the Canadian economy as compared with that of the United States.

Mexico did not escape the effects of the global economic crisis so easily. Its trade declined along with world trade more generally, helped unfortunately by the untimely outbreak of swine flu in April 2008, which hit the tourist industry quite hard. Mexico also saw a reversal of capital flows as investors moved to withdraw capital from emerging economies in general (Jara, Moreno, and Tovar 2009, 54–5). GDP growth slowed from 5% and 3% in 2006 and 2007 respectively to just over 1% in 2008; GDP then declined nearly 7% in 2009 (Canada's State of Trade and Investment Update 2009, 9). Unemployment rose from between 3% and 4% during 2006–8 to over 5% in 2009 (ILO Bulletin of Labour Statistics 2009, 121). Even remittances from Mexicans living and working in the United States were significantly affected, falling by about 20% in 2008–9 (Skelton and Quintin 2009, 5; see also chapter by Gabriel in this volume). In short, Mexico's trade-dependent sectors, which account for a large proportion of its formal economy, were adversely affected by the crisis, primarily because, like Canada, Mexico's chief trading partner is the United States.

Unlike in previous crises, however, Mexican public finances were relatively robust, allowing the Mexican government to respond to the crisis in a manner that directly addressed its worst consequences. The Banco de México entered swap arrangements with the Fed; equally important, Mexico was one of three countries (along with Poland and Colombia) to gain access to the IMF's Flexible Credit line, a new facility designed to extend preauthorized access to a pool of capital available for countries to use to meet liquidity shortfalls during a period of financial instability (Jara, Moreno, and Tovar 2009, 53). As well, Mexico passed a fiscal stimulus package in March 2008 of over $6 billion, which was further augmented in January 2009. Even with this additional spending, however, Mexico's public debt levels are not raising concerns in global credit markets; this is in stark contrast to previous crises.

I would make two observations about the asymmetrical impact of the Great Freeze on North America as a region. First, it has had no discernable direct impact on the *region-ness* of North America. In Europe, there has been both controversy and constructive dialogue about *Europe's* response to the financial crisis. In North America, by contrast, the very idea that NAFTA-related institutions, such as the Security and Prosperity Partnership (SPP) or the Leader's Summit, might be legitimate and useful vehicles through which each state in the region might channel its response, has been largely absent. In other words, the policy horizons of officials across North America have not been stretched to include 'North America' as part of that horizon.

In fact, the American stimulus plan included a Buy America provision, one that has yet to be addressed by Canada and Mexico through NAFTA-related institutions. Instead, each country has negotiated directly with the United States to temper the Buy America provisions as these impact on them alone, instead of (for example) working through NAFTA's dispute-resolution mechanism. And this leads to my second observation – namely, that as each country has responded to the Great Freeze on its own terms, the institutional capacity of NAFTA has become further weakened and hollowed out. NAFTA, in other words, reflects a weak and asymmetrical form of regionalism. By strengthening national policy levers in order to address economic crisis, and by supplementing these efforts with global coordination via the new G20, the countries of North America have reinforced national tools rather than regional ones as the key public policy economic levers, further weakening an already vulnerable sense of *region-ness*. On this basis I argue that the global financial crisis has further undermined North America's already ambiguous sense of *region-ness*.

Quo Vadis Regionalism in North America?

The global financial crisis has altered the context in which North America as a region will evolve. Here I explore the implications of that crisis for the further development of a North American region. There are two possible trajectories: (a) a strengthening of regionalism within the NAFTA framework; or (b) a displacement of NAFTA as the principal framework for regionalism in North America, and a return to a set of mainly bilateral relations among the U.S., Canadian, and Mexican governments. As indicated above, I believe that the second trajectory is the most likely outcome.

Further Integration within the NAFTA Framework?

To the extent that the current crisis has negatively affected international trade and investment among the NAFTA partners as well as between the NAFTA countries and the rest of the world, the situation is most likely going to affect business interests that benefit from international trade and investment. So there is the potential that these interests will pressure their respective governments at national and subnational levels to take measures to revive or increase trade and investment within the region. The case could be made, particularly by business interests and their supporters, that there is a need for a further deepening of NAFTA. This deepening might increase trade and investment levels and enhance the competitiveness of NAFTA countries. The most likely forms of deepening might involve creating a customs union or even a common market among NAFTA signatories.

Governments, however, may not look favourably on the idea of converting NAFTA into either a full customs union or a common market, for several reasons. First and foremost, converting an FTA such as NAFTA into a customs union entails negotiating a common external tariff among the partners. This may not be such an easy or appealing task at this moment, mainly because it will also mean a loss of policy capacity and national sovereignty alongside the concomitant emergence of a single policy horizon. Presently, however, there does not seem to be an appetite to move in this direction. If history is of any guidance, we should expect opposition to be strong in all three countries. For instance, from a Canadian perspective, the issue of free trade between Canada and the United States is a perennial one and has been resisted for fear of American influence on Canada. As Hoberg, Banting, and Simeon (2002, 252) note: 'For Canada, a small open economy overwhelmingly dependent on the world's largest and most dynamic national economy, this anxiety is particularly acute. Indeed, concerns about "Americanization" have been part of Canadian identity, politics, and public policy since before Confederation.' It should not be surprising, therefore, that scepticism towards the benefits of free trade should persist in both Canada and Mexico, where concerns about American influence on their societies historically have been endemic (see, for example, Boothe and Purvis 1997; Clarkson 2002a, 2002b). If we consider the case of deepening NAFTA to achieve a genuine common market, such scepticism becomes even more accentuated. A common market requires not only that the partners institute a common external tariff policy, but also that they negotiate the relatively unconstricted movement of capital and labour as well. In light of the direction in which the United States in particular is moving, this would now be a very hard sell. Similarly, there appears also to be little appetite for rekindling the debate about a common currency (Helleiner 2006), and with the demise of the SPP (see chapters by Bow, Brodie, and Ayres and Macdonald in this volume), few initiatives to deepen NAFTA are on the horizon.

This conclusion is reinforced when we examine the direct implications of the financial crisis and governments' attempts to strengthen their financial systems. There has been minimal integration of banking and financial systems among the NAFTA signatories if we understand integration to mean the seamless ability of financial institutions in each country to operate uniformly across the region. Canadian and Mexican banks – which are better capitalized than their American counterparts – have not expanded significantly into the United States, while American banks have not exploited their competitive advantages to take on Canadian banks or to increase their presence in Mexico, whose banking system is in any case now dominated by foreign-owned banks (including a number of Canadian ones). Similarly, there has not been undue regulatory harmonization of financial systems across the three countries. Under NAFTA, the banks have largely kept their own distinctive regulatory structures intact, and this is unlikely to change in the near future.[15]

Given that NAFTA is unlikely to be deepened in its institutional capacity, is it likely to be widened? Here again, I do not believe this will happen. Although in the early days of NAFTA it was envisaged that Chile would soon be brought into the fold, this option has been dropped. Instead, Canada and Mexico and the United States have all signed separate free trade agreements with Chile and other Latin American states. Effectively, the NAFTA signatories have abandoned the idea that NAFTA is an expandable model, and in tandem with the renewed questioning of the global free trade agenda as the best way of securing economic growth and stability (Germain 2010), the interest of potential recruits to an expanded NAFTA has significantly diminished.

Displacement of NAFTA as the Central Framework of Regionalism?

My examination of the responses in North America to the Great Freeze reveals an interesting common thread: notwithstanding the calls to fight protectionism, the two largest economies have in fact adopted a mild version of protectionism, whether explicitly articulated as such or not. For example, Canada has restricted the building of Coast Guard vessels to domestic contractors in its stimulus package, while the United States has introduced a 'Buy America' clause in its stimulus package. But as it turned out, it was the Buy America clause that drew the most popular attention. And as indicated above, neither Canada nor Mexico has tried to work through NAFTA-related institutions, in part because this agreement does not cover trade (and procurement) at subnational levels, which is where most of the U.S. stimulus funds are ultimately to be spent. So in order to negotiate an exemption, Canada had to agree to permit American firms to bid on provincial-level projects that had hitherto been protected from free trade provisions. Faced with difficult economic conditions, Canadian provinces quickly acceded to these demands. This bilateral resolution of a trade issue is solid evidence that the future of regional integration in North America will reside beyond NAFTA. In the case of Canadian–American relations, it indicates that relations between American states and Canadian provinces are becoming more important, and these relations are not covered by NAFTA (see the chapter by Allan and Vengroff in this volume). This of course is part of a longer historical process, as Jean-François Abgrall has observed: 'Canadian provinces and US states have had bilateral relations for a long time. Yet, these relations are now so frequent and so diverse that, more than ever, they have become an essential part of the relationship between Canada and the United States. New memoranda of understanding, compacts, and agreements continuously confirm and add to the vitality of these relations' (Abgrall 2004, 50).

It is in such a light that I see this outcome and process as moving the regional development of North America into a 'beyond NAFTA' framework. Even if NAFTA itself is not 'deepened,' it is certainly open to being 'widened' to encompass additional areas of economic activity that were originally not subject to NAFTA's provisions. This is the main implication of applying NAFTA rules to subnational government procurement. In other words, the response to the financial crisis (which had triggered a protectionist threat in terms of the Buy America provision) has resulted in a new departure for regional integration in North America. But critically, the extension of integration is not explicitly linked to NAFTA because all of the major post-NAFTA initiatives, such as the Free Trade Area of the Americas initiative and the SPP process, have failed.

The displacement of NAFTA as the central integrating framework of regionalism in North America has had two interesting consequences. First, it has accentuated the power asymmetries that have long marked regionalism in North America. Regionalism 'beyond NAFTA' will remain vulnerable to American decision making, as the negotiations around the Buy America provision suggest. This is reinforced by the observation that nothing in the responses to the Great Freeze of the three governments that are party to NAFTA has actually run through

NAFTA-era institutions. The degree of *region-ness* in North America has not increased, as it has in Europe, for example, or even, according to some readings, in Asia (Higgott and Dieter 2003). In fact, it appears that national policy horizons have been reinforced both nationally and globally. North America, in essence, is being squeezed out by renewed forms of national economic policy making as well as by reinvigorated forms of global coordination.

Second, the displacement of NAFTA as the central integrating framework of regionalism in North America lays bare the social and political limits to the evolution of North America as a region. One of these barriers is the sheer political weight of the United States in North America. With an economy that dwarfs those of its neighbours by magnitudes of 10 or more, and with the global reach of its corporate community driving its foreign economic policy, U.S. officials must look far beyond NAFTA as they seek to shape the economic environment in which they hope to prosper. And where Canada and Mexico were once routinely seen as the two most important trading partners of the United States by a wide margin, today Mexico has been displaced to third place, behind China and Canada.[16] In the current climate of economic crisis and populist response, the United States is simultaneously looking deep inside itself and more broadly towards its largest global trading partners (and especially China) as it negotiates an economic exit strategy. North America as a regional economic focus will get downgraded in this process.

But beyond the political and economic barriers to further regional integration we encounter cultural and nationalist barriers to strengthening the sense of *region-ness* in North America. Critical here are the wellsprings of cultural nationalism in Canada and Mexico, which act as brakes on how far officials in these countries can move to embrace such *region-ness*. Politicians pay a price in these countries for being openly pro-American, and this form of nationalism places limits on how robust the ties of regionalism can become. Recent years have also seen a resurgence of nationalism in the United States, as discussed in the chapter by Bow in this volume. And while such nationalism exists also in Europe, the counterbalancing role of extensive regional institutions works to mitigate such effects. It is because genuinely effective regional institutions do not exist in North America that its regionalism is so peculiarly vulnerable to political developments of the sort that have characterized responses to the Great Freeze across Canada, the United States, and Mexico.

Conclusion

In this chapter I have evaluated the type of regionalism that has developed in North America, the nature of the economic crisis, the ways in which the economic crisis has affected the region's governments, and the possible implications of these responses for further regional developments. I conclude that while it is possible that NAFTA will be deepened as a consequence of the Great Freeze, this is unlikely, despite more recent security perimeter discussions. It is much more likely that the peculiar political vulnerabilities of regionalism in North America will be further exposed and exacerbated. In particular, we believe that the severity of the economic downturn in the United States will make it more difficult for Canadian and Mexican firms to trade with the United States. Part of this arises out of the Buy America provisions of the U.S. stimulus package, although both Canada and Mexico have worked hard to mitigate these. As well, over the longer term, financial regulatory reforms under way in the United States will make it more difficult for banks that are not organized like American financial institutions to operate in the U.S. market. This will hold back regional integration, for both Canada and Mexico are now more than ever reluctant to harmonize their financial institutions along the lines of American ones, given the course of the subprime crisis. Such barriers, small as they may seem, will be complemented by the ongoing thickening of the American border, which will slow down the growth of regional trade (see the chapter by Gilbert in this volume). It may be that American trade with the rest of the world grows more slowly as well, but in any case, North American *region-ness* is very unlikely to grow and/or deepen.

If we add to this the populist backlash against globalization and immigration – as represented most interestingly by the stunning popularity of the Tea Party movement – I can argue with some degree of conviction that the politics of *region-ness* in North America will face increased pressures for some time to come. The North American project has always been an elite-led project, conceived of in fairly narrow economic terms and delivered on the basis that it can achieve real economic gains for its participants. Only in Canada has the argument for NAFTA based on trade gains had any real resonance, and not without significant controversy and debate. The Canadian economy is the most internationalized of the three NAFTA signatories, and it has reaped significant trading gains from NAFTA since its inception. Yet even in Canada, NAFTA and increased regional integration with North America are not easy to sell politically; while in Mexico, strong antipathy towards the United States has always existed. And as Kim Richard Nossal (1985) long ago noted, thus has it always been. And now, as America's insatiable demand for drugs plays into a kind of civil insurgency among Mexico's leading drug cartels (see the chapter by Cadena-Roa in this volume), and as its increasingly strident immigration debate further alienates its own Hispanic community, relations between the United States and Mexico are coming under unprecedented strain. If *region-ness* has an ebb-and-flow quality to it, it appears to be heading towards a period of stress and strain.

Thus the impact of the Great Freeze on regional integration in North America will, I predict, lead to an era of retreat. Regional institutions have become even more hollowed out, while the policy horizons of officials seem to have shrunk, with only a few exceptions. And the political and economic conditions for strengthening regionalism appear to be anemic at best. Unlike in Europe and Asia, regional responses do not even appear to be on the table.

Yet this is not necessarily a 'bad thing.' NAFTA's acknowledged democratic deficits ought to give pause for thought regarding a reflexive response for more regionalization as a solution to economic malaise. If regional solutions are no longer the default option through which a response to economic crisis is organized, perhaps a more robust national response can also be a more democratic response, or at least a response that is more amenable to democratic pressure than a regional one. Democracy, after all, has been most successful at the national (and even subnational) level, when it is organized within the territorial and institutional confines of the nation-state. As the example of the EU suggests, democratic input into public policy is rarely sufficiently realized at the supranational level – indeed, the European sovereign debt crisis is partly connected to this disentangling of the political from the economic. If the response to the ongoing economic crisis is a reduction of *region-ness* but also a movement towards reinvigorating democracy within nation-states, then perhaps the end result will be good for democracy in the states inhabiting North America, if not for North America itself.

Notes

1 This chapter was made possible by the enthusiasm and contribution of Abdulghany Mohamed, who was initially a co-author but had to withdraw from the project before it was completed. The author is grateful

for the initial work done by Mohamed, and for his contributions to the workshop 'North America in Question: Regional Integration in an Era of Political-Economic Turbulence,' held in Atlanta, GA, 5 March 2010. I would also like to thank Laura Macdonald and other participants at the Atlanta workshop for helpful comments on a previous draft.

2 The recession of 1981–2 was also very severe and resulted in unemployment reaching almost 12%, versus just over 10% during the 2007–9 crisis.

3 In the summer of 2008, however, stories began to circulate about the funding difficulties of Fannie Mae and Freddie Mac, the U.S.-government-sponsored enterprises (GSEs) at the heart of the American secondary-mortgage market. As problems in the subprime-linked securities markets became increasingly visible, the capitalization ratios of both GSEs came under scrutiny. Both enterprises were effectively nationalized in September 2008 when the U.S. government officially guaranteed $200 billion of their MBSs. A further guarantee was issued in February 2009 for another $200 billion.

4 This is the main theme of IMF, 'Crisis and Recovery,' *World Economic Outlook* (April 2009), http://www.imf.org, accessed 4 May 2009.

5 All major central banks took part in these efforts, which included creating new credit facilities. In the United States, for example, the Fed designed TALF (Term Asset-Backed Securities Loan Facility) to stimulate commercial paper markets and to allow financial institutions to use newly issued ABSs as collateral for Fed support. Within six months of its creation, TALF had about $1 trillion at its disposal.

6 For example, Citibank lost 90% of its stock market value over 2008–9, while General Motors suffered an even greater slide in the value of its shares prior to entering creditor protection in June 2009. The spike in bankruptcy filings in the United States and Britain is almost without precedent and includes venerable firms such as Lehman Brothers, General Motors, and Chrysler in the United States and Woolworths in Britain. According to the recent figures, almost twenty countries reported year-on-year house price declines in 2009, led by declines of almost 20% in the United States and Britain and nearly 10% in Ireland. Unless indicated, all figures below come from 2009 issues of *The Economist*. Stock market figures come from IMF, 'Global Financial Stability Report: Responding to the Financial Crisis and Measuring Systemic Risks,' *World Economic and Financial Survey* (April 2009), http://www.imf.org, accessed 4 May 2009.

7 Note that these figures represent an improvement over the previous two quarters. Figures taken from 2009 issues of *The Economist*.

8 Plummeting industrial production also feeds through to negative GDP growth rates. Projections for 2009 are as follows: Russia, –7%; South Korea, –1%; South Africa, –2%; Argentina –0.5%; Mexico, –7%. Only a handful of

countries are projected to grow in 2009, among them China, +8%; India, +5%; Poland, +1%; and Egypt, +4%. *Economist,* various issues throughout 2009.

9 'WTO Sees 9% Global Trade Decline in 2009 as Recession Strikes,' Press Release 554, 24 March 2009, http://www.wto.org, accessed 4 May 2009.

10 'ILO Bulletin of Labour Statistics,' 2009–2, 123.

11 *Economic Report of the President,* 2010, Washington.

12 For discussion of these themes, see Schwartz 2009; and Germain 2010.

13 Debt-to-GDP ratios for all countries are taken from the IMF's 'World Economic and Financial Surveys: Fiscal Monitor,' May 2010, 13, http://www.imf.org/external/pubs/ft/fm/2010/fm1001.pdf, accessed 12 July 2010.

14 Interestingly, a federal election ran during the worst weeks of the financial crisis in September and October 2008. During this election, the reigning Conservatives maintained that the unfolding economic crisis would not affect Canada, and their re-election emboldened them to bring in a budget in November that had no fiscal stimulus measures. A parliamentary crisis intervened and Parliament was prorogued. When it met again in February 2009, a stimulus package was announced that did finally acknowledge and address the economic fallout from the crisis.

15 The lack of regulatory harmonization is in stark contrast to the European experience (Fratianni 1997; Fitzgerald 1999).

16 According to the U.S. Census Bureau, China has been the second-largest overall trading partner of the United States since 2005, behind Canada, which remains its largest trading partner. See http://www.census.gov/foreign-trade/top/dst/2010/04/balance.html, accessed 12 July 2010.

References

Abgrall, Jean-François. 2004. 'The Regional Dynamics of Province–State Relations. *Horizons: Policy Research Initiative* 7: 1.

Appendini, Kirsten, and Sven Bislev, eds. 1999. *Economic Integration in NAFTA and the EU: Deficient Institutionality.* New York: St Martin's.

Bhagwati, Jagdish. 1992. 'Regionalism versus Multilateralism.' *World Economy* 15, no. 5: 535–55.

Boothe, Paul, and Douglas Purvis. 1997. 'Macroeconomic Policy in Canada and the United States: Independence, Transmission, and Effectiveness.' In *Degrees of Freedom: Canada and United States in a Changing World.* Edited by Keith Banting, George Hoberg, and Richard Simeon. Montreal and Kingston: McGill–Queen's University Press.

Cameron, Maxwell, and Vinod Aggarwal. 1996. 'Mexican Meltdown: States, Markets, and Post-NAFTA Financial Turmoil.' *Third World Quarterly* 17, no. 5: 975–87.

'Canada's State of Trade and Investment Update 2009.' 2010. http://www.
international.gc.ca/economist-economiste/assets/pdfs/DFAIT_SoT_2009_
en.pdf. Accessed 13 September 2011.

Clarkson, Stephen. 2002a. *Canada's Secret Constitution: NAFTA, WTO, and the
End of Sovereignty?* Ottawa: Canadian Centre for Policy Alternatives.

Clarkson, Stephen. 2002b. *Uncle Sam and US: Globalization, Neoconservatism,
and the Canadian State.* Toronto and Washington: University of Toronto Press
and Woodrow Wilson Center Press.

Duttagupta, Rupa, and Natalia Barrera. 2010. 'The Impact of the Global Crisis
on Canada: What Do Macro-Financial Linkages Tell Us?' IMF Working
Paper WP/10/5. Washington: International Monetary Fund.

Economic Report of the President (ERP). 2010. Washington.

Fitzgerald, E.V.K. 1999. 'Trade, Investment and NAFTA: The Economics of
Neighbourhood.' In *The United States and Latin America: The New Agenda.*
Edited by Victor Bulmer-Thomas and James Dunkerley, London and
Cambridge, MA: Institute of Latin American Studies, University of London
and David Rockefeller Center for Latin American Studies, Harvard Univer-
sity.

Germain, Randall. 2010. *Global Politics and Financial Governance.* Basingstoke:
Palgrave.

Helleiner, Eric. 2006. *Towards North American Monetary Union? The Politics and
History of Canada's Exchange Rate Regime.* Montreal and Kingston: McGill–
Queen's University Press.

Hettne, Björn. 1999. 'The New Regionalism: A Prologue.' In *Globalism and the
New Regionalism*, vol. 1. Edited by Björn Hettne, András Inotai, and Osvaldo
Sunkel. New York: St Martin's.

Higgott, Richard, and Dieter Heribert. 2003. 'Alternative Theories of Economic
Regionalism: Trade to Finance in Asian Cooperation.' *Review of International
Political Economy* 10, no. 3: 430–54.

Hoberg, George, Keith G. Banting, and Richard Simeon. 2002. 'The Scope for
Domestic Choice: Policy Autonomy in a Globalizing World.' In *Capacity for
Choice: Canada in a New North America.* Edited by George Hoberg. Toronto:
University of Toronto Press.

Hveem, Helge. 1999. 'Political Regionalism: Master or Servant of Economic
Internationalization?' In *Globalism and the New Regionalism*, vol. 1. Edited by
Björn Hettne, András Inotai, and Osvaldo Sunkel, New York: St Martin's.

International Labour Organization (ILO). 2009 *Bulletin of Labour Statistics* 2009-
2. Geneva: International Labour Organization.

Jara, Alejandro, Ramon Moreno, and Camilo E. Tovar. 2009. 'The Global Crisis
and Latin America: Financial Impact and Policy Responses.' *BIS Quarterly
Review* (June): 53–68.

Katzenstein, Peter J. 1996. 'Regionalism in Comparative Perspective.' *Coopera-*
tion and Conflict 31, no. 2: 123–59.

Mace, Gordon, and Louis Bélanger. 1999. *The Americas in Transition: Contours of*
Regionalism. Boulder: Lynne Rienner.

Marchand, Marianne H., Morten Bøås, and Timothy M. Shaw. 1999. 'The
Political Economy of New Regionalisms.' *Third World Quarterly* 20, no. 5:
897–910.

Mohamed, Abdulghany. 2007. *Canada's Policy on Financial System Consolidation:*
A Political Economy of Public Policy Transformation in an Era of Globalization.
Unpublished PhD Dissertation. Ottawa: Carleton University.

Nossal, Kim R. 1985. 'Economic Nationalism and Continental Integration:
Assumptions, Arguments, and Advocacies.' In *The Politics of Canada's Eco-*
nomic Relationship with the United States. Edited by Denis Stairs and Gilbert
Winham. Toronto: University of Toronto Press.

Pastor, Robert. 2001. *Toward North American Community: Lessons from the Old*
World for the New. Washington: Institute for International Economics.

Sampson, Gary P., and Stephen Woolcock, eds. 2003. *Regionalism, Multilateral-*
ism, and Economic Integration: The Recent Experience. Tokyo: United Nations
University Press.

Schulz, Michael, Fredrick Söderbaum, and Joachim Ojendal, eds. 2001. *Regional-*
ism in a Globalizing World: A Comparative Perspective on Forms, Actors, Proc-
esses. London: Zed.

Schwartz, Herman. 2009. *Sub-Prime Nation: American Power, Global Capital, and*
the Housing Bubble. Ithaca: Cornell University Press.

Skelton, Edward C., and Erwan Quintin. 2009. 'Mexico's Ano Horrible: Global
Crisis Stings Economy.' In *South West Economy.* Dallas: Federal Reserve
Bank (Third Quarter). 3–7.

2 Immovable Object or Unstoppable Force? Economic Crisis and the Social Construction of North America

BRIAN BOW

> Never allow a crisis to go to waste. They are opportunities to do big things.
>
> Rahm Emanuel (in Zeleny 2008)

Has the ongoing global economic crisis derailed regional integration in North America? As other contributors to this volume explain (see chapters by Clarkson and Golob), regional integration as a trilateral political project never really had much momentum, and most of what it had was lost even before the onset of the current crisis. Recently, there have been some apparent policy coordination breakthroughs – including the new U.S.–Canada Beyond the Border talks – but these have been strictly bilateral and limited in scope and are not predicated on any longer-term commitment to regional integration per se. The recession does seem to have had a smothering effect on the prospects for further integration in North America, but there was nothing automatic or inevitable about this. Economic crisis can be an obstacle to regional integration, but it can also be a catalyst, and in fact – at least in the North American experience – it has more often been the latter. In this chapter I examine the interplay among economic crisis, ideas, and regional integration, drawing on theoretical and methodological insights from the constructivist perspective on world politics, discussed in the introduction to this volume. My main argument here is that the effects of an economic crisis on the prospects for regional integration depend on the wider political context in which it unfolds, and – just as important – on the political meaning ascribed to it.

There are at least three ways in which we might expect an economic crisis to block or even roll back movement towards regional integration, each of which has been raised by others and is intuitively plausible (e.g., Pastor 2008; Gallagher 2009; Parmar 2009): an economic slowdown might undercut business pressures for 'streamlining' trade and investment; it might distract political leaders from other policy questions, such as regional integration initiatives; and it might make voters more receptive to protectionist arguments, and generally more risk averse about complex new policy initiatives. But the same economic trends can be understood as signs of crisis in different kinds of ways, and different ways of thinking about crisis can have very different implications for regional integration.

A crisis might be seen to make integration impossible, but it might also be seen to make integration very possible – or even inevitable – depending on how the crisis itself is diagnosed, what kinds of solutions are seen to be available, and the ways those remedies are related to regional policy coordination. Each of the three previous arguments about the implications of an economic crisis could therefore be turned on its head. Instead of diminishing business pressures for further policy coordination, a crisis could intensify those pressures. Instead of drawing political leaders' attention away from regional integration issues, an economic crisis could focus attention on integration as a possible solution to other policy problems, including the crisis itself. And instead of making the public more wary of the political and economic risks associated with regional integration, a crisis could actually make them more accepting of those risks or even make them disregard those risks altogether.

The political implications of a crisis are contingent and contested, because the meaning of the crisis, and even the identification of crisis itself, is socially constructed. That is not to say, of course, that an economic crisis is imaginary, or that the arguments about what to do about it are disingenuous. But the nature and implications of 'the crisis,' and its relationship to the regional integration agenda, are what we think they are, and what we think is shaped by our debates: What caused the crisis? What exactly is in crisis? Who or what is at risk, and what is the nature of the threat? What policy options are 'available'? Who should decide which option to pursue?

There is a substantial and growing body of literature in international political economy on the role of ideas in shaping both specific policy choices and broad national strategies (McNamara 1988; Hall 1989, 1993; Campbell 1998). More recently, constructivist scholars have gone beyond the idea that ideas are like 'flashlights' guiding policy makers through uncertainty, arguing that even the 'hard facts' of economic life are subject to interpretation and can be framed in different ways by proponents of different policies (Blyth 2003; Kirshner 2003; Abdelal, Blyth, and Parsons 2009). Running through much of this work is a recurring interest in crises, either as windows of opportunity for the advancement of new economic ideas (Gourevitch 1986; Keeler 1993), or – less often – as economic phenomena whose meaning and implications are interpreted and framed by rival political actors, who then use them to advance particular political-economic projects (Glasberg 1989; Boin et al. 2005; Boin et al. 2009; t'Hart and Tindall 2009).

Most of the empirical research in this area has found that crises lead to new economic policies when shifting political alignments create a window of opportunity for policy change and when reform advocates are then able to rally support by framing the crisis in ways that resonate with policy makers (Aberbach and Christensen 2003; t'Hart and Tindall 2009; Chwieroth 2010). My review of regional integration debates in North America confirms these general findings and highlights the importance of several key rhetorical elements. Comparison of debates and policy outcomes in the North American experience suggests that to be effective in rallying support for further regional integration, a particular framing of economic crisis must simultaneously do the following: cast the crisis as part of an ongoing policy 'problem' that is at the forefront of concern for the current political leadership and the wider attentive public; resonate with the current political leadership's basic ideological predispositions; portray potentially controversial policy options as consistent with established national priorities and traditions; and, finally, cast regional neighbours as worthy partners in responding to historical or extraregional challenges.

The remainder of this chapter reviews four economic crises – the recession that hit the United States and Canada in the early 1980s; Mexico's 'lost decade' and the 1990–1 recession in the United States; the constriction of regional trade following 9/11; and the recession of 2008–9 and subsequent economic turmoil – and their effects on (contemporary and subsequent) debates over free trade and other regional integration initiatives.

In each of these four cases, both the proponents and opponents of regional integration attempted to frame the crisis in ways that would support their policy agendas. In the mid-1980s and the early 1990s, advocates of closer economic ties effectively framed the severe recessions their countries had just gone through as proof of a pressing and inescapable need to enhance competitiveness through integration, and thereby galvanized their governments' commitment to the Canada–U.S. Free Trade Agreement (CUSFTA) and North American Free Trade Agreement (NAFTA), respectively. In the early 2000s, proponents of 'deeper' integration successfully cast the constriction of trade caused by post-9/11 border security measures as a new kind of economic crisis, but were only partly successful in translating this into momentum for new policy coordination initiatives. The current economic crisis is widely seen to be the most severe of the four discussed here, and again there have been efforts by integration advocates to frame the crisis in ways that might fuel a renewed push for post-NAFTA integration; but so far these efforts have not resonated with policy makers or with the general public in any of the three countries. In fact, the recession seems to have reinforced anxieties about the economic and political consequences of regional integration, and undercut whatever diplomatic momentum might have remained after the Security and Prosperity Partnership of North America (SPP) process was terminated in 2009. The recent unveiling of renewed talks between Canada and the United States on borders and regulatory coordination may be a reflection of renewed momentum, and, just as in the 1980s and 1990s, economic crisis may end up catalysing further regional integration. But that will depend, just as it has before, on the outcome of ongoing rhetorical struggles over the framing of the crisis itself, and of the connection between post-crisis national economic strategies and regional agendas.

1980–7: Out of the Frying Pan, into the Fire?

Most observers at the time believed that the recession of 1980–3 would intensify the mounting tensions between the United States and Canada, and many worried that the patchwork of sectoral integration agreements connecting the two countries might start to unravel (Leyton-Brown 1985). In the short run, they were right, but within just a few years things turned completely around, and the two governments committed themselves to pursue new forms of economic integration that would have been virtually unthinkable in previous decades. For almost a century, free trade with the United States had been 'the issue that [would] not go away' for Canada, with virtually all Canadian elites in agreement that free trade might be economically advantageous but that it was politically impossible (Granatstein 1985). And then in the early and mid-1980s, many in Ottawa (and then in the rest of Canada) very quickly came to be just as certain that free trade was now not just politically possible, but necessary. Rather than reinforcing Canada's traditional reservations about closer economic integration with the United States, the recession of the early 1980s – or rather, a particular interpretation of the recession – was an essential part of free trade supporters' arguments about why Canada had no choice but to tie itself even more tightly to its southern neighbour. More specifically, by framing the recession as part of a larger crisis of market access and competitiveness, free trade proponents were able to rally the Mulroney government behind free trade, win the support of powerful interests such as the Canadian Manufacturers Association, and deflect criticisms from trade unions and civil society groups. Even after the recession had come to an end, free trade supporters were able to sustain a narrative of crisis and inevitability, which swept aside challengers and built a winning political coalition.

The United States had endured a decade of stagnation and lost confidence when it was hit in 1980 by a severe recession, characterized by bank failures, severe inflation, and spreading unemployment. The contraction of demand in the United States would have been bad enough for Canadian exporters, but it was also accompanied by a wave of protectionism, which threatened to push Canadian producers out of the all-important American market (Frizzell and Westell 1985; Hart, Dymond, and Robertson 1994, 40–53). The United States had gone through hard economic times before, of course – as with the balance of payments crises of the 1960s and the oil crises of the 1970s – but Canadian negotiators had always found ways to deflect protectionist pressures, and secure some kind of special exemption. There were signs, however, that Congress had become much more assertive and more parochial over the last few years, as in the failed East Coast fisheries agreement and the border broadcasting dispute, and there were obvious philosophical and personal tensions between the Reagan administration and the Trudeau government, as played out in the dispute over the National Energy Program.

The Macdonald Commission, created by Trudeau in 1982 and tasked with finding a way out of the crisis, concluded that Canada must focus on enhancing its international competitiveness and that the best way to do so was to undertake market reforms and pursue sectoral trade liberalization with the United States (Inwood 2005). Preliminary talks with American negotiators quickly established that there were no viable sectoral deals to be made; the only way forward, it seemed, was to make sweeping cross-sectoral trade-offs, and that would require an ambitious, across-the-board trade deal. Thus newly elected prime minister Brian Mulroney shook off his initial scepticism and made a fateful 'leap of faith' to free trade.

The recession wound down in 1983, and both economies gained strength over the next few years, with respectable growth rates and gradually declining unemployment numbers; protectionist pressures in the United States slowly but surely subsided (Lewington 1987). But the shadow of the recession hung over Canadian economic policy debates through the next five years. Mulroney's Progressive Conservatives (PCs) justified their commitment to free trade in terms of a set of 'lessons' learned the hard way under the Trudeau governments: the 1980–3 recession, they argued, was an emphatic confirmation of the failure of Trudeau's interventionist agenda, both in trying to keep the United States at arm's length through trade diversion (the 'Third Option') and investment regulation (through the Foreign Investment Review Agency and the National Energy Program), and, more generally, in trying to have the federal government manage and redirect the domestic economy (Hart 2002, 339–91; Inwood 2005, 130–50). Conservative finance critic Michael Wilson derided Trudeau's economic policies as 'a mosaic of failures' (Brown 1982, 13), and Mulroney took office in 1983 announcing that Canada was 'open for business again' (Munro, Murphy, and Ungeheuer 1984).

This interpretation of what was behind the recession was certainly debatable from an economist's point of view,[1] but it resonated with the ideological predispositions of the governing PCs, who were committed to reducing the role of the state in the economy and who saw a free trade deal as a way to 'lock in' their market reform agenda. Equally important, this reading of the lessons of the early 1980s also resonated with broad segments of the Canadian electorate – including a significant number of traditional Liberal voters – many of whom were frustrated by growing deficits and debts as well as fearful of American trade protectionism ('Rout of the Liberals' 1984). Thus the economic crisis of the early 1980s – a relatively straightforward recession driven mostly by trouble in the U.S. economy – was effectively framed as part of a much larger crisis of Canada's foreign economic policy.

Compared to the decades of reserve and risk aversion that came before, the turn to free trade was a radical policy shift. So it is striking that Mulroney managed to present it as a 'conservative' strategy, by emphasizing the need to hold on to markets and investments that Canada had fought hard for and had come to depend on (Golob 2003). Some supporters did trumpet free trade as a bold break from the past, one that would transform Canada's economy and its relationship with the United States. But with the public's post-recession jitters very clearly in mind, most free trade proponents – including Mulroney and his core advisers – tended to downplay ideology and emphasize pragmatism and to focus mainly on present challenges and past (Liberal) mistakes rather than future uncertainties (Hart et al. 1994, 71–86). There were some potential problems with free trade, they acknowledged, but it was still the best option available, and certainly better than what they saw as the most risky alternative: muddling through with the status quo.

The opponents of free trade did not really have a strong counter for these arguments (ibid., 230–2). A few argued that the recession had been caused by the depth of Canada's economic dependence on the United States, not by Trudeau's efforts to scale back that dependence. But most free trade opponents, especially supporters of the Liberal Party, tended to say little or nothing about the tough times of the early 1980s. Their focus instead was on the further past and on the future – more specifically, on the postwar effort to build up a more equitable and developed Canada, and on the future threat that was ostensibly posed to those efforts by free trade. As in the anti-reciprocity coalitions in 1891 and 1911, free trade opponents in the 1980s were primarily concerned with the political and economic consequences expected to follow from a trade agreement: the erosion of policy autonomy and popular sovereignty, the risk of cultural assimilation, and perhaps even a gradual slide towards political annexation (Ayres 1998, 22–4; Doern and Tomlin 1991, 11–18). Polls taken through the late 1980s suggest that many Canadians were concerned about these future uncertainties, and support for free trade eroded as the negotiations went on, though it remained just above 50% and fell far less dramatically than the prime minister's personal popularity (Hart et al. 1994, 131–2).

In the United States, on the other hand, the free trade deal was never really controversial. A few industries and interest groups worried that free trade with Canada might undercut profits or jeopardize jobs in certain communities dependent on import-competing industries. But opposition in the United States tended to be fragmented and weak; and – in stark contrast to the debate over free trade with Mexico just a few years later – there was virtually no argument that free trade with Canada would have significant negative effects on the U.S. economy. Free trade supporters did argue that a deal would bring direct economic benefits to certain industries and/or to the national economy (see Trezise 1988), but their main arguments actually had little to do with U.S.–Canada trade per se. Instead they emphasized two things: first, the prospective agreement's anticipated effects on the U.S. trade position more broadly, especially American global competitiveness; and second, two kinds of diplomatic effects: it would demonstrate the potential for institutional innovation in areas (such as services and investment) that were bogged down within the GATT process; and it would let the Europeans and Japanese know that the United States also had a 'regional option' that it could pursue if the multilateral process reached an impasse (Winham and DeBoer-Ashworth 2000).

The 1980–3 recession played a part in the U.S. debate – albeit a much less prominent part than in the Canadian debate – even after the economy had begun to recover. For U.S. opponents of the free trade deal, the recession fitted into a broader narrative about the harsh effects of trade liberalization on American workers, particularly those in the resource extraction and traditional manufacturing sectors (which competed directly with imports from Canada). Proponents, on the other hand, tended to refer to the recession in much the same way their Canadian counterparts did: as a reflection of an underlying economic malaise and trade policy weakness, one that could only be remedied by supporting exports through negotiated trade liberalization. Thus in the United States, just as in Canada, economic crisis in the narrower sense (i.e., recession) was successfully framed as part of a much broader political-economic crisis (i.e., declining competitiveness, growing protectionist challenge), and thereby made to support the argument that economic integration was necessary and perhaps even inevitable.

1987–93: A New Mexico? A New U.S.–Mexico Relationship?

The North American Free Trade Agreement (NAFTA) was also understood as a response to crisis, or rather to two different and separate pairings of crisis and opportunity, in Mexico and in the United States. In Mexico, the protracted economic crisis of the 1980s convinced the PRI leadership that the import-substituting industrialization (ISI) model the country had long followed was no longer sustainable, and

that Mexico was compelled to pursue closer trade and investment relationships with the United States. North of the border, the George H.W.
Bush administration saw the 1990–1 recession as one manifestation of a
larger crisis in America's place in the global trading order, and saw free
trade with Mexico as a way to improve the United States' international
competitiveness. Notwithstanding intense opposition from organized
labour and environmental activists, the Clinton administration picked
up where Bush left off, but mixed the crisis-and-opportunity theme
with a more complex narrative about 'modernization' and progress, in
both the United States and Mexico.

Signs of serious trouble had been accumulating in Mexican society
since the late 1960s, if not before, but the oil boom of the 1970s allowed
the country to put off a number of difficult choices. When oil prices fell
in the early 1980s, and Mexico found itself compelled to default on its
international debts, capital flooded out of the country and the economy slid into a malaise of slow growth, deep deficits, and technical
stagnation, now often referred to as the 'lost decade.' Some economists
saw this as a straightforward commodity price collapse, but for the
new generation of Mexican elites, each of the many economic setbacks
suffered in the 1980s was part of a much larger political-economic crisis, one that challenged the regime's guiding principles as well as its
grip on power (Pastor and Wise 1994; Golob 2003). Yet they also worried that redirecting the economy might shake the foundations of the
post-revolutionary political order. Rather than retrenching, Salinas and
his advisers were determined to turn the economy around, through
liberal market reforms and the aggressive pursuit of export markets
abroad. Breaking into the U.S. market would be the key to this new
strategy, and the perceived urgency of doing so was only intensified
after the signing of the Canada–U.S. deal in 1987.[2] But, given Mexico's
historical anxieties, the negotiation of a free trade agreement with the
United States was a risky prospect politically, even for a non-demo-
cratic regime, and Salinas held back from openly pursuing it until the
summer of 1990.

Once he had committed himself to free trade negotiations, Salinas
had to figure out how to convince sceptical bureaucrats and business
leaders, as well as the general public in Mexico. Unlike his Canadian
and American counterparts, Salinas – as the leader of a one-party state
– had to be careful about criticizing his predecessors' choices. He therefore argued that the old ISI model had been made obsolete by recent

changes in the world economy, and presented his new export-oriented strategy as the only way to continue pursuing established priorities, which were national autonomy, social stability, and economic development. Thus he was able to 'link his own internationalist goals with the symbols and ideals of the Mexican revolution' (Cameron and Wise 2004; see also Golob 2003). In the early stages of the negotiation, political opposition in Mexico was muted, but there was growing apprehension and criticism both from within the political establishment and from the press and public. Salinas responded by 'selling' the agreement more aggressively, claiming that it would create enormous new export opportunities and draw waves of foreign investment, and implying that this would enable Mexico to make a historic leap from the developing world to the developed one (Hellman 1993).

The U.S. economy was doing reasonably well in the late 1980s but had ongoing problems with fiscal deficits and trade imbalances. Economists in the United States warned of a continuing problem with international competitiveness, and the Reagan and Bush administrations relied heavily on countervailing and anti-dumping duties to try to put pressure on major rivals like Germany, Japan, and South Korea. The onset of the 1990–1 recession provoked criticism of Bush's handling of the economy but did not spark any fundamental rethinking of the Americans' core foreign economic policies (Yankelovich 1992). The administration argued that the crisis was mostly a domestic problem caused by upheaval in the banking sector and that it could be fixed with a domestic bailout and reforms. At the same time, it reaffirmed its commitment to liberalized trade, but with a promise to protect American workers against other countries' 'unfair' trading practices.

U.S. officials welcomed the Salinas government's proposal to initiate free trade negotiations in 1991, partly because they expected that a deal would create new investment opportunities that might enhance American firms' global competitiveness, but mostly because it might bolster Mexico's political stability as well as advance that country's market reforms. By the time negotiations were concluded in December 1992, however, it seemed that the effort might be for nothing, because Bush was losing ground in the polls and the shaky U.S. economy was expected to make voters more protectionist, driving the Democratic Party deeper into the arms of organized labour (Mayer 1998, 70–5). However, the Democratic candidate and eventual election winner, Bill Clinton, was philosophically a free trader, and not particularly sympathetic to the unions; he decided to follow through with NAFTA ratification and to try to deflect pressures from within the Democratic camp by tacking on side agreements to look after labour and the environment.

Clinton's arguments in support of NAFTA were in many ways similar to those of his predecessor – for example, they included frequent references to the recession as a 'wake-up call' for renewed attention to America's global competitiveness. In that vein, he campaigned more ambitiously for trade liberalization abroad (Behr 1993; Bhagwati 1993). But Clinton, not surprisingly, was more inclined to pin the blame for the recession on Bush's inattention to the economy, rather than on any systemic problems with U.S. trade policy. And, bowing to pressures from the Democrats' core constituencies, he was more inclined to acknowledge that free trade with Mexico might cause some economic dislocations in the United States.

Opponents of NAFTA in the United States tended to draw on many of the same arguments and images that we identify with the broader critique of globalization during the 1990s: concern that free trade would destroy jobs, drive down wages, trigger a rush to exploit lower wages and looser regulations abroad, and diminish American quality of life (Mayer 1998, 219–56). Conservatives like Pat Buchanan mixed these economic arguments with existential angst, worrying that economic integration with Mexico would undermine America's traditional values and popular sovereignty (ibid., 232–3). Critics on the left generally avoided these themes, but there were flashes of xenophobia in the warnings of some union leaders and other civil society groups (Skonieczny 2001). In fact, left- and right-wing arguments against NAFTA tended to overlap, emphasizing the plight of 'working families,' the elevation of corporate and other 'elite' agendas above the interests of ordinary Americans, and the subordination of U.S. policy autonomy to international regimes and global markets. Within this very broad critique of NAFTA, there were few direct references to the causes and consequences of the 1990–1 recession, and not much of an effort to directly counter the White House's interpretation of the crisis. However, critics pointed out that the economy was still facing 'hard times,' and appealed to party leaders not to pursue a new trade deal that might make things even tougher on embattled American workers (e.g., Healey 1993).

Free trade supporters countered that the recession and high unemployment had only increased the need for NAFTA, since the deal would create new investment opportunities and reduce costs by providing access to cheaper labour in Mexico, thereby enhancing America's global competitiveness. But economistic arguments about enhanced competitiveness did not resonate much with the general public, especially when those arguments drew attention to lower wages in Mexico – particularly in light of Ross Perot's 'giant sucking sound' argument and NAFTA supporters' previous claims that the deal would raise wages and living standards south of the border. So the Clinton administration focused instead on trying to refute critics' characterizations of the deal and its implications, with particular attention to growth and unemployment.

In both the 1992 election and the 1993 ratification debate, the White House tried to turn its critics' arguments upside down, by framing NAFTA as a 'job maker.' For example, in his showdown with Ross Perot on *Larry King Live*, Vice President Al Gore opened the debate by telling the story of a Tennessee factory worker whose job would be made more secure by free trade, based on the expectation of increased exports to Mexico ('NAFTA Debate' 1993). Facing criticisms from the left and the right, the Clinton administration tried to capture a broad middle ground, casting its opponents as misguided cranks, and pressing voters to renew their self-confidence and their traditional commitment to free trade and international institutions (Golob 2003; Mayer 1998, 311–19, 328–33). 'This,' Gore explained (Lotz 1997, 73), 'is a choice between the politics of fear and the politics of hope. It's a choice between the past and the future. It's a choice between pessimism and optimism ... We're not scared.'

Polls showed that American voters still had serious concerns about the economic and political implications of NAFTA, but these were somewhat tempered by the labour and environmental side agreements, and probably also by moderates' growing mistrust of high-profile NAFTA opponents like Ross Perot and Pat Buchanan. The Clinton administration ultimately failed to build a strong base of popular support for NAFTA, particularly within its own party, but it did blunt enough of the opposition to bring ratification within striking range. The White House's final challenge was to win over nervous Democratic and moderate Republican senators through a mix of side payments and warnings about the supposed consequences of a failed ratification vote: panic in global financial markets, gridlock in the GATT negotiations, and a poisoning of bilateral relations with Mexico (Conybeare and Zinkula 1996; Crutsinger 1993).

Almost immediately after NAFTA came into effect, Mexico was plunged into a series of new crises, including the EZLN uprising in Chiapas, corruption scandals, and – most important – the sudden collapse of the peso in December 1994. Critics of NAFTA argued that some or all of these disasters could be linked in some way to the free trade agreement, if only through the general malfeasance of the PRI leadership (Morris and Passé-Smith 2001). Supporters of NAFTA, on the other hand, maintained that Mexico's troubles in the 1990s were not caused by free trade, but rather by Mexican leaders' failure to follow through properly on the political and economic reforms that were expected to go hand in hand in with trade liberalization (Hufbauer and Schott 2005, 11–14).

In the second half of the 1990s, the U.S. economy was booming, yet public support for NAFTA actually declined. This is attributable in part to the growth of the grassroots anti-globalization movement in the United States and to the continuing association in many Americans' minds between NAFTA and the worst aspects of globalization, such as job losses, environmental degradation, and undermining of popular sovereignty (Hufbauer and Schott 2005; Pastor 2008). But it was also driven by a new wave of populist conservatism, a wave that was fuelled by the growth of talk radio and cable news networks and that stirred up anti-immigrant sentiments as well as scepticism about international institutions. By the end of the decade, there was an unstated consensus that the push to 'deepen' NAFTA – that is, to pursue even closer economic integration and to explore trilateral cooperation in other policy areas – had lost momentum.

But the regional agenda seemed to flicker back to life in 2000 with the election of Mexico's first non-PRI president, Vicente Fox, who elaborated an ambitious agenda for extensive trilateral integration, featuring a new emphasis on labour mobility and regional social transfers. But while there were signs that the new George W. Bush administration was generally supportive of Fox himself, it was also clear that the White House was not prepared to tackle divisive issues like immigration reform and regional institution building. The bursting of the dot-com bubble in 2000–1 would bring an end to the extraordinary growth the United States had experienced in the mid and late 1990s, but the American economy was still doing fairly well, and there was no sense of urgency in Washington around post-NAFTA regional issues. That would change in the autumn of 2001, but not in a way that anyone expected.

2001–8: Drawing Together or Breaking Apart?

The terrorist attacks of 11 September 2001 created a sense of crisis in the United States, and this, of course, created space to advance a variety of previously 'unthinkable' new policy initiatives. But whereas 9/11 was seen in the United States as a (homeland) security crisis, in Canada and Mexico it was seen mainly as an *economic* crisis – one triggered not by market dynamics but by America's new sense of vulnerability and by the subsequent tightening of its borders (Andreas 2003). Canada's and Mexico's dependence on the United States as an export market had grown to extraordinary proportions (about 85% for Canada and 83% for Mexico), and post-9/11 border delays were playing havoc with the transnational production and distribution systems that had grown up under NAFTA. As in the prelude to the free trade debates, proponents of integration in Canada and Mexico argued that their economies' vital lifelines to the U.S. market were at risk and that the only solution was to secure market access through further integration. In Canada, ambitious integration proposals fell on deaf ears, partly because they did not resonate with the political leadership's world view, and partly because of the perception that the United States was simply not interested. In Mexico, the political leadership was at the forefront in pushing for more ambitious forms of regional integration, but that leadership was internally divided, and its appeals were repeatedly rebuffed by the Bush administration. Yet American policy makers understood that they must find some way of managing 'neighbourhood' issues in this new, post-NAFTA, post-9/11 environment. So gradually, a new form of limited regional integration did emerge, one that combined ad hoc bilateral agreements (the Smart Border agreements) with an ongoing process of trilateral dialogue aimed at informal policy coordination (the SPP).

Most proponents of integration in Canada argued that the only way to convince the United States to rethink the new border restrictions was to pursue new unilateral policy changes and policy coordination initiatives designed to reassure the United States that Canada was not a security problem. A few went so far as to argue that 9/11 had created an opportunity for Canada to capture Washington's attention, and to push for much deeper forms of bilateral economic integration; this, they said, would lead to new border regimes, harmonized rules of origin, regulatory convergence, or even new supranational institution building (see Gilbert 2005). These early 'big idea' proposals received a lot of play in the popular media but ultimately made little headway with the Chrétien government, which had a streak of 1970s-style Canadian nationalism running through it and was not receptive to the idea of further integration. Instead, Chrétien took a more cautious, ad hoc approach to U.S. demands, negotiating and signing a bilateral 'Smart Border'

accord that provided for new border procedures and information sharing, and seeking talks on more efficient 'before-the-border' security
measures that would reduce wait times and transportation costs. The
Canadian government also embarked a number of bilateral initiatives
– joint policing, intelligence sharing, military cooperation – designed
to directly address some of America's most pressing security concerns.
These initiatives included Operation Noble Eagle, Integrated Border
Enforcement Teams (IBETs), and the Shiprider program (see Gilbert
and also Clarkson, in this volume).

In Mexico, Fox's PAN party wanted to carry on with the kinds of
market reforms undertaken by Salinas. But in calling for renewed trilateral dialogue, it also appealed to Europe's experience with regional
'cohesion' policies, with particular emphasis on institution building,
transfer payments, and new efforts to build infrastructure and facilitate local development. These ideas were popular at home, at least in
principle; but they were greeted with a measure of cynicism by those
Mexicans who were frustrated by the gap between Salinas's big promises and the post-NAFTA reality, particularly in the south and in rural
areas. Fox, who had staked much of his political capital on closer ties
with the United States, was considerably weakened by the Bush administration's lukewarm response. Beyond the tightening of border check-
points after 9/11, there was a sudden outpouring of xenophobia in the
United States, which ended any momentum for immigration reform,
encouraged the U.S. Congress to build a two-hundred-mile fence along
the southern border, and stirred up a flurry of new legislative efforts
to deny services to undocumented immigrants. The Fox government
was still generally inclined to look to more ambitious forms of trilateral cooperation on the economic and security agendas; but it was less
inclined to propose new initiatives after the fall of 2002, and it grew
increasingly frustrated with the United States and Canada as regional
partners (Castañeda 2003).

In the United States there were a handful of government officials,
business representatives, and academics who saw the post-9/11 security restrictions as a major diplomatic and commercial problem not
only for Canada and Mexico but also for the United States, and who
argued that the White House needed to seize the opportunity to build
on NAFTA's flimsy institutional structure (see, for example, Manley,
Aspe, and Weld 2005). But the Bush administration was almost totally
preoccupied with the war in Iraq in 2003 and 2004 and continued to be
wary of tackling the immigration issue head on. By the spring of 2005,

supporters of post-NAFTA integration had succeeded in convincing the administration that it needed to respond to Canadian and Mexican concerns, and to try to undo some of the economic dislocations caused by the new security regime. The United States therefore agreed to join Canada and Mexico in launching the trilateral SPP initiative.

As discussed elsewhere in this volume, the SPP was designed to facilitate informal dialogue among government officials – with input from the business community – with the aim of identifying and pursuing new policy coordination initiatives that would address both U.S. concerns about security and Canadian and Mexican concerns about market access. This connection between security and market access was the key to building a transnational coalition in support of the SPP process. Leading proponents argued that these two goals were not necessarily mutually contradictory and that the trilateral dialogue's central aim would be to seek creative diplomatic and technological solutions that would maximize both goals simultaneously. Some of the more reluctant participants tended to see the SPP as a simple diplomatic quid pro quo: 'We'll talk about your issues if you'll talk about ours.' The Mexican political leadership strongly supported the process, although it was often unable to follow up that enthusiasm with significant policy changes. The United States was generally in favour of trilateral dialogue; it was not, however, particularly enthusiastic about many of the specific Canadian and Mexican proposals. Canada was somewhat sceptical about trilateralism but ready to use the opportunity to talk about the specific policy problems it cared about most (i.e., border controls).

The SPP was designed to bypass the push-and-pull of domestic politics, especially in the United States, and the three governments did virtually nothing to explain to voters what it was or what it was for; this created the impression of secrecy, or even conspiracy, among sceptics on the farther left and right of the political spectrum; thus, prominent critics like Lou Dobbs decried the SPP as a stepping stone toward some kind of 'North American Union' (Pastor 2008). In fact, the SPP accomplished very little, beyond wrapping up bilateral initiatives kicked off before 9/11 and translating some of the Smart Border commitments into policy outcomes (Anderson and Sands 2007). Some useful 'technical' initiatives were worked out, but the inherent tension between tighter border security and freer-flowing transnational commerce still had not been effectively reconciled, and the SPP process had effectively run out of gas even before the financial crisis erupted in the fall of 2008.

2008–: Regional Problems, National Responses

The current economic crisis was only recognized as such after the wave of mortgage failures in the United States led to massive bank shortfalls in the fall of 2008. Yet there had been signs of impending disaster as far back as 2004–5, when the U.S. housing market began to crumble (Greenspan 2007). By the spring of 2008, it was pretty clear that the U.S. economy was in serious trouble, and there were signs of a shift towards a more protectionist, 'America first' attitude regarding foreign trade and investment (as discussed by Germain and Mohamed in this volume). As the presidential primary races moved through hard-pressed Midwestern states like Ohio and Pennsylvania, Democratic candidates Hillary Clinton and Barack Obama pandered to anti-NAFTA sentiments in the region by pledging to 'renegotiate' the deal. Even at the time, it was pretty clear that neither candidate was really sincere, but business leaders in all three countries worried that – given the public mood at the time – even a free trader Democratic president might be held captive by the same organized labour and environmental groups that had opposed NAFTA back in 1992–3.

Just before the 2008 leaders' summit in New Orleans, candidate Obama promised that, if elected, he would continue to participate in summit meetings with his Canadian and Mexican counterparts. But he explicitly rejected the closed-door model established by his predecessor, and he promised greater 'transparency' and inclusiveness for labour and civil society groups. True to his word, Obama sent a team to the August 2009 summit in Guadalajara, but it came bearing few new policy ideas, and it made no promises to continue the SPP process. However, the leaders' joint statement did suggest a marked shift in tone and priorities, one that reflected Obama's earlier promises to 'ensure that the benefits of our [regional] economic growth are widely shared and sustainable' (White House 2009).

After Guadalajara, the SPP website was updated to indicate that there would be no further updates. The NAFTA Commission met again in October 2009, and there was some optimism that the Leaders' Summit process would continue under some other name. Canada was to host the 2010 summit, but the Canadian and American leaders were both overwhelmed with global summit meetings that summer (Canada hosted both the G8 and the G20), and the decision was eventually taken to quietly drop the 2010 North American summit. There was no summit meeting in 2011. Without the summit process to galvanize compromises and spur policy 'deliverables,' trilateral dialogue ground to a halt (Savage 2010), the SPP working groups were left in limbo, and policy makers quietly reverted to their default approach: ad hoc problem-solving on a purely bilateral basis (see Golob in this volume). There was a trilateral summit in April 2012, but both the format and content of the talks showed off the drift to two separate bilateral agendas.

Throughout the recent recession and subsequent economic turmoil, there have been scattered calls for a renewal of regional policy coordination as a means to enhance the three countries' global competitiveness (NACC 2007; Pastor 2008). Rising economies like China and India have managed to avoid the tremors running through the global economy, and their economies are still growing rapidly, while the United States and many of its traditional partners cannot seem to get rolling again. A number of advocates of further integration have seized on this extra-regional challenge – sometimes mixing their positions with 1970s-style arguments about U.S. relative decline – to try to prod the White House into paying more attention to regional trade and investment barriers, which, they maintain, are an obstacle to enhanced global competitiveness (NACC 2009). But these kinds of arguments have not resonated with policy makers or with the general public in any of the three countries. Rather than catalysing regional integration, the crisis seems to have suppressed it. Why? What was different about this most recent crisis?

One possible difference relates to the *scale* of the crisis. The public mood is darker today than it was during the two previous major recessions, and many observers have referred to the current crisis as the worst since the Great Depression of the 1930s. But economists are divided on whether this recession really has been worse than that of the early 1980s; much depends on which indicators are examined (Gascon 2009; Leonhardt 2009). There are important differences between the two economic slumps, but it is not clear how those differences might explain why regional integration was pushed forward in the 1980s but has not been today. In the 1980s, the causes and implications of the recession were key elements in the debate that led to CUSFTA, and then indirectly to NAFTA. In this most recent crisis, there has again been much hand wringing about the state of the economy, but this time regional integration – in any form – has barely been 'on the radar' in any of the three countries.

In the next few paragraphs, I identify and explain three key differences that help explain why supporters of further regional integration have failed to get political traction this time around: the basic ideological incompatibility between regionalists' proposals and the Obama administration's sense of its problems and priorities; the 'distraction' of the three leaders by other kinds of policy and political challenges; and the shifting momentum between societal players, with the business community apparently discouraged and disinterested, and the unions and civil society organizations confident and engaged. These three differences are discussed in order of their importance, but it is important to recognize that it was the *convergence* of all three that gave them weight as obstacles to further integration.

Ideological 'Mis-Fit'

In the free trade debates, regionalists seeking liberal market reforms encountered new political leaders who were philosophically and politically oriented the same way, and they clicked. The strongest supporters of the free trade option in Canada and in Mexico hoped to secure access to the U.S. market by 'giving up' various forms of state intervention in the economy – such as industry subsidies, quotas, marketing boards, and public monopolies – which they were philosophically inclined to do anyway, with or without a free trade agreement. Mulroney, Salinas, Bush, and Clinton were all generally inclined to free trade in principle, and all tended to think about trade policy in terms of becoming more competitive by letting the market take care of itself. In fact, Mulroney and Salinas both saw the scaling back of the state's role in the economy as one of their most important and urgent policy goals, and both hoped that the negotiation of a formal free trade agreement would help 'lock in' these market reforms. But all four of these leaders were initially worried that while free trade might be the right thing to do, it could not be done politically. In all three countries, the framing of recent economic downturns as symptoms of a larger crisis brought on by the failed policies of previous governments helped break down opposition and build up a broad coalition.

In the 2000s, however, those same arguments did not resonate with the problems and priorities of the political leaderships, particularly in the United States; nor did they resonate with the most urgent concerns of the general public. In the early 2000s, the arguments that integration advocates had been making about 'streamlining' the border were profoundly out of step with Americans' post-9/11 preoccupation with surveillance and control. George W. Bush and his team were of course strong advocates of free markets, but, as U.S. officials often told their

Canadian counterparts, in the post-9/11 world, 'security trumps trade.' And in the late 2000s, integration supporters' arguments about clearing away regulations and other obstacles from the free play of the market did not sit well with the Obama team's emerging neo-Keynesian mindset, or with an American public fed up with corporate recklessness.

Even after his election in November 2008, it was not entirely clear where Obama and his team stood on international economic policy in general, and trade in particular. Throughout the presidential campaign, Obama moved towards the centre, emphasizing his commitment to fostering an 'open' international economic order and to playing a constructive role in world trade. The administration has generally followed up on these commitments but has also sometimes succumbed to pressure from industry lobbies and unions in order to conserve resources for higher-priority initiatives. Thus when Congress attached 'Buy American' provisions to the January 2009 stimulus package, the White House made little effort to fight for special exemptions for Canada and Mexico.

The diagnosis of the financial crisis and the crafting of the stimulus plan seem to have had important 'formative' effects on the Obama administration's economic thinking, in that it has bolstered a pre-existing sense of confidence in government's capacity to guide the economy and has also fostered a new interest in (neo)Keynesian theories and strategies (Krugman 2009; Lindvall 2009). Whatever the president's own ideological leanings, the White House has not been in a position to entertain arguments about cutting back regulations or liberalizing investment rules; the huge bailouts for the banking and auto industries and the catastrophic oil spill in the Gulf of Mexico have undercut public trust in business leaders and shaken Americans' confidence in the market's capacity to take care of itself.

Of course, regional integration does not have to be (only) about removing trade barriers and cutting back regulations. In fact, some of the most prominent critics of the SPP have argued that there should be more extensive policy coordination among the three countries, and a few have called for more extensive state intervention and/or more substantial trinational institutions (e.g., Clarkson 2008; Golob 2008). Robert Pastor (2001, 2011), for example, has continued to advocate for a set of new trilateral regimes to facilitate policy coordination on investment and the environment, to tackle transnational crime, to plan and build infrastructure, and to foster local development in Mexico. Some of these kinds of specific proposals have caught on and have been translated into concrete policies, but the overall approach has not had much traction in the political arena, for a variety of reasons. The business community obviously has little interest in building a bigger state apparatus, and the American public is generally leery of anything that looks like the European Union, which they tend to associate with excessive government interference and bureaucratic inefficiency.

'Bigger Fish to Fry'

The Obama administration's general disinterest in regional integration has been powerfully reinforced by the sheer number of controversial policy challenges it faces. Obama came to office already burdened with two major military interventions abroad, nuclear proliferation challenges in Iran and North Korea, a global financial crisis and severe recession at home, the pent-up frustrations of a Democratic Party out of power for eight years, and extraordinarily high voter expectations. Just as the George W. Bush administration was caught up in Iraq, so the Obama administration has been caught up in the recession, health care reform, and Afghanistan. Having lost its super-majority in Congress, and facing tough prospects in the mid-term elections, the administration felt the need to scale back its ambitions and to conserve political capital for key policy initiatives. And, looking at the world region by region, North America – and the Western Hemisphere more broadly – has been at the bottom of the White House's list (Lowenthal 2010).

In Canada, Harper's Conservatives are philosophically inclined to close ties with Washington and to closer economic integration, but when leading a minority government they were wary of doing anything that might galvanize an effective coalition among the opposition parties. Thus they tended to adopt a cautious, reactive stance vis-à-vis relations with the United States and to steer away from ambitious proposals. Canada has of course always been a reluctant trilateralist, but the current government seems to be even more sceptical than its predecessors, apparently having bought into the argument that including Mexico at the bargaining table tends to drive the conversation away from what Canada wants to talk about, so Canada is better off trying to cultivate its 'special relationship' with the United States (CUCUSP 2009). One manifestation of this ambivalence about Mexico was the Canadian government's clumsy handling of the imposition of new visa requirements on travellers from Mexico, in August 2009, which deeply offended the Mexican public. Harper made some amends the following May when he hosted a visit from Fox's successor, Felipe Calderón, and promised (mostly symbolic) support for Mexico's fight with organized crime, among other bilateral initiatives. These moves were appreciated by Calderón but did little to persuade most Mexicans that there was any real (regional) partnership between the two countries.

Under Fox, Mexico had taken a leading role both in cheerleading tri-lateral dialogue and in proposing specific policy initiatives. But it was often unable to back up its ambitious proposals with concrete policy changes, either because of institutional or infrastructural weaknesses or because of lingering political anxieties about close cooperation with the United States.[3] Calderón has been almost completely preoccupied with the ongoing struggle to contain drug trafficking and organized crime in Mexico. His government has sought support from the United States and Canada through the Mérida Initiative and related programs; but very little of this has been openly talked about as a 'regional' problem or pursued through established trilateral channels. The United States has been slow to deliver on its promises of financial support, and Cana-da's contributions so far have been conspicuously small. Thus Mexican elites are increasingly discouraged about the prospects for any kind of post-NAFTA regional integration, and more circumspect about propos-ing new initiatives.

Business Discouraged, Civil Society on the March

The business community was very active in promoting the free trade agreements, both behind the scenes and in the public arena, and was engaged as a 'stakeholder' in the SPP process as well. While some of the same business associations and executives have actively promot-ed closer economic ties over the past few years, overall the business community has been conspicuously inconspicuous (Greenaway 2008). Frustrations with the SPP, anxiety about the implications of Democratic control over the White House and Congress, and the onset of the finan-cial crisis and recession have undercut business leaders' confidence in terms of pressing for post-NAFTA integration. In all three countries, they have set the regional agenda aside and focused on their own national economies, their own industries, or their own firms.

At the same time, unions and civil society organizations opposed to regional integration have been buoyed by Obama's election and the ter-mination of the SPP. While they are mistaken to think that their efforts effectively derailed the SPP, there is no question that perceptions of active opposition 'out there' have caused many politicians, particularly in the United States, to shy away from these issues (see Ayres and Macdonald in this volume). Where there is little sense of political momentum behind a policy idea, it doesn't take much popular opposition to discourage legislators from engaging with it.

The SPP had been designed as an executive-branch-only, closed-door process, in order to avoid the furor that NAFTA triggered in 1992–3. In retrospect, this effort to avoid trouble succeeded well in evading broad-based opposition, but it also triggered intense suspicion and resentment among trade unions, anti-globalization activists, and 'anti-statist' and anti-immigration groups on the right. By the end of 2008 the SPP had become politically 'radioactive' (Anderson, quoted in Savage 2010). Of course, most of the policy challenges the SPP was meant to confront were still in play, so there was pent-up 'demand' for some kind of replacement regime, be it trilateral, bilateral, or somewhere in between (Davis 2010; Savage 2010). But the acrimony surrounding NAFTA and the SPP made political leaders in all three countries wary of restarting that conversation, especially out in public view.

Crisis, Contingency, and the Future of North American Regional Integration

When we take all four of these episodes together, we see a clear pattern. In the mid-1980s and the early 1990s, advocates of liberal market reforms were able to frame recent economic downturns as reflections of a larger crisis of national competitiveness; then, using that frame, they rallied policy makers and their publics to shake off concerns about the political and economic implications of free trade and to support the CUSFTA and NAFTA agreements. In the early 2000s, proponents of regional integration made similar kinds of arguments in the context of a very different kind of crisis. In this case, this framing of the crisis was enough to convince policy makers to turn their attention to regional issues and to initiate a new trilateral dialogue (i.e., the SPP). But this was not enough to sustain a sense of urgency around these issues in the United States or to generate broad-based coalitions in support of further integration in any of the three countries, so the SPP was not the major regional breakthrough that some proponents had hoped for. In the late 2000s, advocates of deeper integration again tried to frame the most recent economic downturn as a crisis of competitiveness, and to push for a renewal of bilateral or trilateral talks on border controls, rules of origin, regulation, and other post-NAFTA issues. But this time those arguments did not resonate with policy makers – particularly the Obama administration – or with the public in any of the three countries, and the regional integration agenda dropped out of sight.

So the most common rationales for further integration were roughly similar in all of the four cases, and the proposed reasons those arguments did not catch on in the late 2000s sound like the kinds we would expect to hear in a conventional pluralist or political opportunity structure interpretation: change of government, shifting government priorities, and 'activation' of interest groups. We might therefore argue that this proves that states' choices about regional integration initiatives are not governed by ideas and arguments, but rather by national interests. But this 'commonsense' distinction between interests and ideas is overdrawn and misleading. States' decisions about whether to pursue specific regional integration initiatives were indeed driven by leaders' national interest 'calculations,' but in each case there was nothing obvious or straightforward about what the national interest was or how it might be served. In each case, political leaders' choices were powerfully influenced by the framing of a recent or ongoing economic crisis. This narrowed their perceived range of options and steered them towards particular policy choices.

Changing political circumstances are not enough to bring about radical policy shifts; they must be met with creative rhetorical moves that cast the policy agenda in ways that capture the support of policy makers and publics alike and thereby galvanize the formation of winning coalitions. At the same time, it is important to understand that political success is not simply a matter of making 'the right argument.' There are times and places in which certain kinds of policy shifts are virtually 'unthinkable,' given the prevailing perceptions of problems and options within that society. Yet experience suggests that these constellations of political forces can shift suddenly when key players come to think about their interests and options in a new way; and the right framing of a problem can be the catalyst for such an epiphany. Trudeau, after all, switched abruptly from trying to limit trade and investment in 1982 to exploring sectoral free trade in 1983, and Mulroney went from opposing free trade as a candidate in 1983 to making it his central policy initiative as prime minister in 1985–6. Most expected that Salinas would respond to the 'lost decade' as his predecessor (Miguel de la Madrid) had done, with relatively cautious economic policy changes; but instead, he pushed ahead with a radical shift towards aggressive market reforms and free trade. And the Clinton administration defied expectations not only by supporting NAFTA but also by getting it ratified, by effectively coopting or evading critics from within his party's traditional constituencies (labour unions, environmentalists). If nothing else, the free trade debates should teach us that what seems politically impossible may suddenly come to seem possible or even inevitable.

And indeed, the recent announcement of new talks on borders, regulations, and environmental cooperation suggests that new regional integration breakthroughs may be just around the corner. Before thinking about what these new talks might amount to, I will offer some thoughts about where they have come from and why they are coming about now.

Canadian governments have been interested in the idea of 'perimeter security' since 9/11 but have been wary of pursuing it because of anticipated domestic political opposition. In the early 2000s, the concept was symbolically linked by opponents to a number of things that many Canadians hated or feared, including George W. Bush's foreign policy, intrusive surveillance, compromised civil rights, and extraordinary rendition (i.e., the Maher Arar case). The Harper government understood, however, that the 'perimeter' model was pretty much the only one that U.S. security planners were interested in, and was thus the key to unlocking Canada's post-9/11 border problem. Canadian officials and business associations were also interested in negotiated regulatory harmonization as a way to reduce costs and attract attention and support from the U.S. business community.

Mexico was also hoping for some kind of breakthrough with the United States on borders, immigration, and trade. The long-standing dispute over trucking was a major source of resentment for Mexico, and Calderón deliberately framed it as the key test of the Obama administration's commitment to U.S.–Mexico relations. Like the Canadians, Mexican officials saw regulatory coordination as a way to reduce transaction costs and create momentum for closer economic cooperation.

Canadian and Mexican priorities were thus essentially unchanged since 2005; it was new U.S. priorities that opened the door for the new talks on borders, regulation, and the environment. With an eye to the upcoming 2012 elections, the Obama administration had been actively seeking low-risk foreign policy breakthroughs. But the more important catalyst for renewed talks was the changing public discourse in the United States regarding the country's most pressing economic challenges and the proper role of the state in the economy. When first confronted with the financial crisis and the early onset of the recession, the Obama administration had embraced neo-Keynesian ideas and policies. But by the summer of 2010, voters were getting angry about the costs of the bailouts and stimulus packages, and – with encouragement from the president's Republican critics – increasingly worried about mounting public debts and their implications for America's global competitiveness. Thus we are now seeing the early phases of a new political debate in the United States over the 'lessons' of the 2008 crisis – lessons that will have important implications for the future of North American integration.

The Democrats carried the day in the early stages, with a narrative that placed the blame for the crisis on Bush's irresponsibility and neglect and that highlighted the need for renewed state intervention to curb the excesses of the market. But as the crisis continued, the Republicans countered with their own interpretation of it, which skirted over the origins of the financial meltdown and portrayed Obama's stimulus packages as a Trojan horse for an ideologically driven tax-and-spend agenda, and – more generally – for the covert construction of a more ambitious and intrusive federal government. The Obama administration has been at pains to portray its choices as thoroughly pragmatic; it casts itself as having aggressively pursued stimulus when it was urgently needed, then moving quickly to cut spending as soon as it was possible. If the Republicans win in 2012, however, they are likely to turn the debate in a direction similar to the one that was taken in the United States and Canada during the early 1980s; that is, they are likely to blame the crisis on interventionist policies and to maintain that the remedy is freer markets and more extensive economic integration. However, these 'lessons' may not carry over to the most difficult challenges on the regional agenda today, many of which are only indirectly related to trade and investment: border security, immigration, organized crime, and environmental cooperation.

Will the ongoing U.S.–Canada and U.S.–Mexico bilateral talks on border security work out, and catalyse further integration in North America? It is of course still too soon to say, but we can use what we've uncovered in previous episodes to make some educated guesses. Political leaders in all three countries want to show that they are effective managers of crucial relationships with regional partners. All want to frame these new talks in ways that mobilize domestic supporters but that also avoid provoking critics. The decision to refer to the U.S.–Canada border talks in terms of a 'security perimeter' is a double-edged sword for Ottawa, as it instantly cues up thoughts of a breakthrough on the part of Canadian exporters and U.S. security planners, but also stirs up mistrust and opposition among Canadian nationalists and civil liberties advocates. Talk about a new 'partnership' with Mexico on borders and crime helps assuage traditional Mexican anxieties about sovereignty and recognition but also provokes a cynical response from Mexicans, who are weary of the enduring gaps between American rhetoric and policy realities.

These new bilateral talks are likely to challenge the extensive 'security protectionism' that grew up in the shadow of 9/11, but there is no substantial and well-organized constituency in the United States to protect most of those measures. Organized labour in the United States has no objection to border security changes per se, though union members are of course likely to fight some specific proposals. Regulatory cooperation – in both bilateral contexts – is likely to trigger opposition within some affected industries and regions, but so far we do not know enough about which regulations are under review to make any predictions about whether and where strong domestic opposition will manifest itself. So far these new bilateral talks have stirred suspicion but not significant opposition; but that is likely to change over time, especially if the new talks are seen to resemble the old, widely criticized format of the SPP. The long-term economic implications of the recent crisis are still not clear, and the scope and format of the new bilateral negotiations are as yet undefined. But already we are seeing the start of renewed political and rhetorical struggles over the meaning of these developments, and the fight over the framing of this most recent crisis is certain to set the terms for regional cooperation in the years to come.

Notes

1 As free trade supporters frequently pointed out, most Canadian economists supported the free trade option through the mid-1980s. However, there was no such consensus on the root causes of the recession or on the connection between the recession and free trade.

2 Salinas's suspicion that CUSFTA was creating preferential trade area effects that hurt Mexico was probably exacerbated by Canada's negative response to his initial proposal for U.S.–Mexico free trade. Once it became clear that a U.S.–Mexico deal would ultimately go through, regardless of what Canada did, Ottawa insisted on a seat at the (trilateral) negotiating table so that it could better look after its own interests.

3 Interviews with Mexican officials, September 2009 (Mexico City) and February 2010 (Ottawa).

References

Abdelal, Rawi, Mark Blyth, and Craig Parsons. 2009. *Constructing the International Economy*. Ithaca: Cornell University Press.

Aberbach, J.D., and Thomas Christensen. 2003. 'Translating Theoretical Ideas into Modern State Reform.' *Administration and Society* 35, no. 5 (May): 491–509.

Anderson, Greg, and Christopher Sands. 2007. 'Negotiating North America: The Security and Prosperity Partnership.' Hudson Institute Working Paper, Summer, http://hudson.org/files/pdf_upload/HudsonNegotiatingNorth-Americaadvanceproof2.pdf, accessed 21 March 2009.

Andreas, Peter. 2003. 'A Tale of Two Borders: The U.S.–Canada and U.S.–Mexico Lines after 9/11.' In *The Rebordering of North America: Integration and Exclusion in a New Security Context*. Edited by Peter Andreas and Thomas Biersteker. New York: Routledge.

Ayres, Jeffrey M. 1998. *Defying Conventional Wisdom: Political Movements and Popular Contention against North American Free Trade*. Toronto: University of Toronto Press.

Behr, Peter. 1993. 'Clinton Team's Lobbying Campaign Tries to Turn Corner on NAFTA.' *Washington Post*, 11 October, A14.

Bhagwati, Jagdish. 1993. 'The Diminished Giant Syndrome: How Declinism Drives Trade Policy.' *Foreign Affairs* 72 (Spring): 22–6.

Blyth, Mark. 2003. 'Structures Do Not Come with an Instruction Sheet: Interests, Ideas, and Progress in Political Science.' *Perspectives on Politics* 1 (December): 695–706.

Boin, Arjen, Paul t'Hart, Eric Stern, and Bengt Sundelius. 2005. *The Politics of Crisis Management: Public Leadership Under Pressure*. London: Oxford University Press.

Boin, Arjen, Allan McConnell, and Paul t'Hart. 2009. 'Crisis Exploitation: Political and Policy Impacts of Framing Contests.' *Journal of European Public Policy* 16, no. 1 (Spring): 81–106.

Brown, Merill. 1982. "The Fading Allure of Trudeau," *The Age*, September 6.

Cameron, Maxwell, and Carol Wise. 2004. 'The Political Impact of NAFTA on Mexico.' *Canadian Journal of Political Science* 39, no. 2 (June): 301–23.

Campbell, John L. 1998. 'Institutional Analysis and the Role of Ideas in Political Economy.' *Theory and Society* 27, no. 3 (June): 377–409.

Castañeda, Jorge G. 2003. 'The Forgotten Relationship.' *Foreign Affairs* 82, no. 3 (May–June): 67–81.

Clarkson, Stephen. 2008. *Does North America Exist? Governing the Continent after NAFTA and 9/11*. Toronto: University of Toronto Press.

Carleton University Canada-U.S. Project (CUCUSP). 2009. 'From Correct to

Inspired: A Blueprint for Canada–U.S. Engagement.' 19 January. http://www.ctpl.ca/sites/default/files/FINAL-BLUEPRINT-ENGLISH.pdf. Accessed 20 March 2009.

Chwierioth, Jeffrey. 2010. *Capital Ideas: The IMF and the Rise of Financial Liberalization*. Princeton: Princeton University Press.

Conybeare, John A.C., and Mark Zinkula. 1996. 'Who Voted against NAFTA?' *The World Economy* 19 (Spring): 1–12.

Crutsinger, Martin. 1993. 'What Could Happen If NAFTA Is Defeated in Congress.' *New York Times*, 13 November, A12.

Davis, Jeff. 2009. 'The SPP's Death Knell Has Sounded.' *Embassy*. 26 August. http://www.embassymag.ca/page/view/spp_death_knell-8-26-2009. Accessed 26 February 2010.

Doern, G. Bruce, and Brian W. Tomlin. 1991. *Faith and Fear: The Free Trade Story*. Toronto: Stoddart.

Frizzell, Alan, and Anthony Westell. 1985. *The Canadian General Election of 1984: Politicians, Parties, Press, and Polls*. Toronto: Dundurn.

Gallagher, Kevin. 2009. 'Fix America's Trade Regime.' *Guardian*, 15 September. http://www.guardian.co.uk/commentisfree/cifamerica/2009/sep/14/obama-free-trade-nafta. Accessed 12 June 2010.

Gascon, Charles S. 2009. 'The Current Recession: How Bad Is It?' *St Louis Federal Reserve Economic Synopses* 4. http://research.stlouisfed.org/publications/es/09/ES0904.pdf. Accessed 4 January 2010.

Gilbert, Emily. 2005. 'The Inevitability of Integration: Neoliberal Discourse and the Proposals for a New North American Economic Space after September 11.' *Annals of the American Association of Geographers* 95, no. 1 (March): 202–22.

Glasberg, Davita Silfen. 1989. *The Power of Collective Purse Strings: The Effect of Bank Hegemony on Corporations and the State*. Berkeley: University of California Press.

Golob, Stephanie R. 2008. 'The Return of the Quiet Canadian: Canada's Approach to Regional Integration after 9/11.' In *An Independent Foreign Policy for Canada? Challenges and Choices for the Future*. Edited by Brian Bow and Patrick Lennox. Toronto: University of Toronto Press.

– 2003. 'Beyond the Policy Frontier: Canada, Mexico, and the Ideological Origins of NAFTA.' *World Politics* 55, no. 3 (April): 361–98.

Gourevitch, Peter. 1986. *Politics in Hard Times: Comparative Responses to International Economic Crises*. Ithaca: Cornell University Press.

Granatstein, J.L. 1985. 'Free Trade: The Issue That Will Not Go Away.' In *The Politics of Canada's Economic Relationship with the United States*. Edited by Denis Stairs and Gilbert R. Winham. Toronto: University of Toronto Press.

Greenaway, Norma. 2008. 'NAFTA Mired in Security, Trade Slow-Down: Business Leaders Complain Competitors Gaining Ground.' *Ottawa Citizen*, 19
April, A7.

Greenspan, Alan. 2007. 'The Roots of the Mortgage Crisis.' *Wall Street
Journal*, 12 December. http://opinionjournal.com/editorial/feature.
html?id=110010981. Accessed 15 June 2008.

Hall, Peter A. 1993. 'Policy Paradigms, Social Learning, and the State: The
Case of Economic Policy-Making in Britain.' *Comparative Politics* 25 (April):
275–96.

– ed. 1989. *The Political Power of Ideas: Keynesianism across Nations*. Princeton:
Princeton University Press.

Hart, Michael. 2002. *A Trading Nation*. Vancouver: UBC Press.

Hart, Michael, Bill Dymond, and Colin Robertson. 1994. *Decision at Midnight:
Inside the Canada–U.S. Free Trade Negotiations*. Vancouver: UBC Press.

Healey, Robert M. 1993. 'NAFTA Is a Bad Idea That Will Drain Away Jobs.'
Chicago Sun-Times, 26 August, 28.

Hellman, Judith Adler. 1993. 'Mexican Perceptions of Free Trade: Support
and Opposition to NAFTA.' In *The Political Economy of North American Free
Trade*. Edited by Ricardo Grinspun and Maxwell Cameron. New York: St
Martin's.

Hufbauer, Gary Clyde, and Jeffrey J. Schott. 2005. *NAFTA Revisited: Achievements and Challenges*. Washington: Peterson Institute.

Inwood, Gregory J. 2005. *Continentalizing Canada: The Politics and Legacy of the
Macdonald Royal Commission*. Toronto: University of Toronto Press.

Keeler, John T.S. 1993. 'Opening the Window for Reform: Mandates, Crises,
and Extraordinary Policy-Making.' *Comparative Political Studies* 25 (January):
433–86.

Kirshner, Jonathan, ed. 2003. *Monetary Orders: Ambiguous Economics, Ubiquitous Politics*. Ithaca: Cornell University Press.

Krugman, Paul. 2009. 'Fighting Off Depression.' *New York Times*, 4 January.
http://www.nytimes.com/2009/01/05/opinion/05krugman.html. Accessed
22 May 2010.

Leonhardt, David. 2009. 'The Economy is Bad, but 1982 Was Worse,' *New
York Times*, 21 January. http://www.nytimes.com/2009/01/21/business/
economy/21leonhardt.html. Accessed 30 January 2009.

Lewington, Jennifer. 1987. 'Protectionist Fires May Be Going Out.' *Globe and
Mail*, 7 December, A8.

Leyton-Brown, David. 1985. *Weathering the Storm: Canadian–U.S. Relations*.
Toronto: C.D. Howe Institute.

Lindvall, Johannes. 2009. 'Economic Ideas in the Great Recession.' Paper presented to conference on 'Comparative Responses to the Economic Crisis in Advanced Industrial States,' Princeton University, 27–9 March. http://www.princeton.edu/~piirs/projects/Lindvall%20paper%20Econ%20Ideas%20and%20Crisis.pdf. Accessed 2 June 2010.

Lotz, Hellmut. 1997. 'Myth and NAFTA: The Use of Core Values in U.S. Politics.' In *Culture and Foreign Policy*. Edited by Valerie Hudson. Boulder: Westview.

Lowenthal, Abraham. 2010. 'Obama and the Americas: Promise, Disappointment, Opportunity.' *Foreign Affairs* 89, no. 4 (July–August): 45–56.

Manley, John P., Pedro Aspe, and William F. Weld. 2005. 'Building a North American Community: Report of the Independent Task Force on the Future of North America.' Council on Foreign Relations Task Force, Report no. 53 (May). http://www.cfr.org/canada/building-north-american-community/p8102.

Mayer, Frederick W. 1998. *Interpreting NAFTA*. New York: Columbia University Press.

McNamara, Kathleen. 1988. *The Currency of Ideas: Monetary Politics in the European Union*. Ithaca: Cornell University Press.

Morris, Stephen D., and John Passé-Smith. 2001. 'What a Difference a Crisis Makes: NAFTA, Mexico, and the United States.' *Latin American Perspectives* 28, no. 3 (May): 124–49.

Munro, Ross H., Jamie Murphy, and Frederick Ungeheuer. 1984. 'Canada: Hanging Out the Welcome Sign.' *Maclean's*, 24 December. http://www.time.com/time/magazine/article/0,9171,951396,00.html. Accessed 22 July 2010.

North American Competitiveness Council (NACC). 2009. 'Statement to Leaders in Advance of the 2009 North American Leaders' Summit.' 6 August. http://www.as-coa.org/article.php?id=1836. Accessed on-line 11 February 2010.

– 2007. 'Enhancing Competitiveness in Canada, Mexico, and the United States.' Initial Recommendations of the NACC. February. http://www.uschamber.com/reports/enhancing-competitiveness-canada-mexico-and-united-states-private. Accessed 1 September 2009.

'NAFTA Debate: Gore vs Perot.' 1993. *Larry King Live*. 9 November. http://ggallarotti.web.wesleyan.edu/govt155/goreperot.htm. Transcript accessed 2 June 2009.

Pastor, Manuel, and Carol Wise. 1994. 'The Origins and Sustainability of Mexico's Free Trade Policy,' *International Organization* 48, no. 2 (Summer): 459–89.

Pastor, Robert. 2011. *The North American Idea: A Vision of a Continental Future* (New York: Oxford University Press).

– 2008. 'The Future of North America: Replacing a Bad Neighbor Policy.' *Foreign Affairs* 87, no. 4 (July–August): 84–98.

– 2001. *Toward a North American Community: Lessons from the Old World for the New*. Washington: Institute for International Economics.

'Rout of the Liberals [editorial].' 1984. *Globe and Mail*, 7 September, A6.

Savage, Luisa. 2010. 'The End of North American Trilateralism.' *Maclean's*, 29 June. http://www2.macleans.ca/2010/06/29/the-end-of-the-trilateral-dream. Accessed 30 June 2010.

Skonieczny, Amy. 2001. 'Constructing NAFTA: Myth, Representation, and the Discursive Representation of U.S. Foreign Policy.' *International Studies Quarterly* 45, no. 3 (September): 433–54.

t'Hart, Paul, and Karen Tindall. 2008. *Framing the Economic Downturn: Crisis Rhetoric and the Politics of Recessions*. Canberra: Australian National University Electronic Press. http://epress.anu.edu.au/anzsog/global_economy/pdf/prelims.pdf.

Trezise, Philip H. 1988. 'Free Trade with Canada?' *Brookings Review* 6, no. 1 (Summer): 16–23.

White House. 2009. 'Joint Statement by North American Leaders, Guadalajara, August 9, 2009.' http://www.whitehouse.gov/the_press_office/Joint-statement-by-North-American-leaders. Accessed 15 June 2010.

Winham, Gilbert R., and Elizabeth DeBoer-Ashworth. 2000. 'Asymmetry in Negotiating the Canada–U.S. Free Trade Agreement, 1985–87.' In *Power and Negotiation*. Edited by I. William Zartman and Jeffrey Z. Rubin. Ann Arbor: University of Michigan Press.

Yankelovich, Daniel. 1992. 'Foreign Policy after the Election.' *Foreign Policy* 71 (September–October): 1–12.

Zeleny, Jeff. 2008. 'Obama Weighs Quick Undoing of Bush Policies.' *New York Times*, 9 November. http://www.nytimes.com/2008/11/10/us/politics/10obama.html. Accessed 29 February 2010.

3 Continental Governance, Post-Crisis: Where Is North America Going?

STEPHEN CLARKSON

Even before the 2008–9 crisis shook economies around the world, it was clear that North America had missed its chance to become the meaningful political entity, economic experiment, and cultural grafting that many had expected in the first flush of interest about the apparently dramatic new regionalization sparked by the North American Free Trade Agreement (NAFTA). For a considerable period after 1994, when Mexico had joined Canada and the United States to form NAFTA, observers opined that this newly integrating economic space signified that North America formally had entered the club of world regions (Castro-Rea 2006). The eminent expert on hemispheric affairs Robert Pastor affirmed in a similar spirit that for 'the first time, "North America" is more than just a geographical expression,' NAFTA being 'merely the first draft of an economic constitution for North America' (Pastor 2004). While Pastor envisaged a region whose subsequent 'drafts' would approach the sophisticated, multilevel, and transnational governance of the European Union, this chapter maintains that the experiment to form an integrated entity that is more than the sum of its Mexican, Canadian, and American parts had already failed – along with any prospect of what might pass as continental governance – well before the financial crisis had struck and further disintegrated the continent into its component states.

This text will proceed analytically but chronologically by first explaining how the political economy of the relations among NAFTA's three member-states had not evolved in their first decade towards world-region status. In its closing section the chapter will respond to this book's overarching question by explaining how responses to the crisis in the three states have further dimmed prospects for the emergence of a transnational continental governance that could develop a common approach to North America's most pressing challenges.

The Political Economy of North America under NAFTA and after 9/11

The failure of continental governance to take root across the borders of North America can best be understood as principally due to four realities, which are somewhat offset by a fifth:

1. North America was constituted with a set of deliberately weak *continental institutions* designed mainly to settle member governments' and their corporations' legal disputes arising out of NAFTA's provisions.
2. Some economic sectors demonstrated real continental economic integration but did not develop significant *transborder governance*.
3. In other sectors trinational regulatory harmonization resulted less from continental than from *global governance*.
4. Still other industries moved from being continentally to being globally integrated.
5. Since September 2001, traditional forms of Washington-driven *bilateral relations* have predominated in matters of military defence and border security.

The elaboration of these five themes will show how North America's governance trend line was moving away from – not converging with – the hegemony-offsetting, solidarity-boosting model that had energized transnational regionalism in Europe until the economic crisis.

Formal Trilateral Institutionalization

If North America qualified for consideration as a world region, this was thanks to two economic agreements, the first forged bilaterally between the United States and its northern neighbour as the Canada–U.S. Free Trade Agreement (CUSFTA, which entered into force on 1 January 1989). The continent acquired a stronger international image when CUSFTA's provisions were deepened and extended to include Mexico exactly five years later (Leycegui and de Castro, 2000), but the new entity was institutionally empty. With no executive, legislative, or administrative capacity of note, only its judicial bodies could claim any substance. Even as instruments for conflict resolution, these dispute settlement mechanisms proved less effective than those of the World Trade Organization. On issues where powerful U.S. lobbies wielded political clout, Washington repeatedly defied rulings by both NAFTA and WTO arbitral panels when they favoured Canada or Mexico.

NAFTA's institutional vacuum does not mean that its norms, rules, and rights are inconsequential. On the contrary, these three components of what can be understood as each signatory's external constitution (Clarkson 2004) severely disciplined the practices of the two peripheral states, if not those of the centre. For instance:

- The extension of the national treatment *norm* beyond governing goods (as it did under the General Agreement on Tariffs and Trade) to include foreign investment required a wholesale abandonment of Canadian and Mexican industrial strategy policies.
- Dozens of new *rules* prohibited Canada from setting a higher price for the petroleum it was exporting to the United States than that prevailing in the domestic market or from reducing exports to preserve diminishing energy reserves. For its part, Mexico agreed to open up its banking sector to foreign control and imported a complete legal system for addressing trade disputes related to anti-dumping or countervailing duties.
- Important new *rights* were granted foreign corporations to sue host governments from the municipal to the federal levels.

Although these norms, rules, and rights were consequential, NAFTA's legislative and executive institutions were designed to have little substance. To be sure, NAFTA boasts an executive body, the North American Free Trade Commission, but this commission has no staff, no address, and no budget. Despite its substantial responsibilities for managing NAFTA's implementation, it consists solely of sporadic meetings of the three countries' trade minister, secretary, or representative, who have turned out to be loath to make major decisions. As for a legislative capacity to add to or amend NAFTA's new norms, rules, or rights – a necessary feature of any multilateral body that hopes to retain its relevance as conditions evolve – this 'world region' has none. Changes in NAFTA's normative structure require trilateral intergovernmental negotiations by the three states' federal executives and then ratification by their legislatures.

Nor does NAFTA have much in the way of an administrative arm.

Buried in each of the three governments' trade departments, there is a small office responsible for documenting NAFTA-related business. NAFTA's remaining bureaucratic sinew consists of some thirty committees and working groups mandated by the agreement's various chapters. These trinational groupings, which are meant to be staffed by mid-level civil servants from each federal government, barely exist in practice (Clarkson et al. 2005). One interesting continental governance grouping, the North America Energy Working Group (NAEWG), which the George W. Bush administration pressed its neighbours to join in early 2001, was established outside NAFTA and became a forum for information exchange on common issues such as energy efficiency, harmonization of statistical methods, transparency in the marketplace, and renewable energy. Much of the group's work is run by mid-level officials[1] who focus on technical standards and regulations. The NAEWG was folded into the Security and Prosperity Partnership of North America (SPP) as one of its intergovernmental working groups but has barely survived the SPP's subsequent demise at the hands of the Obama Administration.

NAFTA's only institutional features with any strength are judicial (Vega and Winham 2002). But of the half-dozen different dispute settlement mechanisms, two have remained dormant (those relating to energy and financial institutions) and two proved ineffectual (one of the still active North American Commission for Environmental Cooperation and the other of the North American Commission for Labour Cooperation, recently deceased). The agreement's chief conflict resolution processes are specified in Chapters 20, 19, and 11. Disputes between the parties over the interpretation and implementation of NAFTA's provisions were to be resolved by panels established under Chapter 20's clauses, but the panel rulings merely take the form of recommendations submitted to the NAFTA trade commission – that is, the three trade ministers – who in turn can only suggest to their governments how to proceed. When, for instance, after long delays caused by Washington's obstructionism, a NAFTA panel ruled that the U.S. government had failed to honour its obligation to allow Mexican truckers access to its market, Washington was not obligated to change its ways and still persists in its non-compliance (see discussion by Gilbert in this volume).

Putatively binding rulings are made by panels established under Chapter 19, which can replace domestic legal appeals of the anti-dumping or countervailing duty determinations made by individual states' trade administrative tribunals. While useful in the majority of cases, the U.S. government's refusal to comply with these rulings in such high-profile cases as the long drawn out softwood lumber dispute with Canada underlines the point that NAFTA's institutions enjoy strikingly little clout when it comes to containing the unilateral propensities of the region's hegemon.[2]

The single arbitral function with definite muscle is the investor–state dispute process established in Chapter 11, which allows NAFTA corporations to initiate an arbitration process governed by World Bank rules in order to challenge the validity of a domestic measure they claim has expropriated their assets. Because these rulings have direct effect in the defendant jurisdiction, they have caused much dismay among jurists, who lament the derogation of domestic judicial sovereignty, and among environmentalists, who believe that the threat of such actions inhibits the national regulation of corporate polluters. Since the number of Chapter 11 cases remains small and their effects limited, their overall political significance should be considered symbolically important but effectively moderate.

As this overview suggests, the transborder governance established from above by NAFTA's institutions is considerably less than observers had cause to expect when listening either to proponents or to opponents of what President Ronald Reagan, referring to the earlier CUSFTA, had called North America's economic constitution. More important, NAFTA's institutional superstructure did not deepen or broaden. As discussed in the introduction to this volume, traditional theories of regionalism provide little guidance for understanding this phenomenon. Far from developing greater strength over time, as neofunctionalists would have expected, NAFTA's institutions and those that were designed to bolster them, such as the SPP, have actually withered on their respective vines.

Transborder Corporate Governance in Sectors Where Geography Matters

Even if North America is much more institutionally vacuous than the original fanfare over NAFTA had led many to hope or fear, the continent may have a greater political-economic reality in other, more commercial respects (Hufbauer and Schott 2005; Fry and Bybee 2002; Shamsie and Grinspun 2007). Transborder governance can develop from below when clashes of economic interests need to be resolved or when transnational corporations (TNCs) make demands that need to be addressed. In such sectors as agriculture and steel where geographical proximity matters, powerful U.S. transnational corporations have generated elements of a continental political economy.

Agriculture

The North American beef industry is largely integrated across the American, Canadian, and Mexican borders. An embryo from Alberta may cause a calf to be born in Mexico. That animal may subsequently be shipped to the Canadian prairies for fattening in order subsequently to be slaughtered in the United States. This picture of transborder integration was shattered in 2003 when an Albertan cow was diagnosed with BSE. Discovering Mad Cow disease in Canada was a godsend for western American farmers, who invoked health regulations to force the U.S. border to be closed to Canadian beef. Old-fashioned protectionism was good for Montana ranchers, who profited from decreased competition to get higher prices for their herds. In response to Canadian representations, the U.S. Department of Agriculture (USDA) announced a partial reopening of the border to Canadian boneless beef under thirty months of age in August 2003, but the Ranchers-Cattlemen Action Legal Fund (R-CALF) successfully sidetracked the USDA from reopening the Canadian border in May 2004 and again in January 2005. In both cases, the ranchers' lobby argued before a Montana district court that the USDA had failed to justify its decision to reopen the border in terms consistent with the international scientific standards defined by the Paris-based Office of International Epizootics (OIE).

All of this was bad for American food-processing TNCs, which wanted both to import beef from Canada and to export processed beef abroad. Using their superior financial and political muscle, these U.S. TNCs caused the USDA to intervene in the OIE to alter the standards for BSE safety. The OIE consequently approved a reduction in the number of risk categories and recast the criteria used to classify countries under each. Canada and the United States were then put within the 'Controlled BSE Risk' category as countries that posed a negligible risk of transmitting BSE because of their risk mitigation measures. In July 2005 the Court of Appeals for the Montana district reversed the earlier injunction and took specific exception to the district court's interpretation of the scientific standards for reopening the border by making eight specific references to the new OIE guidelines.[3]

A similar battle between U.S. grain growers and U.S. food transportation interests occurred over the Canadian Wheat Board (CWB). When American farmers pushed Washington to impose countervailing duties on Canadian grain exports on the grounds that they were subsidized by the CWB, American food transportation TNCs intervened success-fully within the labyrinthine processes of the U.S. trade administration to defend the CWB, on whose shipments of high-quality durum wheat they depended.

Sectoral Continentalization: Steel

Even though, as a traditional heavy industry, steel provides the back-bone of the old North American manufacturing economy, the Cana-dian and Mexican steel sectors did :not do well under NAFTA. Since the agreement failed to eliminate or even reduce the protectionist anti-dumping and countervailing-duty actions with which the U.S. steel industry had long been harassing imports coming from foreign com-petitors, the more efficient Canadian-owned steel companies found themselves obliged to invest heavily inside the U.S. market. Their American subsidiaries became active members of such U.S. industry associations as the American Iron and Steel Institute, and those sub-sidiaries proceeded to lobby in 2002 – along with the U.S. steelworkers' union, which had fortuitously been run for a decade by Canadian presi-dents – for Canada (and also Mexico) to be exempted from the George W. Bush administration's safeguard duties on foreign steel imports. This collaborative action suggested that in the steel sector a single, if informal, governance space was developing in which Canadian (and later Mexican) firms partially Americanized themselves within the U.S. economy – as opposed to creating a continent-wide industry containing nationally competitive elements.

Symptomatic of this trilateralism was the creation of a modest instrument of trinational governance, the North American Steel Trade Committee (NASTC), which prompted the three governments to inter-act with their respective industry associations in order to develop common North American policy positions at the OECD for the World Trade Organization and for the ultimately aborted negotiations of a Free Trade Area of the Americas. This was a rare example of an eco-nomic sector that would support a functionalist understanding of regionalism, in that interconnectedness in the steel industry led to a short-lived form of multilevel governance with the three domestic industries, their respective national lobby organizations, and the three federal governments, all learning to cooperate in hemispheric and global negotiations.

Having flourished under import substitution industrialization following the Second World War, the Mexican steel industry was seriously weakened by the lifting of government protection in the 1980s. The Canadian industry was much better positioned to participate in the U.S. economy than was its Mexican counterpart, but the acquisition in 2006 of its six largest corporations by Brazilian, Indian, and American conglomerates suggested that NASTC's apparently continental regulatory consolidation had been trumped by the forces of corporate globalization.

Trinational Policy Harmonization within Global Corporate Governance

In some economic sectors where geographical contiguity is of minor importance, signs of trinational policy harmonization may have nothing to do with regional governance. Intellectual property rights for pharmaceuticals makes this point.

Intellectual Property Rights for Pharmaceuticals

Changes to intellectual property rights (IPRs) for pharmaceuticals in North America were driven not by those rights defined in NAFTA's Chapter 17 but rather by the WTO's almost identical TRIPs agreement, which represented the triumph of U.S. Big Pharma and its European and Japanese pharmaceutical counterparts in achieving a new global legal regime for this oligopolistic sector. The fact that Washington has used the WTO's dispute settlement body – rather than NAFTA's – as its legal venue for pressing Canada to make concessions to U.S.-branded drug companies suggests that weak continental judicial governance has been trumped by the stronger alternative established at the global level.

Financial Services

Banking offers a confused picture, because North America turns out – surprisingly – not to be a natural zone for continental commercial and retail banking. Some Canadian banks have operated for decades throughout the hemisphere and, to a lesser extent, globally; and all of them had established large subsidiaries in the U.S. market well before trade liberalization. Between Canada and the United States, the normal economic asymmetry is upended: Canadian banks invest and earn more in the United States than the reverse. As Germain and Mohamed confirm in this volume, U.S. banks have not expanded their operations significantly northwards. Notwithstanding their geographical proximity, it was not American but British banks that predominated among foreign-owned financial services in Canada, whose retail banking system remains primarily in domestic hands. With a much less robust set of banks, which were nationalized in 1982 following one of the country's periodic currency crises, Mexico found itself at the receiving end of transnationalized banking. NAFTA had required it to open its reprivatized banks to foreign ownership according to a defined schedule, but in the shock of the 1994–5 peso crisis, the IMF, the World Bank, and the U.S. Treasury used their financial bailout to force Mexico to drop its timetable restrictions immediately. After a feeding frenzy by foreign TNCs, Mexicans found that all but one of their six largest banks had fallen under foreign ownership. Significantly, Spanish capital took a larger share in the Mexican banking sector than did competing American banks, with the Canadian Scotiabank gaining control over one Mexican counterpart. There is some Spanish–U.S. partnering, as in Bank of America's 25 per cent share in the Spanish bank Santander Sefin's Mexican subsidiary (Clarkson 2008, 306–13). In this way, the financial services sector in North America's three economies has become more globally than continentally restructured, NAFTA notwithstanding.

Although some harmonization of the three banking sectors' regulatory systems has occurred within North America, this is not a result of any transborder governance created by NAFTA. Rather, this apparent continentalization actually reflects the three countries' individual participation in global governance. If banking regulations in the United States, Mexico, and Canada were becoming more similar before the global meltdown of 2008, this was because the three central banks participated in the monthly meetings of the Bank of International Settlements in Basel, whose multilaterally negotiated norms were then applied at home. Instead of banking regulations showing that North America had become a 'world region,' they indicated that the three countries of North America were simply separate players in a global mode of regulation. It thus behooves us to be cautious about inferring a regional significance from signs of harmonization that are happening in North America unless they can be shown to be specific to the continent.

From Continental to Global Sectoral Integration

If NAFTA produced any clear winners, these were surely the three U.S. auto giants and the U.S. textile sector, which managed to obtain rules of origin that gave them protection – at least for a time – from their Asian and European competitors. This section will consider the significance of these two instructive cases.

Automobiles

As the culmination of many years of U.S. automotive TNC lobbying, NAFTA was thought to have set up a fully integrated system of production for those manufacturers – principally the Detroit Three – that could meet its protectionist rules-of-origin requirements. However, the trilateral working groups created to negotiate further continental safety and emissions standards proved incapable of producing the regulatory harmonization necessary for a fully integrated continental production system.

Meanwhile, competition from manufacturers in Europe and Asia undermined the American auto assemblers' oligopolistic dominance on the continent. The resulting transoceanic corporate consolidation through mergers and equity linkages, which created six automotive groups accounting for 80 per cent of world production, was developing a regime of accumulation that was truly global and that was generating pressures to leapfrog over the continental space to create globally harmonized standards for the automotive industry. At the same time, continuing foreign auto and autoparts investment in both Ontario (which boasts an excellent transportation infrastructure and the lower costs for employers that accrue from a public health system) and Mexico (which offers well-trained labour power at one-fourteenth of U.S. wages) reduced the disparity between the two peripheries' automobile sectors but did not reduce their mutual dependence on the vitality of the U.S. market.

Textiles

NAFTA's rules of origin also appeared to succeed in connecting the three countries' disparate textile and apparel industries in a common North American production system in which the interests of U.S. firms combined more intimately with those of their burgeoning Mexican counterparts than they did with shrinking Canadian companies. The asymmetries in this trilateral matrimony grew as the NAFTA-generated continental market governance disintegrated in the face of two exogenous shocks – the expiry in 2005 of the GATT/WTO's Multi-Fibre Agreement (which had allowed industrialized countries to impose draconian quantitative limitations on apparel imports from the Third World) and China's emergence as the dominant low-cost producer supplying the North American market.

Continental production in a severely shaken textile and apparel industry still revolves around an American hub, with the U.S. industry responding unilaterally to its challenges, a battered Mexican industry retreating to the informal economy, and a hollowed-out Canadian sector sitting on the sidelines. Continental governance in this sector amounts to little more than NAFTA's aging rules of origin, which have been made increasingly irrelevant by Washington's bilateral agreements with other trading partners. Far from being a privileged member within a regional regime, Mexico found itself discriminated against by the United States' Central America Free Trade Agreement, because CAFTA gave the Central American republics better access to U.S. markets than Mexico had.

These two examples, along with the takeover of five of the six largest Canadian steel mills by corporations headquartered overseas, show that, whatever sectoral basis may have existed for the establishment of a trinational mode of regulation, North America had become too small a territorial entity to support its own regime of transborder governance. This process of transformation of the regional marketplace by globalization suggests, first, that the economic trend within the three-state area is centrifugal, not centripetal, and second, that the economic basis for a consolidation of North American regional governance is disappearing.

Intergovernmental Security and Defence Relations

In matters of national defence since 11 September 2001, North American governance has reverted to earlier modes of government-to-government relations – and so to an earlier form of regionalism – in which the continental hegemon presses its neighbouring governments to bend to its will – in this case to guarantee the security of the American homeland (Golob 2002).

Defence

Unlike homeland security trilateralism, a reactivated bilateralism characterized Canada's and Mexico's reversion to their Cold War behaviour as they engaged with the military dimension of the U.S. security shift. Responding to U.S. Northern Command – the Pentagon's reorganization of its command structure for North American defence – Ottawa reorganized its own armed forces into a Canada Command, participated in a binational military planning group, and agreed to extend bilateral military integration from its air force to include its navy under the North American Aerospace Defence (NORAD) command.

Just as Canada reverted to its Cold War junior partnership with the Pentagon upon President George W. Bush's declaration of war against terrorism, Mexico reverted to its Cold War estrangement. Far from ingratiating itself with the United States by sending troops to Afghanistan in support of its war against the Taliban and warships to support the U.S. fleet in its war against Iraq (as did Canada), Mexico withheld even moral support, loudly reaffirming its long tradition of non-intervention beyond its frontiers. Although the Mexican fleet was comfortable cooperating with the U.S. Navy on security exercises in the Gulf of Mexico, the Mexican military would not collaborate with the U.S. Army beyond the kind of disaster relief it supplied in the wake of Hurricane Katrina's destruction of New Orleans in 2005. While sending a Mexican military observer to bilateral U.S.–Canadian meetings at NORAD was seen to be a major step forward, the ominous significance attributed to this gesture by Mexican nationalists underlined the enormous discrepancy that persisted between the two bilateral defence relationships and confirmed the absence of any meaningful trinational governance in military matters. But because terrorism involved threats emanating from non-state actors who might send individuals, not armies, to infiltrate the United States, 'homeland security' – as defined by the Bush administration in the aftermath of 9/11 – required the Mexican border to be taken just as seriously by Washington as Canada's.

Security

In contrast with defence issues, the radical shift in U.S. security policies provoked by the terrorist attacks on New York and Washington instantly affected the dynamic driving North American governance. The economic integration fostered by NAFTA had been reducing the government-made economic barriers along the United States' two territorial borders, allowing the marketplace freer flows of humans and goods within the continent. Throughout the 1990s, growth in cross-border traffic of goods and people generated increased attention to border governance issues. Concerned about the efficiency of their continent-wide production systems, business coalitions lobbied their governments to make the increased investments in the transportation and security technologies needed to create a barrier-free continent. President Clinton had signed agreements with Ottawa in the mid-1990s to improve border security management, but his administration did not take significant steps in this direction. As discussed in the chapter by Emily Gilbert in this volume, 9/11 generated the urgent political will that was needed for Washington to commit political capital for partnering with its neighbours to strengthen North America's border security systems.

Washington's sudden replacement of its drive for liberalization with an anti-terrorism security paradigm was dramatized for North Americans on September 11, 2001, by the immediate blockade of its two land borders. This unilateral action demonstrated that, once Washington declared its national security to be at stake, it would simply reassert the control over its policy space that it had previously vacated in the name of trade liberalization. In the post-9/11 handling of border security, traditional binational relations reasserted themselves in response to U.S. unilateralism, with Uncle Sam dealing separately with each neighbour (Bow 2006). Washington's subsequent demands that Canada and Mexico do what *it* felt was necessary to ensure that their exports were secure against terrorism showed how much North American *governance* was driven by American *government*.

These intergovernmental negotiations were supplemented on the Canadian side by an unusually active involvement of business coalitions in the design of high-tech border security systems. This new intensity of heterarchical governance impinged on but did not displace the traditional, government-to-government hierarchy. During the first phase of the U.S. domestic war on terror, a detailed thirty-point U.S.–Canada Smart Border agreement was negotiated, which – thanks to very substantial Canadian input – largely reactivated the Canada–U.S. Partnership established by Prime Minister Chrétien and President Clinton in 1999 to promote enhanced border management. This was signed in Ottawa in December 2001. By March 2002, Washington had used the template it had worked out with Ottawa to impose a parallel, twenty-two-point Smart Border agreement on Mexico. Subsequently, Canada and Mexico's bilateral collaboration added a third but much weaker pillar to intergovernmental security relations within North America.

This reactivated regionalism was unusual. On the one hand, it reinforced Washington's dominance by incorporating Canada and Mexico into an extended zone of U.S.–led continental policy making; on the other, it respected each state's formal sovereignty.

While the first years following 9/11 showed North America to be a more unilaterally, U.S.-defined political space, the proclamation of a Security and Prosperity Partnership for North America (SPP) by the three governments' leaders at their March 2005 meeting in Waco, Texas, appeared to signal a shift towards the trilaterally governed continent that NAFTA had heralded a decade earlier. Nationalist critics in the United States, Mexico, and Canada feared that the SPP was a manoeuvre through which their elites were conspiring to advance their political and economic integration (see Ayres and Macdonald chapter).

As perceived by the Mexican presidency, the SPP was a valuable opportunity to resolve many irritating problems in the bilateral economic relationship and so move NAFTA incrementally towards Mexico's grander vision of an EU-type regional governance.[4] The new strategy involved a trade-off. First, Mexico would comply fully with U.S. demands on security matters. Once it had gained access to the U.S. policy loop, it would negotiate the regulatory corollaries that applied to trade. If SPP negotiations could produce certification standards governing foodstuffs, such Mexican products as avocados would no longer be vulnerable to border stoppages arbitrarily declared by the U.S. Food and Drug Administration. This negotiated regime would then give Mexico's agricultural exporters a competitive advantage in responding to U.S. farm lobby demands over rivals in Latin America, Asia, and even Europe.

While the bulk of the SPP's proposed measures dealt with either the U.S.–Canada or the U.S.–Mexico relationship, the constant informal telephone and e-mail communications among the bureaucrats who had put those measures together suggested that a significant trilateral space was being created in the process. Although the security side of the SPP extended Washington's dominance on the continent beyond any point it had previously achieved, the prosperity issues seemed to offer some counter-asymmetrical power for the periphery. 'Regulatory harmonization' might conjure up images of Mexico and Canada simply having to adopt U.S. standards, but the profound differences among the three countries' multilevel governmental systems implied that this scenario could hardly be achieved by American bullying. Instead, issues would have to be worked out pragmatically, with Washington accepting its incapacity simply to impose its norms on the periphery. In some cases, American officials would still be giving their Mexican counterparts the familiar 'do it our way or your product will not cross our border' message. In others, practical problems would have to be worked out by all parties resolving their problems cooperatively.

Anti-terrorist border security driven by U.S. pressure on its neighbours generated an intergovernmental policy mode that reduced the power asymmetry between the hegemon and the periphery because U.S. security came to depend on the Mexican and Canadian governments' capacity to collaborate in fulfilling their anti-terrorism policy commitments. In this process, the power asymmetry between the continental centre and its periphery was simultaneously intensified and mitigated, a phenomenon that became clearer in the narcotics security dossier (see chapter by Cadena-Roa in this volume). In this domain, the bilateral U.S.–Mexico Mérida Initiative of 2007 signalled a historic sea change, because it represented Washington's realization that security in its border states was endangered by the insecurity generated on the other side of the border by the Mexican drug cartels' battles for turf. Simultaneously the Mexican government recognized that it could not regain control over the cartels without massive U.S. financial and technological assistance.

Another apparently game-changing event was the declaration by Secretary of State Hillary Clinton in 2009 that the United States had to take responsibility for two root causes of the shared narcotics calamity. American consumers' demand for drugs was the primary force driving this illegal, violent, but above all immensely profitable industry. And it was the U.S. firearms industry that was supplying the assault weapons that gave the cartels military superiority over the Mexican army. Attitudes also changed decisively in the Mexican government. Under the PRI, Mexico had generally dismissed the narcotics question as a gringo problem. The Mexican government took on the war on drugs as its own cause following the PAN's presidential election victories, first under Vicente Fox (2000) but more genuinely under Felipe Calderón. (2006). Sending in the army to battle the cartels did not produce victory in Ciudad Juárez, but it did gain the Americans' respect and helped produce a more cooperative binational approach to tackling a desperate, ever-worsening situation.

That the 2001 U.S.–Canada border agreement provided Washington with a template for its arrangement with Mexico also suggested that this process diminished the differences that had once distinguished

Ottawa's relationship with the U.S. government from Mexico City's. Although narco-traffic and immigration pressures were far more intense along its southern than its northern border, Congress pushed the administration to adopt common policies on the Western Hemisphere Travel Initiative, as well as biometric identity cards for all persons crossing U.S. borders. The Bush administration's support for universal technological solutions to the passage of low-risk merchandise across its border and through its ports of entry, and (as Gilbert notes) the Obama administration's insistence that the two borders be treated equally, further reduced the disparity between the two countries' responses to Washington.

The new dynamics of security also helped nourish the continent's *third* dyadic relationship, which had slowly and sometimes reluctantly been developing between Mexico and Canada ever since Ottawa had joined the U.S.–Mexico negotiations leading to NAFTA. North America's third bilateral link was given a boost during the anxious months before President Bush's declaration of war against Iraq, when Prime Minister Jean Chrétien, with President Vicente Fox, developed an oppositional axis in an effort to block the impending U.S. invasion by generating a countervailing coalition of unwilling states at the United Nations. By the mid-2000s it appeared that the two non-neighbours were developing a sufficiently intense relationship that it made sense to take North America's 'third bilateral' as a significant complement to the continent's governance (Clarkson 2008).

The SPP reaffirmed the three federal governments' rhetorical commitment to reconcile the demand for maximum border security with the integrated economy's need for minimum border trade restrictions; yet the DHS's institutional autonomy within the Beltway resulted in ever more onerous border restrictions being imposed on travellers and trucks alike. Corporate leaders in the three countries, who aspired to operate in a borderless North America, criticized the SPP as a mere wish list of low-profile bureaucratic initiatives whose implementation would do nothing to engage with major steps (but as the Germain chapter in this volume shows, politically unachievable ones) towards some meaningful continental governance. Such steps might include a fully integrated market, a customs union, and a common currency. This business animus caused the SPP to establish a trilateral, big-business-led North American Competitiveness Council (NACC) to co-direct the trilateral project. But when the SPP's trinational summitry proved impotent in terms of facilitating cross-border commerce – in the face of the DHS's compulsion to make the border impregnable – the NACC's corporate giants lost interest in co-piloting the new system.[5]

Supplementing the SPP with an annual Leaders' Summit in 2006 did not herald North America embarking on any grander institutional project. Indeed, vehement opposition to the SPP from right-wing nationalists in the United States and left-wing nationalists in Canada and Mexico combined to push the SPP into oblivion. In 2009 the newly elected President Barack Obama met his counterparts in Guadalajara in what proved to be the last of six annual North American Leaders' Summits; after that, under his direction, the SPP disappeared from the agenda. That get-together was so inconsequential that it was not repeated; in fact, it served to confirm the absence more than the presence of continental governance.

The overwhelming U.S. effort to fortify its homeland has created a new kind of regionalism in North America, one that is attempting to extend the U.S. security perimeter to the continent's external boundaries. This is indeed transborder governance, but it remains U.S.-dominated and skewed: Canada's participation in the war on terror is enthusiastic and compliant, whereas Mexico's involvement is more reluctant; Mexico's participation in the war on drugs is enthusiastic and compliant, whereas Canada's involvement is more routine.

Continental Governance before the Crisis

So far we have seen that, even before the financial crisis shook its three countries, the form of transborder governance established under NAFTA and the SPP did not qualify North America for standing as a true world region of the type exemplified by the EU. NAFTA had created a formal structure on paper, but its institutions had been carefully designed to be too weak to construct mechanisms that would generate a self-sustaining dynamic at the continental level. Nor could they offset the power of the dominant member while augmenting that of the smaller ones. On the contrary, while NAFTA's rule changes obliged Canada and Mexico to give up considerable autonomy in order to conform to American legal models, they required few concessions of autonomy by the United States, which in any case refused to comply with major judicial rulings limiting its own trade protection measures.

NAFTA's norms favoured the transnational operations of large corporations, most of which are U.S.-based. Its investor–state dispute settlement panels favoured the strong (transnational investors) over the

weak. In this way, the application to North America of the neoconservative paradigm had successfully constrained the two peripheral governments on the one hand and liberated corporations on the other. As a
result, private actors' involvement in policy areas increased, but mainly
through Washington's policy communities, in which TNCs played
large but spontaneous – and so unpredictable – roles.

In all of the sectors where geographical proximity mattered, North
America became a space in which U.S. hegemonic control increased.
Having failed to gain exemptions from U.S. trade protectionist processes, the two peripheries' industries converged on the centre. Complex
rules of origin caused large structural adjustments in the textile and
apparel industries, though this did not protect them from the impact
of changes in global governance (end of the Multi-Fibre Agreement) or
in the global balance of power (China), or exempt the auto sector from
corporate globalization.

After NAFTA's first decade it was clear that North America was not
evolving towards a continental regime of governance. None of the three
governments gave the continental community priority in its thinking or
paid heed to the interests of its two neighbours.[6] When newly elected
Mexican president Vicente Fox urged his North American counterparts
in 2000 to adopt a solidarity principle that would commit North America's two rich countries to providing Mexico with substantial aid, neither Washington nor Ottawa gave the idea serious consideration.

Continental Governance under and after the Crisis

It is often said that crises bring out the best in people. The 2007 subprime financial crisis brought out the worst in North America, showing its continental governance to be completely irrelevant in playing a
part in its rescue. No trilateral summit convened to work out a North
American position prior to the global governance meetings of the G20
or G8. Like other capitals around the world, Ottawa and Mexico City
simply waited to see what Washington would do. When it came to
bailing out the North American auto industry, Washington made the
structural and financial decisions while Canada's federal and Ontario
governments waited, pens ready, to see how big a cheque they would
have to fill out.

Far from seeing NAFTA as a helpful crutch, Barack Obama had
already identified it as a threat to industrial jobs when he was campaigning for the Democratic nomination. Nor was the spirit of NAFTA

able even to protect existing levels of trinational integration when the Obama administration endorsed the U.S. Congress's attaching Buy-America provisions to the government's massive stimulus package. Because of requirements that all the stimulus money dispensed by Congress be spent on projects having 100 per cent American content, TNCs had to break their cross-border production chains and seek suppliers of all their products' components from within the U.S. market. While walling itself off territorially by continuing to build an impassable fence along its border with Mexico, the United States was also walling itself off in commercial terms.

For its part, Canada's Conservative government preened itself on its banking system (which had been exempted from NAFTA's liberalizing provisions), which was regulated enough to have survived the crisis's turmoil intact. Having first denied the gravity of the crisis, Ottawa then conformed to the international consensus that veered suddenly from neoconservative scorn for government regulation to a Keynesian faith that state intervention in the marketplace could save capitalism from itself.

At the same time, Canada began erecting walls of its own, although these barriers were not so much physical as political. As discussed in the chapter in this volume by Stephanie Golob, the Harper government came to consider that its interests in Washington were being contaminated by its association with Mexico and so proceeded to abandon its previous support for North American trilateralism. Instead, Canadian political and economic elites resolved to re-establish Ottawa's special bilateral relationship, which they nostalgically believed had given Canada a Golden Age of influence in Washington. When it decided to require all Mexicans, including tourists, who wanted to come to Canada to apply for visas – in a process that was humiliating for applicants and that deeply offended the Mexican government – it was signalling its disinterest in sustaining the 'North American idea' (Pastor 2011).

Humiliated by Canada and walled off by the United States, the Mexican government found itself in 2010 isolated from rather than integrated with the two developed economies to the north with which it had implemented NAFTA sixteen years before. Battered by destructive storms, shaken by an influenza panic, displaced by China as the United States' primary source of low-cost products, destabilized by ever more violent drug cartels, and shut out by the U.S. security wall along its northern border, Mexico was left to cope on its own with the disastrous consequences of having hitched its economy to the hegemon's star.

While other economies in the hemisphere merely stagnated during the crisis, Mexico's was the only one to suffer a 7.5% *decrease* in its GDP. It suffered alone and unassisted.

In response to its worsening predicament, the Mexican government made a show of leading a new hemispheric entity, one that included all the Latin American and Caribbean states but that excluded the United States and Canada. It also made an effort to diversify its economic relationships by strengthening the trade and investment agreements it had already signed with other countries. But gestures of solidarity towards its Latin American counterparts and aspirations for economic diversification cannot reverse Mexico's embrace of the United States, if not of Canada. Managing its northern border must be its central preoccupation, although the issues remain too inflamed – witness public outcries over U.S. border agents killing an unarmed migrant, and U.S. drones violating Mexico's airspace sovereignty – for the border's administration to be jointly bureaucratized. Yet regulatory harmonization efforts continue apace: a High-Level Regulatory Cooperation Council was established in May 2010 and delivered an action plan with specific harmonization goals the following March.

Canada upped this ante by agreeing with the White House in February 2011 to establish two frankly bilateral joint executive-level institutions. A Regulatory Cooperation Council (RCC) was mandated to adopt compatible approaches to public regulations in the interests of deepening economic integration. Like its Mexican counterpart, the RCC was to push ahead with the business-inspired agenda already worked out by the SPP's North American Competitiveness Council. While this policy harmonization proceeds, a joint Beyond the Border Working Group was to pick up the traces from the 2001 U.S.–Canada Smart Border agreement and its 2002 follow-up action plan. A decade after these agreements were signed, the United States was still pushing Canada to deliver more Charter of Rights–protected information on Canadian citizens and travellers, and Ottawa was still hoping to persuade the United States that Canadian security policies were so tough that U.S. restrictions on goods and people crossing its border with Canada could be abated.

While Canada's break with trilateralism might suggest that North America has returned to its pre–free trade, hub-and-spoke profile, its two-speed bilateralism is nevertheless different from the cross-border governance of three decades ago. Bilateral relations are lightly institutionalized by regulatory harmonization bodies staffed by government officials and by executive-level consultations such as the Clean Energy Dialogue, established when President Obama visited Ottawa in February 2009, which is designed to have Canada 'parallel' the policies that emerge from the U.S. political process (Hale, 2011). And North America still contains a Mexico whose relationship with Canada has developed significantly under NAFTA and since 9/11.

Theoretical Reflections

North America's failure to conform to regional scholars' expectations raises several implications for thinking about turn-of-the-century regionalism and its ideational underpinnings.

The New 'New Regionalism'

For fifty years, Europe's supranational regional governance was taken to be the prototype for a regionalized global order. Various formulations tried to pinpoint the conceptual kernel of this exciting development. For instance, a 'neofunctionalist' school of thought posited that transborder economic integration would engender a strengthening of community-wide institutions and a corresponding weakening of national state governments. Alternatively, 'intergovernmentalism' would tie the hands of the more powerful member states in the region while strengthening those of the weaker. Neither of these theories found traction on the other side of the Atlantic Ocean. Overall, the three economies became more integrated, but no continental institutions of significance emerged to regulate the new continental economic space. Far from having its hands tied, the hegemon's powers remained unconstrained; it was those of its neighbours that were constrained.

Clearly, as discussed in the introduction to this volume, North American integration did not conform to this theorization of the largely sociodemocratic European experience (Abu-Laban, Jhappan, and Rocher 2008). Even where massive integration is happening, a corresponding governance is not developing. The huge informal cross-border labour market, in which Canada and Mexico respectively constitute the largest suppliers of trained and unskilled labour to the United States, gets no continent-wide regulation. The gigantic illegal cross-border narcotics traffic and the supply of high-powered weapons by U.S. manufacturers to the Mexican drug cartels and Canadian gangs cry out for a trilateral response. There has been none, even though Mexico has lost effective control over several states within its territory due to the cartels' rising power and their indiscriminate violence. A cap-and-trade system to contain the environmental catastrophe of climate warming would function best if the three countries adopted a common system, but nothing happens while all wait for the U.S. Congress to make the first move. Canada and Mexico are very much part of the problem in these three fields, but domestic U.S. politics determines the parameters for their solution (Harrison 2007).

Implications for Neoconservatism

Increased transborder investment flows may have fostered the growth of a more continentalized economic elite, but citizen attitudes in the three countries have remained measurably resistant to developing a continental consciousness. To the extent that there has been a breaking down of the national, either it has been in favour of globalized – rather than continentalized – thinking via the Internet or it has privileged local border issues such as Hispanic immigration into the United States.

For three decades, the nostrums of neoconservatism have prevailed in the corridors of power. This powerful ideology successfully restructured an economically liberalized North America without instituting any capacity for continental governance to address the three member-states' interconnected problems. Having failed to achieve growth rates or real income gains matching those of the previous and much maligned Keynesian era, having redistributed wealth to the super-rich and exacerbated the poverty of the extremely poor, having proven unable to cope with either terrorism or narcotics, either global warming or mass migration movements, it might be thought that neoconservatism has reached the end of its tether.

Neoconservative economic regionalism has been displaced by xenophobic security regionalism, not by a revived Keynesianism that would offer an inclusive, democratic, and solidaristic politics. This leaves North America with a quietly disintegrating economy, a maximally integrating security system, and three federal governments stubbornly disinclined to work together to achieve a greater good. The surprising persistence of an ideology that has failed to deliver its promised prosperity and a North American political economy that does not evolve raises a puzzling possibility for us to consider in conclusion. Although North America's neoconservative contours may offend the liberal mind, it is possible it has set the standard for the regionalisms emerging in the twenty-first century in which can be found:

- A largely autonomous giant that rejects institutional constraints, preferring ad hoc mechanisms for bilateral consultations leading to its neighbours' harmonizing their regulations with its own.
- Decreased autonomy for the hegemon's junior partners, whose policies are increasingly framed, determined, or dictated from the hegemon's capital.
- Substantial integration of major economic sectors.
- Increased capacity for transnational business.
- Diminished access for a polarized civil society to what are becoming ever more inaccessible centres of power.

Politically, we can see that the neoconservative project, which engendered NAFTA in order to accelerate market integration on the continent without creating any institutional capacity to handle the resulting social, environmental, or political repercussions, leaves North America at the mercy of Washington's political processes, for better or for worse. It could be for the better, were Washington to provide a template for a continent-wide approach to mitigating greenhouse gas emissions, decriminalizing the narcotics industry, regulating labour flows, or generating solidarity programs to pull the destitute out of their poverty. But it has largely been for the worse, because cultural xenophobia has prompted the U.S. government to erect higher, longer, and more forbidding walls along the Mexican border.

The disintegration of neoconservative regionalism in North America may be good from a democratic perspective, as Germain suggests. For the two peripheral states, it could induce them to give up their dream that integration with the United States can solve their problems. Instead they might try again to take control of their own destinies by participating more self-directively on the world stage.

But such a rosy prospect seems highly unlikely. Instead, the extensive economic integration that has proceeded in the marketplace and the intensive security integration that Washington has imposed on its two neighbours suggest another way that we should understand North American governance. Far from gradually approaching the elaborate supranational institutionalization achieved in Europe, North America has little chance of comprising more than one giant state towering over its two medium-sized neighbours. Canada and Mexico still maintain separate political systems that sustain real autonomy, which is buttressed by the survival of their substantial public sectors. But where their industrial or resource markets are highly integrated in the American economy, they are largely ruled from Washington, as is clearly the case for Canadian energy governance (Hale 2011).

The 2010–11 bilateral negotiations of further U.S.–Canada and U.S.–Mexico agreements on regulatory harmonization and security integration clarify the extent to which Washington has become recognized as the de facto political centre of an informally operating North America. The continent has retreated from its efforts at trilateralism to two bilateral relationships driven by a Washington that is preoccupied with pushing its anti-narcotics and anti-terrorist security defences not just to the continental perimeter but beyond to Central America and across the seas, where further dangers may lurk in unidentified passengers and unscreened containers heading for the New World.

From what we can see of North America's regressive trends, it may be too anodyne to talk of continental governance 'post crisis' as if we were emerging into a new normalcy. Since there are no discernible signs that its ever-growing problems of commercial barriers, terrorism-focused paranoia, transborder criminality, and environmental degradation are being addressed – or even could be confronted given the present alignment of political and economic forces in the three countries – we may be closer to the mark if we borrow a notion from Leon Trotsky and think of North America's intractable governance problems as having entered a phase of 'permanent crisis.'

Notes

1 Joseph M. Dukert, 'North America,' in *Energy Cooperation in the Western Hemisphere: Benefits and Impediments*, ed. Sidney Weintraub, Annette Hester, and Veronica R. Prado (Washington: Center for Strategic and International Studies, 2007), 138.
2 In contrast with the coercive control exercised by an imperial power, 'hegemon' is used in this chapter to denote the leader of a regime whose weaker members participate in formulating the norms and rules by which the system is governed.
3 U.S. Court of Appeals for the Ninth Circuit, no. 05–35264
4 Confidential interviews in Los Piños, Mexico City, 7 and 14 March 2006.
5 Confidential interview, Mexico City, 1 March 2007.
6 This lack of solidarity was exemplified by the United States excluding Canada and Mexico from its negotiations of a new, transregional Transpa-

cific Partnership and then imposing demanding concessions pre-emptively in 2012 before letting its neighbours join the TPP negotiations.

References

Abu-Laban, Yasmeen, Radha Jhappan, and François Rocher, eds. 2008. *Politics in North America: Redefining Continental Relations*. Peterborough: Broadview.

Bow, Brian. 2006. '"When in Rome": Comparing Canadian and Mexican Strategies for Influencing Policy Outcomes in the United States.' *Canadian-American Public Policy* 65.

Castro-Rea, Julián. 2006. 'Are U.S. Business Priorities Driving Continental Integration?' *Edmonton Journal*, 27 March.

Clarkson, Stephen. 2008. *Does North America Exist? Governing the Continent after NAFTA and 9/11*. Toronto and Washington: University of Toronto Press and Woodrow Wilson Press. Chapter 18.

– 2004. 'Canada's External Constitution under Global Trade Governance.' In *Dessiner la société par le droit / Mapping Society through Law*. Edited by Ysolde Gendreau. Montréal: Les Éditions Thémis, CRDP, Université de Montréal. 1–31.

Clarkson, Stephen, Sarah Davidson Ladly, Megan Merwart, and Carlton Thorne. 2005. 'The Primitive Realities of Continental Governance in North America.' In *Complex Sovereignty: Reconstituting Political Authority in the Twenty-First Century*. Edited by Edgar Grande and Louis W. Pauly. Toronto: University of Toronto Press. 168–94.

Fry, Earl H., and Jared Bybee. 'NAFTA 2002: A Cost/Benefit Analysis for the United States, Canada, and Mexico.' *Canadian–American Public Policy* 49 (2002).

Golob, Stephanie R. 2002. 'North America beyond NAFTA? Sovereignty, Identity, and Security in Canada–U.S. Relations.' *Canadian–American Public Policy* 52.

Hale, Geoffrey E. 2011. '"In the Pipeline" or "Over a Barrel"? Assessing Canadian Efforts to Manage U.S.–Canadian Energy Interdependence.' *Canadian–American Public Policy* 76 (February): 25.

Harrison, Kathryn. 2007. 'The Road Not Taken: Climate Change Policy in Canada and the United States.' *Global Environmental Politics* 7, no. 4 (November).

Hufbauer, Gary Clyde, and Jeffrey J. Schott. 2005. *NAFTA Revisited: Achievements and Challenges*. Washington: Peterson Institute.

Leycegui, Beatriz, and Rafael Fernandez de Castro. 2000. ¿*Socios naturales? Cinco años del tratado de libre comercio de América del Norte*. Mexico: Instituto Tecnológico Autónomo de México.

Pastor, Robert A. 2011. *The North American Idea: A Vision of a Continental Future.* New York: Oxford University Press.

– 2004. 'North America's Second Decade.' *Foreign Affairs* 83, no. 1 (January–February): 124–5.

Shamsie, Yasmine, and Ricardo Grinspun, eds. 2007. *Whose Canada? Continental Integration, Fortress North America, and the Corporate Agenda.* Montreal and Kingston: McGill–Queen's University Press.

Vega, Gustavo, and Gilbert R. Winham. 2002. 'The Role of NAFTA Dispute Settlement in the Management of Canadian, Mexican, and U.S. Trade and Investment Relations.' *Ohio Northern University Law Review* 28, no. 3: 651–706.

4 The Mexican Political Security Crisis: Implications for the North American Community[1]

JORGE CADENA-ROA

This chapter assesses both the extent of the current Mexican political security crisis and its potential consequences for the future of the North American region. Such an analysis is not an easy task because we are witnessing the unfolding of a complex phenomenon whose actual contours and consequences are uncertain not merely across Mexico but over the entire region. It is an unpredictable situation because of the large number of actors involved in conducting illegal business in several countries, because both subnational and national governments are struggling at the same time to enforce prohibitionist laws against drug trafficking, and because of the extent of corruption and the intimidation commanded by criminal organizations. The use of formal and informal rules, the amounts of cash and firepower in the hands of drug traffickers, and the difficulties of telling the 'good guys' from the 'bad guys' are keys to understanding the continued tango of action and reaction between criminals and law enforcers. Clearly, this spiralling and unpredictable conflict has affected negatively continental attitudes towards North American integration; arguably, it has also encouraged what Golob describes in her chapter in this volume as the apparent demise of North American trilateralism with the evolution of 'double bilateralism.' Moreover, the February 2011 announcement by Canada and the United States of joint Perimeter Security and Economic Competitiveness discussions signals a dramatic break from what had been Mexico's more central position in the North American relationship (Wood 2011).[2]

Introduction: The Current Context of Instability

Over the past several years the Mexican security crisis has escalated to unprecedented heights. It is not just affecting the lives, integrity, and belongings of dealers, consumers, and enforcers; it has also become a threat to common citizens and even to the Mexican state. After President Calderón was inaugurated on 1 December 2006, his administration launched what has become a highly contested and controversial war on drugs. As a consequence, Mexico has witnessed an escalation of violence that makes the Mexican state appear weak and the whole country increasingly unstable, unsecure, and violent, and there have been growing tensions between the United States and Mexico. In fact, the U.S. Ambassador to Mexico, Carlos Pascual, resigned from his position in March 2011 after the release of Wikileaks cables four months earlier that revealed U.S. concerns over Mexican security policy (Chase 2011; The Economist 2011).

In addition, over the past few years, rising and sometimes unspeakably violent crime has made obvious the serious limitations of the Mexican state – specifically, its inability to monopolize the use of violence, protect the population under its jurisdiction, and enforce prohibitionist laws. So far, the results of the war on drugs have been paradoxical: the more the authorities try to enforce the law, the more organized crime displays its power and defiance. Recent reports have not been reassuring to governments north of the U.S.–Mexico border: the *Washington Post* reported in June 2011 that the drug cartels are relying on 'narco-tanks' – that is, 'armored assault vehicles, with gun turrets, inch-thick armor plates, firing ports and bulletproof glass' (Booth 2011); and *CNN* noted that same month that Mexican troops were replacing half the police in the northern state of Tamaulipas, which borders Texas (Castillo 2011).

The illegal drug industry is comprised of small cells, criminal networks, and hierarchical groups, which typically conduct business in more than one country, thus representing an informal type of regionalization. These groups and networks sometimes confront yet also sometimes are protected by governmental authorities (federal, state, local), including law enforcement officials. Operations designed to fight these criminal activities regularly provoke adaptive changes in those organizations, which move their activities to other regions of Mexico and which often mutate to survive new methods of persecution. Often these adaptive changes cause new security and enforcement problems: such innovation catches authorities off guard, and while they are learning how to respond effectively, new cycles of violence begin.

This current crisis in Mexico has not emerged out of thin air; indeed, it is widely recognized that narcotics, security, and terrorist threats are negative unintended consequences of globalization (Naím 2003; Love 2011). These threats do not have their origins and effects within single countries; rather, they often spill over from state to state and across regions, reflecting the so-called 'new security dilemma' and strengthening the 'security interdependence' (Ikenberry 2010) of the post–Cold War world. Since drug trafficking is a transnationally organized form of crime, coordination among law enforcers in those countries where the criminal groups operate is vital if they are to be defeated. However, corruption (or suspicion of corruption) is impeding cooperation among officers at subnational, national, and international levels in North America, because where it exists, sharing information would clearly be counterproductive. Policies to fight drug trafficking and corruption must be global or at the very least multilateral; efforts to combat these problems are doomed to failure when they emanate from a single country. Thus, Mexico's political security crisis has many ramifications and potential consequences for the societies and governments of the United States and Canada, as well as for those in Central and South America.

Drug production and trafficking have emerged as criminal activities because of how the law defines them. When states forbid the production and trade of given products and services, there remains a strong demand within populations willing to pay the price for these goods. This in turn encourages the emergence of illegal markets. Drug trafficking is a highly profitable business that obviously, for many people, outweighs the costs and risks involved. Since the demand is mainly in the United States and production is in Mexico (marijuana, heroin, and recently methamphetamines) and South America (cocaine), the drug producers and traffickers have increasingly been using Mexican soil to conduct business, and the Mexican cartels have become the linchpin in the entire operation.

Drug trafficking in Mexico is centred on smuggling, and Mexico has become the main country targeted by the United States for its anti-drug policies. Prohibitionist laws have had harsh consequences in the United States, where the incarceration rate has quadrupled since 1970: one American adult in 100 is behind bars, and one in 9 young African Americans. The federal and state prison population has increased thirteenfold since 1980 ('Rough Justice' 2010; 'Too Many Laws' 2010). As *The Economist* puts it, 'It seems odd that a country that rejoices in limiting the power of the state should give so many draconian powers to its government' ('Too Many Laws' 2010). There is also heightened pressure on source countries to reduce supply. Thus, the way the problem is defined (prohibition should be enforced), and the way that policies are being implemented (on the supply side), are at the root of the current Mexican security crisis. Yet Mexicans rarely contribute to defining the problem and designing policies to solve it; instead, responses are shaped abroad, primarily in the United States. Prohibition is at the heart of illegal drug trafficking (Serrano 2007), and violence in production and transit countries, such as Mexico, is one of its most visible negative consequences.

Given the obviously close connections between the halting progress of North American integration and the Mexican security crisis, the new regionalism and constructivist perspectives are more useful than other theories to understand the interrelated developments in the region over the past decade. As Ayres and Macdonald argue in the introduction to this volume, functionalism offers an apolitical approach to integration, one that is totally inadequate for understanding that process. Institutionalization in North America has remained shallow (Ayres and Macdonald 2009) because there is strong nationalist and sovereignty-based resistance to further integration. The leaders of the three countries have found it easier to advance the integration process through bilateral agreements, out of sight of public opinion and legislative scrutiny, rather than through open debate, public consultation, and formal institutions. Thus, the neofunctionalist assumption that non-governmental actors, beneficiaries of greater cross-border cooperation, would push forward the integration process does not fit the data. Since the new regionalism approach takes into account informal and illicit dimensions, unintended consequences arising from the global environment, and a plurality of actors that push and pull the process in different directions, it seems a more appropriate approach to explaining what has been going on in North America in light of the Mexican political security crisis.

The constructivist approach is also important for understanding how problems, policies, and interests are constructed and redefined. At the root of the Mexican security crisis lies the decision to criminalize the production, transportation, and consumption of drugs and to enforce prohibitionist laws mainly on the supply side. These approaches have been socially constructed; clearly, other ones might have been possible. Similarly, the current security crisis is forcing the Mexican political class to redefine, as a matter of survival, Mexican nationalism and sovereignty.

Finally, theories about regional processes must leave room for unintended consequences. The continued high demand for narcotics in the United States, in tandem with the success of policies to fight supply in Turkey, the Caribbean, and South America, created the conditions for Mexico to become the platform for smuggling drugs into the United States. International criminal organizations were forced to look for Mexican counterparts in order to conduct business within Mexican territory. This chapter will later argue that Mexico's severe poverty and inequality, the inadequacy of old, informal rules when it came to dealing with drug traffickers in the post-9/11 securitized environment, and the corruption that characterized the 'revolutionary family' that ruled the country up to the year 2000 (and that continues to exist at all levels of government), rendered the Mexican authorities unreliable for the country's citizens as well as for its foreign partners. Moreover, the impact of democratization on state power (i.e., it decentralized the state), the regular reshuffling of elected authorities, and the negative consequences of globalization (narcotics, security, and terrorist threats) have combined to create the conditions for the emergence of drug cartels that are powerful enough to confront the state's law enforcers.

In the introduction to this volume, Ayres and Macdonald contend that North American trilateral engagement is at its lowest level since the mid-1990s. Several other contributors stress that U.S. security concerns since 9/11 have recast the agenda of North American integration. Since 9/11 the United States has been demanding more cooperation from Mexico and Canada in security matters and has brought both countries within its security perimeter. Canada has largely been cooperating, while Mexico has been dragging its feet due to nationalist and sovereignty concerns. But undoubtedly, cooperation has also been limited because of the extent of corruption among Mexican politicians and law enforcers. Therefore, if Mexico is going to cooperate more closely with the United States in security matters, Mexico's political class will have to find ways to combine nationalism and sovereignty with closer cooperation with their northern neighbour. This will also benefit the Mexican citizenry, provided that it helps root out corrupt public officials, who at this writing continue to abuse their positions with impunity.

All of this amounts to a sobering challenge for Mexico and the North American region. To this point, Mexico has not been able to see how its national interest is served by being included in the U.S. security perimeter and fighting a war within its borders to stop the smuggling of drugs into the United States. The current political security crisis may serve as the catalyst for building consensus among the Mexican political class and society to move forward in that direction. It takes a national project, as well as sufficient sovereignty to allocate resources purposefully, for a state to serve the national interest; unfortunately, corrupt politicians have often resorted to nationalism to protect themselves from scrutiny, questioning, and prosecution. The ongoing security perimeter discussions between Canada and the United States indicate that those two countries may have already decided not to include Mexico in a security perimeter, or to postpone Mexico's inclusion indefinitely.

With the North American project arguably still unfolding, any advances in a trilateral direction have become conditional on Mexico's increased cooperation in security matters. The United States cannot fully address its security concerns as long as it perceives Mexico as a place where law enforcement officials are difficult to distinguish from drug traffickers. Moreover, Mexican society itself is being heavily strained by a seeming unstoppable flood of corruption, power abuses, and human rights violations; stories about these fill the Mexican news media on a daily basis. The issues touching on the possible continuation of North American integration are extremely sensitive – nothing less than nationalism, sovereignty, and corruption – and they cannot be raised without generating a strong anti-imperialist backlash in Mexico.

It is difficult to assess the magnitude of Mexico's security crisis and its consequences for the North American region because information is scarce regarding its elements and actors, largely because those actors rely on keeping those elements secret in order to continue with their crimes. There is no doubt, however, that organized crime has developed into a clear and present threat to the Mexican state and the North American region. So far, the medicine has been causing the patient more suffering than the disease. Acknowledging at the outset that information is limited, this chapter tries to suggest how destructive the Mexican security crisis has become, what its causes are, and what its implications are for the North American community.

The Background to the Mexican Political Security Crisis

Drug trafficking in Mexico is not a new phenomenon. For decades, drug trafficking operated in Mexico through deals with prominent politicians and members of the 'revolutionary family' (Mexico's political elite, associated with the Institutional Revolutionary Party or PRI), at the local, regional, and national levels. These actors tolerated and closely monitored criminal activities, skimmed some of the profits, and tried to limit the harsher consequences of illegal activities (such as indiscriminate violence and increases in domestic consumption) (Astorga 1996, 2003; Enciso 2009). These politicians never allowed foreigners to run criminal organizations; nor did they let them accumulate sufficient power to take over the business or, least of all, challenge the 'revolutionary family' and the state (Astorga 2004; Serrano 2007). One leading scholar has noted that 'drug trafficking was viewed as just another profitable business that could be run by powerful members of the "revolutionary family," while taking advantage of the political positions they occupied at a given moment' (Astorga 2004, 89). During the Cold War, political stability in Mexico was a higher priority for the United States than preventing drug trafficking, and Washington largely turned a blind eye to these dealings. These were the informal rules that allowed the authoritarian state to control and regulate the drug market, limit the capacity building of drug cartels, and ensure that the state would not be challenged by criminal organizations.

Early Mexican–U.S. Responses to Drug Trafficking

This situation started to change in the late 1960s with Operation Intercept I, during which the U.S. government imposed a thorough inspection of individuals crossing the border, affecting the economy on both sides. The operation was launched on 21 September 1969 and lasted twenty days. Its purpose was to pressure the Mexican government to strengthen its efforts to combat drug production and smuggling. Demand for drugs was increasing in the United States, and because production sites and transit routes were being shut down elsewhere,[3] Mexico became the best available alternative for the production and storage of drugs and for their shipment into the U.S. market. Inevitably, the Mexican criminal organizations became the brokers, and as a result they grew increasingly wealthy and powerful. Between 1975 and 1979, the United States and Mexico cooperated closely in the counter-narcotics Operation Condor, which applied defoliants from aircraft in Sinaloa, Chihuahua, and Durango. This counter-narcotics operation produced a 'cockroach effect': when authorities tried to eliminate traffickers from one place, they moved to the next; thus, the largest traffickers moved their activities to Jalisco and Michoacán.

In 1985, the torture and murder of a U.S. Drug Enforcement Agency (DEA) agent, Enrique Camarena Salazar, and his Mexican pilot, Alfredo

Zavala Avelar, resulted in Operation Intercept II and a crisis in U.S.–
Mexican relations that illustrated Mexico's vulnerability to failures in
anti-drug enforcement. Operation Intercept II partly closed the U.S.–
Mexico border for eight days in February 1985. The DEA had reason
to believe that Camarena and Zavala had been kidnapped and killed
by Mexican drug traffickers or corrupt police. Ever since this incident,
corruption in Mexico has become a principal concern for the U.S. government – and, notably, for the U.S. Congress,[4] which began to see
corruption as the main reason why the Mexican government's drug
enforcement policies had failed (Toro 1995). For some analysts, 'the
Mexican drug problem, as it affects bilateral relations with the United
Sates, is essentially an issue of integrity' (Reuter and Ronfeldt 1992,
130). The Mexican government responded to accusations of corruption and demands for increased scrutiny as if they were violations of
national sovereignty and acts of interference in domestic affairs.

It was clear by the mid-1980s that the informal rules that had long
been in place in Mexico to regulate drug trafficking were beginning to
generate significant tensions in the bilateral relationship. The agency in
charge of dealing with the drug cartels, the infamous Dirección Federal
de Seguridad (DFS) – which also was in charge of the surveillance of
political dissidents, and which was the Mexican counterpart of the Central Intelligence Agency (CIA) – was dismantled by President Miguel
de la Madrid as a result of Operation Intercept II. In 1986, U.S. President
Ronald Reagan signed the National Security Decision Directive, which
declared drug trafficking a threat to U.S. national security, bolstered the
U.S. government's capacity to assert its criminal laws extraterritorially,
and increased pressure on source countries to pass prohibitionist laws
and to police their enforcement. In 1987, drug trafficking was declared
a national security problem by the De la Madrid Administration.

As a consequence of these events, the U.S. government moved from
embracing the cooperation framework exemplified by Operation Condor (1975–9) towards a tougher law enforcement policy that extended
the jurisdiction of U.S. laws to other countries. The Anti-Drug Abuse
Act of 1986 made it a crime to produce or distribute drugs outside the
United States with the intention of exporting them to the U.S. territory.
This new policy included annual certifications regarding the extent to
which other countries were cooperating with the United States against
drug trafficking. Failure to fully cooperate with the United States would
result into sanctions such as cuts in economic and military aid, votes
against in multilateral lending institutions, and loss of trade preferences.

Operación Leyenda (1986–90) was a clear example of the consequences for Mexico of this tougher law enforcement framework. During this operation, the United States sponsored the abduction in Mexico of at least nineteen people who were believed to have participated in the kidnapping, torture, and murder of Camarena and Zavala, and had these people sent to the U.S. for prosecution. This extraterritorial law enforcement operation, arguably unacceptable in any sovereign country and condemned by international law, moved Mexico to protest against what constituted a grave breach of its territorial sovereignty as well as a violation of the 1978 U.S.–Mexico Extradition Treaty (Toro 1995).

The Multifaceted Contributions to the Current Crisis

At the heart of the current explosion of drug-related violence lies the historic reliance of the Mexican authoritarian state on a fair dose of corruption and discretionary law enforcement. It is a well-established fact in criminological studies that increases in the scale and scope of organized criminal activities within and across countries depend on the implicit or explicit support of corrupt public officials (Buscaglia and Gonzalez-Ruiz 2007; Friedrich 1989). Criminal organizations use public sector corruption as a means to confront states with impunity and to subvert or degrade the rule of law. These organizations have the means to distort police investigations, derail criminal processes, bribe judges,[5] and hire the best lawyers available (Buscaglia, González-Ruiz, and Prieto Palma 2006). Criminal organizations operate wherever the risks and costs of doing so are lower. Thus, countries with lower standards in law making and law enforcement are also countries with higher levels of organized crime and corruption (Buscaglia and González-Ruiz 2007). The levels of impunity in Mexico are dismayingly high, and this also encourages crime. Surveys indicate that in the Mexican capital, only 30% of crimes are reported to the authorities; that only half of those reported (15% of the total) are investigated; and that only 10% of those investigated are brought before a judge (1.5% of the total). Put more simply, only 1.5% of the crimes committed in Mexico City are brought before the courts (*Reforma*, 20 April 2010). Without a doubt, this level of impunity is one of the most serious shortcomings of Mexico's democracy (Cadena-Roa and López Leyva 2011).

Drug trafficking is a transnational organized crime (Vellinga 2004). Forty per cent of criminal organizations extend their activities into two or three countries; 17% involve criminal activities in more than three countries (Buscaglia and Gonzalez-Ruiz 2007). So it is vital for countries' law enforcement agencies to share information and coordinate activities regarding the criminal groups operating in their respective jurisdictions. Corruption, or suspicions of corruption, impede this cooperation at the subnational, national, and international levels. Security cooperation between the United States and Mexico requires that the authorities on both sides not be on the payroll of traffickers; when they are, information sharing is counterproductive if not suicidal, compromising the lives of law enforcement officials, witnesses, informants, and their families.

A negative consequence of globalization has been that corruption is no longer a secondary concern for common citizens and businesspeople; in fact, it has developed into a serious challenge to Mexico's social and political stability, and until it is addressed, it will discourage cooperation with foreign partners. When crime breeds with corruption, it becomes a threat to national security. Criminal activity may start as paying a bribe to avoid a speeding ticket and evolve into the capturing of police, prosecutors, judges, law makers, and entire state institutions. Organized crime, corruption, obstruction of justice, and violence are intimately linked and together represent a threat to national and international security.

The large amounts of cash that the cartels control are contributing to the explosion of corruption. When cash fails to buy consciences, there is always an alternative – bullets – of which the cartels also have plenty. Many officials and private businesses conducting legal activities face this sobering alternative: *plata o plomo* (silver or lead). There is no doubt that some areas of the Mexican state have been captured by criminals, and there is no need to go deep into history to document this point. In July 2010, it was uncovered that criminals in custody at the Gomez Palacio prison in Durango were being let out at night with the permission of the director to work as hitmen, using official vehicles and guns. In three separate events from January to July 2010, these hitmen killed thirty-five people, most of them innocent and not related to organized crime. This is but one of an endless list of well-documented examples.[6]

Besides proximity to the largest drug market in the world and the corruption of Mexican politicians, there are other conditions that have allowed drug trafficking to prosper in Mexico. One of these is poverty, which is the lot of more than 50% of Mexicans. Another is the unintended effects of Mexico's transition from authoritarianism (Velasco

Cruz 2005b). Economists had contended that Mexico had the most to gain from NAFTA, yet more than half the Mexican population still lives below the poverty line. The economy has been growing slowly and has been unable to provide work for those entering the job market. As discussed in the chapter in this volume by Gabriel, over the past decade there has been a massive migration of Mexicans to the United States.

The world financial crisis of 2009 and the deterioration of security in large Mexican cities (mainly along the border) have also encouraged Mexicans to join criminal gangs. According to Johnson (2009), the U.S. Assistant Secretary of the Bureau of International Narcotics and Law Enforcement Affairs, some 150,000 people are directly involved in the Mexican narcotics business and another 300,000 in the cultivation and processing of marijuana and opium. The Mexican economy does not depend on income generated from drug trafficking,[7] but it clearly represents an important income in some poverty-stricken regions of the country. According to Johnson, the drug trade – including the trafficking of cocaine and methamphetamines – generates an estimated $13 to 25 billion in earnings per year for the drug cartels. This amount is unevenly distributed among the trade's participants. Prices for drugs increase exponentially from one link of the chain to the next. The most lucrative links in that chain are smuggling drugs into the United States and selling them retail on American streets.

Enormous numbers of people are willing to work for the drug cartels, which offer rapid profits, personal power (from the guns they carry), and a sense of belonging and authority. The risks to freedom and life associated with drug trafficking are high, but these are outweighed by the possibility of making large sums of cash quickly. This is especially so for people who have no other available options. The case of Joaquín Guzmán Loera, aka 'El Chapo' ('Shorty'), the head of the Sinaloa Cartel and one of the main suppliers of Colombian cocaine to the U.S. market, is illustrative. In 1993 he was arrested in Mexico on homicide and drug charges. But on 19 January 2001, he escaped from the maximum security prison of Puente Grande, Jalisco, to seize back control of the organization. He is Mexico's most wanted man, besides being the second most wanted for both the FBI and INTERPOL. The U.S. government continues to offer a $5 million reward for information leading to his capture. 'El Chapo' is #937 on *Forbes Magazine*'s 2009 list 'World's Millionaires,' with a self-made fortune from drug trafficking estimated at more than US $1 billion;[8] he is also #45 on the *Forbes* list 'World's Most Powerful People,' below Osama bin Laden (#37) but above the Russian president Dmitry Medvedev (#43), TV host Oprah Winfrey (#45), former IMF Managing Director Dominique Strauss-Kahn, (#47), Apple co-founder Steve Jobs (#57), World Bank President Robert B. Zoellick (#63), and Venezuela's President Hugo Chávez (#67).[9] 'El Chapo' is one among many self-made men who in just a few years have experienced (and demonstrated) skyrocketing upward mobility that no other legal (and few other illegal) activities provide.

Also facilitating the emergence of independent major drug cartels was Mexico's democratization, which resulted in political parties taking turns in power. In the year 2000, after a world record seventy-one years in power, the PRI peacefully relinquished the presidency to the conservative National Action Party (PAN) under President Vicente Fox (2000–6) (Cadena-Roa 2003).[10] In tandem with democracy came a regular reshuffling in federal, state, and municipal governments that brought new personnel into office who were not privy to the deals that had been struck between the former authorities and the drug cartels, and who were not willing to honour them. Moreover, the drug lords felt that they owed nothing to the newcomers, that they had become strong enough to take over the business all by themselves, without political protection, and that they had no reason to share their profits. In this way, democratization in Mexico cut the drug cartels loose. Higher levels of violence related to drug trafficking in the 1990s were observed in those states where the PRI had lost power, such as Baja California, Chihuahua, Jalisco, Nuevo León, and the Federal District (Astorga 2004, 92). Thus, democracy had the unforeseen consequence of deregulating the drug market by removing third-party intervention from the equation. The business, in effect, had stopped running smoothly, and this encouraged the development of private armies to protect illegal activities from competitors (both local and foreign) and from the strengthened anti-cartel efforts of law enforcement.

All of this also meant that several cartels began warring among themselves to secure the U.S. market and thereby make the largest profits. It also meant that law enforcement officers began fighting this illicit trade with more resolve. This situation somewhat resembles what Hobbes described as the natural condition of mankind – a state of war in which there is 'continuall feare, and danger of violent death; And the life of man, solitary, poore, nasty, brutish, and short' (Hobbes 1979). The market for illegal drugs is highly profitable, and there are no arbiters, courts of justice, or third parties to settle disputes among criminal organizations. As a consequence, each cartel has had to build its own private army to protect its interests from competitors and law enforcers. Violence has coincided with the growth of the illegal drug trade.

Representations of Current Violent Trends

Violence in the cartels' context serves as a private system of justice, again in the Hobbesian sense: each party becomes judge of its own cause and executes the verdict. Many murders are described by the media as means to correct what went wrong (*ajuste de cuentas*) among partners and rivals. Private armies also serve the purpose of protecting the organization, and its drug and money shipments, besides imposing order and discipline within the ranks and sending messages to rivals, authorities, and those law enforcers who are fighting back. Since there is no real competition in terms of drug quality and price, cartels fight one another for control of territory and access to transportation routes and markets. Striking one cartel often has the unintended consequence of strengthening its rivals. After a *capo* is captured or killed, the opportunity arises for promotion within the organization and for rivals to take over what is left: markets, routes, *sicarios* (hitmen), and lower-ranking gangs and criminals. Also, when a *capo* falls, suspicion that rivals gave sensitive information to law enforcers justifies retaliation (de Mauleón 2010).[11] The ensuing disorganization and disruption of the drug trafficking operations usually settles down by means of violence. According to data provided by CISEN, between December 2006 and August 2010, 28,000 people were killed in events related to organized crime (*Reforma*, 8/(/2010).[12] Most of these crimes remain uninvestigated, and since no one claims the corpses, they go to unmarked graves.

According to the media and some scholars (Bailey and Godson 2000; Felbab-Brown 2009; Smith 1999), the absolute and per 100,000 rate of murder in Mexico has risen in the past few years to levels approaching Colombia's. Escalante (Escalante Gonzalbo 2009), however, contends that it has not. He found that the number of homicides in Mexico dropped from 14,520 to 8,507 between 1990 and 2007 and that the number of homicides per 100,000 went from a maximum of 19.72 in 1992 to a minimum of 8.04 in 2007.[13] Compared to the homicide levels in countries such as Colombia, Brazil, and Nicaragua, Mexican figures remain relatively low. This is not to deny that the current upsurge of violence and murder is intolerable (after four years of the Calderón Administration's War on Drugs, Ciudad Juarez has been dubbed the 'murder capital of the world'), but to stress the fact that violence and murder in Mexico have been higher before – but very few noticed and even fewer cared.[14]

Two contrasting patterns led to Escalante's counterintuitive findings. Violence in Mexico's central and southern states (México, Oaxaca, Guerrero), and in rural areas generally, has diminished the most. The end of agrarian reform in 1992 and migration seem to have influenced these trends. In contrast, violence in northern states (Baja California, Sonora, Chihuahua, Tamaulipas), and in urban areas generally, has increased dramatically. Also, about half the murders that took place between 1990 and 2007 in the northern border region were concentrated in two border cities: Tijuana, Baja California (south of San Diego, California), and Ciudad Juárez, Chihuahua (south of El Paso, Texas). Murder decreased in towns with under 10,000 inhabitants, and rose in cities of over 1 million inhabitants.

Several explanations for this phenomenon have been put forward. The population in the northern border cities has doubled in the past two decades, and such cities often lack public services and adequate schools; moreover, a high percentage of the populations of those cities are youth (Bowden 2011). One explanation stands out, however: the smuggling routes converge in these areas, which are the main points of entry for illegal drugs and immigrants to the United States. It follows that in those cities there is a heightened presence and competition among criminal organizations.

But notwithstanding these trends, public perceptions of levels of violence in Mexico have been exacerbated by media representations (Ríos 2011). The national and international media portray Mexico as an out-of-control country, as a failed state that is spiralling into a crisis of violence and murder. Clearly, murder has become much more visible because it is happening more often not in impoverished and remote indigenous towns but in major cities along the U.S. border, where businesses are operating and there is plenty of media presence, along with expectations of security and rule of law. Another trend feeding these public perceptions of violence is that criminals are not shy about their wrongdoings. Quite the contrary – they want to show off their crimes and attract as much media attention as possible. To achieve this, they behead, mutilate, or torture some victims, and leave their corpses out in the open or throw them into public places, including nightclubs and dance floors. The cartels have even uploaded videos of their crimes and murders to YouTube. Obviously, they want their acts and deeds to be known and to have an impact on various publics.

The Mexican government is trying to communicate the message that it is winning the war on crime. To that purpose, it disseminates news about drugs and weapons seized and major kingpins captured, killed, or extradited. When the Federal Police announced the arrest of Santiago Meza López, aka 'El Pozolero' ('The Stew Maker'), they described this criminal as the individual responsible for having dissolved three hundred bodies in acid for a drug cartel.[15] The announcement was intended to demonstrate success in the war on drugs and to reassure the public; however, graphic descriptions of criminals' vicious cruelty, and the use of gruesome nicknames that reflect their activities, increase people's unease.

The Mexican media (followed by the international media) help heighten the visibility of the drug lords and their criminal activities. Jacobo Zabludovsky, a leading anchor on a national radio news program, presents the daily information as coming from different battle fronts. 'From the Michoacán front our correspondent reports,' he announces, and then the correspondent gives the figures of the dead and wounded. Then he continues: 'From the battleground of Ciudad Juárez ...' Almost every day, Mexican newspapers publish front page items about the number of dead bodies found with signs of torture, beheaded or dismembered, and the few criminals captured by the Federal Police, the army, or the navy. In this way, though they are obviously different in many ways, the cartels, the government, and the media compete among themselves to generate images of untamed insecurity, violence, cruelty, and terror in Mexico. All parties concur, however, that violence is out of control and that something has to be done. The atmosphere, then, seems favourable for the formation of new consensus that is a necessary condition for major policy shifts.

Targets and Consequences of the Violence

It is clear that drug trafficking organizations are moving closer to terrorism. Perhaps the first step in that direction was a grenade thrown towards civilians gathered in the main square in Morelia, Michoacán, on 15 September 2008 to celebrate Mexico's Independence Day. Since that attack, terrorist actions without *any* related demands, targeting innocent bystanders for the sole purpose of producing fear, have multiplied. In March 2010 in Monterrey, drug traffickers simultaneously blocked several streets with sixty stolen cars, including streets near police stations. At other times, the cartels have blocked streets and shot at electric power stations, causing blackouts and traffic chaos. Apparently the sole object of these actions is to intimidate the police and show that criminals can do whatever they want with impunity (*Reforma*, 15–16 August 2010). It is fair to describe these actions as terrorist because the casualties are often innocent bystanders in the wrong place at the wrong time. These displays of brutality embarrass the police, the army, and ultimately the government by showing how weak the Mexican security apparatus is and how vulnerable common citizens are.

The North American Free Trade Agreement, signed in 1993, locked in market-oriented reforms in Mexico. Since 9/11, the United States has been seeking more political and military cooperation from Mexico, which, however, has been reluctant to cooperate more fully due to nationalist and sovereign concerns. The cartels' violence is a response to the challenge that has been presented to them by the Calderón administration's war on drugs, and that violence may force the Mexican political elites, as a simple matter of survival, to align themselves more closely with the United States in security matters. It is becoming increasingly clear that Mexico cannot win the war on drugs without U.S. support, intelligence, and resources.

Buscaglia and Gonzalez-Ruiz (2007) report that a study by the UN and the Mexican Unit Against Organized Crime found that 43% of organized Mexican criminal groups are cells, 51% are criminal networks, and only 6% are hierarchical groups. The largest cartels are the Beltrán Leyva Cartel, the Familia Michoacana Cartel, the Gulf Cartel, the Juárez (Carrillo Fuentes) Cartel, the Sinaloa Cartel, the Tijuana (Arellano Felix) Cartel, and the Zetas Cartel.

Some drug cartels have extended their criminal activities beyond drug trafficking. Some charge fees to petty criminals for the right to operate in the territories they control. Others engage directly in robbery, extortion (i.e., selling 'protection' to legal businesses), and human smuggling and operate prostitution rings. There is a close link between drug-related organized crime and kidnapping, which is a primary activity for 23% of organized criminal groups in Mexico and a secondary activity for another 12% (ibid.).

The targets of drug cartels, other than their competitors, include law enforcers. Because Mexico's police forces (municipal, state, and federal) have often been infiltrated by the cartels, the Mexican army and navy have been called to the front lines for eradication campaigns against drug traffickers. In the past few years, military personnel and former military officers have often been appointed as attorneys, as well as to oversee anti-drug activities and to head police departments in violence-stricken cities and towns. This is another paradox of Mexican democracy: areas related to security are increasingly being staffed by military personnel, and this has strengthened the military's influence in democratically elected governments that have been challenged by drug cartels and their private armies.

All of this has led to frequent violations of human rights and to the murder of innocent citizens by the army. In one terrible case, two graduate students at the prestigious Tec de Monterrey were killed on 19 March 2010 by the army, which claimed afterwards that the students had attacked them and they had been compelled to shoot back. The Tec authorities and the victims' families denied such accusations. After an investigation, the National Human Rights Commission (CNDH) found that both victims had been students in good standing, that neither of them had been carrying weapons, that at least one of them had been shot at close range (1 metre), that the soldiers had altered the crime scene and planted weapons beside the dead bodies, and that the civil and military authorities had failed to cooperate with the investigation.[16]

More and more journalists are being targeted by criminal organizations. Journalists Without Borders reports that sixty-nine journalists have been killed on the job since 2000 and that twelve have disappeared since 2003. During President Calderón's mandate, thirty-eight journalists have been murdered (*Reporteros sin fronteras* 2010). Several national and international organizations have denounced the threats, abuses, abductions, and murders of journalists by the drug cartels (Article 19 and CENCOS 2010a; Article 19 and CENCOS 2010b; Hervieu, Flores Martínez, and Julliard 2009).[17] The drug cartels are also increasingly targeting politicians. The PRI candidate for the governorship of Coahuila, Rodolfo Torre Cantú, who was ahead in the polls, was murdered on 28 June 2010, barely one week before election day. Two days later, Calderón convened all political parties to unite against criminal violence. He even suggested that he would be willing to revise the strategy against drug trafficking, and he called for a debate on the legalization of some drugs.[18] Because of partisan politics, his call came to nothing.

Protest groups have developed over the past few years to denounce police involvement in criminal activities such as kidnapping and extortion.[19] These organizations have proposed various initiatives against criminal activities (Reyes Salinas and Castro Guzmán 2008), but to little effect. Also emerging is an anti-violence social movement that is pressing the authorities to improve their security policies and fight corruption and impunity (López Leyva n.d.).

Implications for the North American Community

When NAFTA was signed in 1993, it was viewed as a trade and investment agreement. Some worried about its implications for the environment and labour rights, and subsequently side agreements were included to address these issues. But after the terrorist attacks of 9/11, the United States passed the Patriot Act (2001), the Enhanced Border Security and Visa Entry Reform Act (EBSVERA) (2001), and the Homeland Security Act (2002). Also in 2002, it created the U.S. Northern Command (NORTHCOM) and brought forward the National Security Strategy (NSS) (Benítez Manaut and Rodríguez Ulloa 2006). In this latter document, the U.S. government asserts its right to pre-empt threats to its national security by taking unilateral action wherever those threats seem to be developing. This doctrine allows unilateral pre-emptive strikes without heed to multilateral organizations and international law.

The events of 9/11 catapulted homeland security to the top of the U.S. government's agenda. The case was made that Washington's capacity to safeguard America did not start at the national borders; instead it would require extensive cooperation from trusted allies who were willing to screen travellers and cargo, 'harden' border crossings, and exchange reliable information. Accordingly, the National Commission on the 9/11 Terrorist Attacks concluded: '9/11 has taught us that terrorism against American interests "over there" [i.e., abroad] should be regarded just as we regard terrorism against America "over here." In this same sense, *the American homeland is the planet*' (Kean and Hamilton 2004). In effect, the Americans were locating their security perimeter at every place in the world where people could travel directly to the United States. Thus, the border points of entry were considered critical.

In this securitized environment, trade and economic integration were displaced from the top of the North American agenda. Mexico and Canada were pressed to incorporate U.S. security concerns into their policies by strengthening their collaboration in surveillance, by patrolling their borders more thoroughly, and by coordinating their enforcement activities and sharing information. Canada and Mexico have different histories in their relations with the United States and face different domestic constraints in terms of changing policies. Neither country views itself as a prominent target for foreign terrorists. The changes implemented by both countries since 9/11 have arisen from concerns that the United States might consider them neglectful of U.S. security needs – needs that according to the Americans include a common North American security perimeter that is tailored to fit U.S. standards and procedures. Because of their different relationships with the regional hegemon, Canada and Mexico have responded differently to U.S. demands for increased border security and military cooperation.

Canada signed the U.S.–Canada Smart Border Declaration in December 2001; developed an Anti-Terrorism Plan that same year; passed the Public Safety Act in 2002; revised its Immigration and Refugee Protection Act that same year; and created a permanent National Security Advisory Council and a Department of Public Safety and Emergency Preparedness in 2004. In the military realm, the Canada Command – the equivalent of the U.S. NORTHCOM – has been established as the national operational authority for the defence of Canada and North America. Canada's cooperation in military matters with the United States is nothing new. Canada has long been a member of NATO and NORAD and has cooperated in military operations with the United States, such as the offensive in Afghanistan. Nonetheless, U.S. security concerns have 'Mexicanized' the U.S.–Canada border as well as the two countries' cross-border relations (Andreas 2005, 2009).

The Mexican president at the time of 9/11, Vicente Fox, offered full cooperation with the U.S. security agenda; but in the end, this led to little more than the signing the U.S.–Mexico Border Partnership Agreement in 2002. Not until 2007 did Mexico's Senate approve a package of legislative reforms aimed at combating terrorism. The Mexican government, its political parties, it armed forces, and public opinion have traditionally been wary of collaborating too closely with their U.S. counterparts. Mexican nationalists contend that too much institutional harmonization and cooperation would eventually result in Mexico turning over its security institutions to the United States.

Canada has seemed more comfortable coordinating its security policies with the United States, even at the operational and military levels. Again, Mexico has responded with little more than declarations. Owing to these differences in cooperation, trilateral integration has not been feasible and a double bilateral process has been followed (see the chapter by Golob in this volume). Since cooperation with the United States tends to raise a nationalist uproar in Mexico, most negotiations have been conducted outside public scrutiny, at the executive level, and have resulted in administrative agreements that do not require approval by the Mexican Congress.

In March 2005, the leaders of the three countries, Paul Martin, George W. Bush, and Vicente Fox, met in Waco, Texas, where they announced the Security and Prosperity Partnership of North America (SPP). Clearly, security had replaced prosperity (trade, investment, and economic development) as the Americans' top priority. According to the document they signed, the SPP was based on the principle that 'our prosperity is dependent on our security.' In April 2007, Thomas A. Shannon, U.S. Assistant Secretary of State, described the SPP as a means to improve security cooperation and to protect North America beyond the U.S. borders. The SPP would thus be an effort that

> understands North America as a shared economic space and that as a shared economic space we need to protect it, and that we need to understand that *we don't protect this economic space only at our frontiers*, that *it has to be protected more broadly throughout North America*. And as we have worked through the SPP to improve our commercial and trading relationship, we have also worked to improve our security cooperation. To a certain extent, *we're armoring NAFTA*. We're trying to show that this $15 trillion economy can be *protected against a threat of terrorism* and against a threat of natural disasters and environmental and ecological disasters.[20] [my italics]

In other words, the point of the SPP was to armour the shared economic space of North America against security and terrorist threats. But Mexico lacked incentives for going along with this: it had not been the target of any international terrorist threats, and it had long maintained a foreign policy based on non-intervention. This lack of incentives for Mexico contributed to the demise of the SPP (see the chapter by Ayres and Macdonald in this volume). The declaration signed by Prime Minister Harper and President Obama in Washington in February 2011 regarding a 'North American' security perimeter without Mexico strongly reflected Canada's desire to deepen economic and security discussions with the United States while leaving Mexico behind.

Ever since NAFTA, analysts have repeatedly pointed out the economic, social, and institutional asymmetries among the three countries. Seventeen years later, those asymmetries remain. NAFTA's agenda has been driven by the Americans' geopolitical and economic interests as a superpower, as well as by corporations and free trade promoters in all three countries. The citizenry at large, as well as unions and rural and small business organizations, have been neglected or passed over. As a result of this power imbalance, Canada and Mexico have since 9/11 been pushed to comply with the Americans' demands regarding homeland security and the war on terror and to accommodate their exigencies.

Nationalism and suspicions regarding the United States' real intentions have long made Mexican authorities reluctant to cooperate and harmonize their policies and institutions with those of their northern neighbour. The United States has often in the past been the most salient single threat to Mexico's national security and sovereignty. Such was the case in the 1800s, when Mexico lost more than half its territory to the United States; in the 1910s, when the U.S. Embassy supported the generals who assassinated President Madero in 1913; and in the 1980s, with Operación Leyenda. Thus, Mexico has been reluctant to follow U.S. international policies, admit law enforcement agents and military personnel to operate in its territory, partake in joint police or military operations, or engage in 'hot pursuit' of drug traffickers and suspicious shipments (Toro 1999).

Most analysts say that Calderón started the war on drugs at the beginning of his term on 1 December 2006, not because he wanted to put an end to the criminal activities of the drug cartels, but in order to address legitimacy problems coming from a close election, which the runner-up candidate was openly contesting (Aguilar Valenzuela and Castañeda 2009; Velázquez Flores and Prado Lallande 2009). According to this view, the purpose of the war on drugs was to end the controversy over his electoral victory by bolstering his authority as Chief of the Armed Forces. The unexpected response from the cartels then forced him to continue this policy.

Another hypothesis is that the war on drugs was a response to the United States' interest in expanding its security perimeter and weakening Mexico's resistance to full cooperation with U.S. security needs. In other words, the United States encouraged the new Mexican administration to break the Mexican government's close ties to drug traffickers; the cartels would then respond with violence, and corrupt officials would resist their own government; this in turn would create even bigger problems that ultimately would increase the Mexican authorities' reliance on U.S. assistance. The alternative for Mexico would have been a reputation as a failed state,[21] as a narco-haven, as a threat to U.S. national security, and as a menace once the violence spilled over the border and migrants began to flee the resulting chaos and instability.[22]

The United States would then deliver the assistance requested, but at a price: Mexico must redefine itself, give up part of its sovereignty on security matters, and significantly reduce corruption in order to become a reliable partner in the U.S. security and military agenda. Otherwise it would be left on its own to fall deeper in a spiral of violence.

Surreptitiously, after the SPP was introduced, NAFTA expanded its reach to North American security without public or even legislative debate. This became clear with the Mérida Initiative, a three-year regional security cooperation plan, presented in October 2007 and passed by the U.S. Congress on 26 June 2008. The Mérida Initiative would allocate up to $1.6 billion over three years to Mexico and Central American and Caribbean countries for security aid, particularly regarding counter-narcotics, counter-terrorism, and border security. The aid would go to the military, the police, and the judiciary for equipment and training. The announcement was not unanimously welcomed either in the United States or in Mexico: generally, the concern was that a military approach to drug trafficking would encourage human rights abuses. In Mexico the military forces are not subject to civilian justice, but rather to military courts, which operate in complete secrecy and which rarely convict those who perpetrate abuses. Nonetheless, the funds were released after the State Department indicated that Mexico was willing to respect human rights.

Arguably, the Mérida Initiative is the SPP under another name and in bilateral form. Its unstated objective is to incorporate Mexico into the U.S. security perimeter, thereby gaining Mexico's cooperation and pulling Mexico's national security into the U.S. orbit through the sharing of information and collaboration in security and military operations. As suggested in the chapters by Icaza, Gilbert, Healy, and Brodie in this volume, we should interpret SPP not as a single (failed) project but rather as one of a series of agreements and commitments assumed by the member-states. Thus the SPP, Calderón's war on drugs, and the Mérida Initiative are not unrelated, nor are they responses to short-term problems (such as the contested election); rather, they are stages in a long-term project to draw Mexico into the U.S. security perimeter as a reliable partner. The close connections between corrupt officials and drug lords need be broken as a necessary condition for security cooperation and institutional harmonization between both countries. Mexico's economic dependence on the United States, including its dependence on the resources it needs to wage the war on drugs, is forcing the Mexican government to comply with U.S. demands. After NAFTA, Mexico fell entirely into the U.S. economic orbit; now, with the SPP, the war on drugs, and the Mérida Initiative, Mexico is on the verge of falling into the U.S. security and military orbit as well.

As noted earlier, in February 2011, Prime Minister Harper and President Obama issued a joint statement that established the Beyond the Border Working Group (BBWG) – the next generation of integrated cross-border law enforcement operations. The BBWG would develop and operate a 'perimeter approach to security, working together within, at, and away from the borders of our two counties to enhance our security and accelerate the legitimate flow of people, goods, and services between our two countries.' This bilateral approach would include compatible, interoperable, and joint measures and technologies to ensure timely sharing of information for combined efforts to counter threats; it would also jointly identify, assess, and interdict persons and organizations involved in transnational crime. Until Mexico puts its house in order and significantly reduces corruption in law enforcement agencies, it will not be invited to join this regional security approach; until it addresses its own long-standing concerns about sovereignty, there will be strong social and political opposition to accept such an invitation.

In retrospect, the possibility of reversing neoliberal economic policies was reduced after Mexico signed GATT (1986) and joined NAFTA (1994), declared its central bank autonomous (1993), and signed a free trade agreement with the EU (2000). Together, these measures have institutionalized market-oriented policies and removed these critical areas of policy making from the government's own discretion, thus ensuring policy continuity despite party alternation in the executive branch of government (Cadena-Roa 2003). The Mérida Initiative, writes Carlsen, 'implies much more than a temporary aid program for fighting drug cartels. It structurally revamps the basis of the bi-national relationship in ways meant to permanently emphasize military aspects over much-needed development aid and modifications in trade and investment policy' (2008, 5). The SPP and the Mérida Initiative should be viewed as means not only to precipitate major changes in Mexico (such as breaking the close links between crime and corruption) and in the bilateral relationship (redefining nationalism and reducing sovereignty) but also to lock in those changes.

Conclusion

Mexico's security crisis has had long-developing domestic and international roots. The country's war on drugs has been a response to U.S.

concerns about its own security. But Mexico's drugs policy is wrong-headed, because a policy based on the police and military is doomed to fail. An attack on supply increases prices, thus inviting new entrepreneurs to take even more risks. Plan Colombia increased the production and quality of cocaine even while reducing its price. Similarly in Mexico, cocaine and other drugs are improving in quality even as their prices fall. Four years after the Mexican government launched its war on drugs, the cartels are still in business, killing more people, and presenting bigger challenges to the Mexican state.

Some analysts suggest that the government should cut new deals with the drug cartels and negotiate new informal rules in order to regulate the drug market and reduce the violence (Aguilar and Castañeda 2009). The escalation of the security crisis since 2006 has proved that fighting the drug cartels through prohibition and police and army intervention is not only ineffectual but also counterproductive. In a joint statement, bluntly titled 'The War on Drugs Is a Failure,' former presidents Fernando Henrique Cardoso (Brazil), César Gaviria (Colombia), and Ernesto Zedillo (México) questioned the efficacy of the U.S. war on drugs and proposed that marijuana possession for personal use be decriminalized:

> The revision of U.S.-inspired drug policies is urgent in the light of the rising levels of violence and corruption associated with narcotics. The alarming power of the drug cartels is leading to a criminalization of politics and a politicization of crime. And the corruption of the judicial and political system is undermining the foundations of democracy in several Latin American countries. (*Wall Street Journal*, 23 February 2009)

Former President Vicente Fox went even further, declaring himself in favour of legalizing and taxing the production, sale, and distribution of drugs (Fox 2010).

There is plenty of evidence that the prohibitionist and repressive anti-drug policy driven by the United States has been counterproductive and that the war on drugs cannot be won. A new approach to drug production, trafficking, and consumption is in order. The Obama administration has adopted a new rhetoric of co-responsibility for the drug problem, which is arguably good news. But a more productive approach would be one that evolves along with *actions*. The new approach must include specific policies towards each of the main three pillars of the current security crisis: the drug business, impunity, and corruption.

Regarding the drug business, new policies should be implemented to reduce the demand for illicit drugs in the main consumer countries; treatment and prevention of addiction should substitute criminalization of possession and consumption; more efforts should be made to target the assets, financial structure, and money laundering of organized crime; gun running from the United States to Mexico should be controlled; and the production and consumption of cannabis, which medical evidence shows is roughly as harmful as alcohol or tobacco, should be decriminalized. Marijuana represents by itself more than half the gross profits of the drug business. Legalizing it would cut by half the resources in the hands of the drug cartels, reducing accordingly the money they have available to sustain private armies and to corrupt law enforcers.

To reduce impunity and corruption will require increased transparency and accountability of officers, decisive attacks on high-level public sector corruption, and a revamping of the policing and judicial systems, including the creation of a national police force. There is an important opportunity here for Mexico's citizenry, who may well find international allies in their fight against the impunity, corruption, nepotism, and arbitrariness of Mexican officialdom.

Building a consensus among the legislative, the judiciary, and civil society is a necessary condition for policy change. That said, Mexico's political parties so far are caught in a vicious cycle of partisan competition and backbiting, a cycle that impedes cooperation on any substantive policy. Civil society actors are also divided around the diagnosis of and solutions to the security crisis. Still, the anti-violence social movement 'Estamos hasta la madre' ('We've had it up to here!'), which is demanding a new strategy against organized crime, the solving of slayings and disappearances, and the elimination of impunity, may catalyze the debate and launch Mexico towards a common diagnosis and design viable public policies.

Since President Calderón announced the 'war on drugs,' the death toll has been growing higher and higher and the cartels have grown more violent and increased their defiance of the authorities. To confront this violence, the state is using resources that in other conditions could be invested elsewhere. When the state is challenged in such a way that 'collateral damage' not only affects innocent civilians and bystanders but also damages democracy and civil rights, there is a clear danger that crime-related violence will spill over to Mexico's northern (and southern) neighbours. If this happens, any possibility for extending the trilateral character of the North American project will be undermined. To this point, the ebb and flow of the North American integration project has been subject to the short-term domestic agendas of the superpower and its junior partners. There is no blueprint for what is desirable and achievable in the long term in the North American region.

Notes

1 Thanks to Mario Galicia Gallareta and Victoria Moreno Cárdenas for research assistance, and to Jeffrey Ayres, Laura Macdonald, Valeria Tirado, and Virginia Labiano for their thoughtful and helpful comments.
2 'Beyond the Border: A Shared Vision for Perimeter Security and Economic Competitiveness,' http://www.borderactionplan-plandactionfrontalier. gc.ca/psec-scep/declaration-declaration.aspx?lang=eng.
3 Mexico's emergence as a major smuggling platform has been the result of successful enforcement policies elsewhere. Turkey went out of the opium market in 1971. Since the demand remained high, production of heroin increased dramatically in Mexico. The Caribbean and Florida were also closed for drug trafficking in the 1980s (Serrano 2007). These international events have made Mexico a transit path of cocaine from Colombia and Peru to the United States since the mid-1980s; the U.S. pressure on Mexican authorities to enforce prohibition has increased accordingly.
4 Oddly enough, corruption in Mexico's government and in its police services is rarely considered in Mexican scholars' analyses of the bilateral relationship.
5 It has been estimated that around 40% of organized crime in Mexico resorts to corruption of judicial officers to block investigations or prosecutions. Prosecutors are the most often corrupted group, accounting for almost 90% of the sampled cases (Buscaglia and Gonzalez-Ruiz 2007). Similarly, it has been calculated that each year, each of the major Mexican cartels pays around US $40 million to bribe judges. This is a way to launder money; it also protects cartels from effective law enforcement (Buscaglia, González-Ruiz, and Prieto Palma 2006).
6 Other regrettable examples of high-level corruption in Mexico are the following. In February 1997, General Jesús Gutiérrez Rebollo, Mexican drug czar at the time, was charged with protecting drug cartels. Mario Villanueva, right after he finished his term as governor of Quintana Roo (1993–9), was arrested on drug trafficking charges. He spent several years in jail and was extradited to the United States in May 2010. Noe Ramírez, head of the Unit Against Organized Crime, was charged with taking money from

the drug cartels in November 2008. On 26 May 2009, just weeks before the mid-term elections were held, thirty-five city mayors, most of them from the leftist Democratic Revolution Party (PRD), and chiefs of local police were detained by federal authorities on charges of being on the cartels' payroll. Since then almost all of them have been released because nothing could be proved against them (*Reforma*, 17 August 2010). When the *plata* fails its purpose, *plomo* comes next. The federal official in charge of fighting organized crime, Santiago Vasconcelos, survived three murder attempts, then died when the jet he was flying in crashed near Mexico City in November 2008. The Interior Minister, Juan Camilo Mouriño, died in the same incident. The Commissioner of the Federal Police, Edgar Millán, was murdered in May 2008. In April 2010, a commando fired more than 2,500 bullets and threw several grenades at the Chief of Police in Morelia, Michoacán; miraculously, the target survived the attack. The headquarters of the Federal Police in Monterrey and Ciudad Juárez and army patrols in Apatzingán, Michoacán, and elsewhere have suffered armed attacks.

7 According to Velasco Cruz (2005a, 2005b), the actual income generated by illegal drugs represents between 1.1 to 2.6% of the 2000 GDP, and from 4.9 to 11.8% of legal exports. The income generated by drugs is roughly comparable to the foreign direct investment (FDI), total agricultural exports, and oil export revenues.

8 'The World's Billionaires,' http://www.forbes.com/lists/2010/10/billionaires-2010_The-Worlds-Billionaires_Rank_39.html.

9 'The World's Most Powerful People,' http://www.forbes.com/2009/11/11/worlds-most-powerful-leadership-power-09-people_land.html.

10 Mexico may be a young democracy, but in contrast to much of the recent rhetoric in the American press and elsewhere, it is far from being a failed state. Its political stability has been remarkable in the Latin American context, where coups d'état and barrack rebellions have been frequent.

11 After the Gulf Cartel split, a new group appeared called 'Mexico Unido contra los Zetas' in Torreon and Gomez Palacio, Durango. This group would be responsible for four massacres in bars and nightclubs. Its death toll between January and July 2010 was 44 people killed and 40 wounded.

12 There are significant discrepancies among the figures given by various official sources. The Office of the Attorney General reported 24,826 people killed in the same period. *Reforma* counted 6,587 people killed in 2009 and 7,000 from January to August 2010. Despite the differences in the exact number of casualties of the war on drugs, all sources show an alarming increase. These numbers do not include people who have disappeared or

been kidnapped or corpses that have not been found because they were
buried in mass graves or somehow hidden.

13 These data show that the murder rate in Mexico is closer to that registered
in the United States and well below the rates in Colombia, El Salvador, and
Guatemala.

14 An analysis of homicides in 2008–9 shows a dramatic hike, especially in
those states and municipalities where the armed forces (the Army and the
Navy) disbanded local police forces that protected and collaborated with
criminal organizations. See Escalante Gonzalbo (2011).

15 The nickname comes from *pozole*, a popular hearty soup made of corn and
meat that resembles the floating teeth and phalanges of his victims.

16 CNDH, Recomendación 45/2010. *Reforma*, 13 August 2010.

17 Artículo 19, Asociación Mexicana del Derecho a la Información (AMEDI),
Centro Nacional de Comunicación Social (CENCOS), Amnistía Internacional, Periodistas sin fronteras.

18 Public opinion regarding legalization of drugs in Mexico is divided.
The conservative ruling party, PAN, is against, while several voices are
in favour. The White House has stated that the legalization of drugs in
Mexico is a domestic matter, but has also expressed concern about the consequences for drug demand in the United States. *Reforma*, 5 August 2010, 5.

19 These include Alto al secuestro, Centro de Investigación para el Desarrollo
(CIDAC), Iluminemos México, Instituto para la seguridad y la democra-
cia (Insyde), Mexicanos Primero, México Evalúa, México SOS, Instituto
Ciudadano de Estudios sobre la Inseguridad (ICESI), and México Unido
Contra la Delincuencia.

20 Remarks by U.S. Assistant Secretary of State Thomas A. Shannon, Jr, to the
Council of the Americas. New York, 3 April 2008. http://www.america.
gov/st/texttrans-english/2008/April/20080407164631eaifas0.834347.
html#ixzz102099D6f. Emphasis added.

21 Joel Kurtzman published an article in the *Wall Street Journal* citing 'a new
Pentagon study' that concluded: 'Mexico is at the risk of becoming a failed
state' just like Pakistan, 'where wholesale collapse of civil government is
possible.' As a consequence, 'it may only be a matter of time before the
drug war spills across the border and into the U.S.' Failed states do not just
collapse; they are suitable candidates for establishing protectorates that
restore order and rule of law. See Kurtzman (2009).

22 There have been references to spillover violence that could affect not only
border states but also distant cities. According to the U.S. Ambassador to
Mexico, Carlos Pascual, there has been drug-related violence in Atlanta,
Chicago, Newark, Philadelphia, and other major cities (*Reforma*, 13 August

2010). The United States is deploying more members of the National Guard to surveillance activities on the border (*Reforma* , 20 July 2010), and the U.S. Congress has approved a budget of $600 million for border surveillance (*Reforma*, 11 August 2010).

References

Aguilar Valenzuela, Rubén, and Jorge G. Castañeda. 2009. *El narco: la guerra fallida*. México: Santillana.

Andreas, Peter. 2009. *Border Games: Policing the U.S.–Mexico Divide*. Ithaca: Cornell University Press.

– 2005. 'The Mexicanization of the U.S.–Canada Border: Asymmetric Interdependence in a Changing Security Context.' *International Journal* 60, no. 2: 449–62.

Article 19 and CENCOS. 2010a. *Agresiones contra la libertad de expresión en México. Informe presentado porArticle 19 Oficina para México y Centroamérica y Centro Nacional de Comunicación Social (CENCOS)*. México: Article 19-CENCOS.

– 2010b. *Informe 2009. Entre la violencia y la indiferencia. Informe de agresiones contra la libertad de expresión en México*. Mexico: Article 19-CENCOS-Embajada Británica en México.

Astorga, Luis. 2004. 'Mexico: Drugs and Politics.' In *The Political Economy of the Drug Industry: Latin America and the International System*. Edited by Menno Vellinga. Gainsville: University Press of Florida. 85–102.

– 2003. *Drogas sin fronteras*. México: Grijalbo.

– 1996. *El siglo de las drogas*. México: Espasa Calpe.

Ayres, Jeffrey, and Laura Macdonald. 2009. *Contentious Politics in North America: National Protest and Transnational Collaboration under Continental Integration*. London: Palgrave Macmillan.

Bailey, John, and Roy Godson. 2000. *Organized Crime and Democratic Governability: Mexico and the U.S.–Mexico Borderlands*. Pittsburg: University of Pittsburg Press.

Benítez Manaut, Raúl, and Carlos Rodríguez Ulloa. 2006. 'Seguridad y fronteras en Norteamérica. Del TLACAN a la ASPAN.' *Frontera Norte* 18, no. 35: 7–28.

Booth, William. 2011. 'Mexican Cartels Now Using "Tanks."' *Washington Post*, 7 June. http://www.washingtonpost.com/world/americas/mexican-cartels-now-using-tanks/2011/06/06/AGacrALH_story.html.

Bowden, Charles. 2011. *Murder City: Ciudad Juárez and the Global Economy's New Killing Fields*. New York: Nation.

Buscaglia, Edgardo, and Samuel Gonzalez-Ruiz. 2007. 'The Factor of Trust and the Importance of Inter-Agency Cooperation in the Fight against Transnational Organized Crime: The US–Mexican Example.' In *Borders and Security Governance: Managing Borders in a Globalized World*. Edited by Marina Caparini and Otwin Marenin. Geneva: Center for the Democratic Control of Armed Forces. 269–80.

Buscaglia, Edgardo, Samuel González-Ruiz, and César Prieto Palma. 2006. 'Causas y consecuencias del vínculo entre la delincuencia organizada y la corrupción a altos niveles del Estado: mejores prácticas para su combate.' In *Terrorismo y delincuencia organizada. Un enfoque de derecho y economía*. Edited by Andrés Roemer and Edgardo Buscaglia. México: IIJ-UNAM. 87–102.

Cadena-Roa, Jorge. 2003. 'State Pacts, Elites, and Social Movements in Mexico's Transition to Democracy.' In *States, Parties, and Social Movements*. Edited by Jack A. Goldstone. Cambridge: Cambridge University Press. 107–43.

Cadena-Roa, Jorge, and Miguel Armando López Leyva. 2011. 'La consolidación de la democracia en México: avances y desafíos (2000-2006).' *Estudios Sociológicos* 86: 415–62.

Carlsen, Laura. 2008. *A Primer on Plan Mexico*. Americas Program Special Report. http://www.americaspolicy.org. Accessed 4 April 2011.

Castillo, Mariano. 2011. 'Mexican Troops Replace Police in Half a State That Borders Texas,' *CNN*, 25 June. http://articles.cnn.com/2011-06-25/world/mexico.tamaulipas.troops_1_drug-cartel-gulf-cartel-leader-mexican-troops?_s=PM:WORLD. Accessed 4 April 2011.

Chase, Steven. 2011. 'Sorry, Amigo: Wikileaks Shows Canada Prefers Meeting U.S. without Mexico,' *Globe and Mail*, 2 March. http://www.cdfai.org/PDF/Canada%20prefers%20meeting%20without%20Mexico.pdf.

de Mauleón, Héctor. 2010. 'La ruta de sangre de Beltrán Leyva.' *Nexos* 386: 20–31.

The Economist. 2011. 'North American Integration: To Each His Own, the Push for Deeper Ties Peters Out.' 24 February. http://www.economist.com/node/18229546.

Enciso, Froylán. 2009. 'Drogas, narcotráfico y política en México. protocolo de hipocresía (1969–2000).' In *Una historia contemporánea de México: Las politicas*. Edited by Ilán Bizberg and Lorenzo Meyer. México: Océano. 183–245.

Escalante Gonzalbo, Fernando. 2009. *El homicidio en México entre 1990 y 2007. Aproximación estadística*. México: El Colegio de México-Secretaría de Seguridad Pública.

– 2011. 'Homicidios 2008–2009. La muerte tiene permiso.' *Nexos* 397: 36–49.

Felbab-Brown, Vanda. 2009. 'The Violent Drug Market in Mexico: Lessons from Colombia.' Foreign Policy at Brookings, Policy Paper no. 12.

Fox, Vicente. 2010. 'Drogadicción, crimen organizado y seguridad: momento de reflexión y propuestas.' http://blogvicentefox.blogspot.com/2010/08/drogadiccion-crimen-organizado-y.html. Accessed 4 April 2011.

Friedrich, Carl J. 1989. 'Corruption Concepts in Historical Perspective.' In *Political Corruption: A Handbook*. Edited by Arnold J. Heidenheimer, Michael Johnston, and Victor T. Levine. New Brunswick: Transaction. 15–24.

Hervieu, Benoit, Balbina Flores Martínez, and Jean-François Julliard. 2009. *México. Los entresijos de la impunidad. Escalada de la seguridad pública y pesadez burocrática*. Paris: Reporteros sin fronteras.

Hobbes, Thomas. 1979. *Leviathán*. Madrid: Editora Nacional.

Ikenberry, John. 2010. 'A Crisis of Global Governance?' *Current History*, November, 730.

Johnson, David T. 2009. *Hearing at the Sucommittee on State, Foreign Operations, Related Programs of House Committee on Appropriations*. Washington, DC, 10 March (http://www.state.gov/p/inl/rls/rm/120225.htm).

Kean, Thomas H., and Lee H. Hamilton. 2004. *Commission Report: Final Report of the National Comission on Terrorist Attacks upon the United States*. Kindle Edition, released 9 February 2011.

Kurtzman, Joel. 'Mexico's Instability Is a Real Problem: Don't Discount the Possibility of a Failed State Next Door.' *Wall Street Journal*, 16 January 2009. http://online.wsj.com/article/SB123206674721488169.html.

López Leyva, Miguel A. n.d. '"Ya marchamos ... pero no solucionan el problema": Los movimientos en contra de la inseguridad (1997, 2004 y 2008) y su incidencia en las políticas públicas.' México: ISUNAM.

Love, Maryann. 2011. *Beyond Sovereignty: Issues for a Global Agenda*. 4th ed. Boston: Wadsworth.

Naím, Moisés. 2003. 'The Five Wars of Globalization.' *Foreign Policy*, January–February, 28–37.

Reporteros sin fronteras. 2010. 'Relación de periodistas asesinados y desaparecidos. México.' México.

Reuter, Peter, and David F. Ronfeldt. 1992. 'Quest for Integrity: The Mexican–U.S. Drug Issue in the 1980s.' *Journal of Interamerican Studies and World Affairs* 34, no. 3: 89–153.

Reyes Salinas, Medardo, and Homero Castro Guzmán. 2008. *Sistema de seguridad e impartición de justicia comunitaria costa-montaña de Guerrero*. México: Plaza y Valdés.

Ríos, Viridiana. 2011. 'Violencia mediática.' *Nexos* 397: 50–2.

'Rough Justice: America Locks Up Too Many People, Some for Acts That Should Not Even Be Criminal.' *The Economist*. 2010a.' 22 July. http://www.economist.com/node/16640389.

Serrano, Mónica. 2007. 'México: narcotráfico y gobernabilidad.' *Pensamiento Iberoamericano* 1 (segunda epoca): 251–78.

Smith, Peter H. 1999. 'Semiorganized International Crime: Drug Trafficking in Mexico.' In *Trasnational Crime in the Americas*. Edited by Tom Farer. New York: Routledge.

'Too Many Laws, Too Many Prisoners: Never in the Civilised World Have So Many Been Locked Up for So Little.' 2010b. *The Economist*. 22 July. http://www.economist.com/node/16636027.

Toro, María Celia. 1999. 'The Internationalization of Police: The DEA in Mexico.' *Journal of American History* 86, no. 2: 623–40.

– 1995. *Mexico's 'War' on Drugs. Causes and Consequences*. Boulder: Lynne Rienner.

Velasco Cruz, José Luis. 2005a. 'Drogas, seguridad y cambio político en Mexico.' *Nueva Sociedad* 198: 89–101.

– 2005b. *Insurgency, Authoritarianism, and Drug Trafficking in Mexico's 'Democratization.'* New York and London: Routledge.

Velázquez Flores, Rafael, and Juan Pablo Prado Lallande. 2009. *La Inicitaiva Mérida: ¿nuevo paradigma de cooperación entrre México y Estados Unidos en seguridad?* México: UNAM.

Vellinga, Menno. 2004. 'The Political Economy of the Drug Industry: Its Structure and Functioning.' In *The Political Economy of the Drug Industry: Latin America and the International System*. Edited by Menno Vellinga. Gainsville: University Press of Florida. 3–32.

Wood, Duncan. 2011. 'Perimeter Security in North America: Mexico's Latest, Greatest Rejection.' Canadian International Council. 17 February. http://mexicoinstitute.wordpress.com/2011/02/17/perimeter-security-in-north-america-mexico%e2%80%99s-latest-greatest-rejection. Accessed 4 April 2011.

PART II

North American Problems without
North American Governance

5 North American Community from Above and from Below: Working-Class Perspectives on Economic Integration and Crisis[1]

TERESA HEALY

'Community' is a rich and contested concept. It suggests inclusion, but also boundaries and exclusions. It carries with it a sense of apparently natural connections and self-evident affinities. It may be variously positive and protective, or hierarchical and restrictive. It suggests a space beyond the realm of politics where self-interest may be joined with a more collective impulse in defence of the 'common' good. In its definition, certain political and economic options are privileged and others foreclosed. In the context of economic crisis and ongoing political debates about the future of economic integration in North America, the concept of community has been marshalled by opposing social forces to build support for their respective political projects. On the one hand, the idea of 'North American community' is meant to affirm common cause among business, political, and intellectual elites. It erases borders from the political imagination, rises above national limits, insinuates statelessness, and implicates policy makers in its profoundly liberal economic intentions and conservative security goals. 'Working-class community,' on the other hand, is an idea under siege. It is a way of thinking about workers' lives from a located, embedded, and collective perspective. It is bounded and bordered, and lies well within the national frame, although many workers who come from other national frames, or those facing intersectional marginalization, may find themselves sitting uneasily within such communities. Working-class communities have faced derision, attacks on collective bargaining, political marginalization, and economic dislocation in relation to discourses rooted in the idea of North American community. Even in its most internationalist forms, working-class community is not contained within but exists *in opposition to* the idea of North American community, which is seen by labour as a dominant class project in which democratic practices are actively avoided where possible. On its own terms, transnational labour solidarity is usually project-, issue-, or sector-specific and represents another dimension of the 'shallow governance' regulation of North American social relations (Ayres and Macdonald 2006). In fact, despite the many shared experiences of workers across the borders of North America, 'working-class community' in Canada tends to have a quite local and regional character, which is both its strength and its weakness.

This chapter examines the meaning of community in Canadian contests over economic integration in North America, with a focus on the impact of integration and the recent economic crisis on Canadian workers. I will argue here that the concept of a 'North American community' is not just a disembodied, transnational, political idea. In fact, it is the ideological representation of an employer-led and state-supported attack on economic, political, and social democracy that, from the perspective of working people, has left 'communities in crisis' across the country and the continent.

To make this argument, I begin by outlining some of the reasons why labour movements in North America have been opposed to economic integration in North America. I then move to a discussion of how the concept of 'North American community' has been used by pro–free trade forces in the years since NAFTA came into force. This has been a carefully constructed strategy to create an apparent consensus by avoiding public debate. The chapter then surveys the impact of the 'deep integration' agenda on federal policies and proceeds to reflect on labour's opposition to deep integration before and after the 'Great Recession' of 2008–9. Between October 2008 and August 2009, Canada lost 486,000 full-time jobs. In the midst of this country-wide devastation, the Canadian Labour Congress initiated a research project to examine the impact of the economic crisis on different communities across the country. As project director, I worked with CLC researchers, researchers from affiliated unions, and local activists, who travelled to seven communities across the country, where we conducted in-depth interviews with community leaders and unemployed workers. The final part of the chapter explores the impact of the crisis on a working-class community in Ontario's industrial heartland.

North American Integration: Opposition from Below

From its inception in 1994, the North American Free Trade Agreement

(NAFTA) shaped trinational relationships, not so much by liberalizing trade in goods, but rather by guaranteeing unprecedented investor rights in international law. NAFTA was established to regulate the organization and internationalization of production in North America; but it ignored the question of migration, and it circumscribed the role of the state in industrial policy. Despite fierce opposition throughout the Americas that prevented the NAFTA model from becoming embodied in a Free Trade Area of the Americas (FTAA), NAFTA continues to be advanced as the preferred model for guaranteeing investors' rights in other multilateral and bilateral agreements. Most recently, under the Security and Prosperity Partnership (SPP), North American integration has taken on a securitized dimension in which border controls, policing, surveillance, and military commands have been integrated within the logic of NAFTA, albeit outside the legislative institutions of liberal democracy.

Under free trade, North American workers' wages have stagnated and workers' income share of the economy has declined. Income inequality has increased tremendously. Wealth inequalities have ballooned (Arroyo Picard 2004; Heisz 2007; Hemispheric Social Alliance 2003; Jackson 2007; Whitt 2010). New forms of work organization have relied on increasingly precarious forms of labour (Jackson 2010, 247–70; Vosko 2006). More recently, as a result of the financial crisis and the ensuing Great Recession, Canadian workers have faced massive job losses, especially in manufacturing and forest products. In August 2010, there were 1.51 million unemployed workers in Canada and the official unemployment rate was 8.1%. There were 373,000 more unemployed people in Canada than in October 2008 when the crisis hit. Almost two years later, manufacturing employment reached its lowest in thirty years and the real unemployment rate (which includes discouraged workers and involuntary part-time workers) hovered around 12% (CLC 2010b).

The idea of a North American community floating within the NAFTA and SPP frameworks actively ignores working-class experiences of unemployment and insecurity. Workers' communities have certainly been shaped by the history of power relations that are clearly 'North American,' but workers do not tend to identify their community as such. Unless workers have experienced migration or have engaged in labour education or transnational union activities, the experience of community for most working people remains one constructed in relationships and local geography, as well as through workplace relations, family histories, and the limits of time and place. Some workers are forced into mobility and migrate internally or internationally. Immigrant workers may be doubly dislocated when unemployment hits the foundations of their newly constructed community. Only with great resolve do workers from communities in crisis create solidarity with similarly affected communities across borders, usually by putting pressure on their own Canadian state. The idea of North American community, then, is set in direct opposition to working-class life. North American community is not a geographical idea. It is a way of economic being in which investor rights are granted priority over the spaces and social relations within which most people live and work.

The Canadian labour movement was opposed to North American integration under free trade well before the Canada–U.S. Free Trade Agreement (CUSFTA) came into force in 1989. A statement issued by the Executive Council of the Canadian Labour Congress (CLC) in 1985 declared that

> free trade is ... viewed as reliance on the market to determine economic reality. It is part and parcel of the same philosophy that lends support to the 'downsizing' of government, privatization, deregulation; in short, the package of 'remedies' that place priority on the enhancement of business confidence. One of the implications of free trade is that corporate decision-making in the marketplace is substituted for public decision-making in the political arena. (CLC 1985, 136)

At that time, the CLC predicted that a free trade agreement with the United States 'will mean a further shift from higher value-added labour-intensive industrial activity to capital-intensive, lower value-added primary sector activity. The job content of our economic output and trade will only worsen' (ibid., 139). The public sector unions were concerned that the downward harmonization in standards would mean increased privatization. 'Moreover,' according to the Canadian Union of Public Employees, 'cutting the public sector has been the most widely propounded solution to our economic woes. Slashing government spending, cutting social programs and reducing the influence of government in the economy are widely held as the panaceas for restoring our economy to health' (CUPE 1985).

Labour opposition to free trade continued with the inception of the NAFTA negotiations. The North American Agreement on Labour Cooperation (NAALC – the labour side accord) was opposed by the Canadian labour movement because it offered no effective means to protect labour rights. Furthermore, it was seen to detract attention from the real problems with NAFTA's investment provisions. As Robert White, the CLC's president, said at the time:

> The three governments argued that it would violate 'national sovereignty' if they were forced to live up to a set of minimum labour rights. This is deeply hypocritical since the NAFTA agreement represents a massive loss of national sovereignty when it comes to the ability of governments to regulate transnational corporations with respect to a host of issues ... Second, the agreement creates a tri-national Labour Commission and Secretariat which have no independence from government ... Further there will be no labour participation in either the Commission or the Secretariat ... Third, the sanctions provided for in the side-deal apply only if a country systematically violates its own health and safety, child labour or minimum wage laws. (White 1993)

The general consensus among the Canadian labour movement was that labour provisions in trade agreements were unlikely to lead to improvements for workers.

North American Community from Above

North America's largest employers present a substantially different view of the region than that of labour. NAFTA survived the opposition of labour and other progressive social movements in North America, but the 9/11 terrorist attacks on the United States and the resulting 'thickening' of borders called into question the apparent inevitability of North American economic integration. Wendy Dobson of the C.D. Howe Institute suggested that since the Bush administration was entirely focused on homeland security after 2001, Canadians would need to capture the imagination of U.S. decision makers if they hoped to promote deeper integration with the United States: 'Only a Big Idea will succeed, one that addresses U.S. objectives while creating new economic opportunities for Canada' (2002).

In response, there emerged within the pro–free trade business community in Canada a debate over whether it would be more effective to pursue the strategy of the Big Idea through public bilateral negotiations initiated by Canada or to take a more measured and low-key incremental approach to deeper integration 'under the political radar' (Alexandroff and Guy 2003, 2). In developing their North American Security and Prosperity Initiative (NASPI), the Canadian Council of Chief Executives (CCCE) decided to back the incremental and largely bilateral approach. They pressed the Canadian government to do the following: reinvent borders; harmonize regulations; work towards a North American resource security pact; expand the Canadian military and conclude a North American defence alliance; and develop a new institutional framework for managing North America (Canadian Council of Chief Executives 2003; 2004, 2).

In this volume, Janine Brodie analyses in more detail how the 2005 Security and Prosperity Partnership (SPP) was established along the lines of the corporate proposal. This project was reinforced by the work of an Independent Task Force on the Future of North America, which brought together prominent advocates of deep integration in North America. The Task Force explicitly said that it was not advocating for North America to adopt EU-style institutions. Instead, 'a new North American community should rely more on the market and less on bureaucracy, more on pragmatic solutions to shared problems than on grand schemes of confederation or union, such as those in Europe' (Council on Foreign Relations 2005, 6). Governance, it was thought, could be coordinated through an annual North American Leaders' Summit envisioned by a private sector Advisory Council and carried out by trilateral working groups within ministries.

A year later, government leaders asked top CEOs from across North America to form the North American Competitiveness Council (NACC) to provide 'independent' advice to government in concert with their cycle of leaders' meetings. Documents acquired by the Canadian Labour Congress under the Access to Information Act show that by late 2006, the largest CEOs and their allies continued to avoid public discussion of their vision of the future of North America. CCCE president Thomas d'Aquino was reported to have said at a meeting of corporate, government, and military leaders organized by the North America Forum and held in Banff, Alberta, that ongoing integration would happen only by a strategy of 'aggressive incrementalism.' Indeed, it would be only through 'evolution by stealth on the Big Idea' that a fully integrated North America could be fashioned (Access to Information, Government of Canada, Department of Foreign Affairs and International Trade 2006; World Affairs Council 2007). The Banff meeting was one of an interconnected series of national and trinational meetings by government, military, and business leaders that elaborated the NACC priorities.

U.S. President Barack Obama came to power in the United States in the middle of the worst economic crisis since the Great Depression of the 1930s. At the time, it was unclear how much of a challenge the new administration would pose to the neoliberal agenda in the continent and beyond, or what sort of encouragement Obama's populism would provide for social movements in other countries, including Canada. At a major conference sponsored by the Centre for Trade Policy and Law at Carleton University, presenters urged the Harper government to develop good relations with the Obama administration early on. They expected activist government responses and 'unilateral' Canadian actions to get the attention of decision makers in the United States. It was suggested that Canada reject the nineteenth-century view of the Canada–U.S. border as a division between two countries. They preferred, instead, to see it as 'an area of joint responsibility for managing the security of 'Upper North America' (Carleton University Canada-US Project 2009, v; Healy 2008b).

In this version of North American community, a shared security perimeter and increased integration of Canada's and Mexico's police, intelligence, security, and military forces with those of the United States would diminish national sovereignty but permit the free flow of investments, goods, and service providers. A common trade and investment policy vis-à-vis third countries would mean that the three countries of North America relinquished nationally defined policy making. Common immigration and refugee policies would involve full labour mobility for the most deserving and temporary residence for the least. It would establish two classes of citizenship in North America, along with a third category – the many others who would be excluded altogether. By not mentioning 'social provision' at all, this vision of North American community accepts the inequalities that are created by markets; moreover, it does not permit a role for the state in creating embedded economy. The concept of sovereignty is left unmentioned. The concept of democracy is virtually absent. The idea of North American community is an ideological sleight of hand. It is a means of escaping the national institutions of liberal democracy, and it reveals an effort to create a new common sense that might facilitate a unified economic space in continental North America.

Open for Business: Security and Prosperity in the Harper Government

It was the CEOs' definition of community, and not that of trade unions or other social movements, that the Canadian government embraced.

In the words of one senior Canadian government official, the SPP was taken up in 2005 under the Liberal government of Paul Martin as an effort by the federal executives of the three North American governments to 'see how much we can cooperate on without changing a single law' (Healy 2007b, 2; Government of Canada, Department of Public Safety and Emergency Preparedness Official 2007). By design, the ten 'Security' and nine 'Prosperity' working groups staffed by public servants received direction from the executive branch of government, while bypassing the legislatures of the three NAFTA countries. As an official in the U.S. Embassy recounted to a delegation of civil society groups, the SPP had been set up to deepen the integration process, but it also been structured 'to avoid another bruising NAFTA battle' (Healy 2008a, 13; U.S. Embassy Official 2007).

On being elected in 2006, the minority Conservative government of Stephen Harper took the Security and Prosperity themes into the heart of its political platform, embracing the attendant 'stealth' procedural agenda as well. It then moved forward on harmonizing trade policy, taxation, borders, security and information sharing, and energy integration and regulations, including at the level of interprovincial relations. It also effectively opened up the government procurement chapter of NAFTA. It worked closely with employers' groups to foster a sense of trustworthiness and common purpose among their political counterparts in the United States, especially in the areas of trade, taxation, security, regulation, and energy. As Icaza also points out in this volume, the SPP has had a lasting effect on the Canadian government's policy framework.

For instance, Canada and the United States have very closely aligned trade and investment relations with third parties (Government of the United States 2010; Government of Canada, Department of Foreign Affairs and Intenrational Trade 2010). As well, with the November 2007 Economic and Fiscal Statement, the government adopted a dramatic tax-cutting agenda. It even went beyond the harmonization of corporate income taxes with the United States, announcing a reduction of the general corporate income tax rate from 21% in 2007 to 15% in 2012, which would give Canada a 12.3% advantage over the United States (Government of Canada, Department of Finance 2007a, 75). Together with earlier tax reductions in the budgets of 2006 and 2007, the government cut $58.8 billion from its revenues during 2008–9 and 2009–10 alone, while announcing it would give up $188 billion in tax cuts between 2007–8 and 2012–13 (Government of Canada, Department of

Finance 2007b, 73). A few months later, the government released its 2008 budget, which might have been called the 'SPP Budget' due to its emphasis on border and security issues (Government of Canada, Department of Finance 2008a, 173).

Despite Harper's efforts to unilaterally deepen the integration process, differences emerged between the Conservative government in Ottawa and the Democrats in Washington. These differences became apparent primarily in the scope of their responses to the Great Recession. Canada provided $40 billion, or 2.5% of gross domestic product (GDP), in stimulus spending over two years. With the addition of resources from other levels of government, the stimulus funding was capped at $50 billion, or 3.2% of GDP (Government of Canada, Department of Finance 2009, 68). The Obama administration, in contrast, through the American Recovery and Reinvestment Act, invested $787 billion or 5.7% of GDP. When Washington urged Ottawa to increase its stimulus spending, Ottawa pushed back in a public campaign against the 'Buy American' provisions of the U.S. stimulus bill.

Harper pressed on with domestic reforms that were in line with SPP priorities. The January 2009 Canadian Federal Budget confirmed previous support for the SPP agenda; it also allocated a further $1 billion over five years to the development of carbon capture and storage technologies. This was in clear support of oil producers and Canada's new identity as an 'energy superpower' (Government of Canada, Department of Finance 2009, 179). At the same time, the federal government worked with the provinces to reduce barriers to internal trade by concluding a series of agreements toward full labour mobility and dispute resolution, including a NAFTA-like process by which corporations might sue subnational governments for perceived infringements on their rights (Council of the Federation 2009). As Ayres and Macdonald point out in this volume, the SPP process was formally dropped because the newly elected Democratic administration in the United States was facing pressure to make good on its stated preferences for transparency and inclusiveness. When the North American leaders met once again in August 2009 in Guadalajara, no reference was made to the SPP in the declaration that came out of that meeting. Even without the SPP Leaders' Framework, however, the 2010 Canadian Federal Budget returned to its underlying themes of energy exports, regulatory harmonization, and security integration (Government of Canada, Department of Finance, 2010a, 102). The SPP agenda had been under the radar to begin with; now it had gone completely underground even while the Canadian government continued to work on its central themes.

After being elected in 2006, the Conservative government was careful about which segments of American society it was willing to include in its version of North American community. Harper was long-suffering in his approach to the United States when the security agenda was seen as the reason for border 'thickening.' When it came to issues of social protection, however, the Canadian government quickly made a series of aggressive 'anti-protectionist' statements. Harper began a campaign to counter U.S. 'Buy American' procurement policies in the American Reinvestment and Recovery Act. The government sought an exemption for Canadian suppliers from the provisions that excluded foreign suppliers from bidding on some of the projects funded by U.S. stimulus money. Early in 2010, Canada did get an agreement, but critical analysts expect it will gain Canadian suppliers very little access, while it will cost Canadian communities a great deal (Sinclair 2010). Canadian provinces and municipalities will now be impeded in their efforts to require local content and local benefits of the sort that would enhance job creation and economic development.

By speaking out relentlessly against the Buy American provisions in the U.S. stimulus bill, the Canadian government was in alignment with the demands that the U.S. Chamber of Commerce was making to the U.S. administration (Carnevale 2009). The U.S. Chamber of Commerce did not want to be subject to local content rules either. The government procurement debate, then, must be seen as an exercise in the further creation of a wider economic space for free markets and investor rights against demands for government procurement policies that could ensure 'local benefit.' In Canada, the Conservatives worked to undermine domestic support for 'Buy Canadian' and to forestall the labour movement's campaign, which had been aiming to secure commitments by municipal and provincial/territorial governments to include jobs, environmental sustainability, and local benefit as important priorities in making purchasing decisions. During the depths of the economic crisis, this local and community-based campaign by labour in favour of green jobs and sustainable development was easily eclipsed by the government's campaign against 'American protectionism.'

The strategy of pushing ahead on deeper integration through 'aggressive incrementalism' even continued across borders at the subnational level. For example, during their annual conferences, the New England governors and Eastern Canadian premiers continued to affirm their commitment to the three central issues in the deep integration agenda: energy, security, and 'independence'; cross-border emergency management cooperation; and information sharing (Conference of New England Governors and Eastern Canadian Premiers 2010). Deep integration continued to be carried on as 'common sense' by subnational governments now that the agenda had been set at national levels. This too, was part of community building, North American style.

Canadian Communities in Crisis[2]

With the Canadian government promoting the priorities of the corporate sector before and during the crisis, notions of working-class community continued to be subordinated to those of continentalism. Even so, labour and civil society continued their opposition. In 2002 the rising strength of the Canadian dollar began to affect export volumes and manufacturing employment. From a low of 62.4 cents in January 2002, the Canadian dollar began a steady rise to above parity with the U.S. dollar in October 2007. At the time, the CLC linked the loss of 250,000 jobs with the dollar's rise. In March 2009, in the midst of the financial crisis, the loonie dropped to a low of 0.79 against the U.S. dollar, then increased steadily thereafter. The Canadian dollar approached parity again early in 2010, and averaged 0.98 throughout 2010 and the first 10 months of 2011 (Bank of Canada 2011). Exports were adversely affected during the Great Recession. For example, auto exports fell by 40% and forestry products by 27% in this period – this, after a slump of four years in which both fell by nearly 40% (Cross 2009). Months after the official end of the recession, the crisis in manufacturing continued as factory employment hit a thirty-five-year low in October 2011 (Grant and Keenan, 2011).

The labour movement saw in this a confirmation of its long-held concern about the impact of economic integration on the Canadian economy. Canada's 'petro-dollar' reconstructed regional divisions, which were now based on the energy economy in the 'west' and the manufacturing economy in the 'centre' of the country. The labour movement responded by continuing to campaign on the jobs crisis. Year after year, in lobbying campaigns, pre-Budget submissions, and briefs to Parliamentary Standing Committees, or through the Alternative Federal Budget process, labour and civil society proposals were rejected. Whether they concerned border and security issues, trade policy, regulation, public services, energy and sustainability, migrant labour, procurement, social policy, pay equity, labour rights, women's equality, international development, or any of the issues facing key industrial sectors, their proposals for Canada's domestic or continental relations gained little favour in the Liberal caucus and none whatso-ever within the Harper Conservative government. As the commodities boom turned to bust and the profundity of the global crisis became apparent in 2008, the labour movement pressed the government for a response to these developments and criticized its inadequate stimulus efforts (Canadian Labour Congress 2009).

These concerns were shared by labour movements in Mexico and the United States. The presidents of the AFL-CIO and the Canadian Labour Congress wrote a joint letter to Prime Minister Harper and President Obama on the occasion of Obama's first visit to Ottawa in February 2009. The letter called for NAFTA to be renegotiated in the areas of labour rights, investment, energy, services, and agriculture. It urged Canada and the United States to work together on climate change, green jobs, industrial policy, migration, and development (Georgetti and Sweeney 2009). This letter was followed up by a similar trinational labour statement on the occasion of the 2009 Leaders' Summit. Labour leaders from the National Union of Workers in Mexico, along with the AFL-CIO and the CLC, affirmed their shared concern with the impacts of NAFTA:

> While trade and investment flows did increase, NAFTA did not create more net trade-related jobs, and those that it did were very often less sta-ble, with lower wages and fewer benefits. Instead, increased trade large-ly benefited the corporate elite in all three countries. Income inequality has also grown in the region. We believe that the trade liberalization and investors' rights provisions contained in NAFTA were an important con-tributor to these results. (Hernández Juárez, Sweeney, and Georgetti 2009)

It is important to note that labour's concerns go well beyond concerns about the proper functioning of labour side agreements in NAFTA. Free trade, investment, and related security agreements are concluded not to guarantee the rights of labour, but to solidify the rights of investment and contracts. When labour rights are addressed, they exist within international agreements in a structurally subordinated relationship to the rights of investors. For example, after more than fifteen years in force, not one claim of labour rights violations has proceeded to an arbitration panel set out in the labour side accord.

From the perspective of labour and progressive civil society groups in Canada, in both process and content, the SPP was an even more egregious and direct attack on democracy. A coalition of national non-governmental organizations monitored the efforts of the corporate lobby and continued to promote their own vision of what economic relations on the continent and in the broader hemisphere could become. The CLC established a national SPP Research Network. In March 2007 the Council of Canadians, together with the Canadian Centre for Policy Alternatives and the CLC, organized a 'teach-in' in Ottawa in an effort to break through the media blackout and shed light on the significance of issues being deliberated through the SPP (Council of Canadians 2007).

Oppositional movements to the SPP in Canada promoted a critical discussion of deep integration, one that was informed by years of transnational engagements among trade unions and social movements throughout the Americas. Labour movements throughout the Americas had worked to develop a shared vocabulary capable of recounting the 'free trade' agenda's corrosive effects on domestic social policy and on labour market conditions, as well as the exclusionary politics of international trade and investment negotiations. By the time the Trade Union Confederation of the Americas released its document, 'Labour's Platform for the Americas,' in 2005, labour movements of the Americas had gone a long way towards constructing their vision of what 'a new consensus for development based on justice, employment, inclusion and democracy' might look like (Trade Union Confederation of the Americas 2009). Labour and social partners continued to work across borders through Common Frontiers (in Canada), the Alliance for Responsible Trade (in the United States), and *Red Mexicana de Acción Frente al Libre Comercio*. These relationships solidified when the NAFTA negotiations began in the early 1990s and continued to do so over the following decade, during the period of contestation that resulted in a failure of the FTAA. A transnational coalition called the Hemispheric Social Alliance (HSA) formed in response to the FTAA proposal. The HSA presented an alternative to the free trade agenda, one that called for a strengthening of civil society and for the development of a critical perspective on economic integration based on principles of social justice (Hemispheric Social Alliance n.d.).

When Stephen Harper welcomed Felipe Calderón and George Bush along with their Ministers of 'Security' and 'Prosperity' to the 2007 Leaders' Summit in Montebello, Quebec, the voices of these national organizations and the social movements they represented were present, though security was heavy and they had been excluded from the summit process itself. Just before the summit, the NACC released its report on how effectively the governments had implemented the NACC's fifty-one recommendations (North American Competitiveness Council 2007b). None of the three governments issued a report on the working groups' activities. When protesters came to demonstrate and deliver 10,000 petitions from across Canada to the leaders inside, they were kept at a distance from the Château Montebello, where the meetings were being held. In an inventive use of security cameras, however, the protesters were invited to speak their mind directly in front of a camera from within the protest zone so that their messages would be passed on to the leaders, and presumably to the security forces as well. A scandal erupted over the presence of *agents provocateurs* from the Sûreté du Québec, who attended the event with rocks in their hands and allowed themselves to be 'arrested' by their own forces after being confronted by authentic protesters. The police-issue boots they were wearing gave them away. Eventually, the police were compelled to admit what they had done (CanadiansNanaimo 2007). Meanwhile, Harper ridiculed the opponents, whom he described as people who worry about whether 'the sovereignty of Canada will fall apart if we standardize the jellybean' (MacCharles 2007).

'These Boots Were Made for Working': North America from Below[3]

In direct contrast to the vision of North American community espoused by the country's largest employers, our research with workers has revealed a strong sense of community that is rooted, local, and bounded by relations of family, generation, geography, and time. Trade union activists have an acute sense of how vulnerable working-class communities are to the dynamics of the North American capitalist economy. One devastated industry has certainly been the automobile sector, and Oshawa, Ontario, has been one of the hardest-hit communities. General Motors has been a defining presence in Oshawa for decades, and the community continues to bear the brunt of the loss of good jobs in the auto sector. More than 20,000 workers were employed at the GM plant in Oshawa in the late 1980s. By 2007, only 12,000 were employed there. Their union, Canadian Auto Workers (CAW), has estimated that between 2002, when the Canadian dollar began its rise, and mid-2008, 4,000 auto assembly jobs were lost. For each of these, another 7.5 jobs were lost in the auto parts and services sectors (Trevisan 2008).

In communities where the auto industry was strong, much depended on the strength of trade unions and their ability to shape provincial and federal policy. During the free trade debates, trade unions advocated alternatives. In its 1985 position paper on Canada–U.S. free trade, the CLC stated: 'A strategy of planned trade (alternatively referred to as fair trade or managed trade) combined with an overall economic policy designed to maximise the processing of our raw materials and to stimulate domestic consumption of Canadian goods and services offers the best chance for achieving the twin goals of balanced domestic growth and trading relationships' (CLC 1985, 141). Since NAFTA came into effect in 1994, successive federal Liberal and Conservative governments have openly rejected managed trade. Their inaction led to the WTO striking down the 1965 Automotive Products Trade Agreement (the so-called Auto Pact), which had allowed the 'Big Three' producers to avoid Canadian tariffs if they maintained a certain ratio of production to sales in Canada.

The economic crisis struck with full force in the autumn of 2008 and deepened from there. The region's official unemployment rate rose from 6.3% in September 2008 to 7.9% in July 2009, which is when we conducted our research. A CAW organizer, Joel Smith, witnessed the disaster in its making:

> We went from eight shifts of production to three shifts of production just at General Motors in the span of a year and a half. So, if you can picture an output of just under one million vehicles produced in a year to a level of about 300,000 vehicles, that's a massive decrease in the capacity of the auto assembly plants. So that obviously means less workers. We've seen thousands of workers basically lose their jobs, or those jobs disappear within General Motors. (Smith 2009)

During the summer of 2009 there were just over 3,500 workers, including 2,700 in production and 850 in the skilled trades, left at GM Oshawa.

The crisis took some painful twists and turns. Just two weeks after concluding its collective agreement with the CAW in May 2008, GM announced that the Oshawa truck plant would close. Yet only two weeks before, the company had agreed in writing to locate the next generation of trucks in Oshawa. Instead, the company suddenly announced it would be moving truck production to Mexico and the United States (Canadian Auto Workers Local 222 2008a). Betrayed autoworkers knew that the decision meant the end of 2,600 good industrial jobs, as well as a huge dent in Oshawa's industrial base. The closure of the truck plant was expected to affect 11,000 to 12,000 direct and indirect jobs (Van Alphen 2009). CAW members blockaded the corporate headquarters for twelve days. They could not stop the closure, but they were able to negotiate buyouts and early retirement packages. Nevertheless, all those good jobs were lost to Oshawa.

Sandra Kicinko used to work at Johnson Controls. She was laid off after four years working on the line assembling doors for the Impala. When she was laid off from Johnson Controls in 2008, she and her co-workers were devastated. Many worked at the factory with their spouses, and immediately, entire families were thrown into crisis. 'I saw a woman the other day working in Dollarama, and she looked the other way,' says Kicinko. 'She didn't want me to see her. And I just think that's really sad.' Kicinko remembers nine hundred people working at Johnson Controls. Now there are less than two hundred. Everywhere there are signs of the crisis:

> So, it's devastating in the community. You walk around here and see empty houses that have been taken back by the banks. You see, in my neighbourhood alone, I walk around and I see ... the papers they put up on the windows when a house has been repossessed, 'This property is now being maintained by ... Do Not Trespass.' You see it everywhere. (Kicinko 2009)

By early October 2008, the global economic situation had worsened dramatically. Workers continued to pressure the Canadian government to support Canadian manufacturing. CAW members dumped hundreds of work boots in front of Conservative MP and Finance Minister Jim Flaherty's Whitby office. Laid-off workers from across Ontario tied messages to the boots, such as 'These Boots Were Made for Working' and 'Honestly, "Made in Canada" Matters.' Other signs read 'Lower Gas Prices,' 'Stop Unfair Trade,' and 'Lower Our Rising Dollar.' A CAW poster put it well:

> Dear Mr. Flaherty. Here are my well-used boots. I thought they may be of better use to you, since you have made sure I will never have a need for them again. P.S. Sorry I couldn't remove the blood, sweat and tears from them. (CAW Local 222 2008b).

Late in 2008, GM announced that the third shift at the car plant would be cut. This news came as a blow to seven hundred workers. The company also announced it would be idling the Oshawa car plant in the first week of February and that seven hundred workers would be laid off (Metroland Staff 2008). By the end of 2008 the situation was grim. In January 2009, unemployment in the Greater Oshawa Area hit 8% (Mancini 2009b).

We spoke with Kevin, who had assembled cars at GM for six years, starting right out of high school. Kevin and his girlfriend had been together a year and a half and were moving in together in September so that he could begin retraining. Because she needed a job that would allow her to be with her young son, she worked part-time at the casino. Kevin spoke about having more children:

> We talk about it, and we don't want him to be too much older before, you know, we think about having another one, but it's just, in our financial state, it's not possible. It's not possible to get married for two years, and it's not possible to have children for more than that. So, yeah, it's definitely, this whole situation has been a huge impact on my life.

Kevin and his girlfriend were trying to decide whether they would move in together with Kevin's parents, even though 'it's hard to suck up your pride.' He said that it was common among his friends right now: 'I honestly know about a dozen people right now that have been laid off in all different areas that have gone back home. Back to their parents' house at twenty-six, twenty-eight, thirty.' Connie Snelgrove, a laid-off worker from Lear Corporation and coordinator of the CAW Action Centre, suggested that one of the barriers facing parents who were trying to find work was the lack of child care. 'So parents are looking at how he can work during the week, and maybe a lower paying job, and her on the weekend. Or him during the day, and her at night, so that they're swapping their kids.' The stress on families is enormous (Snelgrove 2009).

By March 2009, GM was facing catastrophe. Despite the continental nature of the crisis (see the chapter by Clarkson in this volume), there were no trilateral governmental discussions to confront it. The CAW and GM concluded an emergency agreement that extended $300 million per year in savings to the company in exchange for a commitment that GM would maintain its share of production in Canada. As the Obama government forced the UAW and GM back to the table in the United States, the Canadian government rejected the CAW–GM agreement and forced CAW to renegotiate its deal with GM Canada to make the Canadian company's labour costs equivalent to those of nonunion Toyota Canada (CAW-GM Master Bargaining Committee 2009). In doing so, the Harper government was challenging the fundamental legitimacy of unions without addressing the real reasons for the company's economic problems. As the CAW had pointed out on numerous occasions, 'direct labour accounts for seven percent of total auto costs: less than capital, less than materials, less than dealer margins. Cutting that to six percent won't sell a single car or truck' (CAW 2009a).

During collective bargaining in the auto industry, wage increases are linked to productivity increases. Canadian autoworkers produce about $300,000 in value-added per worker per year (CAW 2009a). As a result, autoworker wages are $30 to $35 an hour. 'Our labour accounts for seven percent of the cost of producing vehicles. Yet, we got ninety-nine percent of the blame for the automakers' woes,' said a CAW bulletin explaining the restructuring agreement between the CAW and GM to CAW members (CAW 2009b). Laid-off autoworker John Mac-Donald described how in each collective agreement they would negotiate productivity increases in return for better wages and benefits or to maintain them. 'We're now producing three times as many cars, with a quarter of the people that we once did. And it's not really technology changes, it's more they just increased workload on every individual.' John gave an example:

> When I began there in 2004, we had approximately two minutes and thirty-four seconds to do a full install of all the plastic, what we call the garnish, which is all the trim that you put inside a vehicle ... And I left that job and returned back to it nine months later, and we were down to a minute and thirty-two seconds. (MacDonald 2009)

John emphasized that the company had taken time away from workers with no changes in technology and with the same number of people. All that management had done was 'reduce the output by four cars per hour, and that justified taking one minute off of your time.'

In March the union had agreed to a $7-wage-and-benefit cut per hour; yet in May the company came back to ask for more. Thus, the CAW engaged in three rounds of talks with GM in one year. CAW members accepted an agreement to freeze wages and benefits until 2012, and pensions until 2015. The government had permitted the company to underfund its pension in previous years; now, GM was required to fund its pension fully. The union succeeded in preventing wage cuts and any reduction in pensions, but it was compelled to make other painful sacrifices: it lost reimbursements for tuition as well as for time off the job, and it temporarily accepted lower wages for new hires. New hires, however, were not expected anytime soon (Canadian Auto Workers–General Motors Master Bargaining Committee 2009b, 3). As part of its agreement with the CAW and the federal and provincial governments, in order to receive a $6 billion loan, GM promised to maintain 20% of North American production in Canada.

Conclusion

On 1 October 2009, labour and civil society activists met on Parliament Hill to raise a glass of sparkling Canadian apple juice to mark the official demise of the SPP and to celebrate the screening of the Paul Manly's new film *You, Me, and the SPP: Trading Democracy for Corporate Rule* (Manly 2009). It was Manly who earlier had captured the 'matching boots' on tape – a video seen by more than half a million people on YouTube (Manly 2007). Although civil society activists – along with the filmmaker and then-NDP trade critic Peter Julian, who had issued the invitation – knew that the issues behind the SPP process had not gone away, activists felt it was important to take note of the SPP initiative's failure to capture the hearts of Canadians, not to mention that of the new Democratic president in Washington. The public failure of the SPP and of the broader idea of 'North American community' lay in its complete lack of democratic practice. But the economic interests in deeper integration outlived the SPP, and early in 2011, Obama and Harper announced that they would begin immediately to create new mechanisms for a binational definition of North American security. The Beyond the Border Declaration called for a binational working group of civil servants, who would negotiate a new set of bilateral arrangements in areas of law enforcement and surveillance, critical infrastructure protection, and the movement of travellers, goods, and cargo. From the point of view of labour unions in Canada, the North American Security Perimeter, in its efforts to 'push' the U.S. border deep into Canadian society, will pose serious threats to civil rights, privacy, and the human rights of those not deemed worthy of full citizenship rights within North America (Canadian Labour Congress 2011). At the same meeting in Washington, the two leaders announced that progress had been made on their shared energy agenda, and announced as well the creation of a Regulatory Cooperation Council, which would be staffed by senior civil servants of both countries. In effect, the three main issues that defined the SPP were back on the public agenda, this time clearly redefined in binational terms and separated by issue area. Subsequently, members of the Regulatory Cooperation Council and the Beyond the Border working group made contact with oppositional civil society groups to ask for their views as they moved forward with their mandates.

While some in the business community have expressed disappointment that despite all their efforts, the Canada–U.S. border remains 'thick' with security measures, the 'integration by stealth' approach has had a dramatic impact on the North American relationship and within Canada itself. As Golob rightly points out in this volume, the SPP process has always been primarily dual-binational rather than trinational process, reflecting the hierarchies of the interstate system as well as those of the world economy. Any honest effort to achieve what workers could conceive of as a true North American community would have to confront a much broader developmental agenda (Healy 2007a, 15). Given the depth of social problems facing the people of North America, the tragedy of deep integration is that it does nothing to redress the dramatic rise in inequality that each of the three countries had faced since NAFTA came into force in 1994. Canadian capitalists have been unable to accommodate even their own tepid calls for a developmental agenda in trinational North America, and have, as Brodie notes in this volume, now 'erase(d) Mexico from the prosperity map.'

If a transnational community is naturalized by its protagonists, it is with clear intent. Such a concept of community is designed to transcend political boundaries, which are, in the liberal imagination, artificial and steeped in self-interest, captured by the forces of reaction, or outdated instruments of nation building. Borders are a source of irritation for those who would invest, seek larger markets, or produce goods or services on each side of them. National boundaries and indeed national identities, and political movements disrupt the logic of globalization. Markets, however, need to be protected, and a North American community insulates large corporations and their social classes in three ways. First, it casts as small-minded those who have little control of market forces and who would call upon their national governments to respond to the fact that there is no work to be had by strengthening protective legislation and regulations at the domestic level, or by countering the impact of international law and economic forces with active economic policies. Second, by fostering the idea of a North American community in the minds of the ones who govern, corporate CEOs allow that United States' security risks should be externalized and shared by willing neighbouring governments in the interests of freeing up trade and investment flows within the region. Third, the idea of a North American community is also a defensive statement to the rest of the world, one that signals an alliance to defend and promote 'our' way of life within the world order.

Dominant social forces continue in their efforts to frame an understanding of the North American community that is the antithesis of working-class desires and imagination. The economic crisis has visited upon workers not just the effects of an anti-social and anti-democratic economic model, but also the prospects of more of the same going forward. Neither the profundity of the economic crisis nor the shakiness of the 'recovery' has prevented a resurgence of free trade fundamentalism. For labour, the political question is whether and how workers' relational and rooted sense of community can be transformed into a political force that can challenge the neoliberal logic of continental integration as it meets its own contradictions.

Notes

1 I would like to thank the research team from Oshawa, Ontario, who interviewed workers for the Communities in Crisis Research Project of the Canadian Labour Congress, including Tim Eye, Kathie Fowlie, John Macdonald, and Tammy Schoep. I would like to thank the Political Economy Research Institute, University of Massachusetts, Amherst, for welcoming me as a visiting scholar during the writing of this chapter. Finally, I would like to dedicate this paper to the memory of Kathie Fowlie, a courageous CAW activist and advocate for women.

2 This section is adapted from the Canadian Labour Congress's Communities in Crisis research project papers, which can be found at http://www.canadianlabour.ca.

3 Interviewees for the Communities in Crisis Research Project gave their informed consent to have their interviews recorded and used in publications or Web-based materials. They also had the choice of having their real name used or a pseudonym.

References

Alexandroff, Alan S., and Don Guy. 2003. *What Canadians Have to Say about Relations with the United States.* C.D. Howe Institute Backgrounder, Border Papers no. 73. July.

Arroyo Picard, Alberto. 2004. 'El México de Fox y el TLCAN: La dura realidad del pueblo mexicano contrasta con el optimismo de su Presidente.' Red Mexicana de Acción frente al Libre Comercio. http://www.rmalc.org.mx/documentos/fox_tlcan.htm. Accessed 14 September 2011.

Ayres, Jeff, and Laura Macdonald. 2006. 'Deep Integration and Shallow Governance: The Limits to Civil Society Engagement Across North America.' *Policy and Society* 25, no. 3: 23–42.

Bank of Canada. 2010. 'Monthly Average Rates: Ten Year Look-up: August 2000-August 2010.' http://www.bankofcanada.ca/en/rates/exchange-avg.html. Accessed 14 September 2011.

– 2011. 'Monthly and annual average exchange rates.' http://www.bankofcanada.ca/rates/exchange/exchange-rates-in-pdf. Accessed 5 November 2011.

Canadian Council of Chief Executives. 2004. 'New Frontiers: Building a 21st Century Canada–U.S. Partnership in North America.' April. http://www.ceocouncil.ca/en/view/?document_id=365. Accessed 14 September 2011.

– 2003. 'Security and Prosperity: Toward a New Canada–United States Partnership in North America – Profile of a New North American Security and Prosperity Initiative.' January. http://www.ceocouncil.ca/publications/pdf/716af13644402901250657d4c418a12e/presentations_2003_01_01.pdf. Accessed 14 September 2011.

Canadian Auto Workers. 2009a. 'The Economics, and Politics, of Auto Workers' Wages.' *CAW Local 222 News & Events.* 20 April. http://www.cawlocal.ca/222. Accessed 14 September 2011.

– 2009b. 'CAW Canada/General Motors Bargaining Report.' May 2009. http://www.cawlocal.ca/222/newsdetails.asp?NewsID={302E2601-7538-40DA-934C-B8F54C59C5FC}#. Accessed 14 September 2011.

Canadian Auto Workers Local 222. 2008a. 'GM – Bargaining in Bad Faith.' *CAW Local 222 News & Events.* 4 June. http://www.cawlocal.ca/222. Accessed 14 September 2011.

– 2008b. Digital slide-show: 'Giving Jim Flaherty the Boot.' 6 October. http://www.flickr.com/photos/cawlocal222/sets/72157607803683999/show/with/2919113509. Accessed 14 September 2011.

Canadian Auto Workers–General Motors Master Bargaining Committee. 2009. 'We Are Fighting for Our Lives: An Open Letter to GM workers.' 12 May. http://www.caw.ca/assets/pdf/Fighting_for_our_Lives_May_12_09.pdf. Accessed 14 September 2011.

Canadian Labour Congress. 2011. 'CLC Backgrounder on the Canada–United States Declaration: Beyond the Border: A Shared Vision for Perimeter Security and Economic Competitiveness.' March.

– 2010b. 'Government Must Do More for Unemployed: CLC President

Responds to Statistics Canada Job Numbers.' 10 September. http://www.
canadianlabour.ca/national/news/government-must-do-more-unem-
ployed-clc-president-responds-statistics-canada-job-number. Accessed 14
September 2011.

– 1985. 'Surrendering National Sovereignty.' In *Free Trade Papers*. Edited by
Duncan Cameron. Toronto: James Lorimer, 1986. 136.

– 2009. 'Economic Crisis Campaign.' http://www.canadianlabour.ca.
Accessed 14 September 2011.

CanadiansNanaimo. 2007. 'Police Provocateurs Stopped by Union Leader
at Anti-SPP Protest.' 22 August. http://www.youtube.com/watch?v=St1-
WTc1kow. Accessed 14 September 2011.

Canadian Union of Public Employees. 1985. 'Scapegoating the Public Sector.'
In *The Other Macdonald Report*. Edited by Daniel Drache and Duncan Cameron. Toronto: James Lorimer. 43.

Carnevale, Mary Lu. 2009. 'U.S. Chamber of Commerce Hits Back on "Buy
American."' *Wall Street Journal Washington Wire*. 30 January. http://blogs.
wsj.com/washwire/2009/01/30/us-chamber-of-commerce-hits-back-on-
buy-american. Accessed 14 September 2011.

Carleton University Canada–U.S. Project. 2009. 'From Correct to Inspired: A
Blueprint for Canada-US Relations.' 19 January. http://www.ctpl.ca/sites/
default/files/FINAL-BLUEPRINT-ENGLISH.pdf. Accessed 14 September
2011.

Conference of New England Governors and Eastern Canadian Premiers. 2010.
'Resolutions 34-1 – 34-5. July 11–12, 2010.' 34th Conference of New England
Governors and Eastern Canadian Premiers, Lenox, MA. http://www.scics.
gc.ca/new_e.html. Accessed 13 July 2010.

Council of Canadians. 2007. 'Integrate This: Report.' http://www.canadians.
org/integratethis/report/teach-in.html. Accessed 14 September 2011.

Council of the Federation. 2009. 'Agreement on Internal Trade: Tenth Protocol of Amendment.' 7 October. http://www.ait-aci.ca/index_en/ait.htm.
Accessed 14 September 2011.

Council on Foreign Relations, Canadian Council of Chief Executives, and *Con-
sejo Mexicano de Asuntos Internacionales*. 2005. 'Building a North American
Community: Report of an Independent Task Force.' Task Force Report No.
53. May. Washington: Council on Foreign Relations Press

Cross, Philip. 2009. 'Canada's International Trade during the Recession.' *Canadian
Economic Observer*. Statistics Canada, 15 October. http://www.statcan.gc.ca/
pub/11-010-x/2009010/part-partie3-eng.htm. Accessed 14 September 2011.

Dobson, Wendy. 2002. *Shaping the Future of North American Economic Space:
A Framework for Action*. C.D. Howe Institute Border Papers, no. 162. April.
Toronto: C.D. Howe Institute.

Georgetti, Kenneth, and John Sweeney. 2009. 'Letter to Prime Minister Harper and President Obama regarding a New Prosperity Agenda for North America.' 18 February. Ottawa and Washington: Canadian Labour Congress and American Federation of Labor–Congress of Industrial Organizations.

Government of Canada, Department of Finance. 2010a. 'Budget 2010: Leading the Way on Jobs and Growth.' 4 March. http://www.budget.gc.ca/2010/pdf/budget-planbudgetaire-eng.pdf. Accessed 14 September 2011.

– 2010b. 'Press Release: Canada Poised to Become Tariff-Free Zone for Manufacturers Thanks to Budget 2010.' 9 March. http://www.fin.gc.ca/n10/10-019-eng.asp. Accessed 14 September 2011.

– 2009. 'Budget 2009: Canada's Economic Action Plan.' 27 January. http://www.budget.gc.ca/2009/home-accueil-eng.html. Accessed 14 September 2011.

– 2008a. 'Table 4.2: Leadership Abroad.' In 'Budget 2008: Responsible Leadership for Uncertain Times.' 26 February. http://www.budget.gc.ca/2008/home-accueil-eng.html. Accessed 5 November 2011.

– 2008b. 'Table 4.1: Leadership at Home.' In 'Budget 2008: Responsible Leadership for Uncertain Times.' 26 February. http://www.budget.gc.ca/2008/home-accueil-eng.html. Accessed 5 November 2011.

– 2007a. 'Economic Statement: Strong Leadership. A Better Canada.' 30 October. http://www.fin.gc.ca/ec2007/pdf/EconomicStatement2007_E.pdf . Accessed 10 August 2010.

– 2007b. 'Table 3.1: Tax Relief Provided by Budgets 2006 and 2007, the Tax Fairness Plan, and This Economic Statement.' In 'Economic Statement: Strong Leadership. A Better Canada.' http://www.fin.gc.ca/ec2007/ec/ecc3-eng.asp. Accessed 14 September 2011.

Government of Canada, Department of Foreign Affairs and International Trade. 2010. 'Negotiations and Agreements.' http://www.international.gc.ca/trade-agreements-accords-commerciaux/agr-acc/eu-ue/can-eu.aspx?view=d. Accessed 8 August 2010.

Government of the United States. 2010. 'Free Trade Agreements.' Export.Gov Helping U.S. Companies Export. http://www.export.gov/FTA/index.asp. Accessed 8 August 2010.

Grant, Tavia, and Greg Keenan. 2011. 'Steep decline in manufacturing mars employment outlook.' *Globe and Mail Update*. 4 November. http://www.theglobeandmail.com/report-on-business/economy/jobs/canada-sees-biggest-monthly-job-loss-since-2009/article2225234. Accessed 5 November 2011.

Healy, Teresa. 2008a. *The Harper Record*. Ottawa: Canadian Centre for Policy Alternatives. http://www.policyalternatives.ca/sites/default/files/uploads/publications/National_Office_Pubs/2008/HarperRecord/The_Harper_Record.pdf. Accessed 5 November 2011.

– 2008b. 'How Not to Let a Good Crisis Go to Waste.' Conference Report from
    Blueprint for Canada–U.S. Engagement under a New Administration. 8
    December 2008. Canadian Labour Congress.
– 2007a. 'Deep Integration in North America: Security and Prosperity for
    Whom?' Canadian Labour Congress Research Paper no. 42. February.
2007b. 'North American Competitiveness Council and the SPP: Les agents
    provocateurs at the Montebello Leaders' Summit.' Canadian Labour Con-
    gress. Research Paper no. 44. September.
Heisz, Andrew. 2007. 'Income Inequality and Redistribution in Can-
    ada: 1976–2004. Analytical Studies Branch Research Paper Series
    no. 298. Statistics Canada. 11 May. http://www.statcan.gc.ca/
    pub/11f0019m/11f0019m2007298-eng.pdf. Accessed 14 September 2011.
Hemispheric Social Alliance. 2003. 'Lessons from NAFTA: The High Cost of
    Free Trade.' June. http://www.asc-hsa.org. Accessed 14 September 2011.
Hernández Juárez, Francisco, John J. Sweeney, and Kenneth V. Georgetti. 2009.
    'Tri-National Union Declaration on the Occasion of the NAFTA Leaders
    Summit.' Guadalajara, 9–10 August.
Hemispheric Social Alliance. n.d. 'Building a Social Alliance in the Americas.'
    http://www.commonfrontiers.ca/Campaigns/Hemispheric.html. Accessed
    14 September 2011.
Jackson, Andrew. 2010. Work and Labour in Canada: Critical Issues. 2nd ed.
    Toronto: Canadian Scholars Press.
– 2007. 'From Leaps of Faith to Hard Landings: Fifteen Years of "Free Trade."'
    In Whose Canada? Continental Integration, Fortress North America and the Cor-
    porate Agenda. Edited by Ricardo Grinspun and Yasmine Shamsie. Montreal,
    Kingston, Ottawa: McGill–Queen's University Press and Canadian Centre
    for Policy Alternatives. 211–33.
Kicinko, Sandra. 2009. Interview with author. Oshawa. 6 July.
MacCharles, Tonda. 2007. 'Is the Jelly-Bean Up to Standard?' Toronto Star. 22
    August. http://www.thestar.com/article/24865. Accessed 6 November 2011.
– 2009b. 'Unemployment Up in Oshawa Area.' Metroland (Durham). 6 Febru-
    ary, 1.
MacDonald, John. 2009. Interview with author. Oshawa. 7 July.
Manly, Paul. 2007. 'Police Provocateurs stopped by union leader at anti SPP
    protest.' http://www.youtube.com/watch?v=St1-WTc1kow. Accessed 7
    November 2011.
Manly, Paul. 2009. You, Me, and the SPP: Trading Democracy for Corporate Rule.
    Nanaimo. http://www.youmespp.com. Accessed 14 September 2011.
Metroland Staff. 'More Layoffs for Oshawa's GM Car Plant.' 2008. Metroland
    (Durham). 5 December, 1.
North American Competitiveness Council. 2007a. 'Enhancing Competitive-

ness in Canada, Mexico, and the United States: Private Sector Priorities for the Security and Prosperity Partnership (SPP): Initial Recommendations of the North American Competitiveness Council (NACC).' February. Ottawa http://www.uschamber.com/reports/enhancing-competitiveness-canada-mexico-and-united-states-private. Accessed 5 November, 2011.

– 2007b. 'Building a Secure and Competitive North America: Private Sector Priorities for the Security and Prosperity Partnership of North America: 2007 Report to Leaders from the North American Competitiveness Council (NACC).' August. http://www.psp-spp.gc.ca. Accessed 14 September 2011.

Sinclair, Scott. 2010. 'Buy American Basics.' Ottawa: Canadian Centre for Policy Alternatives. 9 February. http://www.policyalternatives.ca/publications/reports/buy-american-basics. Accessed 14 September 2011.

Smith, Joel. 2009. Interview with author. Oshawa. 7 July.

Snelgrove, Connie. 2009. Interview with author. Oshawa. 8 July.

Trade Union Confederation of the Americas. 2009. 'Labour's Platform for the Americas.' http://www.csa-csi.org/index.php?option=com_content&view=section&id=42&Itemid=332&lang=en. Accessed 14 September 2011.

Trevisan, Matthew. 2008. '"A Day of Mourning" at Oshawa GM plant; Workers react with shock, anger as closing of pickup assembly line puts 2,600 out of work.' *Globe and Mail.* 4 June, B7. http://v1.theglobeandmail.com/servlet/story/RTGAM.20080603.wrgmoshawa04/front/Front/Front. Accessed 3 July 2009.

Van Alphen, Tony. 2009. 'Oshawa Reels as Truck Plant Closes.' *Toronto Star,* 15 May, B4.

Vosko, Leah, ed. 2006. *Precarious Employment: Understanding Labour Market Insecurity in Canada.* Montreal and Kingston: McGill–Queen's University Press.

White, Robert. 1993. 'NAFTA Side Deal Changes Nothing for Workers.' Canadian Labour Congress. 25 August.

Whitt, Preston. 2010. 'Negotiating a New NAFTA: What and Why This Is Needed.' 13 September. http://www.coha.org/negotiating-a-new-nafta-what-and-why-this-is-needed/#idc-container. Accessed 14 September 2011.

World Affairs Council. 2007. 'North American Forum.' http://www.itsyourworld.org/wac/North_American_Forum.asp. Accessed 14 September 2011.

6 Environment and Energy: Prospects for New Forms of Continental Governance

DEBORA L. VANNIJNATTEN AND NEIL CRAIK

This book explores the proposition that the future of North America as a meaningful political entity is open to question, given the recent economic turbulence and some rather unexpected political realignments. Has North American integration reached a plateau, is continued integration more likely, or is disintegration inevitable? Certainly, the regulation and governance of environmental and energy issues across North American borders will be affected by potentially fragmenting political and economic forces, as discussed in the introduction to this volume. Yet we argue in this chapter that the factor most likely to impact the amount and nature of North American environmental cooperation in this area is the need to address global climate change on a regional scale. Here we have seen a somewhat different dynamic playing out, one that may be *more* rather than less integrative.

Like other contributions to this volume, this chapter considers the state of play in North America both before and since the recent economic and political turbulence. The first section identifies three broad trends in the trajectory of North American environmental and energy governance, prior to 2008. First, we note that North American states have tended to reject supranational institutions in favour of transgovernmental networks; that is, cooperative arrangements have tended to be informally constituted networks or working groups of government officials. Second, subnational governments have become significant cross-border actors in the environment and energy fields. The shift towards more bottom-up, subregional cooperative structures has not excluded federal actors; rather, the emerging governance structure is multilevel and overlapping. Third, there has been a move towards what we call 'bundled' governance structures, which deliberately link various environmental issue areas or cross-cutting issues such as trade and the environment, and energy and the environment, within a single cooperative framework. The most prominent and most expansive example of bundling was the Security and Prosperity Partnership of North America (SPP), but we would also include the North American Commission on Environmental Cooperation, as well as border-oriented frameworks, such as the U.S.–Mexico Border 2012 Program, as forms of bundling.

In considering the dual trajectories of environmental and energy cooperation, we treat each as a distinct issue area; but as the discussion on bundling discloses, there is a trend – strongly associated with climate change – to treat the environment and energy agendas interdependently. Indeed, we can see the seeds of energy–environment bundling under the climate change mantle as emerging at the 2008 North American Leaders' Summit, where Presidents Bush and Calderón and Prime Minister Harper announced their intention to cooperate on a regional basis to address climate change (Government of Canada 2008), and again in 2009, when the leaders reaffirmed the importance of regional climate change cooperation in a dedicated 'Declaration on Climate Change and Clean Energy' (Government of Canada 2009).

The description and analysis in this first section sets the stage for some more general reflections on the strengths and weaknesses of North American environmental and energy governance arrangements. Of particular interest here is the very 'thin' version of legitimacy that the framers of North American environmental policy have adopted, as discussed in detail in the chapter by Ayres and Macdonald. These claims of legitimacy have been rooted principally in the technical expertise of governmental officials (and a concomitant framing of the policy choices as 'technical') as well as in a formal version of procedural legitimacy that relies on executive delegation and domestic notice-and-comment procedures. We consider the sufficiency of this substantively limited approach to legitimacy for addressing environmental and energy issues effectively, and the potential for renewed governance arrangements to secure continental cooperation in issue areas requiring cross-sectoral and multilevel policy integration.

The third section turns to a discussion of the likely architecture of future regional environmental arrangements. Here our emphasis is on the ability of the three North American states to fashion a regional response to global climate change. Our principal conclusion is that climate change can be expected to increase the *density* (more interactions across more levels) of North American cooperation. Furthermore, bundled transgovernmentalism, as an approach to cooperation, is likely to garner greater purchase in relation to climate change given the technical and cross-cutting nature of climate cooperation. Climate change governance is situated in the broader political and economic context, which currently involves significant spending constraints and deepening competitiveness concerns, but also includes an American administration that is much more engaged than the previous one in the international climate change process. As we consider the impact of these more encompassing political and economic influences, climate change offers some important insights into the role of North American governance as a scale of implementation for global environmental concerns.

Trends in North American Environmental and Energy Governance

Prior to the current economic and political turbulence, we can identify three broad trends in the trajectory of North American environmental and energy governance: a reliance on transgovernmental networks as the dominant mode of transboundary environmental cooperation; the shift towards a more bottom-up, subregional cooperative framework; and a move towards 'bundling,' or linking different environmental issue areas or cross-cutting issues within a single cooperative framework. Each of these is described in detail below.

Transgovernmentalism

Across North America, environmental transboundary interactions occur primarily through ad hoc diplomacy by political officials anchored by a more permanent framework of transgovernmental ties (Craik and DiMento 2009; VanNijnatten 2010). Transgovernmentalism itself has been variously defined. In Keohane and Nye's original and quite narrow formulation, transgovernmentalism resulted from direct interactions among subunits of different governments that employed cross-border activity primarily to achieve domestic policy objectives (Keohane and Nye 1974). Three decades later, Ann Marie Slaughter (2004) used the term to refer to governmental networks aimed at a broader range of purposes, including influencing international policy processes. Baker (2007, 8) notes that transgovernmentalism 'has become a rather complex multifaceted activity that can take several forms, while acting as a mechanism through which state bureaucracies can construct alliances and coalitions with their counterparts in similar bureaucracies.' The key features of transgovernmental networks are that they are composed of regulators rather than foreign office personnel, and that the network itself has limited or no independent authority to impose rules on members (Craik and DiMento 2008, 487). Networks may nevertheless generate commitments, often implemented through non-binding memoranda of understanding. Networks also influence policy choices by sharing technical information and regulatory best practices. The exercise of soft power within the network is translated into hard power because the network participants have the ability to exercise authority within their domestic regulatory spheres (ibid., 486).

Transgovernmental networks in the environmental policy realm in North America exhibit certain characteristics. First, they can be both treaty-based and more informal. Much of the casework on transgovernmentalism focuses on international financial and economic regulation and views the networks constituted in these realms as having been established through more informal means. However, as Craik and DiMento (ibid., 486–7) note, some environmental transgovernmental networks in North America may in fact be established by treaty, with the treaty structure acting to more clearly define the goals of transgovernmental cooperation.

In Canada–U.S. bilateral relations, for example, we have seen a steady succession of focused, formal agreements or treaties under which commissions, boards, or committees of officials meet regularly, monitor implementation, and deal with issues as they arise. From the 1909 Boundary Waters Treaty, the 1919 Migratory Birds Treaty, and the 1932 Glacier-Waterton Lakes National Park Agreement, through to the 1985 Pacific Salmon Treaty and the 1991 Canada–United States Air Quality Agreement, national governments on the northern border have designed cooperative mechanisms to address specific forms of cross-border pollution or the preservation of shared natural resources through administrative cooperation. In many cases the original architecture provided for under the treaty has spawned a broad and differentiated system of cooperative mechanisms; the multitude of boards and task forces (currently numbering twenty-one) associated with the work of the International Joint Commission – itself created under the Boundary Waters Treaty – may be the most extreme example of this.

On the U.S.–Mexico border, an International Boundary and Water Commission was created under the terms of the 1944 Water Utilization Treaty. Its primary mandate has been to oversee matters relating to 'boundary demarcation, national ownership of waters, sanitation, water quality, and flood control in the border region' (IBWC 2010). After the Agreement on Cooperation for the Protection and Improvement of the Environment in the Border Area (known as the 'La Paz' Agreement) was signed by the two governments in 1983, a series of Annexes were concluded between the two governments to facilitate interagency cooperation on specific matters such as the discharge of hazardous wastes and transboundary air pollution caused by copper smelters.

Transgovernmentalism flourishes in less formal forums, of course. For example, in 1992 the United States created the Good Neighbor Environmental Board, composed of delegates from eight federal agencies as well as representatives of state, local, and tribal governments. The board functions as a federal advisory committee concerned with border environmental problems, and its members meet regularly with their Mexican counterparts to discuss border environmental problems. Furthermore, a dizzying array of interagency agreements have been concluded to facilitate information sharing, consultation, and joint action along both borders. The 1999 Agreement for Cooperation in the Boreal Ecosystem Atmosphere between the U.S. National Aeronautics and Space Administration and Natural Resources Canada, and the MOU between the U.S. Department of Agriculture and Mexico's Ministry of Environment and Natural Resources regarding the impact of agricultural practices on the environment, are only two of certainly hundreds of examples.

There are even continent-wide bodies, such as the Canada/U.S./ Mexico Trilateral Committee (for Wildlife and Ecosystem Conservation and Management), which is coordinating interagency efforts by the three countries to implement more than 150 capacity-building projects focused on ecosystem management and preservation of endangered species in Mexico. The Trilateral Committee holds annual meetings where more than one hundred representatives from approximately thirty organizations from the three countries address a broad array of biodiversity priority issues under six 'working tables': Executive, Law Enforcement, Convention on International Trade in Endangered Species of Wild Fauna and Flora (CITES), Migratory Birds, Ecosystem Conservation, and Species of Common Conservation Concern. The Executive Working Table provides overall guidance and oversight.

Transgovernmental cooperation is aimed primarily at joint data gathering and information sharing, technical cooperation (e.g., modelling transboundary air pollution flows), capacity building (particularly in Mexico), and regulatory cooperation (e.g., mutual recognition programs). It appears to work quite well in particular issue areas and with regard to specific pollutants, where a group of officials within complementary agencies may work together on the same file, often for many years. In the air quality realm, for example, officials representing the two governments on the Air Quality Committee and its subcommittees, established under the 1991 Canada–U.S. Air Quality Agreement, have worked to reduce successive air pollutants in border areas – first sulphur dioxide (SO2), then nitrogen oxides, and now particulate matter. The Air Quality Committee also uses an extensive system of transboundary notification for new sources of potential transboundary air pollution. Officials from both the United States and Mexico involved in the Good Neighbour Board have coordinated and submitted twelve annual reports to the President. They also sent former President Bush a letter suggesting ways in which the environmental impacts of the new border fence might be minimized.

The cooperative framework around energy is similarly dominated by transgovernmental networks, but unlike in the environmental field, energy cooperation has been a fairly recent phenomenon. Much of the cooperative activity in relation to energy has been carried out through trade channels: first through the Canada–U.S. Free Trade Agreement and then in Chapter 6 of NAFTA. The trade commitments under NAFTA are aimed principally at ensuring that energy products – chiefly petroleum, natural gas, and electricity – may flow across borders unhindered by trade barriers in the form of export or import taxes and quota restrictions. Mexican trade in energy, while subject to NAFTA, has a number of important exclusions, including a greater ability to restrict trade, as well as exemption from proportionality requirements. Also, Mexico's constitutional requirements place restrictions on foreign ownership of oil and gas assets and related industries.

While trade rules define the contours of the continental energy market, there are significant areas of cooperation attended to through transgovernmental structures. In 2001, Mexico, the United States, and Canada agreed to the formation of the North American Energy Working Group (NAEWG), made up of federal officials from each country. The NAEWG has produced reports on North American energy trends (see, for example, NAEWG's *North American Energy Picture II*); it also convenes a number of expert groups related to specific energy sectors and issues. Much of the cooperative activity is concerned with interconnections between gas pipeline and electricity transmission systems across borders, which are subject to oversight by federal regulatory agencies in each country and coordinated through regular meetings of agency officials. These informal cooperative relationships have been formalized through interagency MOUs. More recently, the NAEWG has also taken on the task of exploring possibilities for enhanced cooperation among the three countries with respect to energy efficiency programs, with the aims of reducing the costs of compliance with standards and mandatory labelling programs in the region, accelerating the replacement of less efficient products, and facilitating the transformation of the regional market for energy efficient products.

The transnational aspects of the electricity sector are also overseen by the North American Electric Reliability Corporation (NERC), a self-regulatory industry body that coordinates reliability standards with the U.S. Federal Energy Regulatory Commission (FERC), as well as with federal and provincial regulators in Canada. The cooperative outputs around energy are similarly focused on information sharing and regulatory coordination. The FERC-(Canadian) National Energy Board MOU, for example, coordinates cross-border interconnection approvals through joint reviews. It also provides a forum for interagency coordination. The NERC has a more explicitly regulatory role in that it seeks to develop reliability standards and to have those standards approved and adopted by the various electricity regulators (see, for example, the NERC-Ontario Energy Board MOU).

Multilevel Governance

Environmental transgovernmentalism in North America is also multilevel, and we can see similar developments in terms of cooperation at the subnational level (see the chapter by Vengroff and Allan in this volume for a broader discussion of cooperation between subnational authorities). Canadian provinces, American states, and Mexican states do not have the constitutional power to conclude treaties, but they do have the political and policy leverage to engage in various collaborative arrangements. Over the past two decades, subnational environmental interactions on both borders have become more numerous, more formalized, more functionally intense, and increasingly multiparty, or cross-border regional (Sanchez-Rodriguez et al. 1998; VanNijnatten 2006, 2009).

Subnational cooperation is quite similar in nature to that at the bilateral level in that it is dominated by executive actors and involves communication and cooperation among officials in related departments of all participating governments. Interactions are typically initiated at annual conferences of subnational regional political leaders. Conference resolutions then provide direction to committees of senior-level officials invested with management responsibilities, after which mid-level officials are assigned project-specific tasks. Cross-border organizations such as the New England Governors / Eastern Canadian Premiers (NEG/ECP), the Conference of Great Lakes Governors and Premiers, and the Great Lakes Commission, as well as the Pacific Northwest Economic Region (PNWER), are particularly active on the northern border. On the southern border, the Border Governors Association and bilateral organizations such as the Arizona–Mexico Commission interact in a similar fashion. The Western Governors Association even encourages participation by both Canadian premiers and Mexican state governors in some of its collaborative projects. Each of these organizations possesses committee systems, which are staffed by relevant agency personnel; these allow participating jurisdictions to run multiple projects simultaneously (VanNijnatten 2009).

Interagency agreements also abound at this lower level. Some have been concluded in order to facilitate the implementation of projects initiated by cross-border organizations; for example, the Interagency Agreement Among the State of Washington Department of Ecology, the Northwest Air Pollution Authority, the Province of British Columbia, and the Greater Vancouver Regional District is intended to make possible the coordination of air pollution monitoring and reduction under the British Columbia–Washington Environmental Cooperation Council. Ontario has signed MOUs on air pollution with New York, Michigan, and Minnesota, dating back to 1974 and covering matters such as monitoring and surveillance, emission source inventories, and exchanges of information on air quality standards. Other agreements exist for agency-specific purposes, such as the Memorandum of Understanding between the State of California and the State of Baja California on Energy Conservation and Renewable Resources.

It should be noted, however, that the increasing importance of subnational governments in the regulation of North American environmental and energy issues has not come at the expense of federal actors. Instead, both levels of government are often occupying common policy and regulatory ground. In some cases, coexistence is institutionalized and the flexibility of transgovernmental arrangements allows for governance arrangements to reflect the complex division of powers between federal and subnational governments across borders. The Canada–U.S. Air Quality Committee, for example, provides for involvement by both federal and provincial regulatory officials. The NERC, which through a series of MOUs coordinates electricity reliability standards with both federal and provincial electricity regulators as well as with private systems operators, provides for involvement of these entities in governance activities. In other cases, the overlapping transborder activities of federal and subnational governments are a source of tension and uncertainty. The rise of subregional climate change regimes, such as the Regional Greenhouse Gas Initiative and the Western Climate Initiative – both of which have transnational reach – has resulted in some concerns over the compatibility of subregional regulatory activities, particularly cap-and-trade programs, with emerging federal policy initiatives. The possibility of the federal government pre-empting some of these activities has been expressly raised in U.S. federal climate legislation, namely the American Climate and Energy Security Act, passed by the House of Representatives in June 2009.[1]

Bundling

Finally, we would note that until quite recently, transgovernmental environmental interactions in North America have not tended to be 'bundled' in any significant way; that is, there has been a preference for addressing issues on a case-by-case basis, generally without institutionalized linkages even where these might be suggested by the nature of the issues being addressed. In the air quality realm, for example, agency officials representing the two governments on the Air Quality Committee have successfully worked to reduce air pollutants in border areas – but one pollutant at a time and each after years of negotiation. Cross-cutting linkages necessary for adopting a more cohesive approach to environmental programming have for the most part been absent. For example, although the IJC has made important progress in cleaning up toxic 'hotspots' in the waters of the Great Lakes, it is only peripherally involved in the projects being implemented by the Canada–U.S. Air Quality Committee, despite their similar geographic focus and even though air deposition is a leading source of pollution in the Great Lakes.

Certainly, there have traditionally been few linkages across the environmental and trade realms – which is, of course, one of the reasons why NAFTA attracted so much criticism in the early 1990s. Neither has there tended to be much in the way of linkages between environment and energy, despite the clear implications each has for the other. The Canada–U.S. Air Quality Committee was reluctant to deal directly with NOx pollution from coal-fired power plants, despite its mandate to address ground-level ozone. Furthermore, the NEG/ECP has developed a number of action plans for reducing air pollutants, although until very recently, its Environment Committee and the Northeast International Committee on Energy (also under the auspices of the NEG/ECP) have operated separately.

One might argue that the IJC is an exception in terms of its ability to make cross-sectoral linkages, given that its role in addressing Great Lakes pollution appears to have become broader under successive iterations of the Great Lakes Water Quality Agreement, from the first version, which directed binational attention to the problem of phosphorous overenrichment; to the 1978 amendments, which highlighted the need for toxic substance regulations; through to the 1987 Protocol, which focused on ecosystem health through the more collaborative Remedial Action Plans and Lakewide Management Plans. At the same time, however, the IJC has encountered significant difficulties with the Canadian and U.S. national governments and their environmental agencies, who have stymied any attempts by the institution (or its advocates) over the years to adopt a more independent and comprehensive view of the border environment. Perhaps for this reason, the IJC has tended to rely more on transgovernmental networking to build support across agencies at different governance levels as well as with the expert community. It might also be noted that the IJC has not devoted significant resources to studying the environmental impacts of energy choices in terms of Great Lakes pollution.

Since the mid-1990s, however, there have been some attempts to create more cohesive frameworks – that is, to bundle initiatives across issue areas, across levels of governance, and even across the environment and energy sectors. At the trilateral level, the North American Agreement for Environmental Cooperation came into force at the same time as NAFTA and established the Commission for Environmental Cooperation (CEC) to help decision makers in the three countries adopt a regional view of environmental concerns. While in some respects the CEC looks like a supranational institution, its structure is actually a more formalized version of transgovernmentalism. The CEC's governing body – the Council – comprises the agency heads of the three environment ministries. The CEC also has an active Secretariat and permanent staff, which allows for the development of a more formalized work agenda, and it is advised by the Joint Public Advisory Committee. But, as is typical of transgovernmental networked arrangements, the CEC has very little ability to impose binding decisions on the parties; instead, its work is implemented by each member through domestic measures. Even the annual program and budget of the CEC remains subject to political oversight from the Council (North American Agreement on Environmental Cooperation, 1993, Art.11.6).

Given these constraints, it is perhaps not surprising that the work plan of the CEC has taken on a fairly narrow and technocratic posture, with projects relating to three priorities agreed upon by political leaders: information for decision making; capacity building; and trade and the environment (CEC 2005, 9). Yet the CEC does attempt to take a cross-sectoral approach to its projects and has, for example, devoted considerable resources to studying the linkages among various forms of electricity generation and transboundary air pollution (see, for example, CEC 2004). But the organization is hampered in this respect, since its governance structure, through the CEC Council, involves only the environment ministers of the three countries; natural resources and energy and trade agencies, for example, are not integrated into the decision making or program structure of the organization. As a consequence, the CEC has not been actively involved in resolving controversial issues related to matters such as the impact of Chapter 11 (investment) proceedings on environmental regulations, the impact of the *maquiladora* industry on border areas, or – until very recently – the challenge that climate change poses for the North American environment.

At the subnational level, there have been a growing number of efforts to bundle transgovernmental cooperative activities, particularly in response to the climate change policy challenge. In fact, it is subnational governments that have taken a leadership role in climate policy, and there are clusters of cross-border regional initiatives – including the NEG/ECP's Climate Change Action Plan, the Regional Greenhouse Gas Initiative in the northeast, the Western Climate Initiative (originally under the auspices of the Western Governors Association), and the Arizona–Sonora Climate Change Initiative – that are adopting cross-sectoral and transnational approaches to carbon reductions. Deliberations are highly technocratic in nature – for example, the creation of emission inventories, the linking of carbon markets, the designing of offsets – although WCI committees and working groups have made efforts to include stakeholders in their discussions, likely due to the considerable distributional implications involved.

Perhaps the most ambitious attempt to date to create a framework for environmental and energy initiatives was unveiled in 2005 under the 'quality of life' agenda of the North American Security and Prosperity Partnership. As discussed elsewhere in this volume, the twin SPP agendas – one for security, the other for prosperity – were developed in response to concerns that the North American integration project had stalled at a time when the region was facing increasing competitive pressures from Europe and Asia. Economic and trade concerns became amplified after the 9/11 terrorist attacks in the United States, which resulted in new border security measures being imposed as well as considerable economic interruptions to the highly integrated North American economy. The immediate U.S. response to the security concerns was the negotiation of separate border security arrangements with Canada and Mexico (see the chapter by Gilbert in this volume). The longer-term response, however, was to establish a process that identified specific issues to be addressed, requiring either bilateral or trilateral cooperation, and to give a mandate to government officials to negotiate the necessary arrangements.

The SPP took the dominant modality of North American cooperation – transgovernmental networks – and deliberately turned it into a more comprehensive governance strategy. The SPP had no foundational treaty, created no permanent institutions, and involved no delegation of authority beyond the state. Instead, the process relied on working groups made up of agency officials to negotiate the various initiatives identified in the security and prosperity agendas. Because negotiators were operating within the confines of existing legislative mandates, the instruments employed were often informal frameworks or ministerial-level MOUs. The subject matter of negotiations tended to be technical in nature – for example, the harmonization of technical standards, mutual recognition of domestic regulatory processes, and cooperation in science and technology. As an approach to regional governance, the SPP was simply an extension of an already preferred approach to cooperation.

As a process for cooperation on environmental and energy issues, the SPP agenda was neither far-reaching nor comprehensive. The agenda items were specific in nature and appeared on their face to be an idiosyncratic mixture of initiatives. This latter characteristic was most likely the result of the agenda items in these areas being made up of pre-existing initiatives, such as transboundary EIA and bird habitat preservation, both of which were previously being addressed under the CEC. There is no noticeable attempt within either the environmental or energy areas to identify and address pressing issues, such as transboundary air and water pollution or climate change (VanNijnatten 2007). None of the prevailing environmental disputes between the parties, such as the Devil's Lake water diversion, or the sustainable use of shared aquifers between the United States and Mexico, were identified as issues suitable for resolution through this process. Instead, the focus was very much on managerial issues with low political salience.

The principal innovation introduced by the SPP was instead to take these disparate matters and bundle them together within a unified process that was subject to high-level executive oversight. By identifying quite specifically the objectives of the process and including within the agendas expected time frames for the successful completion of each item, the SPP focused bureaucratic attention and allowed for the prioritization of resources. The annual North American Leaders' Summit brought increased scrutiny to the progress of various initiatives, as well as a degree of high-level accountability for the outcomes of the process. That said, the quiet demise of the SPP demonstrated the substantial shortcomings of transgovernmentalism.

The process was deservedly criticized for its lack of process legitimacy. The preferential access given to business elites through the North American Competitiveness Council was a powerful symbol for non-governmental groups and confirmed the club-like character of transgovernmental networks, which tend to be able to determine for themselves network membership (see Ayres and Macdonald in this volume; see also Craik and DiMento 2008, 486). The higher profile of the SPP process actually brought greater attention to working group outcomes. However, the negotiation process itself was a black box, with little information being made available regarding membership in working groups or the working group meetings themselves. The framers of the process maintained that the legitimacy concerns were overstated because no formal decisions or actions were taken by the networks themselves and because any change in domestic policies would be subject to domestic administrative procedures. Yet this portrait of networks as benign talking shops misses the mark. Governance through networks is rarely formal and binding, but it retains its governmental nature nonetheless, since network discussions are intended to influence domestic policy choices (Craik and DiMento 2008, 487–9). Lack of access to these channels of policy creation represents a real loss of influence that cannot be compensated for by *ex post* domestic administrative procedures.

While most of the focus of criticism has been on the lack of procedural legitimacy, the absence of any substantive vision, environmental or otherwise, was equally damaging. The SPP framers' failure to articulate any broader purpose beyond improved cross-border efficiencies and enhanced continental security was in fact a deliberate attempt on their part to avoid discussions of more comprehensive and institutionalized forms of continental integration; indeed, their failure actually exacerbated fears that the SPP would threaten national sovereignty, because the process had no clearly defined boundaries. The absence of any normative vision allowed the SPP's critics to project onto the process their concerns that the SPP was 'deep integration' by stealth, regardless of government protestations to the contrary.

It is difficult to assess the success of the SPP's environmental and energy measures in isolation, for the SPP was conceived of as an ongoing process of cooperation, not an ends-oriented negotiation. Among the outcomes of the process were a general agreement on regulatory cooperation and an agreement on energy-related science and technology cooperation (2007 Joint Statement), the harmonization of energy efficiency standards and labelling for appliances (2006 Report to the Leaders), and an agreement on bird conservation (2005 Report to the Leaders). These ought to be considered modest achievements. They reflect the rather anemic ambitions of the environmental and energy agenda items themselves, which were not linked to the core objectives of the SPP in any meaningful way.

Nonetheless, the SPP contains some useful lessons for future regional cooperation. The process-oriented approach coupled with centralized executive oversight creates forums for cooperation among regulators that maintain a good deal of flexibility but that still provide for executive 'steering.' The agenda-setting function allows for the identification of priority issues and provides participating officials with a mandate to negotiate. It also signals to network members those issues which the executive does not want addressed in transgovernmental settings. Climate change, given the Bush (and subsequently, the Harper) administration's equivocal position on the issue, is a clear example of an issue that has lacked sufficient domestic consensus to be addressed at a bureaucratic level. The informal structure of networks enables subnational participation on multilevel governance issues, which characterize the environment and energy fields. The most important lesson relates to the inability of the SPP to engender public legitimacy. Even the relatively benign cooperative issues within the energy and environment agendas resulted in concerns that the process would lead to a 'race to the bottom' and would result in a loss of sovereign control over natural resources.

The Canada–U.S. talks on a 'shared vision for perimeter security and economic competitiveness,' announced by Harper and Obama on 4 February 2011, fail to mention either energy or environmental issues. This dialogue appears to continue many of the patterns associated with the short-lived SPP process. As Ayres and Macdonald discuss in their chapter in this volume, the perimeter talks continue to pay little attention to generating public support and legitimacy, and the omission of environmental issues from discussion of shared risks reflects the ongoing lack of a broader vision that might generate public support. Instead, a more limited 'bundling' of energy and environmental issues has been shifted to a different venue, the bilateral Canada–U.S. Clean Energy Dialogue. Here, the clean energy agenda has been hitched to the climate policy agenda of the Canadian and U.S. governments in a manner that is consistent with previous transgovermental mechanisms (as discussed in more detail below). In this context, it is worth exploring the Border 2012 model on the U.S.–Mexico border, as it provides a national-level framework, bundling together disparate environmental initiatives undertaken by the two national and various subnational governments, across a range of different agencies. It also provides structures for including non-governmental interests in agenda setting and implementation.

Border 2012 is actually the third attempt to develop and implement a comprehensive environmental program on the southern border. Under the terms of the La Paz Agreement, environmental authorities in both countries first developed the Integrated Border Environmental Plan (IBEP) in 1992, which created a broader umbrella under which specific environmental issues, formerly dealt with through the separate interagency agreements referred to above, could be addressed in a more cohesive manner. IBEP dealt specifically with air quality, water quality, and hazardous and solid wastes via working groups of agency officials. However, the implementation of the IBEP was criticized both for its inability to address cross-cutting issues such as environmental health and for a lack of public involvement. These perceived shortcomings led in 1996 to the Border XXI Program, which was intended to facilitate decentralization and cross-sectoral interagency cooperation to a greater degree. Yet there was widespread agreement that Border XXI did not achieve these aims either.

It was clear that the two national governments needed to recognize the diversity of concerns at the local and subregional levels and to marry a 'bottom-up' structure with national-level funding and oversight. Border 2012 thus establishes three types of coordinating bodies: regional work groups (for California–Baja California, Arizona–Sonora, New Mexico–Texas–Chihuahua, and Texas–Coahuila–Nuevo León–Tamaulipas); border-wide work groups, which focus on broad topics (e.g., cooperative enforcement and compliance); and policy forums centred on particular problems (e.g., air, water, and waste). All of these efforts, in which state and local governments play significant roles, are managed by the 'National Coordinators,' the U.S. EPA and Mexico's SEMARNAT.

This attempt to achieve vertical coordination, so that border environmental issues might be more effectively addressed by various levels of government, faces particular challenges. First, while the U.S. federal government has become more enthusiastic recently about promoting local participation, Mexico is much more centralized in a political and budgetary sense, and it is not clear whether and how state and local governments south of the border can actively shape border environmental decision making. Furthermore, as Zorc (2004) notes, the lines of communication and responsibility between the federal bureaucracies and the work groups and task forces is ill-defined; it is assumed that federal officials will take advice from these lower-level deliberations, but there is no formal mechanism for ensuring that they do.

Although there have been some difficulties in terms of realizing Border 2012's participatory vision, the program places great emphasis on a decentralized, cross-border regional approach to programming, and participation by civil society, environmental groups, and indigenous peoples on both sides of the border is expressly encouraged. Border 2012 is described in official terms as a 'results-oriented program' that takes a 'bottom-up approach' to addressing the environmental and public health needs of the border region; in other words, issues and projects are to be identified and implemented at the local level (U.S. EPA 2010). The main mechanisms for achieving this are task forces, which include representatives from local communities; relevant local, state, federal, and tribal governments; and binational, non-governmental, and community-based organizations. Meetings held under the auspices of Border 2012 are to be as inclusive as possible and open to the public.

There are two additional weaknesses in the Border 2012 framework that should be noted here. First, because the program is EPA-led in both an administrative and a budgetary sense (rather than being run from the centre of government), it has not been able to engage continued executive focus and support, as is evidenced by the submersion of Border 2012 programming under the weight of border security and fence building (despite obvious environmental impacts). By contrast, the SPP, with its high-level executive oversight, specified timelines, and prioritization of resources, ensured that – for a time – officials in all three countries were focused on the ends that political leaders endorsed at their annual summits.

Second, Border 2012 is focused primarily on pollution and prioritizes environmental and public health. It involves the federal and state environmental and public health agencies, as well as the Border Environmental Cooperation Commission, the CEC, the Good Neighbour Environmental Board, and the IBWC, along with a range of organizations representing the expert community, civil society organizations, and indigenous peoples. It does not, however, address broader environmental–energy linkages; the U.S. Department of Energy, for example, is not a Border 2012 'partner.' Here, the SPP's ability (if not exactly its willingness) to address cross-sectoral issues is notable.

Economic Crisis, Political Instability, and Transboundary Environmental Governance

As the unceremonious demise of the SPP suggests, the bundling of transgovernmental environmental initiatives is often fragile because it is not accompanied by a robust institutional framework. Bundling, as an alternative to formal institutions, is therefore more vulnerable to short-term shifts in economic and political conditions. The drawing to a close of the SPP can be attributed to the pervasive legitimacy concerns associated with the initiative – these became much harder to ignore as economic pressures mounted over the course of 2008. Indeed, as protectionist sentiments gained traction, the transgovernmental structure of the SPP, particularly its deliberate avoidance of legislative engagement, was viewed as a vice rather than a virtue by the media, the engaged public and – significantly – the newly elected Obama administration.

The bundling of environmental and energy initiatives within the much broader security and prosperity framework of the SPP provided some initial momentum for these activities, but when the underlying conditions that supported the grander security and prosperity bargain faltered, the constituent activities were orphaned. For example, the NAEWG, which predated the SPP but was swept into that initiative, lost much of its momentum after the SPP was discontinued. Similarly, the development of rules for transboundary EIA was an express objective for the CEC, but this also was moved under the SPP umbrella and now has no venue at all for its completion (Craik 2008).

When we consider the SPP experience alongside other forms of transgovernmental bundling in environment and energy, such as the CEC and the Border 2012 Program, we can draw several observations. First – and we think foremost – legitimacy matters. Transgovernmentalism is often conducive to cooperation because of its closed, 'club-like' structure (Craik and DiMento 2008, 486). Network members can be chosen precisely *because* they are like-minded. As Baker (2007, 24) explains, 'it is elitism and exclusion that defines transgovernmentalism as a form of governance, precisely because it rests on dialogues between like-minded officials that share certain overarching ideas and normative beliefs and values.' Despite the efficacy of networked governance, its longer-term stability requires a broader base of support than the network members themselves. Even where the activities are benign and quite technical, as was the case with the environmental and energy agendas under the SPP, the motives of networks are treated with scepticism because they are often not transparent. The privileged position of the North American Competitiveness Council, an advisory group made up of corporate leaders, gave credence to criticisms that the SPP favoured business interests over competing social and environmental interests. The more open structures of both the CEC and the Border 2012 program indicate that it is possible to structure transgovernmental cooperation in more transparent and participatory ways, which can in turn contribute to the resilience of the cooperative framework.

A second observation we would make is that bundling appears to be the result of differing motivations. The SPP was a grand bargain in the sense that it was driven by a high-order linkage between security issues and continued North American prosperity and was anchored in a desire for renewed progress in the broader North American integration project. Environmental and energy matters were subordinate to these ends and were not themselves viewed as subject to cross-sectoral linkages. The bundling within Border 2012 – and to some degree the CEC work agenda

– is more directly motivated by a functional need to address issues across traditional governance boundaries. Considered in this light, functional bundling, because it is less dependent on political conditions, may be better able to weather economic and political turbulence. It also provides a clearer basis for sorting out the roles and contributions of different levels of government, which may all have constitutional and/or policy responsibilities for aspects of environmental and energy challenges, within the transboundary cooperative framework.

A third observation we would make is that the institutional characteristics that surround transgovernmental networks are important. In an obvious way, more formal institutional arrangements provide a more stable environment for transgovernmental activities, particularly in the face of shifting political support. For example, the North American Environmental Cooperation Agreement provides clearly defined roles to the CEC's Council, Secretariat, and Citizen Advisory Committee. It also provides for some set procedures such as the citizens' submission process and Secretariat Reports, both of which allow for a measure of participation.

Perhaps less apparent, though, are the normative influences embedded in institutions, which are often missing – or at the very least inchoately articulated – in most transgovernmental arrangements. The presence of underlying principles provides both purpose and boundaries to transgovernmental activities (Craik and DiMento 2008, 511). In relation to legitimacy concerns, broad principles – such as those found in Article 1 of the North American Agreement on Environmental Cooperation (NAAEC) – insofar as they are widely held, confer legitimacy by establishing the shared basis under which network activities are carried out. In the manner described by Macdonald and Ayres in the introduction to this volume, the NAAEC has served to 'construct' a North America that acts trilaterally in pursuit of environmental sustainability. The cooperative institutions created under the NAAEC, including the CEC, are regarded as having a role to play in pursuit of these objectives. Craik and DiMento attribute the legitimacy concerns associated with the SPP in part to a failure to anchor the SPP process in a shared set of ideas. As a consequence, critics of the SPP process projected a variety of fears onto it, ranging from increased immigration, to a loss of regulatory sovereignty, to concerns over control of natural resources. The SPP's framers dismissed these fears as not being borne out by the actual process; the difficulty was that the boundaries of the process were never articulated.

It follows that normative framing will be particularly important for bundled transgovernmental initiatives because they are potentially more wide ranging and may involve trade-offs among issues. Unlike traditional forms of interstate cooperation, which focus on achieving specific agreements, transgovernmental arrangements tend to be open-ended and incremental, requiring a measure of normative coherence. We do not underestimate the difficulty that finding shared goals in the energy and environmental areas will pose. The CEC provides one model for normative framing whereby the transgovernmental network is nested in a more formal interstate agreement. The Border 2012 process provides a less formal and more bottom-up approach to the development of baseline goals, which involve multilevel agency engagement and extensive public consultation. This has led to the development of a broad mission statement and ten guiding principles, which in turn provide substantive direction and coherence to the program.

Climate Change and the Future of North American Environmental Governance

As we note above, although current economic conditions and political realignments may increase tendencies towards fragmentation in North America, the challenge that climate change presents is likely to work in the opposite direction. We argue that climate change, as the dominant environmental and energy issue, will create increased demand for bundled transgovernmental approaches to governance. While climate change unquestionably raises issues of high political salience, much of the focus of climate change governance in North America will be on implementation. North American climate governance will not be concerned with obligation creation, particularly in relation to targets and timetables, which has been the domain of the UNFCCC negotiations and may include the Major Economies Forum. North America is, however, an appropriate scale for implementation given the open economic conditions in North America, the integrated energy market, and the high degree of existing policy agreement between the three North American national governments.

Most of the existing cooperative activities are technical in nature and are coordinated by agency officials. For example, there has been some harmonization around energy efficiency standards, labelling, and fuel economy standards. There are interagency discussions around research and development cooperation and its supporting infrastructure. These activities have been supported by a Trilateral Energy Science and Technology Agreement as well as by two bilateral frameworks on clean energy development and climate change: the Canada–U.S. Clean Energy Dialogue, and the U.S.–Mexico Bilateral Framework on Clean Energy and Climate Change. The emergence of emissions trading schemes and other carbon pricing measures will also require a high degree of technical coordination if carbon markets are to be linked across borders. These arrangements are anticipated under existing subregional cap-and-trade programs and are currently contemplated under federal proposals in the United States and Canada. The setting of caps and the basic architecture of trading programs is likely to be determined unilaterally, but market linkage measures will require cooperation on accounting, reporting, and verification measures.

Climate change cooperation, particularly if it deepens to include carbon pricing measures, will necessitate a measure of bundling. The packaging of initiatives within a single framework is emerging under the 'clean energy' banner. An example is the Canada–U.S. Clean Energy Dialogue, which includes coordinated activities on energy efficiency, renewable energy development, smart grid development, and carbon capture and storage. Trade and competitiveness concerns should also militate in favour of bundling to address matters – such as proposed border adjustment measures, clean energy subsidies, and climate change–related non-tariff trade barriers – that require expertise to ensure trade rule compliance and environmental efficacy.

One advantage of bundled transgovernmentalism is that aggregating initiatives under an executive framework allows for higher-level direction to bureaucrats, particularly in areas of higher political sensitivity and those which require dedicated spending. The degree of economic disruption that environmentally necessary climate change measures will cause will almost certainly require political leadership. For example, Canada has already expressed concerns over the potential of certain measures – such as low carbon fuel standards and selective renewable portfolio standards – to impact energy trade flows between the two countries. This structure is evident in the clean energy frameworks, which are executive-led initiatives that contemplate further transgovernmental coordination. The approach of the clean energy frameworks is similar to that of the SPP in that the executive does some broad agenda setting to facilitate agency level discussions. With the Clean Energy Dialogue, joint working groups of agency officials have been struck in order to facilitate cooperation, and these groups must report to the two national leaders on their progress.

Bundled transgovernmentalism may also facilitate multilevel policy integration. Having a governance structure that works across vertical *and* horizontal governance arrangements is particularly important in light of the differing constitutional responsibilities for energy, environmental, and financial matters among the three North American states. In Mexico, for example, oil and gas matters are highly centralized within PEMEX; whereas in Canada, oil and gas policy is a jealously safeguarded area of provincial authority. In the case of carbon markets, the absence of any national securities or commodities regulator in Canada, such as the Securities Exchange Commission, will similarly necessitate an informal coordination structure that can accommodate a variety of actors.

The complexity of the current trajectory of climate cooperation in North America is a reflection of the lack of political consensus around climate change at both national and subnational levels. Some subnational governments, such as California and British Columbia, are willing to undertake deeper commitments than other subnational or federal governments. Even among willing government units, the approach to greenhouse gas mitigation is highly diverse and contingent on respective economic attributes. Flexible approaches allow for the development of context-sensitive policies. Indeed, it would be surprising that a policy approach in Quebec, which has abundant hydroelectric power, would be suitable for parts of the southern United States or Mexico. That said, the high degree of economic integration will create strong pressure for comparability of mitigation efforts across jurisdictions. The Canadian government's decision in the wake of the Copenhagen Accord to adopt the U.S. greenhouse gas reduction target speaks to the strong desire for alignment of climate policy as a shield to climate-related trade measures. In addition, each country has affirmed its commitment both to the UNFCCC process and to further trilateral cooperation under the North American Leaders' Declaration on Climate Change and Clean Energy.

Conclusion

As the three countries of North America turn to fashioning a regional response to climate change, these cooperative efforts are likely to increase the density of North American environmental governance arrangements. North American governance, at least in this policy area, is not likely to fade away. To the contrary, we would assume that the continued preference for transgovernmental, networked approaches to cooperation (and the continued reluctance to create any new supranational institutions), along with the technical and cross-cutting nature of climate policy implementation, will militate in favour of bundled forms of transgovernmentalism. In fact, we may even be seeing early signs of bundling in terms of the 'clean energy–lower carbon' policy packages under consideration in the Canada–U.S. Clean Energy Dialogue and the U.S.–Mexico Bilateral Framework on Clean Energy and Climate Change. The CEC's new 'Climate Change–Low Carbon Economy' program is also likely to favour a bundling approach. These particular frameworks – which aim to coordinate energy efficiency, renewable energy, and emissions reduction initiatives – may be more stable given their targeted, functional nature and given the degree to which they have already garnered high-level executive interest. Meanwhile, subnational initiatives such as the WCI and RGGI – themselves also experiments in functional bundling – continue apace.

However, bundled transgovernmentalism as an approach to regional climate policy cooperation must anticipate the kinds of procedural and substantive concerns levelled at the SPP. Although the functional (and highly technical) nature of climate policy cooperation may encourage network commitment and stability, it may also be vulnerable to concerns about a lack of process transparency and exclusivity. The normative aims of the newly instituted climate policy processes must also be made clear. In this vein, the Border 2012 program may supply a useful model for more inclusive and participatory environmental governance, both from a process perspective, as it attempts to achieve both vertical representation across governments and the inclusion of those outside government, and substantively, given its principled commitment to project proposals from local actors and communities.

There can be no doubt that the current political and economic upheaval has certainly impacted the way in which policy makers on the continent view the costs and benefits of climate change policy, particularly given current spending constraints and deepening competitiveness concerns. However, the three countries continue to engage with the international climate change process, and there is, if anything, more coordination among the three governments at the international level, encouraged by a more active U.S. administration. In this context, the dominant modes of regional interaction, through more flexible, transgovernmental networks, seem to be quickly reasserting themselves. In this sense, the impact of political and economic influences offers some important insights into the surprisingly resilient nature of North American environmental governance.

Notes

1 The U.S. Senate has chosen not to act on the legislation, however, and it is now unlikely that climate legislation will emerge from Congress in the near term.

References

'2005 Report to the Leaders – North American Security and Prosperity Partnership.' June 2005. http://www.spp-psp.gc.ca/eic/site/spp-psp.nsf/eng/00098.html. Accessed 4 November 2011.

'2006 Report to the Leaders – North American Security and Prosperity Partnership.' August 2006. http://www.spp-psp.gc.ca/eic/site/spp-psp.nsf/eng/00053.html. Accessed 4 November 2011.

Baker, Andrew. 2007. 'Participation in the Deliberative Spaces of the Global Financial Architecture: A Transgovernmental Analysis.' Queen's University Belfast, GARNET Working Paper No. 21/07 (July 2007).

Commission for Environmental Cooperation. 2005. 'Looking to the Future: Strategic Plan of the Commission for Environmental Cooperation 2006–2010.' Montreal, 17 June.

– 2004. 'North American Power Plant Air Emissions.' Montreal. http://www.cec.org/Page.asp?PageID=122&ContentID=2600&SiteNodeID=437&BL_ExpandID=107. Accessed 4 November 2011.

Craik, Neil. 2009. 'Climate Law and Policy in North America: Prospects for Regionalism.' *San Diego Journal of Climate and Energy Law* 1, no. 1: 1–64.

– 2008. 'Transboundary Environmental Impact Assessment in North America: Obstacles and Opportunities.' In *Theory and Practice of Transboundary Environmental Impact Assessment.* Edited by C.J. Bastmeijer, Kees Bastmeijer, and Timo Koivurova. Leiden: Martinus Nijhoff.

Craik, Neil, and Joseph DiMento. 2008. 'Environmental Cooperation in the (Partially) Disaggregated States: Lessons from the Security and Prosperity Partnership of North America.' *Chicago Journal of International Law* 8, no. 2 (Winter): 479–512.

Government of Canada. Office of the Prime Minister. 2009. 'North American Leaders' Declaration on Climate Change and Clean Energy.' 10 August. Guadalajara.

– 2008. 'Joint Statement by President Bush, President Calderón, Prime Minister Harper – North American Leaders' Summit.' 22 April. Ottawa.

International Boundary Water Commission – United States Section. 2010. 'About Us.' http://www.ibwc.state.gov/home.html.

'Joint Statement by North American Leaders with Key Accomplishments since March 2006.' 21 August 2007.

Keohane, Robert, and Joseph Nye. 1974. 'Transgovernmental Relations and International Organizations.' *World Politics* 27, no. 1: 39–62.

Ministerial Joint Statement – North American Security and Prosperity Partnership. 2008, 22 April.

North American Agreement on Environmental Cooperation between The Government of Canada, The Government of the United Mexican States and The Government of the United States. Montreal: Secretariat of the Commission for Environmental Coopertion, September 1993.

Sanchez-Rodriguez, Roberto A., Konrad von Moltke, Steven Mumme, John Kirton, and Don Munton. 1998. 'The Dynamics of Transboundary Environmental Agreements in North America.' In *Environmental Management on North America's Borders*. Edited by Richard Kiy and John D. Wirth. College Station: Texas A&M University Press.

Slaughter, Anne-Marie. 2004. *A New World Order.* Princeton: Princeton University Press.

U.S. Environmental Protection Agency (EPA). 2010. 'U.S.-Mexico Border 2012 Program.' http://www.epa.gov/border2012.

VanNijnatten, Debora L. 2011. 'North American Environmental Regionalism: Multi-level, Bottom-heavy and Policy-led.' In *Comparative Environmental Regionalism*. Edited by Lorraine Elliot and Shaun Breslin. Routledge/GARNET Series.

– 2009. 'Environmental Cross-Border Regions and the Canada–U.S. Relationship: Building from the Bottom-Up in the Second Century.' In *Transborder Environmental Governance in Canada and the United States*. Edited by Barry G. Rabe and Stephen Brooks. Washington: Woodrow Wilson Center for International Scholars.

– 2007. 'The SPP as an "Indicator Species" for the Emerging North American Environmental Regime.' *Politics and Policy* 35, no. 4: 664–82.

– 2006. 'Building a North American Environmental Regime ... from Below?' Paper prepared for the Annual Meeting of the International Studies Association, San Diego, March 2006.

Zorc, Eileen, 2004. 'The Border 2012 U.S.–Mexico Environmental Program: Will a Bottom-Up Approach Work?' *Georgetown International Environmental Law Review.* http://findarticles.com/p/articles/mi_qa3970/is_200404/ai_n9406127.

7 Borders and Security in North America

EMILY GILBERT

Since the terrorist attacks of 9/11, the borders within North America have become increasingly securitized and also much more complex. While security has been high on the agenda at the U.S.–Mexico border for decades (see Nevins 2002), the new security measures at the Canada–U.S. border are unprecedented. Peter Andreas's observation that a 'Mexicanization' of the U.S.–Canada border is under way reflects both this new dynamic of securitization and the growing convergence of border policies at the southern and northern boundaries of the United States (Andreas 2005). Yet the historic asymmetries in border policies and practices have not been entirely eradicated, and discrepancies continue on the ground (Ackleson 2005). Moreover, border policies are being reconfigured in new ways. This is especially the case vis-à-vis the mobility of people, which is becoming more and more differentiated. While some groups such as refugees and economic migrants are facing more obstacles at border crossings, others, especially the professional class, are being granted expedited access. Finally, at the same time that there has been an evident securitization of borders within North America, there has also been a push for hardening the region's external borders to create a security perimeter. Bilateral and trilateral initiatives are under way to harmonize economic, migration, and security policies, as exemplified by the announcement in February 2011 that the leaders of Canada and the United States would pursue perimeter security (discussed in more detail below).

As a result of these multiple dynamics, border security in North America is highly complicated, contradictory, and often contested. This chapter addresses this complexity of North American border security, with particular attention to post-9/11 developments, including the changing political leadership and the international economic crisis. I argue that no single narrative of protectionism or regionalism is prevailing and that instead there are simultaneous pressures to more forcefully delineate national territoriality *and* to deepen North American integration. The fragmented and contradictory security interests that are at work suggest that the North American region is far from stable and that its future is anything but secure. Security concerns are being mapped onto already existing national and regional challenges and are contributing to a deeper sense of insecurity. Political regime change and the economic crisis have helped exacerbate the challenges facing the North American region. Within nation-states, federal and subnational interests are often working at cross-purposes, as are bureaucracies and organizations representing various public and private groups. Moreover, stated national objectives rest incongruously with federal department initiatives, while there is also considerable pushback by subnational governments, institutions, and actors. At the regional scale, only shallow forms of governance are in place in North America, despite more than fifteen years of free trade (Ayres and Macdonald 2006), and when forms of governance are enabled, they tend to favour U.S. norms and values (Clarkson and Torres-Ruiz 2009, 163). As with other policy domains, regional security is being knitted together by 'bilateral and trilateral agreements in discrete policy areas' that are placing 'restrictions on national governments in an asymmetrical relationship' rather than developing any clear sense of trilateral polity (Jhappan and Abu-Laban 2008, 13).

Addressing this security complexity requires a dynamic and critical concept of borders. In line with the constructivist interpretation outlined in the introduction to this volume, I suggest that borders should not be treated as natural lines in the sand, but as socially, politically, and economically constituted boundaries that are always contingent and contested. In the contemporary context, this more expansive understanding of borders is especially important, for as Etienne Balibar has remarked, 'borders are being both multiplied and reduced in their localization and their function, they are being thinned out and doubled' (Balibar 1998, 220). As recent research in the field delineates, borders are never absolute: they are always porous, whether by design or in practice (Parker et al. 2009). What is therefore interesting is precisely the degree to which a border is open or closed, and for what and whom the border is made permeable or impermeable, and how this has come to pass. This chapter will attend to these issues by examining

North American borders through three frames: (1) transnational border agreements; (2) security policies and practices at the border; and (3) mobility and migration. These three frames help draw out the contradictions around the border; in so doing they also highlight the competing interests and actors implicated in the ongoing securitization of North America.

Transnational Border Agreements

The increased securitization of U.S. borders since 9/11 has had serious implications for the region's economies (e.g., Olmedo and Solden 2005; Ackleson 2005; Drache 2008; Goldfarb 2007; Andreas 2009; Nevins 2009). As discussed in the introduction to this volume, the complete shutdown of the U.S. borders in the immediate aftermath of the terrorist attacks derailed the cross-border just-in-time economy. Shipping trucks were backed up for over 35 kilometres on the Canadian side (Clarkson 2001). Even as borders reopened, new security measures resulted in higher transaction costs and extra delays in processing and crossing times that have affected people on both sides of the border. Ackleson notes that 'retail sales in El Paso, Texas, for instance, have been off in some cases up to 50%, prompting local officials to appeal for emergency economic relief from Congress' (Ackleson 2005, 176). For Canada and Mexico, these challenges have been especially pressing as both their economies rely significantly on cross-border trade with the United States. Both countries have sought to ensure that the border remains as open to trade as possible. This has meant appeasing U.S. security concerns whenever they arise, usually by drawing domestic practices more in line with those in the United States.

To this end, within weeks of 9/11, Canada and the United States negotiated the Canada–U.S. Smart Border Accord (SBA). Although discussions along these lines had been under way for some time, the security impetus emerging out of the United States propelled its quick implementation (Gilbert 2005). The rhetoric of the SBA affirmed the border's importance for both security and the economy: 'By working together to develop a zone of confidence against terrorist activity, we create a unique opportunity to build a smart border for the 21st century; a border that securely facilitates the free flow of people and commerce; a border that reflects the largest trading relationship in the world.'[1] The accord has identified multiple points of collaboration (e.g., managing refugees), common standards (e.g., cargo screening), and reciprocity (e.g., investment in infrastructure) to create a 'smart border' that will facilitate the movement of goods and people deemed low risk, while making the border more impermeable to others. In March 2002, a similar border agreement was signed by U.S. President George W. Bush and Mexico's President Vicente Fox at their bilateral meetings in Monterrey. Their twenty-two point Border Partnership Action Plan was less expansive than its Canadian counterpart; it also reflected Mexico's more limited resources and greater scepticism regarding security collaboration (Díez 2008).

These initiatives have brought North American border security policies more closely into agreement; notably, however, they have been bilateral in their focus. At the same time, proposals to deepen and broaden the trilateral North American Free Trade Agreement (NAFTA) were already in the air, and some effort was made to rethink North American relations along the lines of the European Community (Pastor 2001; Poitras 2001). International economic competitiveness, framed in terms of the rising power of India and China, also helped propel discussions around regional economic integration. It was only post-9/11, however, that these ideas gained real traction, even as the agenda shifted and broadened to include the United States' heightened security interests. Canada and Mexico bent over backwards to appease U.S. security concerns, both with respect to bilateral and trilateral negotiations and implementation of policies related to domestic security. The Security and Prosperity Partnership (SPP), signed by the leaders of Canada, Mexico, and the United States in March 2005, denoted a new agenda around trilateral cooperation, harmonization, and interoperability on both economic and security platforms. The SPP represented a market-based 'partnership' model, one premised on incremental policy harmonization across a wide variety of sectors, from electronic commerce to collaboration in higher education. The harmonization of border security – including information sharing and interoperability of security forces – was a significant component of this agreement. With appeals to the 'quality of life' of their citizens and the shared principles of 'liberty,' 'freedom,' and 'democracy,' the SPP also introduced new possibilities for governing a regional partnership that brought the concept of Fortress North America more clearly into view (Gilbert 2007).

The mandate and expansiveness of the SPP thus seemed to move North America much more in the direction of economic and security integration, with the model of the European Union (EU) looming large as an example of regional governance. Intimations of a regional security perimeter were in the air, and the opening up of internal borders across the continent – also along the lines of the EU – did not seem entirely impossible. Yet, as discussed elsewhere in this volume, the SPP's trajectory would actually be more ad hoc, particularly since bilateral negotiations were permitted, on the understanding that they would eventually become trilateral, much as free trade had been initiated between Canada and the United States and only later extended to Mexico. Also unlike the EU, there was no indication that North America would adopt a political infrastructure, which would have been widely criticized for eroding democratic processes (Gilbert 2007). The only consultative organization established for the SPP was the North American Competitiveness Council, comprised of CEOs from leading multinational companies in each country – which helped affirm that the SPP would uphold the interests of the business community over those of the larger public (see Brodie, Ayres and Macdonald, and Healy chapters in this this volume). Groups reflecting both right and left politics raised numerous concerns that the SPP would erode national sovereignty and human rights (Ayres and Macdonald 2009).

As of August 2009, however, the SPP is 'no longer an active initiative.' This does not mean that its initiatives have faltered; rather, as the current SPP website indicates, they are proceeding under a different guise. The specific reasons for the SPP's demise are unclear. What is important to note in the context of this chapter, however, is that the end of the SPP marks a general waning of enthusiasm for regional initiatives, especially on the part of the United States. President Barack Obama has demonstrated more interest in global politics than in his nearest neighbours. Moreover, the financial crisis has generated a resurgence of economic protectionism, typified by the American Recovery and Reinvestment Act. The Buy American Act, which is bundled into this $800 billion program for reinvestment, states that all goods purchased for public use through the stimulus funds must be manufactured in the United States. Canadian business groups were immediately up in arms over the implications for domestic industry. The U.S. Senate's softening of the protectionist impulses of the House, with the added 'assurance' that these policies would be 'applied in a manner consistent with U.S. obligations under international agreements' such as NAFTA and the WTO, did little to placate Canada's concerns (see the chapter by Healy in this volume).

The Buy American Act is but one indicator of the demise of a preferential trading relationship across North America. Already during the

U.S. election primaries, Obama had placed NAFTA on notice by unilaterally declaring that the agreement would have to be renegotiated. Moreover, under Obama's leadership some NAFTA provisions have been weakened. The 2009 Omnibus Appropriations Act, for example, cancelled a pilot initiative, begun under the George W. Bush administration, to enable Mexican trucks to cross into the United States when delivering their goods (Baughman and Francois 2009). NAFTA had required the United States to admit Mexican trucks, and vice versa, to ensure the smooth operations of just-in-time economies across the border. But concerns around licensing, as well as safety and environmental policies, had long been used to block implementation of this initiative. With the Buy American Act, the Obama administration has returned to a more obstreperous agenda.

It has become startlingly clear under President Obama that Canadian and Mexican assumptions that security cooperation would encourage continental economic integration have been misguided. It is precisely to prevent such acts of unilateralism and protectionism that Canada and Mexico have sought to negotiate trilateral agreements with the United States and have bent over backwards to appease U.S. security concerns. Yet the international financial crisis has made it patently clear that greater security cooperation has not ensured economic openness. As Clarkson and Bow discuss in their chapters in this volume, the crisis *could* have strengthened regional governance but instead has helped bring about its disintegration. Collaboration is proceeding solely on an ad hoc basis; as Stephanie Golob points out in this volume, we have shifted to a model of triple bilateralism across the region. Some of the recent developments on border agreements clearly reflect the return to bilateralism. In March 2010 a new 'United States–Mexico Partnership: A New Border Vision' was signed. That framework rearticulates the SPP principles of 'joint border management, co-responsibility for cross-border crime, and shared commitment to the efficient flow of legal commerce and travel.'[2] Then, on 4 February 2011, the Canadian and U.S. governments issued a 'Declaration on a Shared Vision for Perimeter Security and Economic Competitiveness.' While the details of this new border agreement are still vague, the broad objectives are similar to those of the SPP: boosting economic relations, particularly through trade, with a strong security component that includes early threat detection, integrated personnel, and joint initiatives on infrastructure and cybersecurity.[3]

These separate initiatives clearly suggest that the SPP mandate has not been halted: it has merely been reconfigured into new bilateral agreements. With the re-election of Canada's Conservative Party in May 2011, now with a majority government, there is momentum around border negotiations, which the government has indicated is one of its priorities. Some have called these negotiations 'the most sweeping changes to the Canada–U.S. border since the 1988 free-trade agreement.'[4] Yet as with the SPP, there has been no parliamentary debate in Canada and only limited forms of public engagement (just one government website for the public to record their responses to the intiative).[5] Moreover, and again in line with the SPP process, the only consultative body that has thus far been announced is business-oriented: the Canada–U.S. Regulatory Cooperation Council, whose aim is to smooth the commercial relationship between the two countries. Finally, questions regarding sovereignty and privacy have been prominent among the apprehensions raised in Canada, particularly with regard to the proposed expansion of security interoperability, which is already unfolding at great speed, and which is discussed in the following section.

Security at the Border

North American border policies changed dramatically in the wake of 9/11. The concept of the 'smart border' – one that is open to the 'legitimate' movement of trade and people but impermeable to those deemed 'illegitimate' or 'risky' – has become the prominent trope through which the border is understood. Part of this targeted response involves an intensive securitization and even militarization of the border that belies the emphasis that is placed on openness in these agreements. Having signed the Patriot Act just weeks after 9/11, the United States introduced new legislation and changed existing legislation to permit much more expansive measures of search and surveillance, apprehension and custodial remand. More funds have been directed to border guards; technological directives have been introduced to track visitors into the United States; provisions have been enacted regarding the admissibility of migrants; and new provisions have been introduced with respect to detention. This securitization has entailed a huge investment of money. When the Department of Homeland Security was established in 2003, it became responsible for border security as part of its anti-terrorism mandate. The budget just for the Department of Homeland Security in its first year was $42.4 billion. That department's budget has risen significantly over the years, including under the Obama administration, and is now well over $50 billion.

A significant proportion of the deployed security resources have been directed towards the Mexico–U.S. border. Somewhat paradoxically, NAFTA's opening of the border to trade in the 1990s resulted in the United States *hardening* the border to the passage of migrants, particularly through programs such as Operation Gatekeeper (Nevins 2002, 2009; Andreas 2009). Since 9/11 this securitization has escalated. There are now more than twice as many border guards, with 20,000 agents in place in 2009 (Nevins 2009, 5). The National Guard has also been deployed to that border: more than 6,000 were sent between 2006 and 2008 under Operation Jump Start, and another 1,200 have since been deployed under Obama's administration. In addition to mandated security forces, citizens' groups such as the Minutemen (formed in 2005) are monitoring the border to prevent undocumented crossings (Doty 2009). Their legality has been challenged, but they continue to operate under the radar – a testament to the importance of non-state actors in policing and reinforcing the border. State-funded fortification of the border has also continued apace. Anti-immigration sentiment came to a head around the Border Protection, Anti-Terrorism, and Illegal Immigration Control Act of 2005 (colloquially known as the Sensenbrenner bill after the name of its sponsor in the House of Representatives), which proposed erecting another seven hundred miles of 'security fencing' at the U.S.–Mexico border.[6] This bill did not pass in Congress; however, provisions for extending a double-security fence were rolled out in the Secure Fence Act of 2006. To track undocumented migrants, new surveillance technologies have been deployed, such as unmanned drones, similar to the ones in the skies over Afghanistan and Pakistan (Nevins 2009, 212–13). Other military technologies have been used; for example, a unit of Stryker combat vehicles worked with Border Patrol officers, helping them apprehend about 2,500 undocumented migrants, before the vehicles were shipped out to Iraq (Andreas 2009, 158).

Mexico for its part has introduced more intensive security measures (see Cadena-Roa's chapter in this volume), which target undocumented migrants and drug traffickers. By 2001, Mexico had implemented *Plan Sur*, which entailed erecting physical barriers and deploying military patrols to enforce immigration laws along its border with Guatemala (Coleman 2007a, 622). The aim was to close Mexico's southern border to those Latin Americans who hoped to enter the United States overland through Mexico. These initiatives were undertaken in the shadow of U.S. power; what has *changed* since 9/11 is that Mexico is now more amenable to cooperating with the United States around security measures. In 2003, Mexico launched Operation Sentinel (*Operación Centinela*), in which 18,000 armed forces personnel were specifically assigned an anti-terrorism mandate (i.e., to protect borders and infrastructure) (Díez 2008, 156). Given that terrorism was not high on Mexico's agenda, this mobilization was seen as a response to U.S. concerns rather than to a pressing domestic matter. The administration of Vicente Fox also introduced some limited forms of interoperability across Mexican and U.S. security forces; Mexican personnel, for example, have participated in the U.S. Counter-Terrorism Fellowship Program (ibid., 157).

Since the election of Felipe Calderón in 2006, the border has been shaped by his administration's militarized response to the 'war on drugs,' which has garnered much support from the United States. In 2007, the Mérida Initiative was launched, under which the United States, Mexico, and the countries of Central America agreed to help one another fight the drug cartels (Castro-Rea 2009, 49). The three-year package, worth US $1.4 billion, has been described as a 'regional security cooperation initiative.' The monies are allocated to infrastructure and personnel development. The program allows much greater interoperability across private security forces as well as other government agencies for purposes such as training. The Obama administration has persisted with these objectives. In March 2009, Janet Napolitano, head of the Homeland Security Department, announced an additional $700 million to secure the border. This would include tripling the number of Homeland Security intelligence analysts, implementing more intelligence sharing, and providing more equipment for both U.S. and Mexican forces. Yet, although there has been somewhat more acknowledgment that the cartels' activities are a reflection of the strong U.S. demand for drugs, the onus has been largely on Mexico to close down the cartels. There have been ample criticisms that the agreement has legitimized a militarized engagement with Mexico, along with infringements of human rights (such as torture, illegal arrests, and arbitrary killings), with some arguing that the focus of U.S. policy and funding ought to be on American demand (Brewer 2008). But with respect to security, the program does indicate an important shift toward more cooperation and even interoperability between Mexico and the United States on issues related to border security.

The greater cooperation between the United States and Mexico on security and border matters has been mirrored in Canada–Mexico relations. At the 2009 North American Leaders' Summit in Guadalajara, Prime Minister Harper announced an Anti-Crime Capacity Building Program, which is directing $15 million a year to address criminal activities across the Americas.[7] This includes sending RCMP officers to Mexico to assist with training programs, as well as inviting mid-level officers from Mexico to Canada for training. When President Calderón visited Canada in May 2010, more initiatives were announced that extended funding to train judges and lawyers and to help revise the penal code. But rather than signalling a shift towards regional initiatives, this is more of a case of Canada falling in step with the United States. North American security matters continue to be filtered through the United States and its domestic concerns, including its 'war on drugs.' Security issues at the Canada–U.S. border do not have the same legacy of concerns regarding undocumented migrants and drug trafficking, and the border has historically been much more open. In the wake of 9/11, Canada quickly (much more quickly than Mexico) implemented tighter security at its own borders and began working towards security cooperation and interoperability with the United States (Díez 2008, 158–60; Castro-Rea 2009). Yet much to Canada's surprise, since being confirmed as Homeland Security Secretary in January 2009, Napolitano has stated that because the law does not differentiate between the northern and southern borders of the United States, there is no reason do so in practice. In her first few weeks in office, she identified the Canadian border as one of her top priorities and requested a review of policies and procedures. Infamously, she publicly intimated that the 9/11 terrorists had entered the United States by way of Canada. This oft-repeated fallacy did not endear her to her Canadian counterparts, and she was eventually compelled to retract her statements.[8] Yet the perception of U.S.–Canada border vulnerability persists. A U.S. Government Accountability report dated December 2010 claims that only 1% of the border has an 'acceptable level of security' and that the chances of terrorists entering the United States are highest at its northern border.[9]

These perceptions of vulnerability persist despite the intensification or 'Mexicanization' of security at the Canadian border. As Peter Andreas has noted, prior to 9/11 many Canada–U.S. border posts were unmanned in the evenings; in more remote areas, an orange cone was dragged across the road in the evenings to signal that the border was closed (Andreas 2005, 455). This is no longer the case, and while the numbers are still much smaller than along the Mexican border, the contingent of border guards has increased, from 340 in 2001 to 1,200 today. This latter figure is expected to double in the next few years (Neinast and James 2008). The installation of five air and marine bases near the United States' northern border (such bases have been in place for many years along the southern one) also points to a 'Mexicanization' of the Canadian border (Andreas 2005, 455). U.S. air and marine border surveillance has been increased at the northern border, to twenty-eight aircraft and sixteen interceptor marine vessels. Unmanned surveillance drones (similar to those used in conflict situations) are patrolling the border. These are mounted with extrasensitive radar and with high-definition and infrared video that can capture anything within a 40 kilometre radius. In addition, a high-tech 'virtual fence' is being planned for the Canadian border, although problems with the contractor, Boeing, have meant that monies will now be directed elsewhere (Ackleson 2009, 346).

Yet as with Mexico, even while the Canada–U.S. border is becoming increasingly hardened and restrictive, there are multiple examples of extensive and intensive cooperation and interoperability. Cooperation between Canada and the United States has a much longer and deeper lineage, and the contemporary dimensions of interoperability have followed suit. NORAD is a forerunner for this kind of cooperation between the Canadian and U.S. militaries, and there have been suggestions that the military relationship should be expanded (Robertson 2011). Security cooperation is already expanding and becoming more extensive. The Smart Border Agreement of 2001 created Integrated Border Enforcement Teams (IBETs), which draw together core agencies across the United States and Canada: the RCMP, the Canada Border Services Agency, the U.S. Coast Guard, the U.S. Customs and Border Protection Office of the Border Patrol, and the U.S. Joint Task Force–North, as well as other levels of government. Their primary mission is to monitor border areas between ports of entry, although they also work with border services at those ports in terms of intelligence sharing and coordinated exercises. Joint operations are being undertaken on a more ad hoc basis, and these have been staged between air and marine units and the RCMP (Neinast and James 2008). In the build-up to the Olympics, there was also more marine cooperation, such as the 'Shiprider' agreement signed in May 2009 by Napolitano and then Public Safety Minister Peter Van Loan.[10] That agreement makes permanent a temporary program that had been initiated under the SPP allowing Canadian and U.S. law enforcement agencies to work together on marine law enforcement in boundary waters. It is noteworthy that through this legislation, officers can now enforce the law on *both* sides of the border. As a follow-up, in Parliament on 27 November 2009, Van Loan and Canadian Justice Minister Rob Nicholson tabled Bill C-60, the Keeping Canadians Safe (Protecting Borders) Act, which would designate U.S. police and security agents as peace officers equal to the RCMP in all parts of Canada during joint maritime border operations.[11]

The passage of Bill C-60 was delayed when the 2011 federal election was called. If passed, the bill will allow foreign forces to have operational jurisdiction on Canadian territory in certain circumstances. Already, the Civil Assistance Plan, signed in February 2008 between Canada and the United States, allows forces from one nation to cross over into the other in the case of a civil emergency, *upon request*.[12] The recently announced Canada–U.S. declaration on perimeter security promises to intensify these forms of interoperability. While the details are still vague, it has already been stated explicitly that the agreement will build on the IBETs, the Civil Assistance Plan, and the Shiprider Agreement. Each of these initiatives is pulling border security away from the actual border and inculcating a deeper security state. Interoperability also raises a multitude of pressing questions to which there do not appear to be any clear answers. Who is in charge? Who gets access? Who has legal jurisdiction when the border is crossed? Where are authority, accountability, and transparency located? What if something goes wrong? When do the joint operations begin? Who decides when, and how, they end? Another problematic outcome of interoperability is the potential militarization of security practices both at and away from the border – for example, for crimes such as drug smuggling, contraband, and the undocumented movement of people. It is to this last issue that I turn in the following section, for the immediate impact of this militarized securitization is most visible and most pernicious when it comes to the mobility and migration of populations.

Mobility and Migration

As the previous section has illustrated, North American borders have been increasingly securitized and even militarized since 9/11. Yet even as national markers are more forcefully etched on the ground, there is also extensive collaboration and even interoperability across security personnel. How does this complex landscape of border security affect the populations who are crossing the border? What kinds of *insecurities* are generated, and for whom? The answers to these questions differ substantially across the continent, although there are some important points of coherence. Didier Bigo has argued that there is currently a 'security continuum' at work whereby populations deemed risky in one realm (e.g., 'illegal' migrants) are now targeted as potential security and terrorist threats (Bigo 2002). As a result, undocumented migrants have been stigmatized, ostracized, and terrorized. In this geopolitical discourse of migration, those who are deemed most 'at risk' are in effect turned into risky subjects.

It is clear that the Department of Homeland Security relies on this kind of linkage between migration and terrorism (Ackleson 2005, 178). Yet in the U.S. context, the securitization of immigration and border control against unwanted migrants has a much longer history. The Illegal Immigration Reform and Immigration Responsibility Act (IIRIRA), passed in 1996, earmarked hundreds of millions of dollars for border security and fortification (ibid., 172). The deterrence aims of this legislation resonate with more recent legislation, such as the controversial Patriot Act, passed within weeks of 9/11, which authorized more monies for border patrols and immigration enforcement and provided for the detention and deportation of non-citizens. An initial US $10 billion was allocated to the U.S. Visitor and Immigrant Status Indicator Technology (VISIT) program, which has since expanded. This program mandates that biometric data be captured for all non-citizens entering the United States (although Canadians are exempt). The Secure Border Initiative (SBI) of 2005 sought to further secure the borders by investing resources in technology and infrastructure, drawing together enforcement agencies, creating a more efficient detention process, and clamping down on undocumented workers. As these examples suggest, border security has become increasingly reliant on technology and surveillance (Muller 2008). Populations are being sorted according to their presumed threat to the nation-state (Lyon 2002; Ackleson 2009). The extensive databases that programs such as VISIT draw upon – from police records to records of foreign exchange students – mean that border controls have permeated well beyond the border itself (Amoore 2006).

As noted above, concerns about 'undocumented' migrants along the U.S.–Mexico border are long-standing and have shaped border policy and infrastructure. Yet whereas migration issues in the 1990s were presented as a socio-economic problem, post-9/11 a law-and-order mentality has predominated (Coleman 2007a). Thus the Mérida Initiative, which is ostensibly about curtailing the U.S.–Mexico drug trade, is also targeting cross-border migration at Mexico's northern *and* southern borders (Drache 2008). The blurring of terrorism, law and order, and migration mandates is perhaps nowhere more clear than with regard to vigilante groups such as the Minutemen, who take security into their own hands at the border and rely on discourses of terrorism to secure public support for their exploits (Doty 2009). The targeting of 'undocumented' migrants from Mexico, however, is not just happening at the border; it has been interiorized within the nation. State and local police have been deputized in immigration policing enforcement (Coleman 2007a). As the American Civil Liberties Union has mapped it, the border zone extends one hundred miles inland from the U.S. border, yet it exists outside constitutional purview.[13] The past several years have seen a notable increase in stops and searches in this zone, and these can take place without a warrant. An example is the Roving Border Patrols that were conducted in southern California in June 2004, during which 'exclusively Mexican nationals suspected of working without papers in the US' were targeted, leading to 11,000 ad hoc interrogations and 450 formal detentions and deportations (Coleman 2007b, 60). New legislation in Arizona, SB1070, has given local police officers the power not only to determine someone's legal status if arrested but also to assess someone's status merely on the *suspicion* of being 'illegal.' Since the bill was signed on 23 April 2010 by Arizona governor Jan Brewer, the law has raised significant concerns regarding how 'suspicion' can be justified. In particular, human rights concerns have been raised about racial profiling, particularly of Latinos, who will feel compelled to carry documentation with them at all times in case they are stopped. The new law has delineated an entire population as a potential threat (Thobani 2004).

These examples of technological surveillance and law-and-order mandates illustrate how border politics are being interiorized into the state. This blurring of the line between internal and external security has been typical of the post-9/11 ethos of securitization (Ackleson 2005; see also Bigo 2002). The same examples speak to the ways in which legislation is being innovated at the subnational scale by states and municipalities (Gilbert 2009). Subnational pressures around borders and immigration – as with Operation Gatekeeper, which began as a California initiative – often get taken up at the national level. The chapters by Richard Vengroff and James Allan and Janine Brodie in this volume affirm the importance of subnational governance. Yet there is no clear sense of translation from scale to scale. While the controversial

Arizona legislation aimed at identifying, prosecuting, and deporting undocumented migrants is of great consequence, there has been considerable pushback at the federal level. President Obama has acknowledged failures with U.S. immigration reform, but he has also expressed dismay over Arizona's SB1070 legislation, echoing the concerns of civil liberties groups. More locally, police groups have also opposed the new Arizona law, pointing out that it is pressuring them to act as immigration enforcement agents and that it will make their policing responsibilities more difficult by discouraging non-status residents from reporting crimes. Other civil society actors are voicing their opposition to discriminatory immigration policies (see also Ayres and Macdonald 2009). Academic and trade organizations have called for an economic boycott; even Phoenix's NBA basketball team mounted a protest by changing its team shirts so that they bore the name 'Los Suns' at a playoff game on the Cinco de Mayo in 2010. Yet even while the Arizona law is being challenged in the courts, other states (including Alabama and Georgia) are enacting similar or even more far-reaching legislation that will penalize illegal migrants.

Similar issues are manifest at the U.S.–Canada border, although the agenda has largely been less volatile and has been framed in terms of perceptions that Canada's immigration policies are lax. The fallacious belief that the 9/11 terrorists entered the United States through Canada continues to fuel this perception. As a result, Canada no longer retains special exemptions regarding border crossing. For example, while Canadians were initially exempt from the Western Hemisphere Travel Initiative (WHTI), introduced in 2004, it has been extended to Canadians as of June 2009 so that a passport (or equivalent document) is now required at the land border.[14] This is despite the great efforts that Canada has made in immigration reform to address U.S. concerns (Gilbert 2005, 2007). One such example is the Canada–U.S. Safe Third Country Agreement (STCA), which came into effect in December 2004 as part of the Smart Border Action Plan. The agreement requires that asylum claimants at the Canada–U.S. land border make their application in the 'safe' country of last presence. This effectively means that refugees who arrive first in the United States cannot make an asylum application in Canada, and vice versa. Since this is a provision only at the land border, the unstated intent is to prevent Mexican and Latin American migrants who have been refused asylum in the United States from turning to Canada for a second chance. Since its implementation there has been a dramatic reduction in claims at the land border (Aitken 2007, 190).

Migration advocates have raised many concerns regarding the abrogation of UN conventions on refugees, particularly on 'refoulement' (Macklin 2003). The border has thus been hardened towards refugees; at the same time, a de facto regional perimeter has been established that encompasses Canada and the United States – and that blocks out Mexico. This was entrenched when, on 13 July 2009, Minister of Citizenship Jason Kenney announced that effective immediately, Mexican nationals would require a visa to enter Canada, bringing its visa policy in line with that of the United States. The rationale for this was the near tripling of refugee claims from Mexico since 2005: 9,400 applications in 2008, comprising 25% of total refugee applicants. This has shifted the burden of management offshore and has also limited who can get to Canada, thereby pre-empting opportunities for asylum applications.

Canada–Mexico relations have soured since the announcement of Canada's new visa policy. Prime Minister Harper has sought to patch up the relationship by announcing more security training and cooperation (discussed above). Another initiative is a Memorandum of Understanding on Youth Mobility that will enable 'eligible' youth from both countries to live and work abroad for a year. This is yet another example of specialized mobility agreements of the sort that are proliferating across the continent. The Youth Mobility program, like the temporary worker programs for seasonal labourers that draw thousands of Mexicans to Canada every year, provides a time-limited and highly constrained form of mobility, with no opportunity for participants to apply for status. Temporary labour programs have been promoted in documents such as the SPP as a mechanism to offset domestic labour shortages without encouraging permanent migration (Gilbert 2007). There is a voluminous literature that points to the discriminatory aspects of these programs, particularly in terms of race and gender (e.g., Basok 2002; Stasiulis and Bakan 2003; Sharma 2006). At the other end of the spectrum is a push to expand 'trusted traveller' programs between Canada and the United States. At their November 2009 meetings, Napolitano and Van Loan announced that the NEXUS and Free and Secure Trade (FAST) programs would be expanded and would be available at all land and sea ports. Just over 9% of land crossings are by those enrolled in such programs; the aim is to double these numbers by 2009 (Neinast and James 2008). These programs entitle 'legitimate' travellers to expedited border crossing, using special lanes established at major air and land ports. They are designed for business people and professionals whose work requires frequent cross-border travel, as well as for businesses that rely on networks of cross-border shipping (Sparke 2006). Users are cleared and enrolled in security databases on both sides of the border and are issued with a biometric ID card that entitles them to swift border passage. Napolitano and Van Loan expect that the expansion of these programs will enable a more directed, targeted focus on 'risky' travellers, facilitated by new RFID (Radio Frequency Identification) technology in the membership cards.

The statements that have already been released on the proposed Canada–U.S. security perimeter indicate that biometric and pre-clearance programs will be expanded as the risk management strategy towards border security is being developed.[15] The Beyond the Border statement announces 'an integrated Canada-United States entry-exit system' that will use biometric information sharing to track the entry and exit of *all* visitors, regardless of privacy concerns. The Canadian government has released statements affirming that the perimeter security initiative will develop pre-clearance programs such as NEXUS and CANPASS to ensure the expedited movement of professional travellers, as well as business-oriented programs such as the Partners in Protection (PIP) program.[16] These initiatives will enhance cooperation with the Advance Passenger Information / Passenger Name Record (API/PNR) program, which enables airlines to pre-emptively target foreign nationals who are deemed a potential risk. Unless immigration and criminal legislation is harmonized across the two countries, security initiatives that target 'risky' subjects will not disappear with the implementation of a Canada–U.S. security perimeter. There has been some suspicion that harmonization is the intended – albeit unstated – outcome of this initiative. Such a shift would undermine Canada's historically more open immigration and refugee policies.

New mobility agreements point to a reconfiguration of the differential treatment of low- and high-skill workers under NAFTA that Christina Gabriel describes in her chapter in this volume. The temporary and expedited programs raise difficult questions regarding *how* the borders are being reconfigured and for *whom* (Gilbert 2007). They signal a move away from either/or scenarios – that is, *either* a national border *or* a regional perimeter – but they also suggest that borders are being reconfigured in complex ways that are discriminating against populations deemed 'risky.' One constant is that more and more preventative measures are being put in place to prevent migration from Mexico, or at least to constrain the terms under which that migration can take place, whether this involves the new visa requirements that

Canada has issued for Mexicans, or the fences that are being erected at the U.S.–Mexico border. Ultimately, then, the differentiations being instituted in North American migration policy that delineate between legitimate and 'illegitimate' bodies are being constituted in racialized terms. One result is that Latinos' lives are being made more vulnerable and insecure, both in Mexico and abroad.

Conclusions

This chapter has sought to highlight the complexities surrounding border security issues in North America. There is a constant tug of war between the hardening of internal borders and the push for deeper regional integration. The United States has sought to strengthen its border security and to bolster its national economy; meanwhile, Canada and Mexico have sought to ensure the continuity of regional economic integration and have made a multitude of security concessions to this end. There is thus no clear sense of the region as an emergent political community. There is greater de facto convergence on security and immigration policies, and even harmonization and interoperability; yet almost no regional political structure is in place, nor is there any shared sense of legitimacy and accountability. Especially since Obama's election, the tendency has been towards instrumental bilateral agreements on specific issues, rather than shared governance or a concern for common public interest.

Moreover, as I have illustrated with respect to migration policies, even though there has been some coordination around policy, there is no sense of common citizenship or belonging across the three nation-states. The SPP's rhetoric around shared values has not been realized; neither has the nascent concept of shared community. Rather, Mexicans continue to be treated in discriminatory ways, with more and more impediments constraining their regional mobility. New migration policies have instilled a democratic deficit, since migrants are without citizenship rights, and this has stymied any sense of shared community or belonging. With respect to border security and migration, the discrepancy between federal and subnational governance also poses a challenge to collective belonging. Subnational innovations around border security and attitudes towards immigration are shaping discourses in ways that are often antithetical to a national rhetoric. This cross-purpose activity across different sectors is a further indication of the complexities surrounding border security in North America. As concerns over border security continue to shape inter-state relations across North America, this complexity needs to be drawn clearly into view so that we may better understand the often contradictory pressures that are being exerted, particularly with respect to the mobility of populations. It is only in doing so that we will be able to delineate clearly not only the full impact of border securitization, but also the insecurities that are generated on the ground for certain groups of people.

Notes

1 The Canada–U.S. Smart Border Accord is available at http://www.dfait-maeci.gc.ca/anti-terrorism/declaration-en.asp.
2 The statement is available at http://www.state.gov/r/pa/prs/ps/2010/03/138926.htm.
3 Website of the Prime Minister of Canada, http://www.pm.gc.ca/eng/media.asp?category=1&pageId=26&id=3931.
4 John Ibbitson and Steven Chase, 'Harper and Obama Eye Sweeping Change in Border Security,' *Globe and Mail*, 4 February 2011, http://m.theglobeandmail.com/news/politics/harper-and-obama-eye-sweeping-change-in-border-security/article1891143/?service=mobile.
5 Government of Canada, 'Extension of Public Consultation Period on Shared Vision for Canada–U.S. Perimeter Security and Economic Competitiveness,' http://www.borderactionplan-plandactionfrontalier.gc.ca/psec-scep/news-communiques-20110513.aspx?lang=eng.
6 The violent sentiment against undocumented migrants in the United States was clearly visible in Sensenbrenner bill, which proposed not only to erect more fences, but also to end the catch-and-release of undocumented workers, to make 'illegal' immigration a felony, and to eliminate the ability of cities to offer sanctuary to migrants. The bill passed in the U.S. House of Representatives but was defeated in the Senate. It was nonetheless a crucial fulcrum for mobilizing more than one million protesters in the 'Day without Immigrants' protests of May 2006 (Pulido 2007).
7 Details on the Anti-Crime Capacity Building Program are available at http://pm.gc.ca/eng/media.asp?id=2722.
8 'U.S. Security Boss Clarifies Comments about Border,' http://www.ctv.ca/servlet/ArticleNews/story/CTVNews/20090421/USA_Border_090421/20090421.
9 U.S. Government Accountability Office (2010), 'Border Security: Enhanced DHS Oversight and Assessment of Interagency Coordination Is Needed for the Northern Border,' http://www.gao.gov/new.items/d1197.pdf.

10 'Canada–U.S. Framework Agreement on Integrated Cross-Border Maritime Law Enforcement Operations,' http://www.publicsafety.gc.ca/prg/le/_fl/int-cross-brdr-martime-eng.pdf.

11 The full name of Bill C-60 is 'An Act to implement the Framework Agreement on Integrated Cross-Border Maritime Law Enforcement Operations between the Government of Canada and the Government of the United States of America.' http://www2.parl.gc.ca/Content/LOP/LegislativeSummaries/40/2/c60-e.pdf.

12 Details on the Civil Assistance Plan are available at the website of Canadian National Defence, http://www.canadacom.forces.gc.ca/docs/pdf/cap_e.pdf.

13 The American Civil Liberties Union documentation is available at 'Fact Sheet on U.S. "Constitution Free Zone,"' http://www.aclu.org/technology-and-liberty/fact-sheet-us-constitution-free-zone.

14 WHTI-compliant enhanced drivers' licences have been permitted. Notably, they have been thanks to provincial and state innovation. They were issued first in B.C. and then also in Ontario and Quebec. The states of Washington, Vermont, Arizona, and New York will also produce parallel documents.

15 Available at the Prime Minister of Canada website, 'Beyond the Border: A Shared Vision for Perimeter Security and Economic Competitiveness,' http://pm.gc.ca/eng/media.asp?id=3938. Last accessed 22 November 2011.

16 Available at the Government of Canada 'Canada News Centre' website: 'The Canada–U.S. Border: A Partnership That Works,' http://news.gc.ca/web/article-eng.do?m=/index&nid=587809.

References

Ackleson, Jason. 2009. 'From "Thin" to "Thick" (and Back Again?): The Politics and Policies of the Contemporary Canada–U.S. Border.' *American Review of Canadian Studies* 39, no. 4: 336–51.

– 2005. 'Constructing Security on the U.S.–Mexico Border.' *Political Geography* 24: 165–84.

Aiken, Sharryn J. 2007. 'Risking Rights: An Assessment of Canadian Border Security Politics.' In *Whose Canada? Continental Integration, Fortress North America, and the Corporate Agenda*. Edited by Ricardo Grinspun and Yasmine Shamsie. Montreal and Kingston: McGill–Queen's University Press. 180–208.

Amoore, Louise. 2006. 'Biometric Borders: Governing Mobilities in the War on Terror.' *Political Geography* 25: 336–51.

Andreas, Peter. 2009. *Border Games: Policing the US-Mexico Divide*, 2nd ed. Ithaca: Cornell University Press.

– 2005. 'The Mexicanization of the US–Canada Border: Asymmetric Interdependence in a Changing Security Context.' *International Journal* 60, no. 2: 449–62.

Ayres, Jeffrey, and Laura Macdonald. 2006. 'Deep Integration and Shallow Governance: The Limits to Civil Society Engagement across North America.' *Policy and Society* 25, no. 3: 23–42.

Ayres, Jeffrey, and Laura Macdonald, eds. 2009. *Contentious Politics in North America: National Protest and Transnational Collaboration under Continental Integration*. Basingstoke: Palgrave Macmillan.

Balibar, Etienne. 1998. 'The Borders of Europe.' Translated by James Swenson. In *Cosmopolitics: Thinking and Feeling beyond the Nation*. Edited by Pheng Cheah and Bruce Robbins. Minneapolis: University of Minnesota Press. 216–33.

Basok, Tanya. 2002. *Tortillas and Tomatoes: Transmigrant Mexican Harvesters in Canada*. Montreal and Kingston: McGill–Queen's University Press.

Baughman, Laura M., and Joseph F. Francois. 2009. 'Trade Action – or Inaction: The Cost for American Workers and Families.' 15 September. Washington: U.S. Chamber of Commerce. http://www.uschamber.com/sites/default/files/reports/uscc_trade_action_inaction_study.pdf. Accessed 7 November 2011.

Bigo, Didier. 2002. 'Security and Immigration: Toward a Critique of the Governmentality of Unease.' *Alternatives: Global, Local, Political* 27 (February): 63–92.

Brewer, Stephanie Erin. 2008. 'Rethinking the Mérida Initiative: Why the U.S. Must Change Course in Its Approach to Mexico's Drug War.' http://www.humansecuritygateway.com/documents/HRB_rethinkingthemeridainitiative.pdf. Accessed 14 September 2011.

Castro-Rea, Julián. 2009. 'North American Politics after September 11: Security, Democracy. and Sovereignty.' In *Contentious Politics in North America: National Protest and Transnational Collaboration under Continental Integration*. Edited by Jeffrey Ayres and Laura Macdonald. Basingstoke: Palgrave Macmillan. 35–53.

Clarkson, Stephen. 2001. 'After the Catastrophe: Canada's Position in North America.' *Behind the Headlines* 58, no. 3: 1–10.

Clarkson, Stephen, and Antonio Torres-Ruiz. 2009. 'The Globalized Complexities of Transborder Governance in North America.' In *Contentious Politics in North America: National Protest and Transnational Collaboration under Continental Integration*. Edited by Jeffrey Ayres and Laura Macdonald. Basingstoke: Palgrave Macmillan. 155–76.

Coleman, Mathew. 2007a. 'A Geopolitics of Engagement: Neoliberalism, the War on Terrorism, and the Reconfiguration of U.S. Immigration Enforcement.' *Geopolitics* 12: 607–34.

– 2007b. 'Immigration Geopolitics beyond the Mexico-U.S. Border.' *Antipode* 39, no. 1: 54–76.

Díez, Jordi. 2008. 'Mexico and North American Security.' In *Big Picture Realities: Canada and Mexico at the Crossroads*. Edited by Daniel Drache. Waterloo: Wilfrid Laurier University Press. 153–68.

Doty, Roxanne Lynn. 2009. *The Law into Their Own Hands: Immigration and the Politics of Exceptionalism*. Tuscon: University of Arizona Press.

Drache, Daniel, ed. 2008. *Big Picture Realities: Canada and Mexico at the Crossroads*. Waterloo: Wilfrid Laurier University Press.

Gilbert, Emily. 2007. 'Leaky Borders and Solid Citizens: Governing Security, Prosperity, and Quality of Life in a North American Partnership.' *Antipode* 39, no. 1: 77–98.

– 2005. 'The Inevitability of Integration? Neoliberal Discourse and the Proposals for a New North American Economic Space after September 11.' *Annals of the Association of American Geographers* 95, no. 1: 202–2.

Gilbert, Liette. 2009. 'Immigration as Local Politics: Re-Bordering Immigration and Multiculturalism through Deterrence and Incapacitation.' *International Journal or Urban and Regional Research* 33, no. 1: 15–24.

Goldfarb, Danielle. 2007. *Reaching the Tipping Point: Effects of Post-9/11 Border Security on Canada's Trade and Investment*. Ottawa: Conference Board of Canada. http://www.internationaltransportforum.org/2009/pdf/CDN_TippingPoint.pdf. Last accessed 7 November 2011.

Jhappan, Radha, and Yasmeen Abu-Laban. 2008. 'Introduction.' In *Politics in North America: Redefining Continental Relations*. Edited by Radha Jhappan, Yasmeen Abu-Laban, and Francois Roçher. Peterborough: Broadview. 11–23.

Lyon, David, ed. 2002. *Surveillance as Social Sorting: Privacy, Risk, and Digital Discrimination*. London: Routledge.

Macklin, Audrey. 2003. *The Value(s) of the Canada–U.S. Safe Third Country Agreement*. Toronto: Caledon Institute of Social Policy. 1–23.

Muller, Benjamin. 2008. *Governing through Risk at the Canada/U.S. Border: Liberty, Security, Technology*. Border Policy Research Institute, Western Washington University.

Neinast, Brenna, and Michele James. 2008. Joint Statement of Brenna Neinast, Chief Patrol Agent, Havre Sector, U.S. Border Patrol, U.S. Customs and Border Protection, Department of Homeland Security and Michele James, Director of Field Operations, Seattle Field Office, Office of Field Operations, U.S. Customs and Border Protection, presented before the

Senate Homeland Security and Governmental Affairs Committee Regarding 'Northern Border Security,' 2 July 2008. At Senate Homeland Security and Governmental Affairs Committee, http://hsgac.senate.gov/public/_files/070208NeinastJames.pdf. Last accessed 7 November 2011.

Nevins, Joseph. 2009. *Operation Gatekeeper and Beyond: The War on 'Illegals' and the Remaking of the US–Mexico Boundary*. New York: Routledge.

– 2002. *Operation Gatekeeper: The Rise of the 'Illegal' Alien, and the Making of the US–Mexico Boundary*. New York: Routledge.

Olmedo, Carlos, and Dennis L. Soden. 2005. 'Terrorism's Role in Reshaping Border Crossings: 11 September and the U.S. Borders.' *Geopolitics* 10: 741–66.

Parker, Noel et al. 2009. 'Lines in the Sand? Towards an Agenda for Critical Border Studies.' *Geopolitics* 14, no. 3: 582–7.

Pastor, Robert. 2001. *Toward a North American Community: Lessons from the Old World for the New*. Washington: Institute for International Economics.

Poitras, Guy. 2001. *Inventing North America: Canada, Mexico, and the United States*. Boulder: Lynne Rienner.

Pulido, Laura. 2007. 'A Day without Immigrants: The Racial and Class Politics of Immigrant Exclusion.' *Antipode* 39, no. 1: 1–7.

Robertson, Colin. 2011.'"Now for the Hard Part": A User's Guide to Renewing the Canadian–American Partnership.' Canadian International Council, Strategic Studies Working Group. http://www.opencanada.org/features/reports/cic-working-group-reports/. Last accessed 7 November 2011.

Sharma, Nandita. 2006. *Home Economics: Nationalism and the Making of 'Migrant Workers' in Canada*. Toronto: University of Toronto Press.

Sparke, Matthew. 2005. 'A Neoliberal Nexus: Economy, Security, and the Biopolitics of Citizenship on the Border.' *Political Geography* 25, no. 2: 151–80.

Stasiulis, Daiva K., and Abigail B. Bakan. 2003 *Negotiating Citizenship: Migrant Women in Canada and the Global System*. Toronto: University of Toronto Press.

Thobani, Sunera. 2004. 'Exception as Rule: Profile of Exclusion.' *Signs* 29, no. 2: 597–600.

U.S. Government. 2009. *HR 4321* Comprehensive Immigration Reform ASAP Act of 2009. Introduced in House on 15 December 2009.

8 Continental Dissonance? The Politics of Migration in North America

CHRISTINA GABRIEL

The American television personality and comic, Stephen Colbert, appeared in 2010 before the U.S. House Subcommittee on Immigration – Citizenship and Border Security. Advocating for agricultural migrant workers' rights, he stated:

> I'm a free-market guy. Normally, I would leave this to the invisible hand of the market, but the invisible hand of the market has already moved over 84,000 acres of production and over 22,000 farm jobs to Mexico, and shut down over a million acres of U.S. farm land due to lack of available labour. Because apparently, even the invisible hand doesn't want to pick beans. Now, I'm not a fan of the government doing anything. But I've gotta ask, why isn't the government doing anything?[1]

He called for improvements to the legal status of migrant workers, arguing that immigration reform could afford a measure of protection against exploitation and abuse for these workers in the United States. It is unclear whether Colbert made an impact on the House subcommittee. However, his appearance and active participation in the United Farm Workers 2010 Campaign 'Take Our Jobs'[2] highlights the extent to which the issue of migration – in particular, irregular migration from Mexico to the United States – remains a critical issue in the American public debate.

This is one among many migration issues that are currently playing out across North American space. In contrast to processes of continental economic integration engendered by the North American Free Trade Agreement (NAFTA), migration is characterized by dissonance. This phenomenon was evident during the NAFTA negotiations, when Mexico's migration agenda was sidelined in an effort to secure the trade deal. The failure of Vicente Fox's administration to build on NAFTA to secure a better migration deal, and the recent failure of the Security and Prosperity Partnership of North America (SPP) to include migration, also underline how migration, though a concern for all three countries, has not been the focus of concerted trilateral initiatives. In many ways, migration politics has been characterized by the coupling of double bilateralism with statist agendas at the expense of a more robust continental cooperative migration regime that would ensure free mobility and that would be sensitive to human rights and democracy.

This chapter considers the impact of the recent economic crisis on existing migration patterns and policies in North America. It fits well within a 'new regionalism' approach to contribute to a more pluralistic understanding of North American regionalism. It argues that the immediate impact of the crisis and the responses of the NAFTA member-states in the area of migration underscore how migration politics continues to be marked by dissonances that have significant consequences for those most marginalized – North America's 'precarious residents.' This chapter opens with a brief discussion of some of the dynamics that frame migration politics in North America. This is followed by a brief overview of the asymmetries of continental migration. Together, these two sections frame an assessment of the impact of the economic crisis on migration politics in the region.

North American Asymmetries: Regions, Nations, and Citizens

NAFTA brought three countries into a regional trade agreement. However, processes of integration driven by trade and capital flows obscure the fact that people's mobility rights across the same space are secondary to economic imperatives. The façade of three equal member-states obfuscates the considerable differences between Canada and the United States on one hand and Mexico on the other. As Andrew Hurrell (2006, 561) puts it: 'It is a relationship characterized by extremely high levels of economic and societal interdependence; by high levels of deprivation in Mexico ... and by two rich and privileged partners well able to afford assistance. And yet there is a total absence of debate on even minimal duties of assistance or distributive justice.' For example, during his administration (2000–6), Mexican president Vicente Fox proposed a 'NAFTA Plus' model that would include, among other initiatives, monetary transfers from the north (Canada and the United

States) to the south (Mexico). Ultimately, this call for a robust vision of a North American community collapsed and Fox scaled back his ambitions (Miller and Gabriel 2008, 152–5).

In North America, the issue of migration raises a set of related dynamics that centre on citizenship distinctions *among* countries in a global political economy but also *within* countries. Here the work of Stephen Castles (2005) is useful. He draws attention to two aspects of citizenship associated with processes of globalization. First is the position of states in the new global order. For Castles, the post–Cold War period is marked by a departure from the 'bipolar system' characterized by the competition between the East and West (i.e., the Soviet Bloc and the United States) toward a North–South divide: 'This concept expresses not a geographical configuration but a political and social one. The main division is between the powerful and prosperous post-industrial nations ... and the less powerful and poorer countries of Africa, Asia and Latin America' (ibid., 211). In this context, the United States dominates both North and South and is surrounded by a 'hierarchy of states with varying levels of dependence on the centre and varying levels of power towards other states defined in terms of power (not geography)' (ibid., 211). Castles charts this phenomenon as a series of concentric circles of power or tiers, with the United States in the centre. Countries such as Canada and Australia, along with the European Union, occupy the next circle, while Mexico is farther yet from the centre. This hierarchy characterizes various types of international interactions, including international law, the rules of international trade, and the institutions of global governance (ibid., 214–15).

Second, and relatedly, Castles asserts that the hierarchy of states gives rise to forms of 'hierarchal citizenship,' with U.S. citizens enjoying a high level of formal rights as well as the benefits of democratic institutions. The same is true of citizens of other highly developed countries. But Castles acknowledges that even in these cases, there are minorities who do not necessarily enjoy full membership rights and whose status is a form of 'differentiated citizenship' (ibid., 215). Citizenship as a normative principle refers to inclusion – that is, to the right of each citizen to belong to one member-state. But in practice, there have always been groups that are positioned on the margins and that do not enjoy partial and/or full rights of national membership. Hierarchies of citizenship within nation-states interact with the international citizenship regime: 'Clearly origin in a country which is high in the international citizenship hierarchy is likely to lead to a high position in national hierarchies: few migrants from highly developed countries end up as undocumented migrants or asylum seekers' (ibid., 220).

The rights asymmetry that Castles alludes to is particularly clear in relation to mobility. Some citizens cross borders more easily than others. In terms of labour, countries in the global North have increasingly enacted border controls to keep out those constructed as less desirable – the low-skilled – while competing to attract the most desired – high-skilled workers (even though the former are in demand in many countries). Increasingly, restrictive migration control is being coupled with a demand for low-skilled workers, and this in turn is directly connected to the rise of undocumented migrant workers. For Castles, 'the hierarchy of citizenship helps to construct a *differentiated global labour force'* (ibid., 217). Within North America, the United States and Canada are clearly positioned differently than Mexico. This differential positioning is evident not only in terms of wealth, income, and GDP but also in the fact that Mexico is a *sending* country of migrants while the United States and Canada are clearly *receiving* countries. The ability of Mexico's citizens, including its high-skilled citizens, to cross North America often differs considerably from that of their northern counterparts (see Gabriel and Macdonald 2004).

Differentiation and stratification are becoming increasingly typical of migrant categories within host nations such as the United States and Canada, and this has given rise to multiple statuses. Matthew Gibney, for example, has argued that the 'consequences for ... rights, capability and human development' vary greatly across national contexts and groups of non-citizen migrants (2009–10, 2). Much like Castles, he emphasizes how high-skilled migrants to the global North may enjoy rights and privileges that are akin to those of citizens. In contrast, other non-citizens may find themselves with hardly any rights.

In a useful typology, Gibney refers to the latter groups as 'precarious residents.' He notes that these non-citizens share four characteristics:

- They hold fewer rights than citizens or permanent residents in the countries in which they live;
- They have a high level of vulnerability to deportation or expulsion;
- They have no (or only extremely limited) opportunities for transferring to a more secure immigration status (like citizenship or permanent residence);
- They are residing in the state in question, rather than simply visiting or transiting through it. (ibid., 10)

For Gibney, these groups of non-citizens are defined not by the situations that motivated their exit but by the conditions that constitute their status in host countries (ibid., 10). He notes that while the 'archetypal precarious resident' is the undocumented migrant, 'asylum seekers, guest workers, and individuals with temporary protection from deportation' also fall under this rubric (ibid., 2–3):

> 'Precarious residents' are some of the most vulnerable migrants in the world today. Practically, they may have little or no standing to claim even basic rights because in the eyes of state officials (and large sections of the public) they are *trespassers* with no right to be present in the state in the first place or *barely tolerated guests*, people whom the state is willing or legally obliged to host for a limited period (guest workers or asylum seekers) but who may not be seen as fit for full membership. (ibid., 3)

Thus, the presence of precarious residents raises broader questions of how membership in a national community is defined and practised (Bosniak 2000, 975–7).

In this regard, as Kristen Maher points out, the distinctions between citizen and alien are also about who can claim rights. In the case of migrant workers in the United States – especially low-skilled migrant workers – she argues that universal personhood is secondary to national citizenship as the basis of rights. She contends that this view of citizenship constructs it 'less in objective terms (as a legal status) than as a relational identity defined in opposition to "aliens," particularly in reference to labour migrants from less developed states' (Maher 2002, 21). According to Maher, two discursive rationales situate migrant workers as not having a legitimate claim to rights. The first of these is framed by liberal conceptions of contract and property: 'Liberal thought permits an opposition between contract makers who have legitimate claims to resources and spaces of the public sphere in "their" state and migrants, who, in contrast, are perceived as having forfeited any claims to rights, as criminal invaders, trespassers or usurpers of "privately" held resources' (ibid., 30).

But equally significant is the second rationale, which positions aliens as less entitled to rights than citizens. This reflects a racialized division of labour; it also links First World status with greater entitlement to rights (ibid., 21). Here she highlights three common discourses: that it is temporary workers' home states, not the host countries, that are responsible for safeguarding migrant rights; that labour relations are confined to private arrangements between individual workers and individual employers in the *economic* realm, not the political one; and that the compromising of migrant workers' rights is justified by the supposedly poor conditions in home countries. This discourse, she writes, 'suggests that workers migrating from less developed states must be in desperate circumstances in which they do not or should not expect the human rights to which those from the First World are entitled' (ibid., 35).

Continental regional integration is implicated in the revitalization of debates around race and identity. Within North America, the two rationales that Maher sketches – liberal understandings of property and contract, and neocolonial views – find expression in the situation of precarious residents, namely, irregular migrants and low-skilled temporary workers. According to Hurrell, the view that rights belong to citizens is coupled with a 'depressing lack of concern with the rights of "aliens"; both within the borders and around its periphery, including those who die seeking entry or whose rights are systematically abused in adjacent areas (most obviously Guantanamo)' (2006, 562). He further charges that Canada has sided with the United States 'in remaining outside the regional human rights regime' (ibid.). The next sections explore the dynamics outlined above and consider the extent to which these dynamics have been exacerbated in a time of a global recession.

Patterns of Migration in North America[3]

Migration flows within North America are characterized by two parallel dynamics: Mexico–United States and United States–Canada. In each case the United States is the 'strongest pole of attraction,' just as it is in the hemisphere as a whole (O'Neil, Hamilton, and Papademetriou 2005, 3). Migration dynamics mirror the broader pattern of 'double bilateralism' (see the chapter by Golob this volume). There are few if any trilateral regional institutions to govern continental migration. The double bilateralism that characterizes North American migration coexists – sometimes uneasily – with the more statist dynamics that frame the three NAFTA members' migration policies and regulations. This section sketches some of the key trends characterizing North American migration. It discusses how in many ways, migration in North America epitomizes some of the broader tendencies in global labour migration. Yet developments in migration policies and practices in the region also make it clear that non-citizens (primarily Mexicans) are precarious residents in the other member countries.

Within the global flows of people, some tendencies are particularly noteworthy, according to the OECD (Keeley 2009). First, migration has been rising: in 2005, almost 190 million people (3% of the world's population) were international migrants – that is, they were living outside their country of birth. Second, the impact of cross-border migration is uneven: there has been a shift to the global North, with 'an increasing concentration of international migrants in the developed world' (UN 2009, xiv). Third, it is now recognized that migration is a key element of globalization and that in a national context, migrants play a critical role in stimulating economic growth. 'In the years to come this is likely to translate into increasing competition, especially between developed countries, for highly skilled migrants' (Keeley 2009, 31). These tendencies are certainly evident within the North American region.

Yet the liberalization of trade and investment that characterizes economic globalization has not been accompanied by freedom of movement. More than one social theorist has observed this. Ruhs (2005) has written that the 'asymmetry in the globalization process' is reflected in the actions of countries in the global North that have pushed for trade liberalization even while restricting labour migration. He points out that there are no institutions to govern the liberalization of international labour flows in the same manner as those that govern trade (2005, 12). This tendency is evident within North America. In relation to the United States and Mexico, Andreas (1998) has observed that 'even as the North American Free Trade Agreement (NAFTA) promotes a deterritorialization of the economy, U.S. border control initiatives reinforce state claims to territorial authority. Thus, the apparent paradox of U.S.–Mexico integration is that a barricaded border and a borderless economy are being created simultaneously' (1998, 593). Regional economic integration has not resulted in a trilateral migration regime. Migration in North America is still governed largely by statist agendas and priorities except for some limited mobility provisions within NAFTA.

Asymmetries, Migration, NAFTA, and the North American Region

Sending versus Receiving Countries

Canada and the United States are traditional immigrant-receiving countries. In absolute numbers, the United States is the biggest recipient of permanent immigrants: some 1.2 million in 2006 (OECD 2009,

32). Both Canadian and U.S. migration regimes were once marked by exclusions based on explicit racial criteria. Despite their common origins as settler societies, the policies and practices governing immigration to the two countries have diverged considerably (Woroby 2007, 252). The United States has prioritized family unification in its program and operates a 'demand-driven, employer-led labor market immigration system' (Papademetriou et al. 2009a, 6). In contrast, Canada admits skilled worker immigrants through a points-based selection model and prioritizes economic-class immigrants over others, such as family class members and those in the humanitarian category. As Woroby notes: 'The result of these diverging positions in immigration selection is that approximately two-thirds of immigrants entering the United States do so on the basis of family reunification criteria and only one-fifth because of their skills. In contrast, some 60 per cent of immigrants entering Canada do so based on their skill levels and only one quarter because of family reunification criteria' (2007, 252).

The sources of permanent immigrants to the two countries differ as well. Many immigrants to the United States come from the Western Hemisphere, most notably Mexico (ibid., 251). In contrast, the top three source countries for Canada in 2008 were China, India, and the Philippines (CIC 2008a). Mexico does not place among the top ten sources of immigrants to Canada, whereas the United States does. Additionally, no single source country dominates the flow of immigrants to Canada in the same manner as Mexico does vis-à-vis the United States (Woroby 2007, 251).

In 2005, migrants accounted for 12.9% of the U.S. population and 18.9% of Canada's but only 0.6% of Mexico's[4] (UN 2009). This reflects the fact that the United States and Canada are traditional receiving countries whereas Mexico is a sending nation. According to Terrazas (2010), 'in 2008 there were 11.4 million Mexican immigrants in the United States, accounting for 30.1% of all U.S. immigrants, and 10% of all Mexicans.' More than half of all Mexican immigrants are residing in the United States illegally. In contrast, the Mexican immigrant population in Canada is minimal: 50,000 people in 2006 (Alba 2010, citing Statistics Canada). Quite similarly, the Canadian population in Mexico is estimated to be 75,000 (Canada–Mexico Initiative 2010, 9).

'Skilled' versus 'Low-skilled' Migrant Labour[5]

Migration flows and the regulation of migration within North America point to another strong tendency in international global migration: the dichotomy between 'skilled' and 'low-skilled' migrant labour, with the latter accounting for the majority of global migration flows. However, 'high- and low-skilled immigrants now represent equal shares of migrants to the 30 countries that compose the Organisation for Economic Cooperation and Development, the so-called club of wealthy nations' (Fix et al. 2009, 2). 'Skilled' and 'high-skilled' labour is constructed as something that enhances a nation's global competitiveness. More and more countries now perceive themselves as having joined a global hunt for talent (cf. Kapur and McHale 2005; Kuptsch and Pang 2006). These countries are developing programs to target and facilitate the entry of some desired groups – most notably the 'high-skilled. Simultaneously, they are directing more rigourous control measures at low skilled workers or keeping them out entirely.

In North America the dichotomy between 'skilled' and 'low-skilled' is significant and overlaps with and reinforces the double-bilateral relationship. The linkages between Canada and the United States are on the 'high-skilled' side of the labour market, while Mexico and the United States are more closely tied to the 'less-skilled' end. These linkages are driven by business needs rather than states' actions (Meyers and O'Neil 2004, 46). The existing migration architecture that governs labour mobility, whether continental or statist, privileges high-skilled workers. That is, high-skilled workers and professionals are privileged insofar as they can access NAFTA's provisions and are eligible to apply for entry through permanent resident streams such as the United States' employment-based preferences or Canada's skilled worker category.

There are also specific temporary visas aimed at high-skilled workers – for example, the U.S. H-1B Visa. That visa, introduced as part of the U.S. Immigration Act of 1990, was designed for jobs that 'require theoretical and practical application of highly specialized knowledge to perform fully' (USvisanow 2009, cited by Cerna 2010, 15). The number of such visas was set at 65,000 a year in 2003 (with an additional 20,000 visas for migrant workers with U.S. graduate degrees) (ibid., 15). The recently introduced Canada Experience Class (CEC) category also offers 'skilled' temporary workers a path to permanent resident status. In contrast, the mobility avenues available to 'low-skilled' migrant workers in North America are highly restricted, as is their access to citizenship.

Note that Mexican migrants are found at both ends of the skills spectrum. In the United States, for example, '61.5% of the 9.2 million

Mexican-born adults age 25 and older had no high school diploma or the equivalent general education diploma (GED) compared to 32.5% among all foreign born adults.' Yet at the same time, Mexico was the fourth source country after India, the Philippines, and China of high-skilled migrants to the United States (Terrazas 2010). The skills mix may be a factor in why immigration to Canada from Mexico is low. It is speculated that Mexican migrants do not meet the current criteria of Canada's selection model, which emphasizes higher education (Woroby 2007, 254).

NAFTA

In 2004, the tenth anniversary of NAFTA's ratification, it was observed that the 'trilateral strategy for managing North American migration begins and ends with NAFTA which slightly expanded on migration arrangements made under the 1988 Canada–US Free Trade Agreement and extended some of them to Mexico' (Meyers and O'Neil 2004, 46). This remains true. NAFTA, like many other regional trade agreements, does contain provisions governing mobility. But in contrast to the EU provisions, NAFTA's clauses are restricted to two short sections: Chapter 2 and Chapter 16. This reflects the fact that migration issues were detached from trade issues early in the NAFTA negotiations. The lack of comprehensive migration provisions has been characterized as a 'false dichotomy,' given the close historical ties and geographical proximity of the United States and Mexico (Johnson 1994, 942).

Moreover, a racial discourse imbued the NAFTA ratification debate in the United States. That debate was framed by 'subtle racism and ethnocentrism' (ibid., 952). Johnson points out that among those who pushed for a restrictive immigration policy, some, such as Ross Perot, appealed to nationalist and nativist views:

> [Perot's] suggestion that most Mexicans work for less than human wages and live in substandard conditions played into deeply held stereotypes about Mexican people. The claim that Mexican citizens would work for 'inhuman' wages places their very humanity in question and accentuates the perceived differences between 'us' and 'them.' Similarly the focus on weak environmental controls in Mexico enforced by corrupt government officials plays on popular stereotypes of the corrupt, dirty Mexican. (ibid., 951–2)

Johnson goes on to note that anti-NAFTA positions centred on the characteristics of Mexico and its citizens. In many ways this discourse continues to frame U.S. debates on irregular migration. It should be pointed out that nowhere in the ratification debate did opponents in the United States raise questions about the loss of American jobs to the other member country, Canada. Johnson attributes this to the congruence between Canada and the United States in terms of wealth, class structure, history, and demography (ibid., 952–3). Initially, Canadians were not concerned about NAFTA's impact on migration. In the late 1990s, however, concerns were expressed that skilled Canadian professionals might be lost to the United States (Gabriel and Macdonald 2004, 83).

NAFTA bestows the privilege of mobility on certain select citizens of the three member countries. Under the Chapter 16 provisions, temporary entry is facilitated for four categories of business people: business visitors, professionals, intra-company transferees, and traders and investors. A professional, for example, must:

- be qualified to work in one of the more than sixty professions listed in Appendix 1603.D.1 of Chapter 16 (e.g., accountant, computer systems analyst, engineer, management consultant, technical publications writer); *and*
- have prearranged employment with a Canadian enterprise in an occupation that matches the qualification (CIC 2009).

The professions in Chapter 16's appendix fall into the 'skilled' or 'high-skilled' category. Most of them require higher levels of education (baccalaureate degree, post-secondary diploma or certificate) and, in some instances, a provincial licence and/or three years of relevant experience (ITC 2004, 9–11). NAFTA's provisions have effectively facilitated the entry of the 'high-skilled' while sidelining those considered low-skilled (Gabriel and Macdonald 2004).

NAFTA's provisions gave the appearance that each of the three member countries could expect to be treated the same (ibid., 78). But in practice this did not happen, reflecting Castle's point about a 'hierarchy of citizenship.' In the first ten years of the agreement, the United States imposed a quota on the number of Mexican professionals who could enter the country under Chapter 16's provisions (ibid., 79). Also, the rules for obtaining a visa for the United States differ for Mexicans and Canadians. Mexican citizens must do the following:

The employer has to present a letter of employment stating the position in question requires the professional capacities stipulated in Chapter 16, Annex 1603 of NAFTA. The applicant for his or her part must submit to the United States Consul a letter of offer of professional employment describing the activity to be performed, the purpose of entry and the duration of the stay, together with evidence of the worker's professional status. (Alarcón 2007, 253)

In contrast to the rules governing the entry of Mexican professionals under NAFTA's terms, the rules for Canadians are more liberal. Canadians do not need a visa to enter the United States and can obtain the TN visa at port of entry.

As Alarcón has underscored, what is interesting about this type of visa regime is that while Mexico receives the most 'NAFTA workers' of the three member countries, it sends the fewest. He speculates that this is related to language issues and to there being more professionals in Canada and the United States. Furthermore, there is more Canadian and U.S. investment in Mexico than vice versa. In other words, corporate decision making is playing a key role in the cross-border movement of skilled professionals (Alcarcón 2007, 253–4).

In sum, NAFTA has provided a measure of continental mobility for some select groups: high-skilled professionals, traders and investors, and intracompany transferees. But even these limited provisions are underpinned by continental asymmetries, in that Mexican professionals are treated differently by both the United States and Canada.[6] NAFTA's trilateral provisions exist alongside a statist migration architecture. And those provisions do not supplant domestic immigration policy: 'NAFTA authorizes each member state to restrict immigration from other member nations into its territory and to take whatever steps necessary to ensure border security' (Johnson 1994, 941). As of this writing, NAFTA visas apply to only a small percentage of border crossers. A last point: NAFTA with its emphasis on trade and investment has not provided a space for alternative visions of integration. The more privileged partners, Canada and the United States, have shown little desire to extend development aid to Mexico, and/or to liberalize their mobility policies, on the basis of sharing the continent.

North America's Precarious Residents

A number of non-citizen groups in North America fall under the rubric of 'precarious residents.' It is beyond the scope of this chapter to fully consider all such groups that meet Gibney's schema. That said, two groups are especially noteworthy as they relate to the politics of North American migration insofar as they exemplify migration relationships among the three countries.

Low-Skilled Temporary Work Programs: Canada-Mexico Seasonal Agricultural Workers Program (SAWP)

Both the United States and Canada have visa programs for low-skilled temporary agricultural workers. These workers are recruited from Mexico, Central America, and the Caribbean. Here is one of the clearest examples of the workings of what Castles has termed a differentiated global labour force within North America: Canada and the United States, two countries in the global North, are drawing on a labour force from the global South, Mexico, to provide the agricultural sector with not just 'low cost labour, but also a particular type of labour that through the denial of citizenship can be made more "reliable" than even the most socially vulnerable domestic supplies' (Preibisch and Santamaria 2006, 110). The U.S. program of H-2A visas dates back to 1952, when migrant workers were recruited from Jamaica to work in Florida's sugar cane fields and to harvest apples along the eastern seaboard. Today, now that the sugar cane harvest has been mechanized, most H-2A workers are Mexicans working in 'tobacco and vegetables such as cucumbers and onions in the southeastern states' (Martin 2008, 20). Employer demand for H-2A workers has been increasing: 'Between FY98 and FY07, the number of employers certified to employ H-2A workers more than doubled, from 3,200 to 7,500 and the number of jobs certified to be filled by H-2A workers rose from 35,000 to 77,000.' While most workers return at the end of the contract, a significant number do not (ibid., 19–20).

The Canadian SAWP program functions under a set of bilateral agreements between the Canadian state and Mexico and the Caribbean countries. The program dates back to 1966, when Canada signed an agreement with Jamaica. Mexico followed in 1974. At that time, 203 Mexican workers were participating in the program; by 2010, this number had grown to 15,809 (Becerril Quintana 2011). Mexican workers dominate the SAWP program, with the majority of them working in Ontario (UFCW and AWA 2008–9, 8). Mexican women also participate in SAWP, albeit in much smaller numbers – 609 workers in 2010. A large proportion of male migrant workers are married, whereas the women 'are generally single mothers and divorced, separated or widowed women, with children whom they are still raising' (Becerril Quintana 2011). The different experiences of men and women under the SAWP and in the migration process more generally are now being considered through the prism of social relations such as gender (see Preibisch and Encalada Grez 2010).

There are a number of similarities between the H-2A program and the SAWP, notwithstanding that the former is three times larger. Chief among these is that employers in both the United States and Canada request migrant workers in situations where there is a shortage of domestic labour. However, the H-2A program is highly controversial. Martin points out that 'the H-2A program generates employer complaints because it is more bureaucratic than hiring irregular workers' (2008, 18). In contrast, the SAWP has been hailed as a model of best practice (see Hennebry and Preibisch 2010) on the basis of its administration and design, in which both farm employers and states are involved (Martin, Abella, and Kuptsch 2006, 113). Yet the SAWP still renders non-citizen Mexican migrant workers as precarious residents in Canada. It is useful, then, to briefly consider the ramifications of this form of temporary regional mobility.

The Canadian program allows migrant workers to enter the country for a specified period – anywhere from four to eight months – and to work ten to twelve hours, six days a week (Mueller 2005, 44). The Mexican government is responsible for managing labour recruitment and for monitoring the conditions of work. Employers must guarantee hours of work and provide room and board. There are penalties attached to hiring unauthorized workers and for 'lending' migrant workers to other farm employers (Martin et al. 2006, 112). At the end of the period, migrant workers must return home; there are no mechanisms for changing their status to permanent resident. According to Basok (2007), 'the overstay rate among SAWP workers is negligible ... [A 2006] World Bank report estimates it to be 1.5 percent.'

The SAWP circumscribes the mobility and rights of migrant agricultural workers and places them at a disadvantage vis-à-vis employers. The visa ties them to one specific employer and workplace. Loss of employment usually leads to deportation. These limits and other instruments of control have led scholars to characterize this form of labour as 'unfree' (see Trumper and Wong 2007; Preibisch and Santamaria 2006). Additionally, scholars and activists have identified the ways in which the program gives power and control to farm employ-ers, effectively reducing migrant workers' bargaining power. The requirement to live in employer-provided accommodation gives the employer greater access and control over workers' lives. In addition to the threat of deportation should employment be lost, employers can formally 'name' workers for work in subsequent years; this fosters 'a high degree of worker self-discipline, shores up worker loyalty and ultimately reinforces paternalistic labour relations' (Preibisch and San-tamaria 2006, 111).

Despite being temporary migrant workers, employees who utilize the SAWP are required to meet some social rights obligations, and the workers have certain rights. The workers must pay up their Canadian Employment Insurance (EI), Canada Pension (CP), and income tax. In theory, migrant workers are eligible for provincial health care and workers' compensation. In this respect, the rights available to SAWP workers are more extensive than those provided to their U.S. counter-parts in the H-2A program. The story is more complicated in practice, for the ability to realize rights rests in part on knowledge of those rights and on having a secure position from which to claim them (Gabriel and Macdonald 2011). SAWP workers in Canada are 'precarious residents' in that their rights are fewer and have also been curtailed relative to those of Canadians. Moreover, they are vulnerable to deportation, and there are no mechanisms for them to access a more secure status such as permanent residence. Their precarious position stands at odds with the SAWP program's construction as a best practice model.

Irregular Migrants

There are fewer 'irregular' migrants in Canada relative to the United States. Estimates place the irregular population in the United States at around 10.8 million in January 2009. While that population includes migrants from a variety of source countries such as China, Brazil, Hon-duras, and Ecuador (Chishti and Bergeron 2010), a critical proportion of this population is Mexican. (Some are Canadian.) Much like low-skilled migrant workers on H-2A or SAWP participants, these non-citizens in the United States are precarious residents. As was made clear by Stephen Colbert's appearance before the U.S. subcommittee, the issue of irregu-lar migration not only dominates U.S. policy debates and public opinion but also plays a role in the highly politicized immigration debate more generally. In Canada, this is much less true. First, the undocumented population in Canada is much smaller. Estimates place it at 200,000 to 500,000, and questions have been raised about how this population should be defined. 'There is an absence of systematic empirical analyses' (Goldring, Berinstein, and Bernhard 2009, 242). Second, debates in the United States often focus on those who clandestinely cross the Mexico–U.S. land border (ibid., 245; OECD 2006). Most unauthorized migrants to Canada do not normally enter in such a manner; 'rather than unauthorized land entry, other pathways to illegality and precarious immigration status are more common' (ibid 246): family sponsorship breakdown, visa change/expiration in the case of temporary workers, or a change in refugee status (Goldring et al. 2009, 248–50). These are the reasons why the issue of irregular migration tends to be positioned very differently on the Canadian and U.S. policy agendas and why there is little common ground on this issue between the two countries. As Goldring and colleagues write: 'In Canada, migrant illegality is largely a non-issue and certainly not a significant research area. Public debate regarding immigration may address immigrant integration, the non-recognition of foreign credentials, the refugee determination backlog or sector-specific labour shortages' (2009, 240). Nevertheless, it would be useful to briefly consider the status of Mexicans in the United States as 'precarious residents,' because this issue dominates the migration agendas of two of the three NAFTA partners and has, it follows, important implications for the broader bilateral and regional agendas.

Most of the unauthorized irregular migrants in the United States are from Mexico. It is estimated that Mexicans account for 62% (6,650,000) of unauthorized migrants in that country. This figure has increased since 2000 by some 42% (Terrazas 2010). The Pew Hispanic Center reports: 'Mexicans accounted for more than three-quarters of all unauthorized immigrants in Arkansas, California, Colorado, Idaho, Indiana, Mississippi, Nevada, Oregon, Texas and Wisconsin. They accounted for 90 percent or more of unauthorized immigrants in Arizona, Colorado and New Mexico' (cited by Terrazas 2010).

As Gibney points out, these people's status prohibits them from working legally. Nevertheless, they work primarily in in construction, manufacturing, agriculture, and services. If they come to the notice of authorities, they are vulnerable to expulsion; if they used false documents to obtain employment, they have committed a more serious crime. Irregular migrants are not eligible for social services such as welfare, unemployment benefits, or public housing. The insecurity of this population is increased further by the actions of the Department of Homeland Security, which 'has undertaken vigorous new efforts to locate and deport undocumented migrants, adding to a new wave of insecurity amongst unlawfully present populations that has forced many to limit interaction with the authorities even further' (Gibney 2009–10, 13). This phenomenon is related to the broader securitization of borders and border control (see the chapter by Gilbert in this volume).

A Tale of Two States: Canada and the United States

As Germain discusses in his contribution to this volume, the 2008 economic crisis started in the United States and then went global. Thus the present recession is markedly different from previous times of economic turbulence, such as the 1970s oil shocks. It has been argued that this crisis 'has had a deeper and more global effect on migration than any other economic downturn in the post-World War II era' (Migration Information Source 2009). That said, the impact of the recession has varied between countries and regions.

Conventional wisdom suggests that migration should fall during a recession and that non-citizens return to their home countries in the absence of sufficient jobs and/or state incentives. However, effects vary considerably by the type of migrant flow – permanent, temporary, irregular, humanitarian – between sending and receiving countries,and in terms of the region in the world (Fix et al. 2010, 2). This section uses some of the asymmetrical migration dynamics discussed earlier as markers to consider the impact of the economic crisis on migration within the North American region. It is here that continental dissonance becomes most apparent. The settler societies of the United States and Canada have pursued their own migration paths during the global recession. Many of North America's most precarious residents are Mexicans in the United States, and these non-citizens have navigated the crisis in some unexpected ways as well. In no respect, however, has the continental dimension of the impact of the recession on migrants been addressed in a concerted regional manner.

As noted earlier, the United States and Canada differ in their approaches to immigration. The United States focuses on family reunification coupled with a demand-led, employer-driven system; Canada uses a points-based selection model for skilled workers and has family sponsorship provisions. In Canada, economic criteria are prioritized within the immigration system. One would expect Canada's system to display considerable vulnerability to global changes because its skilled worker category is tied to the labour market. This has not happened in the immediate wake of the economic crisis. The permanent legal streams of immigration in the two countries in North America have been affected in different ways. And to some extent, a critical portion of immigration flows to the United States may be less affected:

> The number of immigrants receiving legal permanent visas in the United States (or 'green cards') has been stable despite the economic downturn. One explanation is that would-be immigrants – especially family-based immigrants who account for two thirds of all US permanent immigrants— have to wait in line for years to obtain a US permanent visa. Thus, many would be unlikely to postpone their plans based exclusively on economic considerations. (Fix et al. 2009, 22)

That said, immigrants entering the United States on employer-supported visas may be vulnerable to the changing economic conditions. It is reported that 'the number of applications for US permanent visas that require direct employer sponsorship fell by more than 50 percent between 2007 and 2008 … and only 36,000 applications were submitted in the first eight months of fiscal year 2009' (ibid., 22). In contrast, Canada has been characterized as 'swimming against the tide': the federal government has pledged to maintain permanent immigration levels, and admissions remain stable. Where other countries have adjusted their immigration policies (ibid., 6), Canada has not. The Minister of Immigration has emphasized that Canada will 'maintain its current policy of encouraging immigration in order to meet identified labour shortages in key areas despite the financial crisis' (cited in Cerna 2010, 14). The number of skill-based permanent immigrants to Canada increased between 2007 and 2008 from 131,244 to 149,072, or by 14 per cent (Fix et al. 2009, 23). Similarly, Canada has not moved to reduce the number of temporary workers, either skilled or low-skilled, entering the country.[7]

Canada's actions in the midst of the economic crisis highlight its commitment to 'skilled' and 'high-skilled' migrants. In this respect, the Canadian state's actions reflect the Migration Information Source's contention that 'gloomy economic forecasts do not seem to have slowed the hunt for highly skilled migrants or foreign students, whose locally earned degrees and language skills make them an obvious talent pool' (Migration Information Source 2008). Indeed, Canada introduced a new immigration category in 2008: the Canadian Experience Class (CEC). Under CEC provisions, international students and some groups of temporary workers (those with professional, managerial, and skilled work experience) will be allowed to apply for permanent resident status. According to the Canadian Minister of Citizenship and Immigration, 'with the Canadian Experience Class fully in place, Canada will be more competitive in attracting and retaining individuals with the skills we need ... [It] will go a long way in bringing Canada in line with its global competitors (CIC 2008b).

Unlike Canada, the United States has moved to place limits on high-skilled migration in response to changing economic conditions. Analysts have noted that demand for high-skilled temporary migrants was affected by the crisis: 'The demand for migrant workers with US advanced degrees remained the same, [but] the demand for migrant workers from outside the US was only half the available cap' (Cerna 2010, 15). It is reported that the number of H-1B petitions fell by nearly 20% between 2007 and 2009. Also, 'five countries – India plus Canada (6.5 percent or 22,156), the United Kingdom (4.3 percent or 14,610), Mexico (4.2 percent or 14,352), and China (3.8 percent or 12,922) accounted for 55.1 percent (187,042) of all H-1B admissions in 2009' (Batalova 2010). Additionally, the United States has moved to limit H-1B visas for certain firms. In February 2009, under the terms of The American Recovery and Reinvestment Act (2009) (i.e., the U.S. stimulus bill), banks and other financial institutions receiving support from the Troubled Assets Relief Program (TARP) were prohibited from hiring H-1B workers in jobs in which they had made U.S. workers redundant (ibid.).

To date, in their responses to the economic crisis, the United States and Canada have chosen different approaches regarding permanent and temporary migration. Meanwhile, the impact of economic turbulence is being experienced directly by various groups of non-citizens. According to the OECD, 'in the United States, the unemployment rate of immigrants increased 10.5% in February 2009, more than twice the unemployment rate recorded in March 2007.' These outcomes are related, in part, to the fact that migrant workers are overrepresented in sectors that have been adversely affected by the recession: construction, wholesale trade, and hospitality (OECD 2009, 4).

As discussed in the previous section, the Mexican irregular population in the United States constitutes a significant group of precarious residents. 'In 2008, there were 11.4 million Mexican immigrants in the United States, accounting for 30.1 percent of all US immigrants and 10 percent of all Mexicans. Over half of all Mexican immigrants reside in the United States illegally' (Terrazas 2010). Their position as precarious residents means that they will not necessarily be shielded from the effects of the crisis by a social safety net. These effects could include unemployment, lower earnings, and the loss of a home due to interest rate flunctuations and will be experienced in a broader context of anti-immigrant sentiment (Orozco 2009, 7–8). Orozco also points out that 'welfare reform has excluded recent undocumented immigrants who lack citizenship from accessing major federal benefit programs, such as food stamps and cash welfare ... In general unauthorized immigrants are ineligible from all federal benefit programs and services except for a few emergency services' (ibid., 8).

Given this situation, to what extent has the flow into the United States and return to Mexico been affected by the weakened economy? The Pew Hispanic Center reports that the annual flow of immigrants from Mexico to the United States in 2008–9 'was lower than at any point during the decade and only about half of the average for the previous two years' (Passel and Cohn 2009, 3). Again, analysts point to the vulnerable position of precarious residents. In this case they are working in industries disproportionately affected by the recession – construction, manufacturing, hospitality – and their status often means they lack the security of an employment contract. Also, 'unauthorized immigrants tend to have less secure contractual arrangements with their employers than do native-born and lawful-immigrant workers' (Chishti and Bergeron 2010). In spite of rising unemployment, there has been no significant change in the number of Mexican-born migrants returning to Mexico. According to Papademetriou and Terrazas (2009), a number of characteristics of this population as well as developments along the southwestern border and in Mexico and Latin America indicate that large returns may be unlikely. These include:

- unauthorized immigrants' high degree of attachment to the labour force;
- unauthorized workers' greater mobility between sectors and high geographic mobility within the United States;
- the rising cost of illegal entry to the United States, which has contributed to reducing back-and-forth migration dramatically over the past two decades; *and*
- increasing drug-related violence in Mexico and Central America (ibid.).

The Pew Hispanic Center, relying on U.S. government data, reports that there is little evidence to support the contention that Mexicans are returning home (Passel and Cohn 2009, i).

That said, the recession has also been marked by increasing border enforcement and by the rise of anti-immigrant sentiment (Orozco 2009, 8). This has contributed to further insecurities in this group of precarious residents.

Lastly, the recession's impact – be it in terms of unemployment, loss of earnings, and/or loss of a home – coupled with increased border enforcement, has noticeably dampened the volume of remittances to Mexico from the United States. One report found that remittances have declined significantly:

> Remittances to Mexico declined 4 percent in 2008 and to date in 2009 they have declined an additional 12 percent. In total, remittance flows to Mexico are about 18 percent below their 2006 peak. The average amount of remittance sent to Mexico has also declined from about $343 per transaction in January to June 2007 and 2008 to about $329 in January to June 2009 (Fix et al. 2009, 83–4).

As discussed in the chapter in this volume by Cadena-Roa, the decline in remittances has heightened the impact of the economic crisis in Mexico. This in turn has worsened the country's security crisis.

Conclusions

The case of North America illustrates the importance of migration dynamics, an element of regional integration emphasized in the 'new regionalism' approach discussed in the introduction to this volume. The number of migrants from Mexico to the United States (and to a much lesser extent Canada) has increased since NAFTA was implemented. This stands in contrast to claims by NAFTA advocates that the agreement would reduce migration. The failure of the deal's negotiators to include provisions relating to low-skill migration has aggravated the asymmetries and dissonances of the North American region and has contributed to the growing numbers of 'precarious residents.'

That same failure, along with the limitations placed on high-skill migrants, continues to affect the character of the North American region. And all of the consequences have been aggravated by the recent global economic crisis. The impact of that crisis on migration policy and politics in North America has demonstrated the ways in which Canadian and U.S. mores diverge, however close their bilateral relationship. Canada has chosen not to make significant adjustments in levels of migrants or in its selection model, perhaps because the recession's impact has not been as severe in Canada as in the United States (see the chapter in this volume by Germain). In contrast, the United States has moved to limit some high-skilled temporary migration, and its employer-driven system of permits has been adversely affected.

These experiences must be understood as predicated on the existing relations among the three NAFTA members – relations in which statist frameworks have tended to prevail over more weakly institutionalized trilateral measures such as NAFTA's Chapter 16 provisions. However, within North America, Mexico and its citizens face unequal relations with the two other partners. It is no accident that North America's most precarious residents – 'low-skilled' agricultural workers in the H-2A and SAWP programs, and irregular migrants in the United States – are Mexican nationals whose position has worsened since the crisis. The Democrats' recent loss of the House of Representatives to the Republicans in the November 2010 elections does not bode well for comprehensive migration reform in the United States. Moreover, the demise of the SPP means that no trilateral mechanism seems to exist for addressing the regional dimensions of labour mobility. Other models of regional integration based on labour mobility (such as the EU) also involve processes of inclusion and exclusion and do not guarantee full citizenship rights for all residents. The North American model is a clear case of regional integration exacerbating the situation of precarious residents.

Notes

1 This quote is taken from Stephen Colbert – 'Opening Statement – Subcommittee On Immigration – Citizenship and Border Security.' http://lybio. net/stephen-colbert-opening-statement-subcommittee-on-immigration-citizenship-and-border-security/people. Accessed 28 September 2010.

2 The campaign 'Take Our Jobs' is led by United Farm Workers. It is 'aimed at hiring U.S. citizens and legal residents to fill jobs that often go to undocumented farm workers. The effort spotlights the immigrant labor issue and underscores the need for reforms, without which the domestic agricultural industry could be crippled, leading to more jobs moving offshore. As part of the movement, the campaign is sending a letter to U.S. lawmakers, offering up farm workers who are "ready to welcome citizens and legal

residents who wish to replace immigrants in the fields."' See About the Campaign - http://takeourjobs.org. Accessed 8 November 2011.

3 Some of the arguments in this section were introduced in 'Canada and Mexico's Migration Relationship: Retrospect and Prospect,' North American Dialogue Series no. 11 (Mexico City: CEDAN Technologico de Monterrey, January–June 2010).

4 The UN figure is based on the number of persons born outside the country or area.

5 As Cerna points out, there is no standard definition for 'highly skilled immigrants'; such definitions vary by national contexts. 'But highly skilled immigrants are commonly defined as "having a university degree or extensive/equivalent experience in a given field" (Iredale 2001, 8; see also Salt 1997, 5). Definitions also consider education, occupation, and even salary. Highly skilled immigrants often work in private, internationally competitive sectors ... but also in public sectors, such as education and healthcare' (2010, 1).

6 In 2009, Canada also imposed a visa requirement on Mexicans.

7 This situation may change. In February 2011, media outlets reported that figures obtained through Access to Information indicate that plans were under way that would see a cut in 'all [Canadian] economic class visas by nearly seven per cent and federal skilled worker visas specifically by 20 percent in 2011' (Elliot, CBC News, 2011).

References

Alba, Francisco. 2010. 'Mexico: A Crucial Crossroads.' Migration Information Source. Washington: MPI. February. http://www.migrationinformation.org/feature/display.cfm?ID=772. Accessed 2 March 2010.

Alarcón, Rafael. 2007. 'The Free Circulation of Skilled Migrants in North America.' In Migration without Borders. Edited by Antoine Pécoud and Paul de Guchteneire. New York: Berghahn.

Andreas, Peter. 1998. 'The Escalation of U.S. Immigration Control in Post-NAFTA Era.' Political Science Quarterly 113, no. 4 (Winter 1998–9): 591–615.

Basok, Tanya. 2007. 'Canada's Temporary Migration Program: A Model Despite Flaws.' Migration Information Source. Washington: MPI. 12 November. http://www.migrationinformation.org/Feature/display.cfm?ID=650. Accessed 8 November 2011.

Batalova, Jeanne. 2010. 'H-1B Temporary Skilled Worker Program.' Migration Information Source. Washington: MPI. 7 October. http://www.migrationinformaton.org/USFocus/print.cfm?ID=801. Accessed 18 November 2010.

Becerril Quintana, Ofelia. 2011. 'A New Era of Seasonal Mexican Migration to Canada.' Canadian Foundation for the Americas (FOCAL). http://www.focal.ca/en/publications/focalpoint/467-june-2011-ofelia-becerril-quintana-en. Acessed 15 November 2011.

Bosniak, Linda. 2000. 'Universal Citizenship and the Problem of Alienage.' *Northwestern University Law Review* 94 (Spring).

Canada–Mexico Initiative. 2010. 'The Canada–Mexico Relationship: A Backgrounder.' October. http://www.focal.ca/images/stories/Canada-Mexico_FOCAL_Backgrounder_October%202010_e_sm.pdf. Accessed 8 November 2011.

Castles, Stephen. 2005. 'Nation and Empire: Hierarchies of Citizenship in the New Global Order.' *International Politics* 42: 203–24.

Cerna, Lucie. 2010. 'Policies and Practices of Highly Skilled Migration in Times of Economic Crisis.' International Migration Papers no. 99. Geneva: International Labour Office. http://www.ilo.org/public/english/protection/migrant/download/imp/imp99.pdf. Accessed 15 November 2011.

Chishti, Muzaffar, and Claire Bergeron. 2010. 'Increasing Evidence That Recession Has Caused Number of Unauthorized Immigrants in US to Drop.' Migration Information Source. 15 March. http://www.migrationinformation.org/USFocus/display.cfm?id=774&feed=rss. Accessed 18 November 2010.

Citizenship and Immigration Canada (CIC). 2009. 'Working Temporarily in Canada: Special Categories – Business People.' http://www.cic.gc.ca/English/work/special-business.asp#php. Accessed 16 November 2010.

– 2008a. 'Facts and Figures 2008 – Immigration Overview: Permanent and Temporary Residents.' http://www.cic.gc.ca/english/resources/statistics/facts2008/index.asp. Accessed 8 November 2011.

– 2008b. 'News Release: Canadian Experience Class Now Open For Business.' 5 September. http://www.cic.gc.ca/English/department/media/releases/2008/2008-09-05c.asp. Accessed 10 June 2009.

Elliot, Louise. 2011. 'Visas for Skilled Workers Set to Drop.' CBC News, 16 February. http://www.cbc.ca/news/canada/story/2011/02/15/pol-visas-skilled-workers.html. Accessed 8 November 2011.

Fix, Michael, Demetrios G. Papademetriou, Jeanne Batalova, Aaron Terrazas, Serena Yi-Ying Lin, and Michelle Mittelstadt. 2009. 'Migration and the Global Recession.' Washington: MPI. http://www.migrationpolicy.org/pubs/MPI-BBCreport-Sept09.pdf. Accessed 8 November 2011.

Gabriel, Christina, and Laura Macdonald. 2011. 'Citizenship at the Margins: The Canadian Seasonal Agricultural Workers Program and Civil Society Advocacy.' *Policy and Politics* 39, no. 1 (February): 45–68.

– 2004. 'The Hypermobile, the Mobile, and the Rest: Patterns of Inclusion and

Exclusion in an Emerging North American Migration Regime.' *Canadian Journal of Latin American and Caribbean Studies* 29, nos. 57–8: 67–92.

Gibney, Matthew. 2009–10. 'Precarious Residents: Migration Control, Membership and the Rights of Non-Citizens.' UNDP Human Development Research Paper. April. http://hdr.undp.org/en/reports/global/hdr2009/papers/HDRP_2009_10.pdf. Accessed 8 November 2011.

Goldring, Luin, Carolina Berinstein, and Judith K. Bernhard. 2009. 'Institutionalizing Precarious Migratory Status in Canada.' *Citizenship Studies* 13, no. 3: 239–65.

Hennebry, Jenna, and Kerry Preibisch. 2010. 'A Model for Managed Migration? Re-examining Best Practices in Canada's Seasonal Agricultural Program.' International Migration, early view (February), no. DOI 1-33.

Hurrell, Andrew. 2006. 'Hegemony in a Region That Dares Not Speak Its Name.' *International Journal* 61, no. 3: 545–66.

International Trade Canada (ITC). 2004. 'Temporary Entry into the United States and Mexico under the North American Free Trade Agreement: A Guide for Canadian Businesspersons.' Cat. no. IT4:2/2004E-PDF. Ottawa.

Johnson, Kevin R. 1994. 'Free Trade and Closed Borders: NAFTA and Mexican Immigration to the United States.' In 27 *U.C. Davis Law Review* (Summer) 937.

Kapur, Devesh, and John McHale. 2005. *Give Us Your Best and Brightest: The Global Hunt for Talent and Its Impact on the Developing World.* Washington: Centre for Global Development.

Keeley, Brian. 2009. *International Migration: The Human Face of Globalization.* Paris: OECD.

Kuptsch, Christiane, and Pang Eng Fong. 2006. *Competing for Global Talent.* Geneva: ILO.

Maher, Kristen Hill. 2002. 'Who Has a Right to Rights? Citizenship's Exclusions in an Age of Migration.' In *Globalization and Human Rights.* Edited by Alison Brysk. Berkeley: University of California Press. 19–43.

Martin, Philip. 2008. 'Global Forum on Migration and Development (GFMD) Roundtable 2.1 – Fostering More Opportunities of Legal Migration in North America.' http://www.migrationanddevelopment.net/research-publications/fostering-more-opportunities-for-legal-migration-in-north-america. Accessed 8 November 2011.

Martin, Philip, Manolo Abella, and Christiane Kuptsch. 2006. *Managing Labor Migration in the Twenty-first Century.* New Haven: Yale University Press.

Meyers, Deborah W., and Kevin O'Neil. 2004. 'Immigration – Mapping the New North American Reality.' *Policy Options* 25, no. 6: 45–9.

Migration Information Source. 2009. 'Top 10 Issues 2009 – Issue #1: The Recession's Impact on Immigrants.' Washington. 2 December. http://www.migrationinformation.com/Feature/print.cfm?ID=757. Accessed 18 November 2010.

– 2008. 'Top 10 Migration Issues of 2008 – Issue #2 – The Recession-Proof Race for Highly Skilled Migrants.' Washington. December. http://www.migrationinformation.org/Feature/display.cfm?id=712. Accessed 11 May 2010.

Miller, Mark J., and Christina Gabriel. 2008. 'The US–Mexico Migration Honeymoon of 2001: A Retrospective.' In *Governing International Labour Migration*. Edited by Christina Gabriel and Hélène Pellerin. London: Routledge. 147–62.

Mueller, Richard E. 2005. 'Mexican Immigrants and Temporary Residents in Canada: Current Knowledge and Future Research.' *Migraciones Internacionales* 5, no. 1: 32–56.

Organisation for Economic Co-operation and Development (OECD). 2009. 'International Migration: Charting a Course through the Crisis.' *Policy Brief.* June. http://www.oecd.org/dataoecd/10/24/43060425.pdf. Accessed 8 November 2011.

–. 2006. 'Policy Note: Mexico and International Migration.' http://www.oecd.org/dataoecd/52/11/38120155.pdf. Accessed 8 November 2011.

O'Neil, Kevin, Kimberly Hamilton, and Demetrios Papademetriou. 2005. 'Migration in the Americas.' Global Commission on International Migration. September.

Orozco, Manuel. 2009. 'Migration and Remittances in Times of Recession: Effects on Latin American Economies.' Washington: Inter-American Dialogue. http://www.oecd.org/dataoecd/48/8/42753222.pdf. Accessed 8 November 2011.

Papademetriou, Demetrios G., Doris Meissner, Marc R. Rosenblum, and Madeleine Sumption. 2009. 'Aligning Temporary Immigration Visas with US Labor Market Needs: The Case for a New System of Provisional Visas.' Washington: MPI. http://www.migrationpolicy.org/pubs/Provisional_visas.pdf. Accessed 8 November 2011.

Papademetriou, Demetrios, and Aaron Terrazas. 2009. 'Immigrants in the United States and the Current Economic Crisis.' Washington: MPI. 1 April. http://www.migrationpolicy.org/pubs/lmi_recessionJan09.pdf. Accessed 18 November 2010.

Passel, Jeffrey S., and D'Vera Cohn. 2009. 'Mexican Immigrants: How Many Come? How Many Leave?' Washington: Pew Hispanic Center. 22 July.

http://pewhispanic.org/reports/report.php?ReportID=112. Accessed 8 November 2011.

Preibisch, K., and E. Encalada Grez. 2010. 'The Other Side of *El Otro Lado*: Mexican Migrant Women and Labor Flexibility in Canadian Agriculture.' Special Issue on Women in Agriculture. *Signs: Journal of Women in Culture and Society* 35, no. 2: 289–316.

Preibisch, Kerry, and Luz Maria Hermoso Santamaria. 2006. 'Engendering Labour Migration: The Case of Foreign Workers in Canadian Agriculture.' In *Women, Migration and Citizenship: Making Local, National, and Transnational Connections*. Edited by Evangelia Tastsoglou and Alexandra Dobrowolsky. Farnham: Ashgate. 107–30.

Ruhs, Martin. 2005. 'The Potential of Temporary Migration Programmes in Future International Migration Policy.' Global Commission on International Migration. September. http://economics.ouls.ox.ac.uk/12666/1/TP3.pdf.

Terrazas, Aaron. 2010. 'Mexican Immigrants in the United States.' Washington: MPI. February. http://www.migrationinformation.org/USfocus/display.cfm?id=767. Accessed 12 November 2010.

Trumper, Ricardo, and Lloyd L. Wong. 2007. 'Canada's Guest Workers: Racialized, Gendered, and Flexible.' In *Race and Racism in 21st Century Canada*. Edited by Sean Hier and B. Singh Bolaria. Peterborough: Broadview. 150–70.

UFCW and AWA. 2008–2009. *The Status of Migrant Farm Workers in Canada 2008–2009*. Toronto: UFCW.

United Nations. Department of Economic and Social Affairs, Population Division. 2009. 'International Migration Report 2006: A Global Assessment.' New York. http://www.un.org/esa/population/publications/2006_MigrationRep/report.htm. Accessed 8 November 2011.

Woroby, Tamara M. 2007. 'North American Immigration: The Search for Positive-Sum Returns.' *Requiem or Revival? The Promise of North American Integration*. Washington: Brookings Institution.

PART III

Democratic Deficits, New Actors, and Responses to the Crisis

9 *Plus Ça Change*: Double Bilateralism and the Demise of Trilateralism

STEPHANIE R. GOLOB

Even as the three NAFTA nations struggle to adjust to times of 'political-economic turbulence,' one aspect of the North American regional system that has shown resilience in the face of crisis is its double-bilateral structure. After over a decade of free trade and over a century of other forms of de facto economic, societal, and environmental interdependence, what remains solid is the orientation of the region's 'Three Amigos' towards two parallel bilateral relationships, each one 'special' to its respective members, and each one a well-worn channel for managing conflict and cooperation. Notably underdeveloped, if not entirely missing because of these ingrained patterns, is a core of trilateral regional institutions that might mitigate against the negative effects of double-bilateralism, most notably the 'Othering' of the region's less wealthy and less politically stable partner. Rather than questioning these divisive tendencies and moving towards greater mutuality to confront the crisis, today's North American leaders appear to be taking refuge in the certainty and the political ease of time-worn patterns.

To be fair, *double-bilateralism* in North America makes a certain amount of practical sense, for it reflects structural asymmetries. First, the region is naturally dominated by the United States as a global military superpower and as the world's primary consumer market and leading financial centre. Thus, the main dyads in North America are those in which the United States is a partner. Second, these two U.S.-linked dyads are very dissimilar in many ways and require different sets of norms to govern cooperation and to adjudicate conflict. The Canada–U.S. bilateral relationship links two highly industrialized nations, both members of the NATO alliance and partners in NORAD's continental air defence system, sharing at least one common dominant language and a shared

British colonial history, not to mention a twentieth-century history of economic interdependence, shared democratic norms, and the oft-cited 'special relationship.' Conflict in the Canada–U.S. dyad often centres on discrete issue areas of domestic (federal or provincial) policy in which Canada seeks to assert its difference from the United States, but those areas can be cordoned off in order not to jeopardize the overall operation of the relationship.

By contrast, the Mexico–U.S. dyad spans divides in development level, language, culture, and history, the latter viewed in Mexico as one of American interventionism and in the United States as one of Mexican lawlessness through illegal migration and drug trafficking. One-party authoritarianism in Mexico, lasting for seven decades and ending only in 2000, has added a normative divide; meanwhile, the current wave of drug-related violence is contributing to the media-fuelled image of Mexico as a 'failed state' (see the chapter by Cadena-Roa in this volume). Thus, Mexican governments both before and after NAFTA have laid claim to a 'special relationship' similar to the one between its two northern neighbours; but in practice and reality, 'irritants' on the agenda – migration and drugs primary among them – are the agenda itself, and conflict on those issues often overshadows other forms of ongoing cooperation.

Finally, the two border regions and their respective geographic, demographic, and infrastructural characteristics further distinguish and differentiate the Canada–U.S. and Mexico–U.S. dyads. This divide was starkly reflected in the two-track 'Security' portion of the Security and Prosperity Partnership (SPP; ASPAN in Spanish), based as it was on two separate 'Smart Border' accords rather than on a vision of an integrated 'North American' security space. Given these realities, and in the spirit of change and transparency promoted by the newly minted Obama administration, the quiet demise of the SPP in 2009 could have the effect of releasing North America from its pretensions to trilateralism, leaving behind a more honest system that – in the context of economic crisis – is shifting increasingly scarce resources towards the two bilateral relationships that matter most. Indeed, the Canada–U.S. Beyond the Border Declaration of February 2011, which is paired with a new agreement on regulatory cooperation, makes no apologies for celebrating interoperability between the two advanced members of NAFTA and awards the 'perimeter approach' to border management to the more advanced border (White House, Office of the Press Secretary, 2011).

Yet this outcome, as logical as it sounds, must be recognized as a departure from expectations. Obama's campaign rhetoric appeared to promote a far more critical and possibly confrontational position vis-à-vis NAFTA, while his foreign policy agenda was firmly pointed towards greater, rather than diminished, multilateralism. As I will contend in this chapter, the current context of 'political-economic turbulence' has not produced a path-altering *critical juncture* as foreseen by historical-institutionalist analysis. Instead, the convergence of the *structural* shake-up of the U.S.-centred global financial crisis with Obama's *ideational* move towards pragmatism is likely to reinforce or even accelerate long-standing, path-dependent processes that have shaped North America into an underinstitutionalized, double-bilateral regional governance system.

I begin this analysis with a brief history of double-bilateralism in North America, demonstrating first how choices made by powerful political and economic actors at the very birth of the region set it firmly on a path away from Europe's high-concept supranationalism *and* its lower-concept 'spillover' dynamics, with *double-bilateralism* as a key element in that strategy. Over time, and under the political radar, NAFTA-based North America continued to integrate economically and socially, both within and outside the agreement's confines, in the absence of high-level political will to articulate commonalities and enforce broader shared standards to govern this growing continental system. Instead, the region has been managed on mostly parallel bilateral tracks, in line with the primarily bilateral intergovernmental networks and working groups developed to implement the NAFTA accord.

Following this overview, I present an analysis of regional integration after 9/11, identifying the SPP as the apotheosis of the double-bilateral ethos at the heart of North American integration. Rather than providing a critical juncture that would shift the region towards greater mutuality and institution-based cooperation, the 9/11 attacks merely brought to the surface the hub-and-spoke realities of Canadian and Mexican vulnerability to U.S. unilateralism. In response, and in distinct ways, both Canada and Mexico embraced double-bilateralism with renewed vigour. Rather than create new institutions with trilateral reach, the SPP merely empowered an already existing web of mainly bilateral intergovernmental relations linking bureaucrats across borders. Thus, the patterns established at its origins – with the limitations on 'spillover' enforced in part through double-bilateralism – were perpetuated by the SPP process, which kept North America firmly on its incremental, intergovernmental path.

That this continues to be the case, even after the historic election of

Barack Obama in November 2008 and his administration's retirement of the SPP brand the next year, further underscores the powerful impact of past choices on present patterns of regional economic integration in North America. Path dependency also helps explain how the global financial crisis and its domestic manifestations in the United States have been perceived by the Obama team, and how those perceptions have further *reinforced* the appeal of a double-bilateral North America. In the next section of this chapter, I demonstrate why this external shock was not enough to send the United States and its neighbours down a new tri-lateralist path, and conclude that double-bilateralism is likely to become more pronounced and visible under the Obama administration. I then present two scenarios for the future of North American governance: the first sees NAFTA-premised cooperation returning 'underground' via the perpetuation of the sectoral 'working group' model of transbureau-cratic interaction; the second suggests that the North American regional idea will simply be tossed 'overboard' in favour of a more high-profile double-bilateralism, one that emphasizes parallel bilateral mechanisms, including subnational cross-border initiatives.

In the final section of the chapter, I take a somewhat provocative approach to the question of NAFTA's third bilateral – the underde-veloped Canada–Mexico relationship – and its future in a context of deepening and hardening double-bilateralism. Under what circum-stances would it be more optimal, in the double-bilateral context, to deepen Canada-Mexico cooperation, leading to a *triple-bilateral* govern-ance system? Two publicly promoted initiatives – the Canada–Mexico Partnership and the Canadian Fund for Local Initiatives (*Fondo Canadá*) – raised expectations for greater cooperation within NAFTA's third bilateral; however, the controversy over Canada's July 2009 decision to impose travel visas on Mexicans has underscored the not-so-neigh-bourly perception that Canada has preferred to mark distances with Mexico rather than view it as a regional partner. These disappointments and conflicts reveal yet another truth of North American integration: governments are more often the *brakes*, not the engines, of integration, most notably in their fierce defence of sovereignty-as-state prerogative. By taking a second look at these initiatives, however, we can also see an alternative model of regional 'governance' in an emerging 'triple-bilateral' region, albeit one that echoes the predictions of 'new region-alist' approaches that have paired globalization and regionalization as processes that would unleash the international influence of non-state actors (Hettne, Intoi, and Sunkel 1999, 7–8). Specifically, I contend that the construction of a 'triple-bilateralist' model would be led by civil society and private sector actors, which are ahead of governments in generating and recognizing mutuality of interests and identities. The final section of the chapter explores this society-driven model, with the Canada–Mexico relationship – long playing catch-up in state-to-state and trade-and-investment terms – potentially emerging at the forefront of informal governance innovation.

A Brief History of Double-Bilateralism in North America: The Trilateral Path Not Taken

In his pioneering monograph *Politics in Time*, Paul Pierson (2004) brings together research across the social sciences to make the temporal-dynamic argument that sequence, timing, and path dependency offer key insights into phenomena that are often viewed only in static terms. Not only does 'history matter,' he contends, but it matters in very specific ways, in that it generates *positive feedback effects* whereby certain decisions and behaviours become self-reinforcing and change to other behaviours becomes excessively costly (2004, 18). Historical-institutional analysis also examines the *mechanisms of reproduction* that consolidate these effects over time and suggests that rare *critical junctures* – brought about by external factors such as economic crisis or war, or local economic and political upheavals – may short-circuit previously stable mechanisms of reproduction both material (patronage networks) and ideological (bureaucratic insularity) may be short-circuited (Thelen 1999). Otherwise, institutions and policy projects tend to develop along paths defined mainly by continuity; as Pierson effectively argues, such *path dependency* emerges because under positive feedback, *the costs of switching or leaving paths is often very high for individual as well as collective actors*. In the case of regional economic integration, which often involves large investments of political capital at the founding as well as the empowerment of vested economic interests in the perpetuation of the arrangement, I would argue that regional 'paths' are, to a great degree, laid out by initial sets of rules and norms, and that institutional innovation over time may be encouraged or inhibited depending on these *founding social contracts*.

In North America, regional integration was characterized from the start by a rejection of multilateral institution building and by strict limits on the construction of regional mutuality – that is, by a deliberate short-circuiting of the mechanisms of reproduction that had consolidated positive feedback effects encouraging Europe down its path towards integration. These ground rules and formative underlying assumptions can be traced to ideological and strategic orientations of powerful actors in government and the private sector in the three member-states. Ideologically, there was a convergence at this time in all three countries towards a *neoliberal* view of the relationship between states and markets among political and economic elites. This convergence was due in large part to the external shock of the 1981–2 recession, which can be viewed as a 'critical juncture' that delegitimated earlier, more interventionist models of economic policy making while breaching the 'policy frontier' that had rendered the free trade option taboo in Canadian and Mexican foreign policies (Golob 2003). In Canada, experiments in economic nationalism such as Trudeau's National Energy Program (NEP) and the Foreign Investment Review Agency (FIRA) were rolled back; in the United States, Ronald Reagan preached the 'magic of the market' and championed deregulation and privatization; in Mexico, a new generation of young '*técnicos*' with doctorates in economics from American universities transformed the domestic economy and opened it to foreign investment and competition. While the European Union was itself a market-expanding enterprise, the burgeoning bureaucracy in Brussels was easily viewed, through the lenses of the Reagan/Thatcher Revolution and the Chicago Boys, as a retrograde bastion of welfare state inefficiency, bent on overregulation. Thus, 'world-historical' timing, along with ideological shifts among elites brought on by external shock, help explain the rejection of the institution-centred European model.

At the same time, within the crowded and highly asymmetrical confines of the North American continent, the European formula for 'pooling sovereignty' was equally rejected on all sides. Europe's nation-state members agreed over time to cede degrees of unilateral control over certain policy levers in order to give force and legitimacy to EU-wide norms; by contrast, NAFTA's members viewed free trade as a limited form of economic cooperation that should not and would not involve such derogation of authority. Canada and Mexico had each spent the better part of the preceding century fending off pressures from the dynamic and expansionary U.S. economy; the last thing either country wanted was to open the door to continental standards that, it could be assumed, would be determined by the more powerful United States. Both countries also insisted on negotiating exceptions to free trade involving 'sacred sectors' – examples include 'cultural industries' such as publishing and film for Canada (Goff 2000), and oil for Mexico (Lock 1993). Indeed, the United States itself had no interest in a more institution-centred agreement of the sort that would limit its policy autonomy and offer its neighbours undue influence over domestic (or immigration) policy. Growing U.S. 'sovereigntism' – reflected in the 1980s in a preference for forging 'hub and spoke' bilateral deals and retaining unilateral levers such as retaliatory anti-dumping legislation known as 'Super 301' – in turn led its future NAFTA partners to despair of U.S. support for the multilateral GATT process and to wager on a regional accord. Thus, NAFTA's architects rejected European-style integration in favour of a model that would allow maximum autonomy for governments and minimum supranational institutional constraints for both governments and markets.

Riding these trends, two key sets of powerful (and empowered) actors preferred a minimalist NAFTA and were able to infuse the agreement with their preferences for limited institutionalization. First, the big corporations favouring the deal had already spent much of the 1980s pursuing a continentalization strategy, moving their supply chains and expanding their consumer bases across borders in response to greater competition from Asia and, to some extent, a unifying Europe (Blank and Haar 1998, 21–44). They also had an eye on avoiding the bureaucratic and regulatory strictures on labour market and tax regimes represented by the more institutionalized European model. Chapters 11 and 19 of the NAFTA accord, which recognize corporate rights to an extent unheard of in the EU, further reinforced the fundamental aversion to developing a shared *public* interest in North America (Gutiérrez Haces 2006). Big business also benefited from the 'green room' model established during the NAFTA negotiations, whereby private sector leaders and their representatives had direct, informal access to their own national government's negotiators and trade officials in order to communicate their views, thus evading European-style formalized supranational institutions.

The second key group of actors favouring a minimalist NAFTA was national politicians. NAFTA turned out to be a hard sell in hostile domestic political arenas, both during ratification and in the immediate, tumultuous aftermath. In Mexico, NAFTA was blamed for the crisis that followed the devaluation of the national currency in late 1994. Former president Carlos Salinas de Gortari, the leading architect of NAFTA and neoliberalism in Mexico, left office – and the country – in a cloud of scandal, and in 2000 the ruling *Partido Revolucionario Institucional* (PRI) lost its first presidential election in more than seven decades. In Canada, free trade was already a hot-button political issue, as seen in the mobilization against the bilateral Canada–U.S. Free Trade Agreement (CUSFTA) and the 1988 'Free Trade Election' (Ayres 1998). The 1993 federal elections were themselves a referendum on free trade, which was blamed for Canada's own economic slowdown. The party most associated with NAFTA, the Progressive Conservatives, was reduced to a handful of seats in Parliament and was consigned to years in the political wilderness, coming close to disappearing altogether. Perhaps the most bruising political battle, however, was in the United States, where a rancorous public debate revealed intense opposition to NAFTA specifically, and to free trade in general, on both the right (anti-immigration sovereigntists) and the left (activists opposing 'corporate-led globalization' and the victory of corporate values over citizen values such as labour rights and environmental protections).

Given this panorama, it is not surprising that politicians breathed a collective sigh of relief when an *institution-lite* NAFTA went into operation as it was designed to do, through mainly bilateral intergovernmental bureaucratic channels well away from the public eye. Without any institutions in sight, NAFTA could fly metaphorically 'under the political radar' of most of the public in all three countries, and 'North American integration' could be left to the professionals, where it belonged. Even the commissions for labour and the environment created by the side accords were far less 'trilateral' than they appeared on first glance, in that they held states accountable only to their own laws rather than to 'North American' standards, and lacked independent means of enforcing their decisions (Graubart 2008). The resulting model reflected an anti-European, 'privatized' governance model favouring informality, depoliticization, and market-driven integration. But it also set North America on an institutional path of *incrementalism and intergovernmentalism without regional mutuality*. Specifically, without the shared project of constructing trilateral institutions, there has been little to generate regional mutuality even at the governmental level, let alone at the societal level. This lack of mutuality has been most keenly felt by Mexico and Mexicans, who, unlike their counterparts in Europe's 'Poor Four,' have not seen the commitment of resources necessary to 'level up' their national economy or to protect them from abuses as they cross borders seeking opportunity (Pastor 2007; Peacock 2006). It is not surprising that, in the absence of a broader, *political* consensus around even limited goals for the region as a whole – both within the three national societies and across the national governments – only the narrowest and most 'privatized' of goals can be achieved.

Finally, perhaps the most curious part of the North American integration story relates to the interactions among these foundational constraining institutional (or deinstitutionalized) choices and the dynamics of integration these choices have unleashed. As the 'new regionalism' literature discussed in the introduction of this volume notes, regionalism is forged through transnational ties below the level of the state, ties that often produce unintended consequences. Without the top-down orientation seen in Europe, North American integration has been a bottom-up affair, meaning that private actors – the private sector primarily, but also civil society actors such as transnational advocacy networks, undocumented migrants, border communities, and even senior citizens in Florida purchasing drugs from Canadian pharmacies – have responded to the incentive structures of regional economic integration by deepening cross-border economic and social ties even while political ties remain underdeveloped (Ayres and Macdonald 2006). At the same time, the operation of the free trade area, and the subsequent informal communications that have kept disputes from going public, have largely been ensconced within federal government bureaucracies and intergovernmental working groups, thus forging 'epistemic communities' of experts across borders (P. Haas 1989).

Looking carefully, and with an eye to the literature on European integration during its first, uncertain decade, we see the conditions that Ernst Haas contended would produce 'spillover,' the process whereby cooperation within narrow areas (such as coal and steel in Europe) would build trust, first among technical experts and later among the broader public; this in turn would spill over into broader and more comprehensive integration initiatives (such as a customs union in Europe) (E. Haas 1964, 291–2; 1968, 407). In historical-institutionalist terms, spillover was one of the mechanisms of reproduction that generated positive feedback and sent Europe down its integrationist path. Why, then, have we not seen spillover in a region that, by design, has counted on integration to be self-regulating and self-sustaining?

The answer, I would venture, lies in the disconnect between the two elements of spillover as identified by Haas. In North America, the NAFTA experts within the executive-level bureaucracies who are talking to one another have been purposefully insulated and isolated from the public sphere; in addition, they are not fully engaged with or accountable to political society beyond their masters in the Executive

Branch. Meanwhile, much of the 'on the ground' integrative activity has limited or sporadic contact with NAFTA experts, who themselves are often hostile to groups critical of the accord. Even where we have seen positive synergies – described in this volume in Craik and Van-Nijnatten's analysis of 'deliberative transgovernmentalism' linking government climate change experts across borders – those synergies have had limited projection towards the public sphere. The result has been pockets of elite cooperation among experts rather than broader networks fostering a regional outlook among citizens. It is the self-reinforcement of anti-spillover ideas, rather than the expansion of the circle of integration-invested constituents, that has led to a short-circuiting of this potential mechanism of reproduction. North America was never intended to become Europe; indeed, it has become virtually impossible, in practical terms, for Europe's experience to be repeated.

Because of these foundational choices, neither formal trilateral institutions nor informal spillover chains have been in the cards for North America. Instead, the region has grown haphazardly out of a *double-bilateral* structure: first the bilateral CUSFTA in 1989 (Doern and Tomlin 1991; Hart, Dymond, and Robertson 1994), followed in 1990 by the Mexican initiative towards its own bilateral FTA, which subsequently became subsumed in the NAFTA negotiations (Rohter 1990; Cameron and Tomlin 2000). From its very inception, NAFTA was less a regional integration accord than an economic and political security pact in which the two weaker partners, Canada and Mexico, attempted to 'lock in' certain policies or make policy reversals more costly for their mutual partner, the United States. Aside from 'locking in' its FTA gains, above all Canada wanted to 'lock in' market access for its exports, over 80% of which were destined for the United States. Meanwhile the Salinas government in Mexico wanted to 'lock in' both domestic economic reforms and flows of foreign investment from the United States. Without countervailing pressure favouring trilateral approaches, the logic of double-bilateralism became a self-fulfilling prophecy: Canada and Mexico feared that the United States would impose its preferences in any trilateral negotiations, yet by leaving the field, they were acquiescing to U.S. preferences for the *institution-lite*, asymmetrical, double-bilateral governance model.

For the remainder of the 1990s, an 'invisible' North America continued to integrate along the narrow, double-bilateralist lines favouring informality, depoliticization, and market-driven integration. The double-bilateral model also limited North America's potential to bring about qualitative change in the region, in the form, for example, of a comprehensive transportation system, an environmental strategy, a public health emergency preparedness system, or a regional approach to drug trafficking that might have mitigated what is presently happening in Mexico. In the absence of effective regional governance, by the end of the 1990s even the private sector was acknowledging the need for investment in public goods in the form of infrastructure (roads and bridges, most notably at the border, as well as ports, rail, airports, etc.) (Blank 2007). Cross-border trade expansion also led to negative environmental externalities that both burdened local communities and raised questions about how these problems would be documented and defined and who should pay for their abatement (Melious 2006). Meanwhile, the Northeast blackout of August 2003 and the mad cow disease scare earlier that year demonstrated how deeply energy and food supplies were intertwined and how the absence of coordinated regional governance could place publics at risk. Clearly, NAFTA's architects had underestimated how integration could expand beyond the confines of their privatized vision.

Other limits of this approach were by now visible in the area of unauthorized migration (described in greater depth by Christina Gabriel in this volume). In the wake of the Mexican peso crisis in 1994–5, which was followed closely by agricultural liberalization under NAFTA and by the unanticipated 'giant sucking sound' of Mexican assembly jobs leaving for China, Mexican out-migration exploded during NAFTA's first decade. However, unlike other such moments, when the 'safety valve' allowed Mexicans to leave the United States during a crisis and return when it had abated, new border controls were keeping these workers from returning and thus created a new market for human smuggling as families sought to reunite and as more established workers promised relatives help in finding work over the border. Unregulated and unprotected Mexican undocumented workers in the United States were responding to regionalized incentives (and being rewarded with work by equally unregulated business) yet lacked any sense of belonging to 'North America.' And nowhere in this process was Canada going beyond its own limited involvement – its own guest worker program – to challenge the notion that this was a purely bilateral U.S.–Mexico issue.

It's (Still) Alive! Double-Bilateralism after 9/11

Following the years of North American 'invisibility,' a new phase in the consolidation of double-bilateralism began after 9/11, when borders became sources of insecurity rather than opportunity. By some measures, the new phase had begun the year before, when Vicente Fox became the first Mexican president from an opposition party to be democratically elected, and he and his foreign minister, Jorge G. Castañeda, began to fashion a comprehensive bilateral migration accord. Announced with much fanfare on the fateful day of 10 September 2001, the Fox–Castañeda plan was the first casualty of the Bush administration's response to 9/11 (Bumiller 2003), but its bilateralist spirit lived on. Subsequently the United States and Canada moved quickly to quash any discussion of a 'North American Security Perimeter' – an idea that challenged the double-bilateral ethos by considering North America as a single security zone, such that Mexico and Canada would both be equally 'inside.' It is hardly surprising that the unilateralist Bush team, focused on maximum control and minimum multilateralism, discarded the idea. More surprising, however, is its rejection by Canada, where 'NAFTA-plus' ideas were being floated by the private sector (Dobson 2002; d'Aquino 2003) and where a parliamentary commission would shortly table a report, titled 'Partners in North America,' arguing that Canada's approach to regionalism should include Mexico more holistically (Canada, House of Commons, 2002). For the private sector as for the Chrétien government, and most notably for Deputy Prime Minister John Manley, the priority was 'economic security': keeping the border open for Canadian exports to the United States, exports that had been summarily denied entry while the United States sealed its borders in the wake of the attacks. The spectre of losing market access reactivated bilateralist tendencies, and the priority to position Canada as the 'good neighbour' further militated against viewing Mexico as an equal regional partner (Golob 2008). Meanwhile Mexico, which had come in for heavy criticism in Washington for its lukewarm official response to 9/11 and for the public expression of anti-Americanism among its population, found itself left behind by Canada's rapid move to negotiate a bilateral Smart Border accord (Canada, DFAIT, 2001), and soon followed suit (Andreas 2004), further consolidating the double-bilateral governance model.

Thus we arrive at the 2005 founding of the Security and Prosperity Partnership of North America (SPP), ostensibly a trilateral arrangement but actually a further extension of double-bilateral patterns. By inserting its preferred security agenda into NAFTA-based North American governance, the Bush administration was sending a strong signal to its partners that first and foremost, the SPP would advance protection of the U.S. 'homeland.' This would mean a hub-and-spoke system whereby negotiations on the economic front to secure market access would be contingent on acceptance and furthering of these U.S. priorities. Double-bilateralism was also entrenched in the SPP's rhetoric of devising joint 'strategies' and finding 'compatible' practices and 'equivalent' approaches. Such language avoided the European term 'harmonization,' which would have implied a separate, 'North American' standard under which the three governments had to bring their practices and regulations into alignment. Similarly, while there was both implicit and explicit mention of 'shared goals,' the SPP materials only sparingly referred to strategies as 'North American'; also, NAFTA was virtually absent either as a descriptor or as the basis for the SPP's work.

Furthermore, whatever the outward ambitions of the two agendas, in practice the regulatory reform and cooperation that the SPP claimed to be advancing was heavily circumscribed by sensitivities about national sovereignty and, even more notably, by the limits of national lawmaking authority. In other words, the SPP was seeking to make changes in practices that did not require any new laws or revisions of laws already passed. For example, as Debora VanNijnatten (2007) has observed, in the area of environmental policy the SPP focused on 'end of the pipeline' projects, aiming to complete what had already been started. This choice of 'low-hanging fruit' also purposefully avoided legislative oversight or public media scrutiny, which was generally viewed as obstructionist. Instead of a grand bargain, the SPP was, in the end, the sum of multitudinous meetings and incremental reforms, often dealing with quite marginal and technical aspects of its broader, substantive agendas.

Finally, organizationally, also in line with the anti-European NAFTA model, the SPP never established a separate secretariat; instead, it was to be managed by existing Executive Branch ministries and departments (Ackelson and Kastner 2006). The SPP did enjoy a higher public profile, complete with photo ops at annual Leaders' Summits and preparatory ministerial meetings that produced progress reports, which were dutifully posted on SPP websites. Remaining far from public, however, was the day-to-day business of integration, which still resided firmly in the hands of insulated and insular expert networks. Specifically, the key actors were low-profile offices in ministries that till then had handled NAFTA-related issues (in the United States, for example, the Office of NAFTA and Interamerican Affairs in the Department of Commerce), as well as assorted working groups, many of which on the Prosperity side had already been established in the mid-1990s under NAFTA, and which were made up of government officials from specific agencies and offices within the functionally indicated department or ministry (McKinney 2000, cited by Clarkson, Ladly, and Thom 2002). For example, the NAFTA Working Group on Customs was the precursor to the SPP Working Group on Movement of Goods; meanwhile, the North American Energy Working Group (NAEWG), established during the first year of the George W. Bush administration, assisted with proposals in the energy sector (Dukert 2007). As one former U.S. government official put it, '[the administration] didn't have to change any flowchart in government to make the SPP' (confidential interview, Washington, 17 January 2007). The same civil servants, technical experts, and trade hands from the three NAFTA countries who had been working on these issues together for years were simply given a new context in which to continue talking about and doing what they had been talking about and doing before.

Besides eschewing all forms of trilateral institution building, the SPP reinforced double-bilateralism by pushing Canada to differentiate itself from Mexico in order to prove itself a more equal partner. The SPP, with its emphasis on intergovernmentalism, allowed Canada to play to its strengths vis-à-vis Mexico – that is, to the historic close and nearly interoperable relations between their respective government officials (Lyon 1968). This was specifically true in the security realm, which was the priority area for the Bush administration in the SPP, in that historic Canada–U.S. military cooperation through NATO and NORAD far outstripped the less developed (and law enforcement–based) ties in the Mexico–U.S. relationship (Kilroy 2007). Similarly, the rapid negotiation of the Canada–U.S. Smart Border Accord sent reassuring signals to Washington. Canada also benefited from a de facto SPP norm often referred to as 'Three Can Talk, Two Can Walk' – in practice, a two-speed, parallel-track structure that further consolidated double-bilateralism and that situated Canada within the core of the North American integration project. Such an arrangement suggests even greater asymmetrical effects than a 'multispeed' Europe does, given the absence of a more developed trilateral institutional core that might compensate – in material or symbolic ways – for the 'odd man out' dynamics.

To sum up, rather than create new institutions with trilateral reach, the SPP merely empowered an already existing web of mainly bilateral intergovernmental relations linking bureaucrats across borders. These networks, along with the national leaders they served and the business 'stakeholders' who advised them, remained committed to an institution-lite, spillover-free North America along double-bilateral lines as a bulwark against the risks of more institutionalized, publicly visible, trilateral regionalism. Thus North America, despite the turbulence of 9/11, remained on its underinstitutionalized, double-bilateral path.

Plus Ça Change ... Double-Bilateralism after Obama

As we have seen, despite their global impact, the 9/11 attacks did little to shift the incentive structure within the North American regional system away from its historic path of double-bilateralism. This volume assesses the impact on the region of two more recent shifts of historic proportions, both emanating from the world economy's hegemonic core: the U.S.-driven global financial crisis that began in 2008, and the nearly coincident election of President Barack Obama. From the standpoint of the three NAFTA partners, the international and domestic realms both appear caught in what Ayres and Macdonald have termed 'political-economic turbulence,' an unsettled context that has suggested crisis yet has not generated (or has yet to generate) the path-altering consensus usually associated with 'critical junctures.' As discussed in this volume's chapter by Brian Bow, unlike during the crisis of 1981–2, no ideological consensus has swept the globe. The initial reaction to the crisis may have appeared to empower states over markets; but in 2010 Europe shifted towards austerity and more recently critical voices among its citizenry have protested their government's abdication to the dictatorship of the market. Similarly, the Obama administration's ambitious, change-oriented domestic and foreign policy agendas have faced bruising reversals, with Tea Partiers rallying against government regulatory 'usurpation' and the G20 refusing to endorse global standards for financial sector reform. I would suggest that in the context of this ideological turbulence, governments are likely to act in pragmatic ways, which in the North American context means hewing to the low-cost, low-profile model of incremental and intergovernmental double-bilateralism that has been consolidating itself over the years.

I would further argue that the shape of the crisis itself, and of the Obama administration's response to it, has augured specifically *against* a shift towards the trilateralization of North American regional governance. First, the crisis has, if anything, revealed weaknesses in the mutuality-based foundations of Europe, which is the most deeply integrated of regions. Despite recent achievements in supranational institution building – the approval of the quasi-constitutional Lisbon Treaty, the naming of key EU officials akin to a president and a foreign minister, and the formation of an EU foreign service – when financial markets gave the Greek economy a vote of no-confidence and then proceeded to batter Spain, Portugal, Italy, and Ireland (disparagingly referred to as the PIIGS), the richer countries of Europe initially balked at stabilizing the currency zone. Despite the successful mustering of rescue packages for Greece and later Ireland and Portugal, mutuality in the EU continued to decline as a 'second wave' of the crisis hit in 2011. That mutuality has been frayed by, among other things, the resistance of the average German voter to 'bailing out' Europe's profligate periphery ('A Second Wave' 2011). Second, when the crisis in the United States struck the most iconic of domestic industries – the automobile sector – the U.S. response was not to view the industry as 'North American,' which is what it had been since the Auto Pact of 1964. Similarly, whatever their limited practical impact, the 'Buy American' provisions passed by the U.S. Congress (and subsequently revised vis-à-vis Canada through a bilateral accord in February 2010) struck Canadians as a further indication of rising economic protectionism and political insularity, as well as stunted mutuality.

Finally, the Obama administration may have given rhetorical and symbolic primacy to restoring U.S. support for multilateralism in the international context, but it has been practising its foreign policy in strongly bilateral ways. In almost every conceivable region, in an effort to defuse conflicts and 'reset' relations, Secretary of State Hillary Clinton and Obama's special envoys have been complementing the president's own personal rapport with leaders with a reinvigorated and bilaterally based State Department. It comes as no surprise, then, that we see this trend operating in the North American triad. For example, though he was confronted with many other foreign policy priorities, Obama made Ottawa his first foreign destination after his inauguration, if only for a few hours, in order to solidify key bilateral ties with an ally that had troops fighting and dying in Afghanistan. Similarly, to support President Felipe Calderón and to demonstrate U.S. commitment to and responsibility in the 'war on drugs' in Mexico, Obama travelled to Mexico in April 2010, having been preceded by Secretary of State Clinton, Homeland Security Secretary Janet Napolitano, and Attorney General Eric Holder. By way of contrast, the North American Leaders' Summit held in Guadalajara in August 2009 was not publicly announced until just prior to the meeting, and without the SPP there was far less channelling of meetings towards trinational, let alone tri-lateral, initiatives. This left the leaders to focus instead on bilateral talks and bilateral agendas.

My conclusion, then, is that we are more likely to see greater and more overt double-bilateralism in North America in the Obama years. Given this orientation, I see two potential scenarios for how North America will develop as a regional project in the short term:

Scenario One: Underground North America

President Obama has come in for criticism from his own left flank as he demonstrates a strong pragmatic streak and an affinity for technical expertise. With 'bigger fish to fry,' and with trade continuing to be a lightning-rod issue pitting angry constituents against nervous foreign trading partners, Obama and his economic team may be happy to learn that North American integration can continue to advance – incremen-tally and intergovernmentally – without the SPP or any other overarch-ing program. Obama, like President Clinton after the bruising NAFTA approval process, may prefer that whole issue disappear from public view. Moreover, also like Clinton, Obama has foreign economic policy aims that favour multilateralism, and he is likely to want to advance *global* trade as part of a multilateral response to the crisis. Given these incentives, the obvious solution would be to send North American integration back 'underground' and to entrust its operation to technical experts with deep knowledge of the system's inner workings. Indeed, the Obama/Harper perimeter accords of February 2011 announced the launch of two new bodies in the 'working group' model – the Beyond the Border Working Group (BBWG) and the Regulatory Cooperation Council – aimed at deepening the grooves and connections among spe-cialized government officials (Sands 2011, 20–1).

At the same time, by trusting these in-house experts, Obama may be able to engage at home in some electorally friendly populism (as the Buy American provisions have been labelled), while trusting that all can be smoothed out on a bilateral basis behind the scenes. Indeed, the rapid and highly collegial solution of the Buy American controversy through a bilateral accord with Canada negotiated mainly by teams of interoperable trade hands demonstrates the model that Obama may seek to replicate if conflict arises in the future with his country's NAFTA partners.

Scenario Two: North America, Overboard

If going 'underground' would appeal to Obama's pragmatic, incre-
mentalist, and technocratic side, sending the whole project of NAFTA-
based regional integration 'overboard' would resonate with his stated
commitment to government transparency and accountability. Specifically, it would address the main criticisms of the integration process
emanating from both sides of the political spectrum in the United
States, as well as from major critical voices in Mexico and Canada (as
analysed in this volume by Ayres and Macdonald). All of these groups
have called for greater legislative oversight over, and citizen input into,
integration-oriented policies as well as for more attention to how integration affects local communities such as those in cross-border regions
(Policy Research Initiative 2006). As Ayres and Macdonald, as well as
Gabriel, point out in this volume, citizenship issues in the region are
so fraught because NAFTA and (later) the SPP have been perceived
as empowering corporations without providing any institutions that
would be sensitive either to citizen input or to mobility rights capable
of protecting border-crossing citizens from exploitation. Embracing,
ironically enough, the European principle of *subsidiarity* – that is, keeping the level of regulation and rule making as close to the citizen as
possible – this new approach to integration would look to 'cross-border
microregions' and subnational paradiplomacy of the kind described by
Vengroff and Allan in order to overcome North America's 'democratic
deficit.' A number of such proposals and initiatives are already at work,
such as the Borders 2012 initiative discussed in this volume by Van-
Nijnatten and Craik. There is also potential for the Mérida Initiative to
be revised, localized, and opened to civil society input. This approach
would, however, also base its legitimacy on a rejection of the fantasy
of trilateralism and embrace double-bilateralism as an indication that
the United States has moved from a position of ideologically driven
regional dominance towards one of pragmatic leadership favouring
targeted, citizen-led problem solving.

What Ails North America: Is *Triple Bilateralism* the Answer?

Given the extent to which double-bilateralism has consolidated itself
as the dominant mode of inter-state cooperation and conflict resolution in the region, it is clear that trilateralism is not now, nor has it ever
been, a viable governance model for North America. At the same time,

this *empirical* observation does not necessarily preclude the *normative* assessment that the current state of North American governance is suboptimal. Rather than viewing Mexico's development as a *regional* goal, deserving of the commitment of *regional* resources, the United States has used double-bilateralism to further leverage its asymmetrical advantage over Mexico in both security and economic agendas, while Canada has tended to treat Mexico as a threat to its 'special relationship' rather than as a partner or even an ally to counterbalance the United States. Mexico's marginalization has not been beneficial either to the United States – which has felt most directly the impact of undocumented migration flows and, more recently, the effects of increasing drug violence – or to Canada, which has also begun to absorb more Mexican workers (George 2008) and asylum seekers, the latter often fleeing their home country's growing drug-related violence. That marginalization promises to be detrimental to both countries into the future (Hausmann and Macdonald 2009, 333–4). But if trilateralism is not a realistic option, what other dynamic could potentially shift these ingrained double-bilateral practices towards a more balanced and, ultimately, just relationship between the three NAFTA partners?

Here I would put forward an unlikely candidate for this job: the 'triple-bilateral' approach, which envisions a more prominent role for a third North American bilateral dyad – one between Canada and Mexico. There is nothing new in recognizing the potential of this relationship for bringing the region into better balance. In the post-9/11 period, for example, this point has been made quite eloquently, if only rhetorically, in the 2002 'Partners in North America' parliamentary report, and it was the main argument of a 2005 binational study group, which also noted with dismay that the SPP lacked even a single Canada–Mexico initiative (Goldfarb 2005, 8). More recently, the Canadian Foundation for the Americas (FOCAL) and the Mexican Council on Foreign Relations (COMEXI) launched a binational working group based on the premise that the bilateral relationship 'is of critical and rising importance to both countries' (Canada–Mexico Initiative 2010).

These voices point to a number of key synergies linking these two North American partners, among them shared multilateralist foreign policy traditions, a commitment to playing a 'middle power' role in the Americas, and, most notably, a historic vocation to individuate themselves from the overwhelming, identity-crushing proximity of the United States. Other synergies emerge, ironically, from the very asymmetry between them, in the form of complementarities: Canada's much-celebrated educational, high-tech, and NGO sectors could help equilibrate Mexico's economic and social deficits while diminishing dependence on U.S. expertise, while Mexican unskilled and skilled workers – for example, nurses – could help fill growing labour market shortages in Canada. To date, however, the only 'special relationship' in North America that has mattered consistently for Canada has been with the United States, and Canada has shown little interest in leveraging this relationship to 'level up' Mexico. Indeed, Athanasios Hristoulas (2006, 330–2) critically notes that, in light of its much-trumpeted commitment to promoting 'human security' internationally, Canada's less than generous attitude towards its NAFTA partner smacks of moral hypocrisy as well as practical short-sightedness.

Clearly there has been a yawning gap between the potential and the actualization of the 'third bilateral' in North America. But that gap may be bridged by looking beyond national governments – whose incentives still lean against spillover and towards containment of regional mutuality – towards non-state actors. Civil society groups, labour unions, microcredit and other not-for-profit sources of development assistance, the private sector (small and medium businesses as well as traditional continental enterprises), academic networks (students and professors), and transnationalized migrants all have the potential to generate a bilateral and even regional mutuality that heretofore has been stymied in the governmental sphere. Following the demise of 'big ideas' such as the SPP, the future of North American integration may yet lie in this context, in which Canadian and Mexican citizens may start talking and listening to one another and a hundred small ideas may take shape.

Official bilateral cooperation between Canada and Mexico is hardly extensive. However, two recent programs point in the direction of leadership in the 'third bilateral' by non-state actors. The Canadian Fund for Local Initiatives (CFLI), or *Fondo Canadá*, is a development assistance program of the Canadian Institute for Development Assistance (CIDA), administered by the Canadian Embassy in Mexico City, whose purpose is 'to finance small development projects which provide technical and economic support to projects focusing on democracy, human rights, governance, rural development, health and education … [thus enabling] Canada to work directly with local communities (through NGOs)' ('What Is the Canada Fund …?' n.d.). The CFLI is not exclusive to Mexico; it also operates in Africa, Asia, and Eastern and Central Europe. Also, the program is matched at CIDA by programs that seek out Canadian citizens – students, Aboriginal Canadians, members of the 'voluntary sector' – as 'partners' for NGOs receiving grants for their projects. Thus, not only is there a traditional use of aid as a diplomatic tool, but there is also an attempt to connect non-state actors to one another.

Meanwhile, the Canada–Mexico Partnership (CMP), founded in 2004, promises to do for the private sector what the CFLI is doing for NGOs – that is, to give them an equal seat at the table in shaping bilateral cooperation in a variety of issue areas, such as trade, investment, science and technology, agribusiness, energy, labour mobility, environment, and forestry ('Canada-Mexico Partnership' n.d.). Following the same working group structure as NAFTA and the SPP, the CMP innovates by adding non-trade issues to the discussion. It also offers a vehicle for greater communication across borders by non-state actors, in terms of organization, legitimacy, and resources. Thus, whether or not state elites in Canada and Mexico ever overcome double-bilateral obstacles to (re)discover one another and, as Andrew Cooper puts it, move 'from a relationship of convenience to a relationship of commitment' (Cooper 2008), these programs speak to the potential of non-state actors to develop North American interests and identities that are independent of NAFTA-centric, state-based models.

Similarly, recent research on North American integration has shown that it is *non-state* actors that are innovating and challenging received wisdom about governance in the region. For example, Jeffrey Ayres and Laura Macdonald and their colleagues document and analyse the development of, and struggles within, North American transnational civil society coalitions that are organizing to resist what other authors have also identified as the 'disciplining' nature of neoliberal continental integration after NAFTA (Ayres and Macdonald 2009). Joe Bandy, for example, profiles the Coalition for Justice in the Maquiladoras (CJM), which he views as a trinational group that has transcended borders but that has also had to confront the asymmetries of understanding and of perspective that mirror differences in race, social class, and education within the otherwise normatively cohesive coalition (Bandy 2009). What is notable is that the ethos of civil society – self-organizing, focused on participatory practices and on holding the state accountable – offers not a romanticized egalitarian sphere, but rather a venue for debate over what a group values and who can speak for the group. Such issues are at the heart of what it means to participate democratically in a political community.

Finally, it bears noting that the North American Competitiveness

Council (NACC), the trinational business lobby group organized in 2006 to give continentalized business a unified voice in the SPP 'stakeholder' process, went further than its government partners in devising a genuinely trilateral internal governance structure ('North American Competitiveness Council' n.d.). Rather than replicating the 'green room' model mentioned earlier, the three national secretariats of the NACC innovated and operated on a *consensual* basis, producing single trinationally endorsed documents. While business may find its SPP/NACC-defined broader role shrunk to fit the more regulation-specific function of the new Regulatory Cooperation Council (RCC), the relationships forged between Mexican and Canadian corporate members set a precedent for continued *direct* consultation between them, overcoming the double-bilateral divide, while the model of consensus-based governance suggests an innovation that could be replicated among other non-business groups in the region.

There is, however, one sector that provides a less optimistic view of the 'triple-bilateral' approach advanced here: migration. On the one hand, the greater influx of Mexicans into Canada noted earlier, whether as students, workers, or asylum seekers, suggests more interaction, more direct contact, and possibly greater participation of Mexicans in Canadian-based groups, just as hometown associations, immigrants' rights groups, and even labour unions are providing direct experience for Mexicans in the U.S. political system. On the other hand, the Canadian government has asserted its control over this process by instituting a visa requirement for *all* Mexicans entering Canada as of July 2009 (CIC 2009a). Canada's visa requirement, vigorously denounced by Mexican officials, technically does not target Mexicans alone – indeed, Canada requires such visas from nationals of over 140 other countries, and on the same day in July 2009 citizens of the Czech Republic were also faced with a new visa requirement ('Czech Republic Recalls Ambassador' 2009). Furthermore, with Mexican refugee claims tripling in the previous four years and Mexico topping the list with one-quarter of all claims in 2008, the visa is of a piece with Minister Jason Kenney's aim to avoid special treatment for any country within Canada's refugee policy (CIC 2009b), and to give preference to asylum seekers outside of Canada over those (such as most Mexicans) who enter first and then seek refugee status (Christina Gabriel, personal communication).

Still, while the visa may be designed to prevent abuse of the system, it has also served as a disincentive for legitimate travellers –

including short-term students, artists, and tourists from Mexico – to visit Canada, and it could potentially short-circuit the 'triple-bilateral' dynamic (Garzu 2010). But more than that, the visa has underscored the regional mutuality deficit. Its symbolic impact is arguably greater because Mexico is not just any Latin American source of inward migration or asylum seekers: it is Canada's NAFTA partner, and Mexicans seeking refuge from drug violence are not simply economic migrants. Perhaps as the transnational effects of this humanitarian crisis deepen, a new realization will be made: that what has been compartmentalized as a U.S.–Mexico bilateral issue is, in fact, one that does and should matter directly to Canada in the context of the 'third bilateral.'

Concluding Remarks: A New 'Third Option' for North America

In this chapter I have argued that, rather than forming an obstacle to North American regional integration, double-bilateralism is a central truth of the project, one that is unlikely to change. Deliberate choices made – starting with the negotiation of a trinational free trade agreement from a distinctly 'double-bilateral' ethos, through the 'silent integration' years, then the response to 9/11 and the 'homeland security' imperative, right through the nominally trilateral but effectively two-speed SPP – have added up to a region that is little more than the sum of two bilateral relationships.

At the same time, in contemplating what the future of North American integration might look like after Bush and the SPP, I argued, first, that a more honest approach would recognize the primacy of double-bilateralism in governing conflict and cooperation in the region. Unlike Europe, which was a political project from the start and which responded to various 'great leaps forward' engineered by intellectuals and political leaders, North America continues to resist such grandiose designs. This may mean that, in the absence of U.S. presidential leadership such as that provided for the SPP by George W. Bush, and in the presence of severe economic hardship (particularly in Mexico), North American integration may be entering a time of quiescence and even of drift. Or, as the recent perimeter accords have suggested, the Obama administration's aim towards greater honesty in North American relations may translate simply into a more open pursuit of double-bilateralism.

However, another way to look at this reality is to recognize that moments of breakdown and failure can also be moments of great self-awareness and creativity. For that reason, I have suggested that a 'third option' could emerge now to counterbalance this dominant pattern through non-state interactions that bridge the gap in NAFTA's third bilateral between Canada and Mexico. While the first wave of post-NAFTA regional integration has been dominated by one set of non-state actors – the continentalized private sector – perhaps this new wave will have the effect of empowering civil society, particularly groups in Canada and Mexico, to question the double-bilateral divide and to demand of national governments a more inclusive and responsive regional model. Just as the Third Option discussed in the 1970s sought to liberate Canadian foreign policy from rigid notions of necessity, perhaps the 'triple-bilateral' trend will liberate North America from its own suboptimal patterns of division, inequality, and injustice.

References

Ackelson, Jason, and Justin Kastner. 2006. 'The Security and Prosperity Partnership of North America.' *American Review of Canadian Studies* 36, no. 2 (Summer): 207–32.

Andreas, Peter. 2004. 'U.S.–Mexico Border Control in a Changing Economic and Security Context.' Working Paper (December). Washington: Woodrow Wilson International Center for Scholars.

'A Second Wave (Briefing: The Euro Crisis).' 2011. *The Economist*, 18 June, 29–31.

Ayres, Jeffrey M. 1998. *Defying Conventional Wisdom: Political Movements and Popular Contention against North American Free Trade*. Toronto: University of Toronto Press.

Ayres, Jeffrey, and Laura Macdonald. 2009. *Contentious Politics in North America: National Protest and Transnational Collaboration under Continental Integration*. Basingstoke: Palgrave Macmillan.

– 2006. 'Deep Integration and Shallow Governance: The Limits of Civil Society Engagement across North America.' *Politics and Society* 25, no. 3 (Spring): 23–42.

Bandy, Joe. 2009. 'Paradoxes of a Transnational Civil Society in a Neoliberal World: The Coalition for Justice in the Maquiladoras.' In *Contentious Politics in North America: National Protest and Transnational Collaboration under Continental Integration*. Edited by Jeffrey Ayres and Laura Macdonald. Basingstoke: Palgrave Macmillan.

Blank, Stephen. 2007. Preface to Jean-Paul Rodrigue, 'Managing Rail Expansion and Congestion in North American Freight Transportation: The

Thruport Concept.' Working Paper no. 4 (December). North American Transportation Competitiveness Research Council.

Blank, Stephen, and Jerry Haar. 1998. *Making NAFTA Work: U.S. Firms and the New North American Business Environment*. Miami: North–South Center Press of the University of Miami.

Bumiller, Elisabeth. 2003. 'White House Letter: Two Presidential Pals, Until 9/11 Intervened.' *New York Times*, 3 March. http://www.nytimes.com/2003/03/03/us/white-house-letter-two-presidential-pals-until-9-11-intervened.html. Accessed 9 November 2011.

Cameron, Maxwell A., and Brian Tomlin. *The Making of NAFTA: How the Deal Was Done*. Ithaca: Cornell University Press.

Canada, Department of Foreign Affairs and International Trade (DFAIT). 2001. 'Canada-U.S. Smart Border Declaration.' http://www.dfait-maeci.gc.ca/anti-terrorism/declaration-en.asp. Accessed 19 November 2009.

Canada, House of Commons, Standing Committee on Foreign Affairs and International Trade. 2002. 'Partners in North America: Advancing Canada's Relations with the United States and Mexico.' Tabled 12 December 2002. http://www2.parl.gc.ca/HousePublications/Publication.aspx?DocId=1032319&Language=E&Mode=1&Parl=37&Ses=2. Accessed 19 November 2009.

Canada–Mexico Initiative. 2010. 'The Canada–Mexico Relationship: A Backgrounder.' Working Paper. http://focal.ca/images/stories/pdfs/Canada-Mexico_FOCAL_Backgrounder_October%202010_e_sm.pdf. Accessed 15 October 2010.

'Canada-Mexico Partnership.' n.d. http://www.canadainternational.gc.ca/mexico-mexique/cmp-pcm.aspx?lang=en. Accessed 15 October 2010.

Citizenship and Immigration Canada. 2009a. 'Canada Imposes a Visa on Mexico.' http://www.cic.gc.ca/english/department/media/releases/2009/2009-07-13.asp. Accessed 13 July 2010.

– 2009b. 'Facts and Figures: Immigration Overview, Permanent and Temporary Residents.' Research and Evaluation Branch. http://www.cic.gc.ca/english/pdf/research-stats/facts2008.pdf. Accessed 19 November 2009.

Clarkson, Stephen, Sarah Davidson Ladly, and Carlton Thorn. 2002. 'De-Institutionalizing North America: NAFTA's Committees and Working Groups.' Paper presented to the Third EnviReform Conference, Toronto, 8 November 8. http://www.envireform.utoronto.ca/conference/nov2002/clarkson-paper2.pdf. Accessed 15 October 2010.

Cooper, Andrew F. 2008. 'Thinking Outside the Box in Canada–Mexico Relations: The Long Road from Convenience to Commitment.' In *Big Picture Realities: Canada and Mexico at the Crossroads*. Edited by Daniel Drache. Waterloo: Wilfrid Laurier University Press, 237–49.

'Czech Republic Recalls Ambassador.' 2009. *Globe and Mail*, 14 July. http://www.theglobeandmail.com/news/politics/mexico-czech-republic-criticize-visa-requirements/article1216687. Accessed 13 July 2010.

D'Aquino, Thomas. 2003.'Security and Prosperity: The Dynamics of a New Canada–United States Partnership in North America.' Presentation to the Annual General Meeting of the Canadian Council of Chief Executives, Toronto, 14 January.

Dobson, Wendy. 2002. 'Shaping the Future of the North American Space.' The Border Papers, no. 162 (April). Toronto: C.D. Howe Institute.

Doern, G. Bruce, and Brian Tomlin. 1991. *Faith and Fear: The Free Trade Story*. Toronto: Stoddart.

Dukert, Joseph M. 2007. 'North American Energy, 2000–2007: What a Difference Those Years Make!' *American Review of Canadian Studies* 37, no. 1 (Spring): 57–76.

Garzu, Anca. 2010. 'Mexicans Declare "Surprise, Anger" at Visa Application Process.' *Embassy Magazine*, 28 April. http://www.embassymag.ca/page/view/visa-04-28-2010. Accessed 13 July 2010.

George, Usha. 2008. 'Mexican Migration to Canada: Case Study Report.' *Journal of Immigrant and Refugee Studies* 6, no. 3 (2008): 463–74.

Goff, Patricia M. 2000. 'Invisible Borders: Economic Liberalization and National Identity.' *International Studies Quarterly* 44 (December): 533–62.

Goldfarb, Danielle. 2005. 'The Canada–Mexico Conundrum: Finding Common Ground.' The Border Papers, no. 91 (July). Toronto: C.D. Howe Institute.

Golob, Stephanie R. 2008. 'The Return of the Quiet Canadian: Canada's Approach to Regional Integration after 9/11.' In *An Independent Foreign Policy for Canada? New Directions and Debates*. Edited by Brian Bow and R. Patrick Lennox. Toronto: University of Toronto Press. 83–99.

– 2003. 'Beyond the Policy Frontier: Canada, Mexico, and the Ideological Origins of NAFTA.' *World Politics* 55, no. 3 (April): 361–98.

Graubart, Jonathan. 2008. *Legalizing Transnational Activism: The Struggle to Gain Social Change from NAFTA's Citizen Petitions*. University Park: Penn State University Press.

Gutiérrez Haces, Teresa. 2006. 'Entre la protección a la inversión extranjera directa y la disciplina sobre gobiernos: el caso del capítulo XI del TLCAN.' In *Diez años del TLCAN en México*. Edited by Mónica Gambrill. Mexico City: UNAM CISAN-IIE-Facultad de Economía. 383–420.

Haas, Ernst. 1968. *The Uniting of Europe: Political, Social, and Economic Forces, 1950–1957*. Stanford: Stanford University Press.

– 1964. *Beyond the Nation State: Functionalism and International Organization*. Stanford: Stanford University Press.

Haas, Peter. 1989. 'Do Regimes Matter? Epistemic Communities and Mediter-
ranean Pollution Control.' *International Organization* 43 (Summer): 377–403.
Hart, Michael, Bill Dymond, and Colin Robertson. 1994. *Decision at Midnight:
Inside the Canada–U.S. Free Trade Negotiations*. Vancouver: UBC Press.
Haussman, Melissa, and Laura Macdonald. 2009. 'Introduction: Canada–U.S.
Relations under Obama: Continuity or Change? ACSUS Enders Sympo-
sium, Carleton University, 24 October 2008.' *American Review of Canadian
Studies* 39, no. 4 (Enders Symposium Issue, December 2009): 323–35.
Hettne, Björn, András Inotai, and Osvaldo Sunkel. 1999. 'Globalization and
the New Regionalism: The Second Great Transformation.' In *Globalism and
the New Regionalism*. Edited by Björn Hettne, András Inotai, and Osvaldo
Sunkel. New York: St Martin's in association with UNU/WIDER.
Hristoulas, Athanasios. 2006. 'Canada in Latin America: A Foreign Policy of
Ambivalence, Pragmatism, or Inconsistency?' In *Handbook of Canadian For-
eign Policy*. Edited by Patrick James, Nelson Michaud, and Marc J. O'Reilly.
Lanham: Lexington. 317–35.
Kilroy, Richard J., Jr. 2007. 'Perimeter Defense and Regional Security Coop-
eration in North America: United States, Canada, and Mexico.' *Homeland
Security Affairs Journal*, Supp. 1. http://www.hsaj.org/?special:article=suppl
ement.1.3. Accessed 15 October 2010.
Lock, Reinier. 1993. 'Mexico–U.S. Energy Relations After NAFTA.' *U.S.–Mexico
Law Journal* 1 (1993): 235–54.
Lyon, Peyton. 1968. 'Quiet Diplomacy Revisited.' In *An Independent Foreign
Policy for Canada?* Edited by Stephen Clarkson. Toronto: University League
for Social Reform. 29–41.
Melious, Jean O. 2006. 'Environmental Regulation of Marine Vessel Emissions
and Port Competitiveness in Canada and the United States: An Analysis of
the Port of Vancouver and the Ports of Seattle and Tacoma.' Paper presented
at the ACSUS-in-Alaska Colloquium, 'Canada in the North Pacific,' Anchor-
age, 28–30 September.
McKinney, Joseph. 2000. *Created from NAFTA: The Structure, Function, and Sig-
nificance of the Treaty's Related Institutions*. Armonk: M.E. Sharpe.
'North American Competitiveness Council.' n.d. http://coa.counciloftheameri-
cas.org/group.php?id=10. Accessed 15 October 2010.
Pastor, Robert A. 2007. 'The Solution to North America's Triple Problem: The
Case for a North American Investment Fund.' *Norteamérica* 2, no. 2 (July–
December): 185–207.
Peacock, Nina. 2006. 'New Lessons from the Old World: Side Payments and
Regional Development Funds.' *Norteamérica* 1, no. 2 (July–December):
99–125.

Pierson, Paul. 2004. *Politics in Time: History, Institutions, and Social Analysis.* Princeton: Princeton University Press.

Policy Research Initiative. 2006. 'North American Linkages Briefing Note: Canada-U.S. Relations and the Emergence of Cross-Border Regions.' (February). http://policyresearch.gc.ca/doclib/XBorder_BN_e.pdf. Accessed 15 October 2010.

Rohter, Larry. 1990. 'Free Trade Talks with U.S. Set Off Debate in Mexico.' *New York Times,* 29 March, A1, D23.

Sands, Christopher. 2011. 'The Canada Gambit: Will It Revive North America?' Security and Foreign Affairs Briefing Paper (March). Washington: Hudson Institute.

Thelen, Kathleen. 1999. 'Historical Institutionalism in Comparative Politics.' *Annual Review of Political Science* 2: 369–404.

VanNijnatten, Debora. 2007. 'The Security and Prosperity Agreement as an "Indicator Species" for the Emerging North American Environmental Regime.' *Politics and Policy* 35, no. 4 (December): 664–82.

'What Is the Canada Fund for Local Initiatives (Canada Fund)?' n.d. http://www.canadainternational.gc.ca/mexico-mexique/dev/c_fund-fonds.aspx?lang=en. Accessed 15 October 2010.

White House, Office of the Press Secretary. 2011. 'Declaration by President Obama and Prime Minister Harper of Canada – "Beyond the Border: A Shared Vision for Perimeter Security and Economic Competitiveness."' Washington, 4 February. http://www.whitehouse.gov/the-press-office/2011/02/04/declaration-president-obama-and-prime-minister-harper-canada-beyond-bord. Accessed 22 November 2011.

10 Paradiplomacy: States and Provinces in the Emerging Governance Structure of North America

JAMES P. ALLAN AND RICHARD VENGROFF

As noted in the introduction to this volume, the character of the North American region is increasingly complex and multilayered. While the process of regionalization seems to be faltering at the level of nation-states, subnational relations appear to be flourishing. As discussed in this chapter, the number of contacts, official meetings, signed accords, cooperative agreements, collaborations on policies, and trade delegations traversing the U.S.–Canadian border and far beyond has grown dramatically in the past decade. Several international organizations composed of subnational units (states, provinces, and even cities and metropolitan areas) have grown, developing regular meetings and coordinated programs. These include associations in border regions across both countries and even some organizations linking interior states with Canadian provinces such as the Southeastern United States / Central and Eastern Canadian Provinces Alliance. In the Pacific Northwest, as William Yardley noted in a *New York Times* article on 27 February 2010, 'Business leaders and elected officials took the Cascadian dream and worked to make it a brand, a cross-border powerhouse of trade and tourism tilted toward Asia, the Arctic and the new, all to be linked by high-speed rail, a green economy and a sense of independence from Ottawa and Washington.' The same article suggests that not all signs are quite that positive, arguing that the new security regulations and the downturn in the economy have put on hold the emergence of 'Cascadia' as a region spanning the Pacific Northwest.

These international contacts, discussions, and agreements often occur without benefit of direct formal involvement by either the Government of Canada or the Government of the United States. Yet the states and provinces involved have introduced new policies and regulations to conform to these agreements. Recently, France and the Province of Quebec launched a joint trade mission to Mexico. Although Quebec has been a leader of the paradiplomacy movement (Michaud 2003; Balthazar 1993, 1999; Bélanger 1993; Bernier 1996), as of this writing all of Canada's ten provincial governments maintain either an international office or a separate international ministry to handle their external relations, here identified as 'paradiplomatic' activity. Our concern in this chapter, as with the chapters throughout this volume, is the impact of the current global economic crisis on an emerging governance network (or perhaps structure) in North America. More particularly, we are here interested in examining how these economic challenges influence the nature, direction, and levels of paradiplomatic activity and hence North American governance. Our focus here is on relations among subnational actors in Canada and the United States, but similar processes are at work in U.S.–Mexican relations (Schiavon Uriegas and Velázquez Flores 2009).[1]

While all of Canada's provinces and the U.S. states have engaged in this type of activity for some time now (Kukucha 2009), they are not alone or even at the cutting edge in terms of paradiplomacy (Hocking 1999a, 1999b; Michaud 2002; Duchacek, Latouche, and Stevenson 1988). In Europe, Belgium's regions of Flanders and Wallonia regularly sign treaties and other agreements with sovereign states and have an international role that equals and sometimes surpasses that of the Belgian state (Paquin 2003a). In Spain, Catalonia maintains a presence abroad, not only in Europe but much farther afield (Paquin 2003b), while in the United Kingdom the devolved Scottish government maintains offices in the United States and China (Allan and Vengroff 2008). The U.S. states have significant involvement in international economic issues and trade (Fry 1993, 2004). In other federal countries such as Australia and Germany, federal and state/*Land* governments jointly participate in a variety of foreign policy decisions (Michaud 2002; Craven 1993; Ravenhill 1999). Elsewhere in Europe, calls for greater regional autonomy 'from below,' and recognition of subnational regions 'from above' (i.e., the European Union), have combined to create a new dynamic in foreign policy making. These are just a few examples of the growing international presence and action of subnational governments.

How has this situation come about? Are not international relations under the purview of central governments? Why is this type of activity becoming more and more prevalent – indeed, at a rate that far exceeds the growth of international activity among the traditional representatives of sovereign states? And how do these developments affect regional governance and integration?

As Ayres and Macdonald demonstrate in the introduction to this volume, traditional explanations for regional integration have largely reflected the broader theoretical concerns of international relations and international political economy. Scholars have disagreed over the motivations underlying decisions to form regional organizations, particularly among leaders of those national states that prior to the growth of regionalization had been seen as the predominant actors in the international system. European integration in particular has, perhaps unsurprisingly, attracted the most scholarly attention, but after successive waves of integration, attention has also turned elsewhere.

While European integration continues to attract considerable attention, particularly as the process has widened and deepened in recent decades, the defining feature of the most recent wave of integration has been the proliferation of regional organizations around the world. As efforts to reach binding agreements through multilateral trade negotiations in venues such as the World Trade Organization have faltered, hundreds of regional trade agreements have been signed that have created scores of free trade areas, many with overlapping memberships.

The growth of agreements during this second wave of regional integration continues to be interpreted through traditional theoretical lenses. The shift in U.S. policy away from championing liberal multilateralism towards joining regional trade agreements such as CUSFTA and NAFTA has been particularly notable (Taylor 2008). Realists have viewed this as a declining economic hegemon seeking to maintain its position in the face of rising economic challenges from Japan and Europe. Greater access to the U.S. market also has served the interests of Canada and Mexico, notwithstanding that NAFTA has created large asymmetries of economic power. Liberal institutionalists, while preferring multilateral trade agreements through the GATT/WTO, have viewed agreements such as NAFTA as preferable to no agreements at all.[2]

While traditional theoretical lenses continue to be applied to the new wave of regionalism – a wave that has included the negotiation of regional agreements in North America – other scholars have seen the process as emanating from a different set of conditions and priorities that have made this wave of regionalism distinct from that of the postwar era. In particular, the onset of globalization has created a new set of imperatives that are distinct from those of the bipolar world of the immediate postwar era (Hettne 2003).

Absent from much of the previous discussion of regional integration, however, has been the role of substate actors – the focus of this chapter. The unitary actor approach of realism assumed away such internal state differences, while liberal approaches typically have privileged the interests of economic actors over political ones. More recent work, however – including studies employing the 'new regionalism' approach – has given greater attention to such entities. Keating (2006) stresses the emergence of the 'politics of territory' in both Europe and North America. Jessop (2003) argues that microregions and 'cross-border regions' often have emerged as microregional responses to globalization and to the restructuring of economic and political activities from the national to the subnational level.

A review of the growing literature on paradiplomacy suggests a number of key factors that have contributed to this trend. Among the most commonly cited factors are increasing globalization; international, including continental, trade agreements; the ongoing impacts of federalism, nationalism, and decentralization; existing but somewhat ambiguous constitutional provisions; and the expansion of international activity into spheres heretofore reserved for subnational units. Duchacek was among the first scholars to talk of various types of paradiplomacy. He labelled these respectively: *regional* paradiplomacy – regionally confined interactions among peripheral local, provincial, state, and cantonal governments; *transregional* paradiplomacy – institutionalized contacts among non-central governments that are not neighbours but whose governments are; and *global* paradiplomacy – contacts among non-contiguous countries' governments (Duchacek 1984, 1986, 1988; see also Aguirre 1999). In this chapter, we examine these aspects of paradiplomacy in general and then compare how they play out in several Canadian provinces – Quebec, Ontario, Alberta, and British Columbia – and how they in turn impact North American governance.

First, however, it is important to define the key term for discussion: paradiplomacy. Rosenau's perspective seems to underlie the thinking of many scholars on this issue. He argues that there has been a 'proliferation of relevant actors' on the world stage and an increasing 'density of actors that sustain world politics' (Rosenau 1997, 67). 'Glocalization' – the simultaneous push of globalization, regionalization, and local concerns – is at the root of these changes. Paradiplomacy fits under what he calls 'the other world of world politics.' Nossal (1997, 292) suggests that there is emerging 'a diffuse multi-centric world consisting of numerous international actors such as local governments, NGOs and transnational corporations.' Hocking, making the case for the grow-ing importance of non-central governments (NCGs), argues that they have made 'the boundaries demarcating state and non-state actors far more permeable than hitherto and creat[ed] ambiguities about the sta-tus and character of each' (1999a, 2). He concludes that foreign affairs have been at least partly removed from the exclusive control of central states and have become the concern of many subnational governments as well – a change he regards as having positive implications. Aguirre (1999) suggests that the nation-state has become 'polyvocal' – that is, it now speaks with more than one legitimate voice.

Dyment (1993) characterizes these many changes in diplomacy as international relations among 'perforated sovereïgnties' or as 'substate paradiplomacy' and 'paradiplomacy' with other states. Telford (2003, 3) makes the case that 'considerable political activity is happening along the multiple frontiers between the local, provincial, federal, Aboriginal and international spheres of governance.' In identifying this process in Canada, Telford argues that 'contemporary political problems do not fit neatly into distinct jurisdictional boundaries, if they ever did, and the governments of Canada are increasingly enmeshed in a complex network of relationships' (ibid., 3).

According to Paquin (2003a, 2003b), paradiplomacy comes into play when a subnational government gives its representatives a mandate to negotiate with other international actors. He emphasizes the importance of ethnic and linguistic diversity. Identity paradiplomacy occurs when the main objective of these foreign policy actions is to reinforce the 'con-struction' of the nation in the context of a multi-national (ethnic) coun-try. When the goal of 'para-diplomatic' activity becomes 'independence' or the creation and recognition of a new state, he labels such activity as qualitatively different and employs the term 'protodiplomacy.'

Some substate actors have even developed more important net-works and links than many state actors. There are literally hundreds of such actors in federal states alone. These units negotiate 'treaties' and agreements with sovereign actors, participate in international forums and international organizations, and even involve themselves in that most sacred function of the central state – human security issues. Their actions include sending economic, trade, and political missions abroad; participating in commercial fairs, regional organizations, and academic and student exchanges; and promoting investments, tourism, and cul-tural exchanges and even international development activities.

In sum, Kaiser (2005), drawing on the works contained in Michelmann and Soldatos (1990) and Aldecoa and Keating (1999), says that paradiplomacy refers to the external relations of subnational actors. He goes on to say that such relations either can be coordinated with and complementary to activities of the central state level, or are pursued in conflict or concurrence with traditional 'macrodiplomacy.' It is this broad perspective on paradiplomacy that will guide the analysis in this chapter.

Globalization, Federalism, Culture, and Paradiplomacy

Several common themes regarding the origins of paradiplomacy run throughout the literature. Most prominent among them are globalization and federalism–decentralization, the latter often complemented by the notion of 'subsidiarity.' Lecours (2002a, 2) argues that paradiplomacy gained prominence in the 1990s as a result of interactions among both international factors (economic globalization and the construction of supranational institutions) and domestic ones (a surge in territorial politics and decentralization). The core of this thinking is that paradiplomacy grew out of, or expanded directly with, increasing levels of globalization. Now that the world economy is becoming increasingly global and increasingly integrated in a variety of ways, subnational units (regions, states/provinces, even cities) have found their functions and activities circumscribed by the global system (Fry 2004; Michaud, 2002; Gosselin and Mace 1994).

What were once conceived of as strictly regional or local functions now have major international dimensions (Gerin-Lajoie 1989; Hooghe and Marks 2003; McIlroy 1997). Treaties signed at the central government level are impinging more and more on local policy or local areas of shared or full competence. Social policies, health care, education, transportation, and local tax regimes are all subject to agreements such as the WTO, NAFTA, the EU, and numerous other organizations. Global competition and dispute adjudication mechanisms are vital to regional economic development activities. Wages, environmental issues, labour conditions, and investment all are subject to external influences and in some cases control. One prominent example of this, among many, is the impact of the Chapter 11 dispute settlement procedures under NAFTA.

Federalism is another key contributor to the growth of paradiplomacy (Michaud 2002). Subnational actors such as states and provinces, which have a formal legal personality, are necessarily more likely to engage in international activities designed to promote and protect local or regional interests and prerogatives (Craven 1993). In some cases, such as Mexico, constitutional provisions relating to foreign affairs may clarify the matter. Mexican states are constitutionally highly constrained from engaging in foreign policy activity. In other cases, constitutional arrangements may lack clarity as well as mechanisms for limiting or coordinating subnational diplomatic activity. The added legitimacy associated with elected subnational governments provides another encouragement to action. Indeed, it is in federal states that paradiplomatic activity finds its greatest activity and support.

The changes that took place in Belgium when it became a federal state in 1993 stretch the limits of such activity; nevertheless, they are instructive. Both Flanders and Wallonia have signed numerous international agreements, including even treaties; also, both have many representatives abroad and participate directly in foreign policy decision making (Paquin 2003a). Catalonia has developed extensive international connections and initiatives in the context of the asymmetric quasi-federal relations it has in Spain (Paquin 2003b). German *Länder* are less independent in this regard but still exercise considerable influence over policies directly affecting their local interests (Craven 1993; Michaud 2002).

In Australia and Canada, the lack of constitutional clarity regarding the role of the federal and provincial/state governments in foreign policy has made paradiplomacy a more common and generally 'acceptable' activity. On the other hand, constitutional clarity on the division of other functions, such as education and social policy, means that the central government, while able to sign international treaties and agreements, depends on the subnational governments to implement those very same agreements (McIlroy 1997). That implementation, or lack thereof, can be quite contentious.

Canada is a federal state, but one in which there is a lack of constitutional clarity regarding the distribution of authority over foreign policy. The provinces' role in foreign policy is governed by provisions of the British North America Act (BNA) of 1867 and the Constitution Act of 1982, particularly Sections 91 and 92. These provisions 'specify the division of powers but fail to explicitly assign competence in foreign affairs to either the federal or provincial levels' (Nossal 1997, 292). The provinces were not specifically denied a role in either act. Nossal suggests that the provinces, not being prohibited from getting involved internationally, naturally sought to do so in order to protect and promote their own interests.

Although the 1982 constitution gives the central government the power to act to maintain 'peace, order, and good government' (clause

91), the courts have ruled that the 'federal government could not enact legislation in an area explicitly given to provinces under section 92, even if it was designed to fulfill obligations under an international treaty' (Nossal 1997, chapter 11). Furthermore, 'Parliament cannot amend provincial legislation or pass a new statute in an area of provincial legislative jurisdiction. Thus a treaty or a specific section thereof whose subject matter falls within the legislative competence of the provinces cannot be implemented unless the provincial legislatures intervene with respect to the matters within their jurisdiction' (Dupras 1993, 6).

This is consistent with the precedent codified by the Privy Council in 1937 in the 'Labour Conventions Case.' After Canada became a member of the International Labour Organization (ILO), the federal Parliament enacted legislation to implement it. Upon judicial review, however, the British House of Lords held that 'there was no such thing as a general federal power to implement international treaties' (McIlroy 1997, 434). In addition, they held: 'If the legislation dealt with a matter allocated to the federal Parliament, then Ottawa had the power to implement the treaty; however, if the subject matter was allocated to the provincial legislatures, then Ottawa could not enact treaty implementing legislation' (ibid.). Here, the legislation was struck down because the Parliament in Ottawa had enacted legislation dealing with labour, which is a provincial concern. Thus, 'sovereignty is not just an issue between nations; sovereignty is also an issue within some trading partners' (ibid.; Nossal 1997). In the United States, this has been an ongoing problem in a number of areas. For example, consular treaties specify that foreign nationals should have access to consular services when accused of a crime in the United States. States such as Texas have regularly violated or ignored this provision, even in high-profile murder cases involving Mexican citizens.

Hypotheses, Data, and Methods

As discussed elsewhere in this volume, with the impact of the 9/11 terrorist attacks, the change in administrations in Canada and the United States, and the global recession, the North American system is in a state of flux. It therefore seems like an opportune time to consider what impact these are having on North America as an emerging entity. What is the future of the North American community? This section examines changes, real and potential, in the nature and levels of paradiplomatic activity generated by the global economic crisis. As Figure 10.1 shows, the recent recession had a strong impact throughout Canada. One per-

Figure 10.1. Annual Real GDP Growth (% Change), Canada and Provinces (2010 figures are projected)

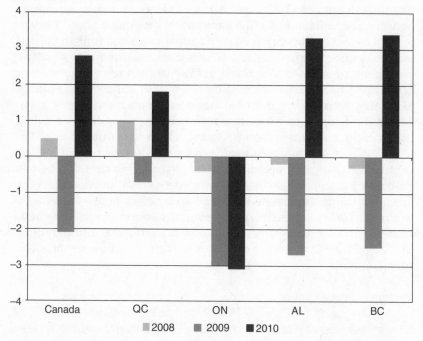

Source: Government of Alberta, Weekly Economic Review for week ending 10/16/2009.

spective suggests that, given the need for budgetary restraint and even cutbacks at the state and provincial levels, paradiplomatic activity is an obvious and politically painless area to cut. On the other hand, it can be argued that just the opposite is true. With the need to expand markets wherever possible, state and provincial governments may choose to increase or at least maintain current levels of paradiplomatic activity in the hope of ensuring their economic status when the world and North American economies recover. There is also some indication that some Canadian provinces see the current economic downturn as an opportunity to build on their comparative advantage in the banking and credit sector in order to enhance their position in the market. For example, Quebec opened a new business office in Atlanta in 2009 in order to look for new investment and partnership opportunities that have arisen in the current economic downturn.

To test our competing hypotheses, we have collected data on parad-iplomatic activity by subnational actors over time, focusing on Quebec, Ontario, Alberta, and B.C. These data include international agreements between subnational units (the paradiplomatic equivalent of treaties), as well as agreements between subnational units and foreign national governments. We also look at activity levels in provincial ministries and states' departments involved in international relations and trade. Have these bodies been affected by changes in budgets and staffing? Have they increased or decreased their involvement in North Ameri-can trade delegations? Are they maintaining, expanding, or cutting back on their representation in states or provinces outside the bor-ders of their respective countries? What roles do they play in regional organizations of provinces and states? What is the direction of their paradiplomacy? Is it heavily concentrated in North America, or has the economic downturn resulted in their looking elsewhere – for example, to China? We begin here by considering these questions in terms of the four provinces that are leaders in Canada's economic and paradiplo-matic activity. We then shift our focus to regional groupings of subna-tional units.

Paradiplomacy in Quebec

Quebec has been by far the most active Canadian province in its level of paradiplomatic activity. It has a well-institutionalized forty-year-old ministry dedicated solely to international relations, and that ministry employs an astonishing seven hundred staff. It is organized into four units, each roughly equivalent to a subministry: multilateral and fran-cophone affairs, bilateral affairs, protocol and missions, and adminis-tration. Two of the ministry's principle activities are developing and maintaining relations between Quebec and the francophone world, and promoting and maintaining ongoing trade and cultural relations with the United States, to which Quebec sends about 75% of its exports.

Since 1964, Quebec has signed more than six hundred international agreements, more than three hundred of which are still in effect with seventy-nine different countries. In addition, the province has a con-siderable presence overseas, with a network of twenty-eight offices in seventeen countries in the United States, Latin America, Europe, and Asia. Quebec has signed nine agreements within China, including three directly with the Chinese central government regarding educa-tion, science, and technology. Similar agreements have been negotiated out of the Quebec Government Bureau in Munich, which has facilitated thirty-five bilateral cooperation projects.

Quebec's government and people have been among the strongest supporters of CUSFTA and NAFTA and of free trade in general. Quebec has developed surprisingly strong ties with Mexico, which is its second-biggest trade partner in the hemisphere after the United States. Since the formation of a task force in 1982, Quebec and the Mexican government have signed ten cooperation agreements on issues that include forestry, the environment, education, vocational training, and culture.

Beyond this, Quebec has been an active participant in educational exchanges and cultural and language promotion. It has astutely maintained its French cultural heritage even while opening itself to economic globalization. The province is a member of the *Organisation Internationale de la Francophonie* (OIF), in which it plays a role similar to that of a sovereign state.

One important albeit largely symbolic feature of Quebec's foreign relations has been its support of international treaties. For example, it has incorporated the Kyoto Protocol into its international and domestic policies, coordinating both with the federal government. Also, provincial policy makers are currently working for the approval of two UN human rights treaties regarding children: the Optional Protocol to the Convention on the Rights of the Child on the Sale of Children, Child Prostitution, and Child Pornography; and the Convention on Protection of Children and Cooperation in Respect of Inter-Country Adoption.

Quebec has adjusted its paradiplomacy to shifts in domestic politics, particularly with regard to the controversial question of Quebec sovereignty. Under 'sovereigntist' Parti Québécois (PQ) governments in Quebec City, the province's international activity often crossed the line from paradiplomacy to proto-diplomacy. Proto-diplomacy, here, was part of Quebec's effort to lay the groundwork for international recognition and support for PQ aspirations for statehood. Conversely, under federalist Liberal (Liberal Party of Québec – PLQ) governments, Quebec has collaborated more closely with the federal authorities that implement foreign policy. According to Louis Balthazar, 'the development of transnational relations and of regional transborder transactions coupled with an awareness of globalization and interdependence seems to be the main reason why Québec has created and cultivated so many relations with foreign political entities' (1993, 150). Thus, it could be argued that regardless of who is in power, the overwhelming thrust

Figure 10.2. International Agreements by Governing Party in Quebec

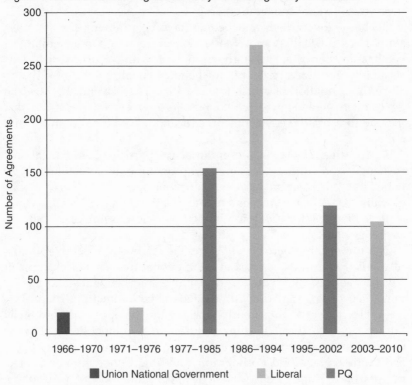

Source: Compiled from Quebec Ministry of International Affairs, Quebec Relations,
http://www.mri.gouv.qc.ca/en/relations_quebec/.

of international activity by Quebec is aimed at economic self-interest
rather than political independence. Consistent with this position is the
fact that whichever party has been in power in Quebec City, the PQ or
the PLQ, there has been an ongoing assertion of Quebec's right to participate in treaty negotiations and to approve any treaties that impinge
on areas of provincial authority.

As can be drawn from Figures 10.2 to 10.5, the overall level of paradiplomatic activity engaged in by Quebec is by all measures very high,
certainly among the highest in the world. Figure 10.2 shows the total
number of agreements made during periods when the Liberals and the
PQ respectively were in power. Somewhat surprisingly, the highest

Figure 10.3. Number of International Agreements by Year in Quebec

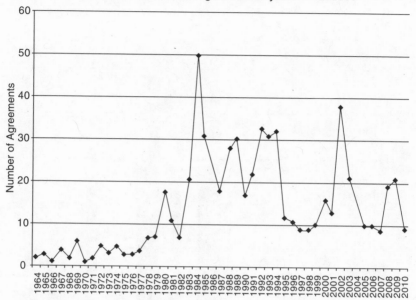

Source: Compiled from Quebec Ministry of International Affairs, Quebec Relations, http://www.mri.gouv.qc.ca/en/relations_quebec/.

level of activity was during the Liberal governments of 1986 to 1994 (268 agreements). This is followed by the PQ governments of 1977 to 1985 (156 agreements) and 1995 to 2002 (118 agreements). The Liberal government from 2003 to 2007 signed 66 agreements, and the Liberals from 1970 to 1976 signed 22 (3 per year). The two annual peaks (Figure 10.3) both occurred in the last year of a PQ government: 1984–5 and 2002. Perhaps these reflect flurries of activity designed to complete negotiations in progress during the life of those governments.

Because of the different lengths of time served by the various parties in government, it is important to consider the average number of agreements signed per year. The Liberal governments from 1984 to 1995 were a period of high but relatively stable levels of activity. The average for this period was 33.5 agreements a year. For the three other major periods, including two PQ governments and one Liberal government, the levels of activity are fairly consistent, averaging 19.5 per year under

Figure 10.4. Number of International Agreements by Type and Governing Party in Quebec

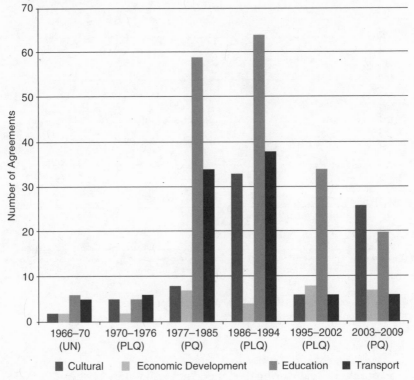

Source: Compiled from Quebec Ministry of International Affairs, Quebec Relations, http://www.mri.gouv.qc.ca/en/relations_quebec/.

the first PQ government and 16.8 under the second. During the current period of PLQ leadership, there has been an average of 16.5 agreements per year.

We expected to find differences between PQ and PLQ governments in both the types of agreements (Figure 10.4) and with whom those agreements were signed (Figure 10.5). But the only difference here is the somewhat greater emphasis on agreements regarding economic development under the PQ as opposed to the Liberals. This is linked to the emphasis the PQ places on ties with francophone Africa. In general, the direction of agreements towards certain countries also shows little dif-

Figure 10.5. Quebec's International Agreements – France, the United States, and Total

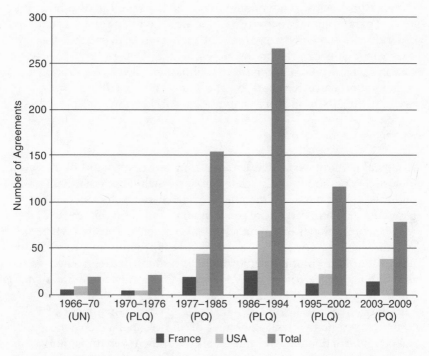

Source: Compiled from Quebec Ministry of International Affairs, Quebec Relations, http://www.mri.gouv.qc.ca/en/relations_quebec/.

ference between governments. For example, agreements between Quebec and various U.S. states between 1976 and 2009 remain very similar regardless of the Quebec regime in power. The same is true for Quebec's other most important international partners. The twenty-four agreements with Belgium and the eighty-five with France do not show significant differences from one government to the next.

Overall, it seems that the decision to involve Quebec in international activity was initially stimulated on a large scale by the sovereigntist governments of 1977 to 1985. Once the floodgates were opened, the Liberal government that followed outdid its PQ predecessor by demonstrating its strong commitment to representing Quebec's international interests. It seems that as this involvement grew and as CUSFTA and then NAFTA came into play, the global economic imperative became the dominant force. The influence or potential influence of domestic partisanship seems to have thereby receded. As we can also note, the level of paradiplomatic activity has not waned with the global economic downturn. Involvement remains quite high; one can even argue that it is increasing. Quebec's role in the New England–Eastern Provinces association remains pivotal. Thus, at the subnational level, cooperation and collaboration consistent with greater integration is still occurring and even growing in the face of a changing global economy.

Paradiplomacy in Ontario

Another of the most active provinces in terms of paradiplomacy is Ontario. Its paradiplomatic-related projects include international trade and investment missions, memberships in cross-border associations of subnational (state/provincial) governments, bilateral treaty-like agreements with national or subnational governments, and its own representation abroad. Ontario is Canada's largest province in terms of both population and volume of international trade. It currently houses its international office within the Ministry of Economic Development and Trade.

Ontario depends for about half its GDP on exports, most of them to the United States. The economies of all of Canada's provinces rely heavily international trade, and their governments are thus motivated to engage in paradiplomatic activities to represent, protect, and expand their interests. In this regard, Ontario and Quebec especially stand out. Before the current economic crisis, the Ontario government had undertaken fifty-six international missions to some twenty countries, including Germany, Italy, South Africa, and South Korea, with the goal of improving its position in the global market. In 2002, Ontario also negotiated three memoranda of understanding with the federal government so that the province could post Senior Economic Officers at the Canadian missions in Shanghai, New York, and Munich. On the diplomatic front, between 2001 and 2002 Ontario had more than 139 official interactions with foreign leaders and representatives. The province participated in separate summits with New York State and Michigan, signing memoranda to strengthen bilateral cooperation in tourism, transportation, energy, and technology. Early in 2004, the Ministry of Economic Development and Trade, which houses the Office of International Relations and Protocol, underwent a reorganization. The new

Office of International Relations and Protocol (OIRP) was moved to the Ministry of Intergovernmental Affairs. Its focus would now be on foreign relations, with a separate office dedicated solely to relations with the United States. That office's relatively high status was underlined by the fact that it reported directly to Ontario's Deputy Premier.

The current Liberal government of Ontario has moved most of its international activities back to the Ministry of Economic Development and Trade. The ministry has six divisions, including a Division of International Trade and Marketing, which runs ten international marketing centres in eight different countries, including one each in New York and Los Angeles. All of these are located in the Canadian government's consular offices. The New York office is especially important, given that nearly two-thirds of foreign investment capital in Ontario comes from that city. The Los Angeles office oversees exports to California that exceed any of Ontario's exports to international markets beyond the United States. In addition to the efforts of the Ministry of Economic Development and Trade, the Ministry of Intergovernmental Affairs provides advice to the premier on international affairs, protocol, and promoting the international image of Ontario. The Ministry of Research and Innovation funds a small program of strategic international collaboration between research institutions in Canada and those abroad (primarily in the United States). Recent paradiplomatic activities include trade missions to Miami and New York.

In general, Ontario's international activities are heavily focused on economic and trade issues and are closely tied to federal efforts as opposed to being independent in scope. The province does, however, play an active role in the Great Lakes Association of Governors and Provincial Premiers. While activity remains high, the economic downturn has had a somewhat dampening effect on paradiplomacy. Even so, it remains a core activity for the province.

Paradiplomacy in Alberta

Paradiplomatic activity by the Government of Alberta is channelled mainly through the Ministry of International and Intergovernmental Relations. The minister who leads the department has a fairly high profile within the Alberta cabinet, being listed fifth in order of precedence, ahead of such ministries as Energy (crucial in the oil-rich province) and Justice. Previously called the Ministry of Intergovernmental and Aboriginal Affairs, the department was renamed in 1999 to reflect the growing importance of the international arena for Alberta's activities. The ministry's mission is to 'advance Alberta's interests by leading government-wide strategies that capitalize on Alberta's regional, national, and global relationship and opportunities' (www.international.alberta.ca).

Within Canada, Alberta promotes its interests in a number of ways. Like all Canadian provincial governments, Alberta participates in the Council of the Federation and the First Ministers' Conferences. With its regional western neighbours, Alberta also participates in a number of cooperative ventures. The Western Premiers' Conference, which is similar to the Western Governors' Association in the United States, brings together the four western provinces as well as the three territories. Joint cabinet meetings are held on a regular basis with the provincial cabinets in B.C. and Saskatchewan as well as with Yukon.

Economic cooperation among the Western provinces has also become more prominent in recent years. In 2006, Alberta and B.C. signed the Trade, Investment, and Labour Mobility Agreement (TILMA), which went into full effect in early 2009. The purpose of TILMA was to remove barriers to trade between the provinces, as well as to make it easier for workers in licensed or regulated professions to move between provinces without having to be relicensed in their new place of work. In March 2009 the TILMA became the basis for a new agreement, the Western Economic Partnership, which promoted economic cooperation among Alberta, B.C., and Saskatchewan. Notably, the Western Economic Partnership includes a MOU devoted to promoting cooperation between the three provinces in the area of international marketing. That cooperation includes joint trade missions and the sharing of marketing intelligence (Alberta Ministry of International and Integovernmental Affairs n.d.). We now turn to the international dimension of Alberta's paradiplomacy.

Alberta has long had an international presence. Its first overseas international office was opened in Japan in 1970, and as Table 10.1 shows, it now has ten international offices in Asia, Europe, Mexico, and the United States. In recent years several of these offices have added additional (local) staff. In 2008 a review of Alberta's international activities recommended that additional offices be opened in India, Brazil, Shanghai, and California and that the province establish a presence in the Middle East, Russia, and the European Union (Alberta Foreign Offices Review Committee 2008). In addition, Alberta has twinning relationships with eleven regions in eight countries, as well as transboundary partnerships with Montana and Alaska in the United States.

Table 10.1. Alberta's international offices and staffing levels

	Opened	2006–7 Staff	2007–8 Staff	2008–9 Staff
China	2000	7	7	7
CNPC (Petroleum China)	1989	3	4	4
Hong Kong	1980	4	4	5
Taiwan	1988	2	2	2
Japan	1970	6	6	7
Korea	1988	3	3	3
Germany	2002	2	2	2
Mexico	2002	3	3	3
UK	2003	3	3	5
USA	2005	3	4	4
Total		36	38	42

Source: Compiled from Government of Alberta, Ministry of International and Intergovernmental Relations, http://www.international.alberta.ca/5.

In terms of international agreements signed with other states and regions, Figure 10.6 does not indicate any clear trend in terms of growth or retrenchment in such agreements over the past decade. What *is* clear is that Alberta continues to look well beyond North America. About one-quarter of its international agreements are with authorities in either the United States or Mexico (most of the latter being with its twinned state of Jalisco), but there have not been many signs of growth vis-à-vis the rest of the world in the past decade or so. The international agreements cover a wide range of areas, including commerce, education, culture, and research and development. In 2010, two further energy-related agreements were signed with states in the United Arab Emirates.

When other indicators are examined, however, there is some evidence that the economic downturn of 2008–9 is having an effect on Alberta's paradiplomatic efforts. First, as Figure 10.7 shows, since the late 1990s Alberta has steadily increased its number of international missions. Seventeen missions, the most in recent history, were undertaken in 2009. It is notable, however, that of these seventeen missions, fourteen were to the United States, including four visits each to Texas and Idaho alone.

Second, the recent trajectory of the Ministry of International and Intergovernmental Relations' budget reflects the more austere fiscal climate in which Alberta now finds itself. Figure 10.8 shows that in 2006–7

Figure 10.6. Alberta's International Agreements, 1998–2009

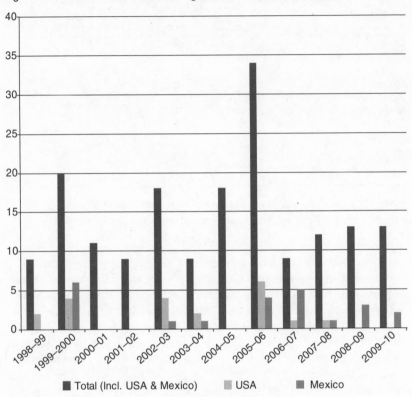

Source: Compiled from Government of Alberta, Ministry of International and Intergovernmental Relations, http://www.international.alberta.ca/5.cfm.

(the first year in which international offices' expenses were included), the department budget was roughly $24.5 million. In fiscal year 2008–9, the budget grew to over $29 million, but since that time the department – like most others in the province – has seen considerable retrenchment as the government attempts to keep its promise to balance the provincial budget within three years. Thus, the 2010–11 budget calls for a 7.7% reduction in the ministry's budget relative to the previous year. Of the approximately $24 million allocated to the ministry, over $15 million is intended for international activities. Overall, Alberta's international links and paradiplomacy in North America remain quite significant even in the face of global recession.

Figure 10.7. Alberta's International Missions, 1998–2009

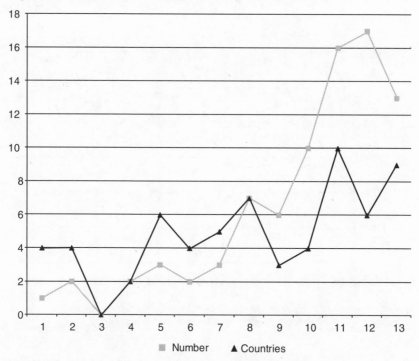

■ Number   ▲ Countries

Source: Compiled from Government of Alberta, Ministry of International and Intergovernmental Relations, http://www.international.alberta.ca/5.cfm.

Paradiplomacy in British Columbia

Unlike its neighbour to the east, B.C. does not have a separate ministry for paradiplomatic activities. Instead it has an Intergovernmental Relations Secretariat, a central agency contained within the Premier's Office. There is, however, a Minister for Intergovernmental Relations. That ministry's secretariat has three subsections: a Federal–Provincial Section, an International Section, and a Strategic Services Section. Like Alberta, B.C. promotes its interests within the Canadian federation through conventional channels. It also participates in the same regional and cross-border intergovernmental organizations and conferences discussed above for Alberta, including the PNWER, the Western Premiers' Conference, and the Council of State Governments – West.

Figure 10.8. Alberta's International and Intergovernmental Relations Budget

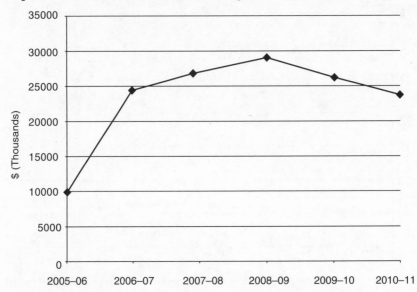

Source: Compiled from Government of Alberta, Ministry of International and Intergovernmental Relations, http://www.international.alberta.ca/5.cfm.

While the International Section of the Intergovernmental Relations Secretariat claims 'overall responsibility for British Columbia's relations with international governments' on its website, the main hub for promoting the province's economic interests lies with the Ministry of Small Business, Technology, and Economic Development. Within that department, the Asia–Pacific, Trade, and Investment Division 'develops and maintains trade and investment relations with key international markets' and promotes the interests of B.C. businesses. The division's name points to the main focus of the province's international activities: according to its website, in 2008, 30% of B.C.'s exports went to the Asia–Pacific region and India (note that during the last census, more than one in five B.C. residents identified themselves as Asian). However, the division also manages relations with Europe and the United States. Trade and investment representatives are located in nine offices worldwide: three in China, the others in India, Japan, South Korea, Britain, Germany, and the United States.

The same division promotes and manages twinning relationships

Figure 10.9. British Columbia's International Agreements by Country/Region (Selected)

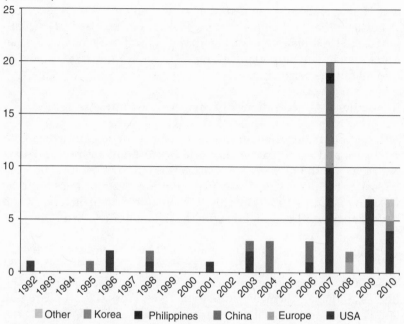

Source: Compiled from Government of British Columbia, Ministry of Small Business, Technology and Economic Development, http://www.gov.bc.ca/tted/.

between local governments in B.C. and those elsewhere. Again, the focus is on the Asia–Pacific region: more than half of the province's hundred-plus twinning relationships are with localities in China and Japan. But these relationships have also been forged with communities in Africa, Europe, Australasia, Latin America, and elsewhere in North America.

As Figure 10.9 indicates, B.C.'s international activities have increased considerably in recent years. Much stronger impetus for the development of international agreements came in 2007 with the launch of the Asia–Pacific Initiative. The aims of that initiative were to make B.C. the 'Pacific Gateway' for Canada and for North America more generally, and to expand business, investment, and educational links with the region. During the period shown in the figure, China ranked only behind the United States in the number of agreements reached.

According to the 2008–9 annual report on the Asia–Pacific Initiative, a further twelve MOUs of educational cooperation have been reached with China and Korea, and further educational MOUs are expected to be signed in 2010 with Vietnam, Taiwan, China, Qatar, the Philippines, and Colombia. Overall, paradiplomatic relations with American states remain very important, even as B.C. looks for market expansion throughout the Pacific Rim.

International Organizations of Provinces and States

The key international organizations in North America in which both provinces and states participate include those linking New England with the Eastern Provinces and Quebec; the Great Lakes and Midwestern states with the central provinces; and the western states with the western provinces. Levels of activity in all of these remain modest and have perhaps declined slightly with the economic downturn.

The Council of the Great Lakes Governors and Central Canadian Provinces

This council represents eight U.S. states and two Canadian provinces: Illinois, Indiana, Michigan, Minnesota, New York, Ohio, Wisconsin, and Pennsylvania as well as Ontario and Quebec. Its mission, according to its website, is to encourage an 'economically sound and environmentally conscious' world. Current projects include the restoration of the Great Lakes, for which a budget of $475 million has been allocated.

The New England Governors and Eastern Provinces Premiers Conference

This organization comprises six U.S. states and five Canadian provinces: Maine, Massachusetts, Connecticut, New Hampshire, Rhode Island, and Vermont, as well as New Brunswick, Newfoundland and Labrador, Nova Scotia, Prince Edward Island, and Quebec. These eleven have undertaken a multitude of projects together, relating, among other issues, to the following: economic development, health care, energy, the environment, transportation, sustainable development, and security. At present, the strongest focus is on energy efficiency and climate change.

The Western Governors and Premiers Association

This group includes eleven U.S. states and two Canadian provinces:

Arizona, California, Colorado, Idaho, Montana, Nevada, New Mexico, Oregon, Utah, Washington, and Wyoming, as well as Alberta and B.C. (the Mexican state of Baja California is also included in this project). This association has tackled issues such as climate change, forest and wildlife conservation, and transportation fuels. Its members have also engaged in around US $26 billion worth of trade. Currently, the association is undertaking a project to develop 'a consensus proposal ... on how best to develop and deliver energy from renewable resource area throughout the region to load centers.'

Southeastern United States / Central and Eastern Canadian Provinces Alliance

This relatively new organization links a number of states and provinces that do not share a border. Its first meeting was held in Canada in 2007; this was followed by another in Savanna, Georgia, in 2008. Although interest remains high, collective activities seem to be relatively limited, with bilateral state/provincial relations as the most important related activities.

Pacific Northwest Economic Region (PNWER)

Established in 1991, the Pacific Northwest Economic Region incorporates both public and private sector representatives from the states of Alaska, Idaho, Montana, Oregon, and Washington and the provinces of Alberta, B.C., and Saskatchewan, as well as Yukon and the Northwest Territories. In recent years, the organization has embraced a wide variety of issues, including disaster preparedness, energy, border security, livestock health, tourism, and the environment. The PNWER holds an annual conference; its twentieth meeting was held in Calgary in 2010.

Western Premiers Conference

A conference bringing together the four western premiers and the three northern territories is held annually. The conference is organized with the help of the federal government (through the Canadian Intergovernmental Conference Secretariat). The proceedings are an opportunity for the regional leaders to discuss issues of common concern, such as energy policy and relations with the United States. The 2009 conference was held in Dawson City, Yukon.

Conclusions

Looking at North American integration through traditional theoretical lenses provides only an incomplete picture of the extent of cross-border linkages. As highlighted by Ayres and Macdonald in the introduction to this volume, the largely state-centric theories used to explain earlier waves of regional integration have for the most part overlooked the great extent to which economic and political linkages have been fostered at the subnational level, regardless of relations between states at the national level. In this respect, approaches derived from the 'new regionalism,' with their greater recognition of the multilayered quality of regional integration, offer a useful alternative for examining integration on the North American continent.

The above discussion demonstrates that, notwithstanding the economic challenges that have followed the economic crisis of 2008, the development and strengthening of paradiplomatic activities across North America seems likely to continue largely unabated. Our provincial case studies show that with economic hard times, some subnational units have seen opportunities to expand their linkages and their economic reach both within North America and beyond. To the extent that fiscal budgetary crises have temporarily impaired international activities by some subnational governments, they have if anything strengthened contacts within North America as governments look for economic and political partners 'closer to home.' But this recent trend should not be overstated; our evidence also suggests that forging paradiplomatic links within North America is not inconsistent with paradiplomatic activities farther afield.

Given the desire to attract investment during a period of large fiscal imbalances, it should not be surprising that paradiplomatic activities are driven largely by economic imperatives. Quebec – the North American leader in paradiplomacy – is perhaps the exception here, as historically it has placed considerable emphasis on cultural and educational linkages. Indeed, its efforts have sometimes veered towards protodiplomacy, though it too has more recently given more attention to trade and economic development. As VanNijnatten and Craik's contribution to this volume makes clear, however, environmental concerns have also underpinned cross-border ties between subnational governments. All of the regional associations highlighted above place great emphasis on environmental cooperation, particularly when their members share an environmentally sensitive resource such as the Great Lakes.

The recent economic turbulence has likely dealt a blow to North American integration in the short term, when integration is viewed through a traditional theoretical lens. Elite-driven integration at the national level is less likely when political leaders, particularly in the United States, face electorates that are already sceptical of existing trade agreements. This chapter, however, taking a view that is more consistent with the 'new regionalism' approach, suggests that the paradiplomatic activities of subnational governments are key to integration in North America. Indeed, the strongest political/economic structures and activities in North America may come from this important source rather than from Mexico City, Ottawa, and Washington. Interactions and networking appear to be far easier to develop at the subnational level than at the national one. Regardless of the direction of national policy on North American integration, it has a solid foundation in paradiplomatic relations and activities. These developing ties are strong and hard to break. It seems that the provinces, states, and regional groupings and organizations examined in this chapter may provide the real cement that holds the idea of North America together.

Notes

1 While relations between subnational actors in Mexico and Canada exist (e.g., between Alberta and Jalisco, discussed below), they are generally much more limited.
2 Article 24 of GATT allows for the creation of regional trade agreements as long as they are trade creating, and not trade diverting.

References

Aguirre, Inaki. 1999. 'Making Sense of Paradiplomacy? An Intertextual Inquiry about a Concept in Search of a Definition.' In *Paradiplomacy in Action: The Foreign Relations of Subnational Governments*. Edited by Francisco Aldecoa and Michael Keating. London: Frank Cass. 185–209.

Alberta Foreign Offices Review Committee. 2008. 'Final Report to the Minister of International and Intergovernmental Relations on Alberta's International Office Network.' http://www.international.alberta.ca/documents/Alberta_Foreign_Offices_Review_Committee.pdf. Accessed 4 November 2011.

Alberta Ministry of International and Intergovernmental Affairs. n.d. 'Western Economic Partnership.' http://www.international.alberta.ca/documents/WesternEconomicPartnership.pdf.accessed. Accessed 4 November 2011.

Aldecoa, Francisco, and Michael Keating, eds. 1999. *Paradiplomacy in Action: The Foreign Relations of Subnational Governments.* London: Frank Cass.

Allan, James P., and Richard Vengroff. 2008. 'Paradiplomacy and Government Change: Quebec and Scotland in Comparative Perspective.' Paper presented at the 49th Annual Meeting of the International Studies Association, 26–30 March, San Francisco.

Bache, Ian, and Matthew Flinders, eds. 2004. *Multi-Level Governance.* Oxford: Oxford University Press.

Balthazar, Louis. 1999. 'The Quebec Experience: Success or Failure?' In *Paradiplomacy in Action: The Foreign Relations of Subnational Governments.* Edited by Francisco Aldecoa and Michael Keating. London: Frank Cass. 153–69.

– 1993. 'Quebec's International Relations: A Response to Needs and Necessities.' In *Foreign Relations and Federal States.* Edited by Brian Hocking. London: Leicester University Press. 140–52.

Balthazar, Louis, Louis Bélanger, and Gordon Mace, eds. 1993. *Trente ans de politique extérieure du Québec.* Québec: CQRI/Septentrion.

– 2003. 'Les relations internationals du Québec.' In *Québec: État et Sociétés.* Edited by Alain-G. Ganon. Montréal: Québec/Amérique.

Bélanger, Louis. 1994. 'La diplomatie culturelle des provinces canadiennes.' *Études internationales* 25, no. 3: 421–52.

– 1993. 'Les espaces internationaux de l'État québécois.' Paper delivered at the annual colloquium of the Canadian Political Science Association, Carleton University, 6 June.

Bélanger, Louis, Guy Gosselin, and Gérard Hervouet. 1993. 'Les relations internationales du Québec: Efforts de définition d'un nouvel objet d'étude.' *Revue québécoise de science politique* 23: 143–70.

Bernier, Luc. 1996. *De Paris à Washington. La politique internationale du Québec.* Montréal: Presses de l'Université du Québec à Montréal.

Boeckelman, Keith. 1996. 'Federal Systems in the Global Economy: Research Issues.' *Publius* 26: 1–10.

Brown, Douglas M. 1993. 'The Evolving Role of the Provinces in Canada–U.S. Trade Relations.' In *States and Provinces in the International Economy.* Edited by Douglas M. Brown and Earl H. Fry. Berkeley: Institute of Governmental Studies Press. 93–144.

– 1990. 'The Evolving Role of the Provinces in Canadian Trade Policy.' In *Canadian Federalism: Meeting Global Economic Challenges.* Edited by Douglas M. Brown and Murray G. Smith. Kingston and Montreal: Institute of Intergovernmental Relations and Institute for Research on Public Policy.

Brown, Douglas M., and Earl H. Fry, eds. 1993. *States and Provinces in the International Economy.* Berkeley: Institute of Governmental Studies Press.

Chambers, Edward J., and Nataliya Rylska. 2000. *The Alberta and Western Canada Export Experience under the Free Trade Agreements: 1988–1999.* Edmonton: Western Centre for Economic Research, University of Alberta.

Craven, Greg. 1993. 'Federal Constitutions and External Relations.' In *Foreign Relations and Federal States.* Edited by Brian Hocking. London: Leicester University Press. 9–26.

Duchacek, Ivo D. 1988. 'Multicommunal and Bicommunal Polities and Their International Relations.' In *Perforated Sovereignties and International Relations.* Edited by Ivo D. Duchacek, Daniel Latouche, and Garth Stevenson. New York: Greenwood. 3–28.

– 1986. *The Territorial Dimension of Politics Within, Among, and Across Nations.* Boulder: Westview.

– 1984. 'The International Dimension of Subnational Self-Government.' *Publius: The Journal of Federalism* 14, no. 4: 5–31.

Duchacek, Ivo D., Daniel Latouche, and Garth Stevenson, eds. 1988. *Perforated Sovereignties and International Relations.* New York: Greenwood.

Dupras, Daniel. 1993. *NAFTA: Implementation and the Participation of the Provinces.* Ottawa: Parliamentary Research Branch, Background Paper. Provided by the office of the NAFTA Secretariat in Ontario.

Dyment, David K.M. 1993. 'Substate Paradiplomacy: The Case of the Ontario Government.' In *Foreign Relations and Federal* States. Edited by Brian Hocking. London: Leicester University Press. 153–69.

Fry, Earl. 2005. 'Sub-State Strategies in an Era of Globalization and the Information Technology Revolution.' In *Mastering Globalization; New Sub-States' Governance and Strategies.* Edited by Guy Lachapelle and Stéphane Paquin. London: Routledge. 116–23.

– 2004. 'The Expanding Role of State, Provincial, and Local Governments in North American Economic Relations.' Paper presented at the Annual Meeting of the International Studies Association, Montreal, 20 March.

– 1998. *The Expanding Role of State and Local Governments in U.S. Foreign Affairs.* New York: Council on Foreign Relations Press.

– 1993. 'The U.S. States and Foreign Economic Policy: Federalism in the New World Order.' In *Foreign Relations and Federal States.* Edited by Brian Hocking. London: Leicester University Press. 122–39.

Gerin-Lajoie, Paul. 1989. *Combats d'un révolutionnaire tranquille.* Montréal: Centre éducatif et culturel.

Gosselin, Guy, and Gordon Mace. 1994. 'Asymétrie et relations internationales: les provinces canadiennes, l'Europe et l'Amérique latine.' *Études internationales* 25: 523–51.

Hetne, Bjdm. 2003. 'The New Regionalism Revisited.' In *Theories of New*

Regionalism: A Palgrave Reader. Edited by Fredrik Söderbaum and Timothy
M. Shaw. New York: Palgrave Macmillan. 22–42.

Hocking, Brian. 1999a. 'Patrolling the "Frontier": Globalization, Localization,
and the "Actorness" of Non-Central Governments.' In *Paradiplomacy in
Action: The Foreign Relations of Subnational Governments.* Edited by Francisco
Aldecoa and Michael Keating. London: Frank Cass. 17–39.

– 1999b. 'Managing Foreign Relations in Federal States: Linking Central and
Non-Central International Interests.' In *Paradiplomacy in Action: The For-
eign Relations of Subnational Governments.* Edited by Francisco Aldecoa and
Michael Keating. London: Frank Cass. 68–89.

– 1993a. *Localizing Foreign Policy: Non-Central Governments and Mutilayered
Diplomacy.* London: St Martin's.

– 1993b. *Foreign Relations and Federal States.* London: Leicester University
Press.

Hooghe, Liesbet, and Gary Marks. 2003. 'Unraveling the Central State, But
How? Types of Multi-Level Governance.' *American Political Science Review*
97: 233–43.

Jessop, Bob. 2003. 'The Political Economy of Scale and the Construction of
Cross-Border Micro-Regions.' In *Theories of New Regionalism: A Palgrave
Reader.* Edited by Fredrik Söderbaum and Timothy M. Shaw. New York:
Palgrave Macmillan. 179–96.

Kaiser, Robert. 2005. 'Sub-State Governments in International Arenas: Paradi-
plomacy and Multi-Level Governance in Europe and North America.' In
Mastering Globalization: New Sub-States' Governance and Strategies. Edited by
Guy Lachapelle and Stéphane Paquin. London: Routledge. 90–103.

Keating, Michael. 2006. 'Territorial Politics in Europe.' In *Developments in European Politics.* Edited by Paul M. Heywood, Erik Jones, Martin Rhodes, and
Ulrich Sedelmeier. New York: Palgrave Macmillan.

– 1999. 'Regions and International Affairs: Motives, Opportunities, and Strategies.' In *Paradiplomacy in Action: The Foreign Relations of Subnational Governments.* Edited by Francisco Aldecoa and Michael Keating. London: Frank
Cass. 1–16.

Kincaid, John. 1999. 'The International Competence of U.S. States and Their
Local Governments.' In *Paradiplomacy in Action: The Foreign Relations of
Subnational Governments.* Edited by Francisco Aldecoa and Michael Keating.
London: Frank Cass. 111–33.

– 1993. 'Consumership versus Citizenship: Is There Wiggle Room for Local
Regulation in the Global Economy?' In *Foreign Relations and Federal States.*
Edited by Brian Hocking, London: Leicester University Press. 27–47.

Kukucha, Christopher J. 2009. 'Dismembering Caada? Stephen Harper and the

Foreign Relations of Canadian Provinces.' *Review of Constitutional Studies* 14: 21–52.

– 2005. 'From Kyoto to the WTO: Evaluating the Constitutional Legitimacy of the Provinces in Canadian Foreign Trade and Environmental Policy.' *Canadian Journal of Political Science* 38: 146–7.

Lagasse, Charles-Étienne. 1997. 'Le systéme des relations internationales dans la Belgique fédérale.' *Courrier Hebdomadaire* 1549–50.

Lecours, André. 2002a. 'When Regions Go Abroad: Globalization, Nationalism, and Federalism.' Paper presented at the conference on 'Globalization, Multilevel Governance, and Democracy: Continental, Comparative, and Global Perspective,' 3–4 May 2002, Queen's University, Kingston.

– 2002. 'Paradiplomacy: Reflections on the Foreign Policy and International Relations of Regions.' *International Negotiation* 7: 104–10.

Léger, Jean-Marc. 1992. 'Vingt-cinq ans de relations internationales: un acquis riche de promesse.' *Forces* 100: 129–35.

McIlroy, James P. 1997. 'NAFTA and the Canadian Provinces: Two Ships Passing in the Night.' *Canada–United States Law Journal* 23: 431–40.

Michaud, Nelson. 2003. 'Québec and the Americas: A Federated State's Answer to the Challenges of Continentalization.' Paper presented at the 2003 biennial meeting of the Association for Canadian Studies in the United States, 20–3 November, Portland, Oregon.

– 2002. 'Federalism and Foreign Policy: Comparative Answers to Globalization.' In *The Handbook of Federal Countries.* Edited by Ann L. Griffiths and Karl Nerenberg. Montreal and Kingston: McGill–Queen's University Press. 319–415.

Michelmann, Hans J., and Panayotis Soldatos, eds. 1990. *Federalism and International Relations: The Role of Subnational Units.* Oxford: Oxford University Press.

Nossal, Kim R. 1997. *The Politics of Canadian Foreign Policy,* 3rd ed. Toronto: Prentice-Hall Canada.

Paquin, Stéphane. 2003a. 'Paradiplomatie identitaire et diplomatie en Belgique fédérale: le cas de la Flandre.' *Canadian Journal of Political Science* 36: 621–42.

– 2003b. *Paradiplomatie identitaire en Catalogne.* Québec: Les Presses de l'Université Laval.

– 2002. 'Globalization, European Integration and the Rise of Neo-Nationalism in Scotland.' *Nationalism and Ethnic Politics* 8, no. 1: 55–80.

Ravenhill, John. 1999. Federal–State Relations in Australian External Affairs: A New Cooperative Era?' In *Paradiplomacy in Action: The Foreign Relations of Subnational Governments.* Edited by Francisco Aldecoa and Michael Keating. London: Frank Cass. 143–52.

Rosenau, James. 1997. *Along the Domestic–Foreign Frontier: Exploring Government in a Turbulent World*. Cambridge: Cambridge University Press.

Schiavon Uriegas, Jorge A., and Rafael Velázquez Flores. 2009. 'La paradiplomacia de las entidades federativas en México.' In *Regionalización y paradiplomacia*. Edited by Zidane Zeraoui. Puebla: Tecnológico de Monterrey. 67–85.

Taylor, C. O'Neal. 2009. 'Of Free Trade Agreements and Models.' *Indiana International and Comparative Law Review* 19: 569–609.

Telford, Hamish. 2003. *Expanding the Partnership: the Proposed Council of the Federation and the Challenge of Glocalization*. Montreal: Institute for Research on Public Policy.

11 (Re)Thinking the 'New' North America through Women's Citizenship Struggles in Mexico[1]

ROSALBA ICAZA

The editors of this book ask a provocative question: Does North America exist at all as a meaningful political entity, economic region, cultural idea, or community? This chapter deals with that question from the perspective of working-class and indigenous women in Mexico who have contested the North American Free Trade Agreement (NAFTA) and the Security and Prosperity Partnership of North America (SPP) as a project for regional governance. My central argument is that despite the constraints that NAFTA and the SPP have placed on Mexican women's exercise of their citizenship rights, those women's strategies and activities of localized[2] resistance help unveil the violent and unsustainable nature of those agreements. Furthermore, those strategies and activities may be contributing to an open-ended questioning of regions and regionalism, exposing those entities as cultural and imperial constructs that produce and reproduce particular ways of understanding the world, and in which certain experiences are actively produced as irrelevant by the International Political Economy and International Relations academic communities.

To develop these ideas, this chapter questions the idea that the SPP has 'failed,' echoing the arguments made by Gilbert and Brodie in this volume regarding the persistence of its basic framework in the ongoing dynamics of regional and bilateral (Mexico–U.S.) governance. Specifically, I analyse the SPP framework of 'security' *as* militarization and 'prosperity' *as* free trade from the perspective of the constraints it has placed on working-class and indigenous women's rights-claiming activities and strategies. The chapter also examines those activities and strategies in order to identify how they may be helping challenge 'commonsense' assumptions about North American regionalism specifically and ideas about 'region' and regional governance more generally (Walters and Larner 2002, Clarkson 2007). Following Catherine Walsh, the chapter highlights these resistances as both disruptions and (re)constructions of dominant views of the political economy (Walsh 2007).

This chapter has four sections. The first section situates these issues within the current literature on regionalism and resistance. It discusses the contributions made by the international political economy and international relations (IPE/IR) literature regarding resistance to regionalism as well as the limitations of that literature. Here I argue, following Santos, that this literature fails to make visible the gendered, imperialist, and culturally specific dimensions of dominant interpretations of 'region' and 'regionalism'; as a result, women's struggles are actively rendered as non-existent and irrelevant 'knowledge' for IPE/IR theorizing (Santos, Nunez, and Meneses 2007). The second section reviews the material conditions and institutional shifts and continuities that Mexican women now confront in a post-NAFTA/SPP era as workers, activists, and members of indigenous groups. The third section examines women's resistance to NAFTA and the SPP by examining the urban, Mexico City–based feminist Network on Gender and Economy (REDGE) as well as rural, Chiapas-based *Zapatista* women. The fourth section focuses on key aspects of these women's resistance to NAFTA and the SPP in Mexico, identifying some ways in which these are inviting us to critically (re)think 'North American regionalism.'

This contribution does not take for granted IR/IPE theoretical approaches to social resistance to regionalism; rather, it explores how conventional IPE/IR representations of regionalism are being challenged by women's resistance activities and strategies in Mexico (Escobar 2008). This approach aims to go a step beyond the interest that 'new regionalism' theories take in the everyday practices of social mobilization as drivers of regionalism, by displaying some of the ways in which women's resistances are challenging and transforming our understandings of regions and regionalism (Marchand, Boas, and Shaw 1999, 904; Icaza 2009). This chapter is based on interviews, participant observation, and dialogues with women activists from Mexico City and San Cristóbal de las Casas and with indigenous women of Mayan Tzetzal and Tzotzil descent at Oventik (in *Zapatista* territory).[3] I am approaching these voices from the position of a Mexican *mestiza* feminist working as an academic in a European research centre on international development.[4] Inevitably, these interconnected identities mark and limit the interpretations I present in this analysis, which nonetheless seeks to contribute to the current critical intercultural exchange on IPE/ IR themes, including as that exchange relates to resistance to North American regionalism.[5]

Thinking Resistances to Regionalism

In IPE/IR mainstream literature on regionalism, expressions of resistance to the North American model of integration have been marginalized, labelled as 'nationalist' or 'populist,' or rejected as conservative and protectionist. Meanwhile, critical IPE/IR scholars who have closely analysed women's and indigenous peoples' resistances to the NAFTA model of integration have focused on the dynamics of 'bottom-up' cross-border solidarity and the role of contentious forces in the forging of ideas, institutions, and policies for the region (Ayres and Macdonald 2010). Within this literature, it is possible to identify a number of approaches to analysing resistance to NAFTA regionalism and, in particular, women's resistance.

In the IPE/IR literature, some researchers have taken a liberal democratic perspective on civil society activism. In examining the creation of 'hemispheric' networks contesting the contemporary politics of trade, they tend to pay too much heed to the 'impacts' of civil society actors, without considering how structural conditions drive and/or constrain such interventions. As a consequence, they portray social transformation as a product of purposeful actors' resistances, so much so that the making and remaking of regions is seen as a product of their interventions (Bulow 2010; Korzenewiz and Smith 2001; Natal and Gonzalez 2003).

This perspective portrays resistance to free trade as an expression of individuals' 'private' interests. The implication here is that resistance is a purposeful and rational behaviour. This perspective, however, does not allow for unexpected, unplanned, or 'irrational' attitudes. Furthermore, the context in which active resistance is analysed is characterized, from this perspective, as composed of networks of 'opportunity structures,' which in turn conveys the idea that the political 'marketplace' is fixed, that is, a 'given.' Thus, groups that oppose regionalism are described as if they were demanding that governments and inter-state organizations open the political economic regime to them so that reforms will be possible. It follows that these scholars analyse 'change' in terms of policies and regimes, and then declare the agents' 'interventions' to have succeeded to the extent that they have generated reforms (and implementations thereof) of particular policies. This literature focuses strongly on the policy outcomes achieved by civil society groups and networks; hence, it ignores or oversimplifies the structural conditions that actually drive or constrain these 'impacts' (Bulow 2010; Korzenewiz and Smith 2001; Natal and Gonzalez 2003).

Acknowledgment of the above limitations to 'liberal' perspectives on resistance to NAFTA has given rise to a second wave of analyses of resistance to NAFTA in the IPE/IR literature: so-called neo-Gramscian and neo-Marxist analyses of social movements (Drainville 1999; Morton 2000, 2007). These 'structuralist' accounts tend to focus on the dominant forces that generate social resistance.

For some, structuralist approaches have been quite useful for conceptualizing the transformations that have stimulated the emergence of social forces that are critical to the NAFTA model of regionalism in the Americas. However, these researchers have tended to conceptualize this resistance as either the product of powerful structures or as actually comprising those structures; hence, they do not provide an adequate perspective for understanding the complexities of localized resistance to regionalism. For example, some neo-Gramscian authors tend to address 'agency' from the perspective of the structures (the whole). As a result, 'agency' appears to be in the hands of unproblematic and unified actors, which does not take into account their diversity or social location (Icaza 2006).

Meanwhile, as discussed in the introduction of this volume, constructivist perspectives within the so-called new regionalism approach, by focusing on how regions are socially created, have helped bring to light the complex and multilevelled nature of regionalism (Hettne and Soderbaum 2000; see also chapters by Bow and Golob in this volume). This approach opens up the possibility of identifying key agents and social forces (material, institutional, or discursive) that are shaping and being shaped by the formation, expansion, and transformation of regions (Icaza 2009). However, this approach tends to take 'regions' as socio-political, discursive, or spatial and temporal realities that existed *before* they were interpreted through cultural and imperial discourses inscribed in the very notion of 'regions' (Coleman and Johnson 2008). This ontological option, as discussed below, has deep epistemological implications for a critical (re)thinking of regions and regionalism, a (re)thinking that goes beyond colonial frameworks and provides epistemological alternatives.

Finally, Foucauldian approaches to NAFTA have contributed to our understanding of the role that discourse plays in depoliticizing decisions and in producing counter-discourses to this model of integration (Donegan 2006; Gilbert 2005; see also the chapters in this volume by Gilbert and Brodie). From this perspective, feminist IPE approaches to women's resistances display NAFTA discourses as sites where meaning is produced, thus exposing those discourses as gendered, exploitative, disciplinary frameworks for women's lives and bodies (Marchand 1994 and 1996).

Overall, these four approaches help reveal the complexities of regionalism; the limitations of mainstream theories; and the limitations of EU regionalism as yardstick for assessing all other regionalisms (Marchand et al. 1999; Icaza 2009). Parallel to this, some attempts have recently been made in IPE/IR studies to 'integrate' the politics of those "subaltern" groups that are resisting the NAFTA style of regionalism (Morton 2007). Meanwhile, others have attempted to 'bring in' perspectives from 'Southern' academia to describe what IPE is from a Chinese, Latin American, Indian, and/or British perspective (Blyth 2009).

Nonetheless, some IR/IPE scholars have reminded us that regions emerged as a 'subject of study' during a post–Cold War moment in which area studies proliferated in the United States (Coleman and Johnson 2008; Escobar 1995; Szanton 2004). In particular, Coleman and Johnson have emphasized the cultural and imperial nature of regions as a concept:

> The notion of 'region,' might be seen as a particular way of seeing and organizing the world that began with Euro-American, Japanese, and perhaps Chinese imperialism. Within the academy, it might be reinforced through government support for 'area studies' that, in turn, reifies a dominant notion of 'region' in the West. 'Regions' in this sense are constructed as places with 'natural resources,' 'consumer markets,' and 'strategic importance' and given life by powerful states acting on these constructions. So we would need to accept at the outset that the notion of 'region' is a cultural construct, coming from hegemonic power centers. (2008, 9)

Accepting the cultural and imperial connotations of 'region' as a concept with heavy historical significance has had various implications for how IPE/IR authors have explained 'North America' and regionalism. One epistemological implication has been the active production of certain experiences as non-existent, which has helped 'erase' those experiences in cognitive terms (Santos et al. 2007).

For example, Walsh (2007, 20) and Rojas (2007) note the absence in IPE/IR literature of non-Western philosophical frameworks that are *not* centred in the individual, and of economies and subjectivities that were *never* fully capitalist. From the perspective of Quijano (2000), this reveals 'the coloniality of power' as established relations of domination, superiority/inferiority divides, and Western 'control,' in this case, of IPE/IR frameworks for thinking about regions and regionalism. This, following Mignolo (2000) would in turn explain the subordination of non-Anglo/European modes of knowing conceptualizing, and representing regions and regionalisms. This epistemological subordination precludes a rethinking of certain meanings of and/or commonsense assumptions through the prism of localized women's resistance to NAFTA.

Next, this chapter examines the material conditions set by NAFTA and the SPP; presents urban-based feminist and rural-based *Zapatista* women's experiences of resistance to both those agreements; and identifies key disruptions and possible (re)constructions of taken-for-granted views on North America and regionalism.

Landscapes of Change and Continuity

In North America, economic liberalization had long been the dominant discourse and policy option for region building. However, as discussed in the chapters by Gilbert and Bow in this volume, securitization became the dominant objective after 9/11. By the end of 2001, the SPP had been created and Smart Border Agreements had been signed between the United States and Canada and the United States and Mexico; all of these were steps towards a North American security perimeter (Sandoval Palacios 2005). The SPP, like NAFTA ten years earlier, was opposed by Mexican, Canadian, and U.S. civil society networks, which were critical of the effects it would have on development and citizens' rights (see the chapter by Ayres and Macdonald in this volume). But unlike NAFTA, which, being a treaty, had to be ratified by the legislatures, this time national legislatures offered restricted possibilities for citizens' input. The SPP was an executive-level agreement that did not need to be ratified by the legislatures of any of the countries involved. In addition to this, civil society groups and networks faced the huge challenge of finding ways to bring wider public scrutiny to the SPP's security objectives.

Women's organizations in Mexico that opposed the SPP confronted major hurdles to voicing their concerns both in official circles and within civil society, regarding this new partnership's gendered nature and its possible implications for women's security (Interview A). For example, they were confronted by a shifting context in which multidimensional forms of regulation increasingly emanated 'from multiple locales at the same time' (Scholte 2004; see also Interviews A and B and Workshops A, B, and C). In the case of NAFTA and the SPP, these forms of regulation included the three countries' state apparatuses (federal, provincial, and local governments; judicial and legislative systems; and the military and national security forces), private corporations and firms with regional and local outlets, and intergovernmental organizations and regional bodies (WTO, ILO, NAFTA).

Furthermore, this trend in governance seems to have been reinforced by the fact that states and governmental apparatuses did not lose their relevance – rather, certain aspects of *how* state power was to be exercised or claimed (e.g., regarding territorial sovereignty) were being reshaped by a multitude of globalizing processes, such as migration, criminal networks, remittance flows, and terrorist threats, which challenged previously sacrosanct state power and authority. This 'decentralization' trend has since unfolded through an uneven dispersion of public sector governance among various authorities and through the involvement of non-traditional policy arenas and actors, including civil society actors. In the case of the SPP, trilateral working groups were projected as the real decision makers (as with NAFTA's ad hoc working groups). These working groups were supposed to include public officials, private corporations' representatives, and security specialists – that is, people with the technical capacity and 'knowledge' to be included in regional decision making (Interview C).

Similarly, trends towards the privatization of governance in North America have meant that private corporate actors are increasingly involved in formulating, implementing, monitoring, and enforcing control, consent, and decision making with regard to public and general concerns such as trade, development, macroeconomic policies, and (more recently) the securitization of borders. This has been the case with the North American Business Committee (NABC) and the North American Competitiveness Council (NACC), which have since their inception promoted linkages between policy issues and business priorities (Carlsen 2007; Lendman 2007).

Moreover, as control unfolds through regional, subregional, and extraregional means of governance, diverse formal and informal practices, mechanisms, and arrangements for regulating and coordinating social life in North America have become increasingly connected to various processes of regional integration. NAFTA and the SPP are only two of the state-supported initiatives that are consequences of increasing regionalization of governance. Meanwhile, civil society mobilizations and regional forums have been pointed out as examples of 'informal' trends in regional solidarity building – trends rooted in a shared identity stemming from common identified grievances – grievances that include democratic deficits generated by NAFTA and the SPP.

Continuities and Resistance

In Mexico, changes in how global relations are governed have resulted in both changes and continuities in some of the traditional corporatist and authoritarian practices of the Mexican state. For example, some spaces have emerged for citizen participation and for the public scrutiny of governing authorities in relation to foreign policy. Yet the executive – whose role has been vital to the consolidation of neoliberal reforms through NAFTA – continues to play a key role to avoid NAFTA's renegotiation (Icaza 2008).

Furthermore, citizenship rights and entitlements in Mexico remain poorly enforced and are constantly being violated by the formal authorities. The emphasis in this chapter on Mexican women will highlight some of the consequences for their everyday lives when their formal rights as citizens are simply not enforced.

These changes and continuities constrain women's rights-claiming efforts in different ways and with different intensities. The conjuncture of dominant material, institutional, and discursive neoliberal frameworks and their accompanying structural reforms reflecting global markets' requirements has had important implications for the capacities of certain sectors in Mexican society to protect, claim, enforce, and expand citizenship rights relating to trade policies and the militarization of borders. This is especially true for women, including working-class and indigenous women in Mexico.

Analyses of gender and NAFTA have also pointed out that the gendered hierarchies in civil society organizations are a key limiting factor for any meaningful democratization of trade governance (Domínguez 2002; Gabriel and Macdonald 1994, 536; Macdonald 2002). This literature has noted that gender-related issues have rarely been the focus of national civil society organizations or of trilateral coalitions in the

Americas campaigning against NAFTA. Generally speaking, civil society initiatives and campaigns have often interpreted feminists' concerns regarding the gendered nature of trade liberalization as exclusive to women. This has been the case with Mexico's networks of civil society organizations and social movements, which have privileged, for instance, NAFTA's democratic deficits above any gender-related concerns (Domínguez 2002, 2007). For example, in the national campaign 'Sin maíz no hay país' ('Without corn there is no country'), which opposed the implementation of NAFTA's agricultural chapter, women played an important role as activists, but gender concerns were simply not highlighted within the main campaign (Icaza et al. 2008).

Furthermore, the incorporation of a gender perspective into civil society's multisectoral alliances and networks – such as the Mexican Network on Free Trade (RMALC) – has not been easy or automatic; rather, it has been the result of strong mobilizations of women from popular sectors allied to middle-class organizations in national and transnational campaigns (Domínguez 2002 and 2007). In Mexico, women have had to confront the lack of gender equality in decision making within civil society organizations, which have long resisted providing them with opportunities for meaningful participation (Domínguez 2002, 2007; Macdonald 2002). Certainly, in many cases this may be the result of unconscious assumptions; in general, however, civil society groups are not immune from the asymmetrical relations that exist among their own members.

Women Resisting NAFTA

Women's resistance to NAFTA and the SPP has faced multiple constraints in Mexico. That said, their right-claiming discourses and practices indicate that neoliberal regionalism is far from a *fait accompli* in North America. This does not mean that NAFTA and the SPP are not powerful governance frameworks with gendered and imperialist mechanisms of control, but certainly those agreements do not represent the only views of how social life should be and actually is organized in 'North America.' In particular, the actions of the urban-based Network Gender and the Economy (REDGE), and rural *Zapatista* women promoting the right to participate in trade negotiations as well as the right to autonomous governance of the political and the personal, help illustrate alternative ways in which 'North America' can be been imagined and organized (Icaza 2010).

NAFTA and SPP under Women's Eyes

Since the early 1990s, REDGE has been coordinating joint actions by working-class urban and rural women and feminist organizations to oppose NAFTA. Its main objective has been to transform women's experiences of poverty and violence while generating alternatives to neoliberalism and free trade agreements through participatory methodologies, popular education, and solidarity. Accordingly, in 2005 REDGE joined the Mexican Action Network on Free Trade (RMALC) and the Women's Committee of the Hemispheric Social Alliance (HSA), two networks that have been actively involved in hemispheric campaigning against free trade and neoliberalism in the Americas (Icaza et al. 2008).

For REDGE coordinator Leonor Aida Concha, Mexico's neoliberal governments have been using NAFTA to consolidate structural reforms while downsizing social programs for working-class women: 'Free trade agreements, such as NAFTA, have meant the prosperity of the few and the poverty of the majority' (Interview A).

Zapatista Struggle

On 1 January 1994 the southern Mexican state of Chiapas was turned into a key site of resistance against neoliberalism and NAFTA. The direct cause was the public appearance of the *Ejercito Zapatista de Liberación Nacional* (EZLN). The EZLN defined itself as the armed wing of the indigenous communities of Tzotzil, Tzetzal, Chol, Tojolabal, and Mame descent. When they took over some cities in Chiapas, including San Cristóbal de las Casas, the *Zapatista* men, women, and children shocked the world and helped launch an intense cross-border resistance to neoliberalism.

When I visited Oventik, one of the five *Zapatista* communities, male and female *Zapatistas* told me that their fight was against the Mexican state and neoliberalism, NAFTA and the Mesoamericano Project (Plan Puebla Panama).[6] The participants at this meeting did not explicitly mention the SPP, but the increasing militarization that had accompanied the SPP framework was a common concern often voiced by *Zapatista* women.[7] The Center for Political Analysis and Social and Economic Research (CAPISE) reported in 2007 the presence of seventy-nine military compounds in Chiapas, fifty-six of them within indigenous territories. CAPISE also reported that elite military groups had been deployed to areas near the *Zapatista* autonomous territories (CAPISE 2007). Furthermore, when neoliberalism and free trade agreements were raised, *Zapatista* women expressed their opposition to them, describing them as contrary to land rights, fair employment and salaries, fair access to housing, health care, and education, real democracy, freedom, justice, and political autonomy.

Strategies of Resistance

Since 2005, *Zapatista* women's resistance to NAFTA has become part of a larger project of political autonomy, the 'Sixth Declaration of the Lacandon Jungle' or '*La Sexta*.' This program expresses *Zapatista* communities' anti-capitalist, anti-neoliberal agenda, which is part of the process for building autonomous local governance. One of the first strategies to flow from this agenda was the organization of a campaign that ran parallel to those run by the major political parties in Mexico's 2006 presidential election. Branded 'The Other Campaign, the Other Politics,' it promoted a radical break with the institutional systems of representative democracy; this included rejecting exercise of the right to vote in the 2006 elections.[8]

La Sexta calls for the strengthening of the *Zapatistas'* political and economic autonomy through the creation of parallel governments in rebellion. The *Zapatistas* have developed new territorial jurisdictions called *caracoles* (snails), which often operate semiautonomously from federal and local government apparatuses (Workshop C). The *caracoles* are administered by 'good government *juntas*,' which are elected by majority vote every three years and which are ruled by the principle of 'governing by obeying' (Burguete Cal y Mayor 1995, 2003).

The *juntas* are responsible for health, education, productive programs, and the enforcement of the Zapatista Women's Revolutionary Law of 1992. A *Zapatista* woman explains some of the reasons underlying this strategy:[9] 'We decided that if the Mexican government would not do what they had promised to do [grant them political and territorial autonomy] and what their representatives previously signed [the San Andrés Agreements of 1996], then we would have to put into practice what we have said on paper.'[10] *La Sexta* emphasizes the *Zapatistas'* struggle for 'real democracy, freedom, justice and political autonomy' but also their rejection of the militarization of southern Mexico that has occurred since the SPP was announced, the Merida Initiative was implemented, and military forces were deployed by President Calderón for his war against drugs (see the chapters by Gilbert and Cadena-Roa in this volume).

The country's increasing militarization, coinciding with the announcement of the SPP, helped REDGE focus its activism. In particular, REDGE's national campaign amounted to one of the few critical voices from feminist organizations concerned about the negative effects that the SPP's 'Prosperity' component would have on women's rights through the privatization of water services, unaffordable health and education services, and so on. At the same time, the security component resonated with REDGE's long-term work on gender violence and its campaign for a General Law Against Violence Towards Women. According to REDGE, the SPP framework would increase violence against women because security would now be promoted through militarization.

As part of their anti-SPP activities, REDGE organized a Women's World March, which began in San Cristóbal de las Casas and ended in Ciudad Juárez, a border city where U.S. women activists continued the mobilization across the United States. According to a member of REDGE's Mexico City office, this caravan helped link the South to the North, indigenous women of Chiapas and Guatemala to *maquiladora* workers of Ciudad Juárez and working-class women in the United States (Interview B). For the REDGE coordinator, it had begun a new chapter for the network's activism, one that promised an overdue return to the organization's grassroots: 'A women's movement is not possible as we were at that point. We were purely acting as an NGO. We realized that grassroots women, indigenous women, wouldn't be able to exercise any leadership if we stayed like that' (Interview A).

This marked a new stage in REDGE activism on women's rights and the SPP, one that entailed a decentralization of its activities and decision making to local counterparts. At present, the Centre for Action–Research on Latin American Women (CIAM), headquartered in San Cristóbal de las Casas, is coordinating REDGE's nationwide campaign for the security of women's lives in Mexico (Interview A).

Identifying Duty and Power Holders

REDGE and *Zapatista* women's resistance to NAFTA-related structural reforms and SPP-related militarization have unfolded parallel to complex processes for identifying holders of power and duties. REDGE statements and policy briefings highlight the growing influence of NAFTA institutions on national and local economic governance. Nonetheless, the Mexican state itself remains ultimately responsible for promoting equitable development for all and for upholding women's rights. 'This is a paradox,' REDGE's coordinator says, 'because the state apparatus is also the main perpetrator and reproducer of gender-based violence by direct actions or by omissions of their responsibilities' (Interview A).

Having acknowledged this paradox, REDGE has mixed its strategies in relation to NAFTA and the SPP. These have included direct engagement with or frank opposition to state authorities. Thus, the network has organized workshops for women leaders on gender and economics in collaboration with local governments in Mexico City and Campeche. Access to the authorities in order to influence their agenda is possible thanks to the fact that former members of the REDGE staff have entered local governments – for example, REDGE's former coordinator now works in Mexico City's Women's Institute.

But acknowledging the paradox mentioned earlier does not mean that REDGE has avoided the costs of campaigning against NAFTA and the SPP: 'Now we need to be actively involved in cross-border networking and coordination efforts, to actively seek the decentralization of our decision-making processes as much as possible to our local counterparts, to reach as many authorities as possible [that are] open to our demands in Mexico and abroad, to lobby every single instance that opens among private corporations and labour unions, and do all of this at the same time! This has had a huge cost for our relationship with our grassroots' (Interview B).

Regarding the *Zapatistas'* resistance to NAFTA and the SPP as part of a larger project for political autonomy, it has meant that their resistance has turned against formal mechanisms of representative democracy. In the case of *Zapatista* women, it has also meant a struggle for personal autonomy and the implementation of the 1992 Zapatista Women's Revolutionary Law. That law grants *Zapatista* women the right to choose a partner, to have the number of children they can care for, and to occupy positions of leadership, among other rights (Hernandez Castillo 2007).[11] *Zapatista* Commander Hortensia has indicated that 'the work that women have been doing in the five *Zapatista* [autonomous] zones is to try to exercise our rights and duties as *Zapatistas*. It hasn't been easy for us, but we are working and we will continue to do so in order to accomplish what the Women['s] Revolutionary Law states.'[12]

For *Zapatista* women, the notion of rights is highly significant and is often raised in their discourses and communiqués – just as it is in their Revolutionary Law – even if it is not explicitly linked to questions of citizenship (Hernandez Castillo 2002, 2007). The Revolutionary Law declares that their struggle is for the survival and recognition of their rights as both women and indigenous people; it also provides them with a concrete framework of rights against patriarchal power. According to one *Zapatista* woman of the good government *junta* at Oventik, there have been important changes since the Zapatista Women Revolutionary Law: 'Before, we didn't have any rights, but now [no one] can say that we cannot do something, because the law says that we have rights. It clearly says that!'

For Hernandez Castillo (2007, 126), a key aspect of this law is that it challenges not only official nationalism and ideas of a *mestizo* (mixed-race) Mexico but also the ethnic essentialism of the sort heralded by some sectors of the indigenous movement. This law acknowledges the discriminatory living conditions faced by indigenous women arising from their ethnicity, gender, and social class – the 'triple oppression' – conditions that had remained frankly overlooked until the *Zapatista* uprising. But according to some *mestiza* activists in San Cristóbal de las Casas, the law's articles are often not enforced in *Zapatista* communities, let alone in non-*Zapatista* communities (Workshop C, Cacho Niño 2007). Furthermore, given the gender hierarchies that continue to prevail among indigenous communities in Chiapas, domestic and community violence by husbands and relatives has often been the cost that women have paid for their political involvement and for their challenge to those hierarchies (Hernandez Castillo 2007).

Even so, the same *mestiza* activists in Chiapas emphasize the subtle but important differences between communities that are *Zapatista* and those that are not, stressing that in the former, those women who have exercised responsibilities in the *juntas* display a transformation that is quite important for other younger indigenous women in their communities to see: 'These women know that their right to speak and be heard is now a possibility' (Workshops A and B). A *Zapatista* woman at Oventik described her involvement in the *juntas* as follows: 'Little by little we have advanced here and there. It hasn't been easy, we don't have resources or experience to organize ourselves. This won't be quickly, we can't speak our mind and say what we think, we need to learn that … and our daughters too.'

To sum up, the *Zapatista* women's localized construction of political and personal autonomy suggests that it would be too narrow to understand their struggles for citizenship in Mexico in the NAFTA/SPP era as merely to obtain political rights and responsibilities, for the state itself to then enforce. Furthermore, their experiences tell us that citizenship may well be an ongoing struggle, one that is open to different renegotiations with diverse holders of power and responsibility at the national, local, and community levels. These renegotiations are taking place at multiple sites of governance and in diverse sites of politics and power (state authorities, households, communities) but also through de facto institutions and mechanisms such as good government *juntas* (Mukhopadhyay 2004, 20; Meer and Sever 2004).

(Re)Thinking the 'New' North America

In this section, key REDGE and *Zapatista* women's practices of rights claiming as resistance to NAFTA and the SPP are explored to highlight their contributions to (re)thinking 'North America' in IR/IPE literature.

Rethinking SPP 'Failure'

As was indicated in the introduction to this collection, NAFTA's economic failure as a model for regionalism has been increasingly accepted in Mexico on the basis of its failure to generate employment and raise incomes. Nonetheless, the notion that the SPP was 'quietly dropped by the three North American governments, without public announcement or consultation' (see the editors' introduction in this collection) can be contested, and indeed has been contested by REDGE activists and *Zapatista* women, who every day experience violence from the military and the drug traffickers, both in their communities and on their bodies.

In other words, the SPP as a discourse on security as the militarization of borders has not failed at all; rather, it has become a 'reality of] intergovernmental regulatory transformations that have taken place under Washington's insistence since September 11, 2001' (Clarkson 2007, 87). Indeed, it has been quite successful as a violent practice that is affecting the lives of women in concrete ways. For REDGE activists that monitor the increasing militarization of border zones in northern and southern Mexico, this trend is hitting hard migrant women workers arriving in the south of Mexico from other Latin American countries or leaving Mexico for the United States (Interviews A and B).[13]

Meanwhile, *Zapatista* women's resistance in Chiapas faces pressing dilemmas owing to increased militarization, and their activities to strengthen their political and personal autonomy are becoming too dangerous for their own security (Olivera Bustamante 2007). In Mexico, since the Calderón government's offensive against the drug cartels, launched in 2007, and the U.S.–Mexico Mérida Initiative (2008), the militarization of Mexican cities and towns has been on the rise as well. This militarization has meant that highly unaccountable bearers of power and authority, such as the military, police forces, and drug cartels and their mercenaries, are acting with impunity. According to a report of the International Federation for Human Rights, both the United States and Mexico 'openly disregard their human rights obligations under national and international law, including the right to life' (IFHR 2008). In this context, gender-based violence and discrimination have come to characterize the landscape of women both as migrants and as residents of border cities in northern and southern Mexico.

In sum, the increasing militarization of cities and small towns in Mexico, instigated by the SPP and implemented through U.S.–Mexico bilateral efforts such as the Mérida Initiative, has meant that women's physical integrity is under threat in a country that ranks high on levels of impunity.[14] It is well known that violence against women in Mexico reflects a complex intersection of class, ethnicity, and gender, an example being the 370 unsolved murders of young working-class women in Ciudad Juárez and rapes of indigenous women in the southern states of Chiapas, Veracruz, and Oaxaca (the latter committed by military forces deployed there for Calderón's offensive against the drug cartels) (Staudt 2008, Hernandez Castillo 2007).[15]

In Chiapas, one feminist activist (Workshop A) observed: 'Violence against women happens every day, but due to recent militarization women cannot do their "normal" duties and activities, like going to the river for water. Women are afraid.' Furthermore, it has been reported that *Zapatista* women members of the good government *juntas* are often unable to carry out their political work because of the drug cartels' and military forces' presence on their territories (Olivera Bustamante 2007, 2009). *Zapatista* women's involvement in the *juntas* hasn't come free of costs to them, and killings of women and children by paramilitary forces in Chiapas have been reported. For some, this suggests 'counter-insurgency practices' – in other words, these women and girls were attacked because of their gender (Hernandez Castillo 2007, Workshop C).

These experiences invite us to critically rethink the SPP as a 'failed project' and to question the assumptions underlying that view. Lack of formal implementation of the SPP security component has not necessarily meant that security as North American militarization is no longer a reality for those women who are facing direct violence. The securitization trend opened by and legitimized through the official SPP discourse is shaping and redefining Mexico–U.S. bilateral relations; more important, it is also affecting women's everyday practices of resistance and mobilization against NAFTA.

Rethinking Oppression

As has already been argued, women's rights discourses and practices indicate that neoliberal regionalism in North America is far from a *fait accompli*. The concrete experiences of indigenous women in parallel governments through leadership positions in the *Zapatista* good government *juntas* help highlight this and contribute to rethinking a supposedly all-encompassing domination by the NAFTA model of regionalism in the organization of social life in North America.

The following observation of a *Zapatista* woman on her community leadership helps illustrate this sort of questioning: 'In the *juntas* we learn how to make decisions, how to speak. It is not to solve our problems. It is a place to play a role in the discussions, organization, and administration. It is where we exercise our resistance.'

The *juntas* are meant to help build *Zapatista* women's political and personal autonomy. This becomes especially relevant when we take into account the overall and persisting conditions of sexual inequality and discrimination within Mexican households and in Mexican society. Furthermore, given the pressing structural constraints of their 'triple oppression,' *Zapatista* women's participation in the *juntas* defies the role they were supposed to play as poor indigenous women in the new North America, mainly as *maquiladora* workers or maids in the cities.

Rethinking Dialogue

Since its first appearance in 1994, the EZLN has organized numerous public dialogues, starting with the Intercontinental Gathering for Humanity and Against Neoliberalism in 1997. Ten years later, the first Gathering of Zapatista Women with Women of the World took place, bringing together various strands of feminism to listen to women *Zapatistas'* testimonies. In particular, *Zapatista* girls and women talked about recent changes in their communities. Said one young woman: 'As a single woman my father now let me go to school and outside the town.' Another mentioned that 'before they [male relatives] rejected us because we were born woman and said that we had no value. Now, this is starting to change.' Both mentioned how difficult it had been to promote these changes and that 'there is still a lot to be done.'[16]

Feminists are increasingly aware of the potential that critical inter-cultural dialogue has – indeed, its indispensability – as a means to con-struct 'affinities' among women in national and transnational arenas (Desai 2002; Hernandez Castillo 2002, 2007; Marcos and Waller 2005; Marcos 2008; Otzoy 2008). Walsh describes critical interculturality as a process that 'initiates with a profound questioning of this system and seeks its major transformation in social, political, epistemic, and existential terms'; by contrast, functional interculturality is 'an institu-tional strategy that seeks to promote dialogue, tolerance, coexistence, and inclusion without necessarily addressing the causes of inequality; it makes diversity "functional" to the system' (Walsh 2007, 21). From this perspective, a critical intercultural dialogue would be attentive to relationships of inequality that have characterized the urban / rural Western / non-Western divides.

These divides might be grasped in the contentious topic of sexual and reproductive rights, particularly abortion rights, which have been rejected by many indigenous women, including *Zapatista* women. An attentive attitude to the previously mentioned divides could be under-stood through the following observation by a young Italian feminist working for the rights of undocumented women migrants in Europe: 'Our challenge is not how to "convince" women about their right to have a safe abortion, but to let them know that our grandmothers and mothers fought for this right while at the same time listen and under-stand why they don't want this right' (International Seminar 2009).

This kind of listening and sharing has characterized *Zapatista* gather-ings. As such, these hold a radical yet fragile potential: the possibility of cutting across geographical, class, and ethnicity divides – a potential that seems especially relevant when demands to protect and enforce formally granted citizenship rights in national and local arenas (life and bodies free of violence) and/or the extension of those rights across borders with regard to trade policies (whose prosperity?) and the mili-tarization of borders (whose security?) are voiced by both *Zapatista* indigenous women and *mestiza* women.

Furthermore, the sort of critical intercultural dialogue that is described here might open a questioning of IPE/IR (re)thinking on North America and regionalism, in particular regarding academic research practices that have contributed to reproducing the hegemony of knowledge, hence promoting the epistemic inequality that character-izes North/South, Western/non-Western, urban/rural, male/female divides. Opening up research to other forms of knowledge would mean taking seriously the need for an epistemic justice if we are to attain any sort of social justice (Santos et al. 2007). In particular, everyday constraints on women's rights-claiming experiences resulting from the NAFTA/SPP governance framework, together with those same women's resistance strategies in the form of networking and political and personal autonomy, are taken here as first-order questions in the process of theorizing the 'new North America.'

Notes

1 I would like to thank Laura Macdonald, Jeffrey Ayres, and John Gaventa for their comments on earlier drafts of this chapter. The ideas presented here have been shared with various colleagues in Mexico, the Netherlands, and Great Britain. My deepest gratitude, also, to REDGE activists and to the *Zapatista* women of Oventik as well as to their supporters for their trust and support. Fieldwork activities were possible thanks to the financial support of the HIVOS-ISS Knowledge Program on Civil Society Building (http://www.hivos.net) and a Marie Curie Reintegration Grant from the European Commission.
2 The term 'localized' is understood as place-based and is used in contrast to 'placeless' views of resistance (Escobar 2001).
3 See list of interviews and workshops attended at end of this chapter.
4 My analysis is inspired by the work of Mexican feminists Rosalva Aida Hernandez Castillo and Sylvia Marcos and that of American feminist anthropologist Donna Haraway.
5 There are, however, some examples of ongoing critical dialogue. These include the Canadian-based project Globalization and Autonomy; the British-based project Building Global Democracy; the U.S.–Latin America research project on Modernity/Coloniality/Decoloniality; the network Other Knowledges; and the Programa de Democracia y Transformación Global (PDTG).
6 I participated in a meeting with the 'Good Government Juntas' of the autonomous *Zapatista* territory of Oventik in the summer of 2008 as part of a team of academics from a European research centre based in The Hague.
7 *Zapatista* women include girls as well as young and senior indigenous women who support the *Zapatista* demands, and/or who live in *Zapatista* autonomous territories, and/or who are part of the Zapatista National Liberation Army (EZLN).
8 Enlace Zapatista, http://enlacezapatista.ezln.org.mx. Accessed 22 November 2011.

9 This and other statements by *Zapatista* women are part of a conversation I held with them and their male partners as members of the Oventik Junta of Good Government in the summer of 2008. All comments translated from Spanish are my own.

10 Even though the 2001 Law on Indigenous Rights and Cultures was approved by all political parties in the National Congress, the view of the *Zapatistas* is that this law did not include the agreements on autonomy and self-determination previously reached between them and President Zedillo in 1996.

11 This Revolutionary Law has been met with both approval and scepticism by feminist and women's groups worldwide. It includes the following rights: to participate in the revolutionary struggle, to work and receive a just salary, to primary attention in their health and nutrition, to education, to be free of violence from both relatives and strangers, and to hold military ranks in the revolutionary armed forces.

12 'Fifth Wind: A Dignifying and Feminist Rage.' Commander Hortensia's discourse on the First Festival of the Dignifying Rage. http://enlacezapatista.ezln.org.mx/varios/1250.

13 In March 2009, the newspaper *Excelsior* reported that 8,500 soldiers had been deployed just to Ciudad Juárez.

14 Indeed, the IFHR reports that female migrants are sexually harassed or raped by local, state, and federal authorities in Mexico. The perpetrators have never been judged (IFHR 2008, 27).

15 Examples of gender-based violence without any prosecution of identified perpetrators are abundant in Mexico. REDGE has followed up a dozen of cases dating back to 1994. REDGE staff provided me with a copy of this list, which includes both girls and elderly women, in most cases of working-class and indigenous origin.

16 This statement can be watched at: http://vodpod.com/watch/514088-3-encuentro-de-mujeres-zapatistas.

References

Ayres, Jeffrey, and Laura Macdonald. 2010. *Contentious Politics in North America: National Protest and Transnational Collaboration under Continental Integration.* Basingstoke: Palgrave Macmillan.

Blyth, Mark, ed. 2009. *Routledge Handbook of International Political Economy (IPE): IPE as a Global Conversation.* London: Routledge.

Bulow, Marisa von. 2010. *Building Transnational Networks: Civil Society and the Politics of Trade in the Americas.* Cambridge: Cambridge University Press.

Burguete Cal y Mayor, Araceli. 2003. 'The de Facto Autonomous Process: New

Jurisdictions and Parallel Governments in Rebellion.' In *Mayan Lives, Mayan Utopias: The Indigenous Peoples of Chiapas and the Zapatistas Rebellion*. Edited by Jan Rus et al. Lanham: Rowman and Littlefield. 191–218.

– 1995. 'Autonomia Indigena. Un camino hacia la paz.' *Revista CEMOS-Memoria* 75: 14–25.

Cacho Niño, Norma Iris. 2007. 'La triple discriminación: un breve bosquejo de la mujer indígena en Chiapas y en México.' Equipo de CIEPAC, no. 539, 30 July. http://www.ciepac.org/boletines/chiapasaldia.php?id=539.

Carlsen, Laura. 2007. '"Deep Integration": The Anti-Democratic Expansion of NAFTA.' Centre for International Policy, Americas Program. 30 May. http://americas.irc-online.org/am/4276.

CAPISE. 2007. 'La embestida del Estado Mexicano contra los indigenas y sus territorios' and 'Cara de Guerra: un Ejercito Federal Mexicano, unos indigenas, su territorio.' http://www.capise.org.mx.

Clarkson, Stephen. 2007. 'Does North America Exist? Transborder Governance after NAFTA and the Security and Prosperity Partnership.' *Norteamérica* 1–2: 85–104.

Coleman, William D., and Nancy A. Johnson. 2008. 'Building Dialogue on Globalization Research: What Are the Obstacles and How Might These Be Addressed?' Paper prepared for presentation to the workshop on Building South–North Dialogue on Globalization Research: Phase II, Centre for International Governance Innovation, Waterloo, 22–23 August, 4. http://www.globalautonomy.ca/global1/dialogue.jsp. Accessed 22 November 2011.

Desai, Manisha. 2002. 'Transnational Solidarity: Women's Agency, Structural Adjustment, and Globalization.' In *Women's Activism and Globalization: Liking Local Struggles and Transnational Politics*. Edited by Nancy Naples and Manish Desai. London: Routlege. 15–33.

Domínguez, E. 2007. 'Transnational Class/Gender Networking between the North and the South: Overcoming Diversity or Reproducing Dependencies?' In *Remapping Gender in the New Global Order*. Edited by Marjorie Griffin Cohen and Janine Brodie. London: Routledge. 223–43.

– 2002. 'Continental Transnational Activism and Women Workers' Networks within NAFTA.' *International Feminist Journal of Politics* 4: 216–39.

Donegan, Brendan. 2006. 'Governmental Regionalism: Power/Knowledge and Neoliberal Regional Integration in Asia and Latin America.' *Millennium: Journal of International Studies* 35, no. 1: 23–51.

Drainville, André C. 1999. 'Social Movements in the Americas: Regionalism from Below?' In *The Americas in Transition: The Contours of Regionalism*. Edited by Gordon Mace and Louis Bélanger. London: Lynne Rienner. 219–54.

Escobar, Arturo. 2008. *Territories of Difference, Place, Movement, Life, Redes*. Durham: Duke University Press.

– 2001. 'Culture Sits in Places: Reflections on Globalism and Subaltern Strategies of Localization.' *Political Geography* 20: 139–74.
– 1995. *Encountering Development: The Making and Unmaking of the Third World*. Princeton: Princeton University Press.
Gabriel, Christina, and Laura Macdonald. 1994. 'NAFTA, Women, and Organizing in Canada and Mexico: Forging a "Feminist" Internationality.' *Millennium: Journal of International Studies* 23, no. 3: 535–62.
Gilbert, Emily. 2005. 'Inevitability of Integration? Neoliberal Discourse and the Proposals for a New North American Economic Space after September 11.' *Annals of the Association of American Geographers* 95, no. 1: 202–22.
Hernandez Castillo, Rosalva Aida, ed. 2007. *La Otra Palabra. Mujeres y Violencia en Chiapas, antes y despues de Acteal*. Mexico: CIESAS/IWGIA.
– 2002. 'Indigenous Law and Identity Politics in Mexico: Indigenous Women Recreate Multiculturalism.' *PoLAR: Political and Legal Anthropology Review* 25, no. 1: 90–99.
Hettne, Björn, and Fredrik Söderbaum. 2000. 'Theorizing the Rise of Regionness.' *New Political Economy* 5, no. 3: 457–72.
Icaza, Rosalba. 2010. 'Global Europe, Guilty! Contesting EU Neoliberal Governance to Latin America.' *Third World Quarterly* 31, no. 1: 123–39.
– 2009. 'Alternative Regionalisms and Civil Society: Setting a Research Agenda.' *Pensamiento Propio* 29, no. 14: 235–44.
– 2008. 'The End of Neoliberal Regionalism in Mexico?' In *Canada-Mexico at the Crossroads: Big Picture Realities*. Edited by Daniel Drache. Waterloo: Wilfrid Laurier University Press. 185–204.
– 2006. '"To Be or Not to Be": The Question of Transborder Civic Activism and Regionalization in Mexico: A Critical Account of Neo-Gramscian Perspectives.' *Globalizations* 3, no. 4: 485–506.
Icaza, Rosalba, Peter Newell, and Marcelo Saguier. 2008. 'Democratizing Trade Politics in the Americas: Insights from the Women, Environmental, and Labour Movements.' IDS Working Paper. http://www.ids.ac.uk/files/dmfile/Wp328.pdf. Accessed 22 November 2011.
International Federation of Human Rights (IFHR). 2008. 'Walls, Abuses, and Deaths at the Borders.' http://www.fidh.org/FIDH-Releases-its-Investigative-Report-Walls,5334. Accessed 22 November 2011.
Korzenewiz, Roberto Patricio, and William C. Smith. 2001. 'Protest and Collaboration: Transnational Civil Society Networks and the Politics of Summitry and Free Trade in the Americas.' *North-South Agenda* 51 (September). Miami: North-South Centre, University of Miami.
Lendman, Stephen. 2007. 'The Militarization and Annexation of North America.' *GlobalResearch.ca*. 19 July. http://www.globalresearch.ca/index.php?context=va&aid=6359.

Macdonald, Laura. 2002. 'Globalization and Social Movements: Comparing Women's Movement Responses to NAFTA in Mexico, the U.S.A., and Canada.' *International Feminist Journal of Politics* 4, no. 2: 151–72.

Marchand, Marianne H. 1996. 'Selling NAFTA: Gendered Metaphors and Silenced Gender Implications.' In *Globalization: Theory and Practice*. Edited by Eleonore Kofman and Gillian Youngs. London: Pinter, 1996. 253–70.

– 1994. 'Gender and New Regionalism in Latin America: Inclusion/Exclusion.' *Third World Quarterly* 15, no. 1: 63–76.

Marchand, Marianne H., Martin Boas, and Tim Shaw. 1999. 'The Political Economy of New Regionalisms.' *Third World Quarterly* 20, no. 5: 897–910.

Marcos, Silvia. 2009. 'Otro camino feminista.' Paper presented at Sexto Viento: una otra digna rabia. First Festival of Dignifying Rage, 5 January. Audio: http://dignarabia.ezln.org.mx/?p=456.

Marcos, Silvia, and Margarite Waller, eds. 2005. *Dialogue and Difference: Feminisms Challenge Globalization*. London: Palgrave.

Meer, Shamin, and Charlie Sever. 2004. *Gender and Citizenship: Overview Report*. Brighton: IDS/Bridge.

Morton, Adam David. 2007. 'Peasants as Subaltern Agents in Latin America: Neoliberalism, Resistance. and the Power of the Powerless.' In *Everyday Politics of the World Economy*. Edited by John M. Hobson and Leonard Seabrooke, Cambridge: Cambridge University Press. 120–38.

– 2000. 'Mexico, Neoliberal Restructuring. and the EZLN: A Neo-Gramscian Analysis.' In *Globalization and the Politics of Resistance*. Edited by Barry K. Gills. London: Palgrave. 255–72.

Mignolo, Walter. 2000. *Local Histories / Global Designs*. Princeton: Princeton University Press.

Mukhopadhyay, Maitrayee. 2004. 'Introduction: Gender, Citizenship, and Governance.' In *Gender, Citizenship, and Governance: A Global Book*. Edited by Minke Valk, Sarah Cummings, and Henk van Dam. Amsterdam: KIT (Royal Tropical Institute) and Oxfam GB. 13–28.

Natal, Alejandro, and Tonatiuh Gónzalez. 2003. 'La Participación de la Sociedad Civil en Procesos de Integración Comercial: El Caso del ALCA en México.' *Foro Internacional* 43, no. 4: 852–92.

Olivera Bustamante, Mercedes. 2009. 'Militarizacion de la Frontera Mexico–Guatemala.' Paper presented at the 53rd International Congress of Americanists, Mexico City, 20 July.

– 2007. 'Acteal: Los efectos de la Guerra de baja intensidad.' In *La Otra Palabra. Mujeres y Violencia en Chiapas, antes y despues de Acteal*. Edited by Rosalva Aida Hernandez Castillo. México: CIESAS/IWGIA. 114–24.

Otzoy, Irma. 2008. 'Indigenous Law and Gender Dialogues.' In *Human Rights in the Maya Region: Global Politics, Cultural Contentions, and Moral Engage-*

ments. Edited by Pedro Pitarch, Shannon Speed, and Xochitl Leyva Solano. Durham: Duke University Press, 2008. 171–86.

Quijano, Anibal. 2000. 'Coloniality of Power, Eurocentrism, and Latin America.' *Nepantla: Views from South* 1, no. 3: 533–80.

Rojas, Cristina. 2007. 'International Political Economy/Development Otherwise.' *Globalizations* 4, no. 4: 573–87.

Sandoval Palacios, Juan Manuel. 2005. 'La "Nueva Estrategia" estadounidense para el continente americano.' In *La Hegemonía Estadounidense después de la Guerra de Irak.* Edited by Juan Manuel Sandoval Palacios and Alberto Betancourt Posada. México: Plaza y Valdes. 101–24.

Santos, Boaventura, J.A. Nunez, and M.P. Meneses. 2007. 'Opening Up the Canon of Knowledge and Recognition of Difference.' In *Another Knowledge Is Possible: Beyond Northern Epistemologies.* Edited by B. de Sousa Santos. London: Verso. xix–lxii.

Scholte, Jan Aart. 2004. 'Globalization and Governance: From Statism to Polycentrism.' CSGR Working Papers 130, no. 4.

Staudt, Kathleen. 2008. *Violence and Activism at the Border: Gender, Fear, and Everyday Life in Ciudad Juarez.* Austin: University of Texas Press.

Szanton, David L. 2004. 'The Origin, Nature, and Challenges of Area Studies in the United States.' In *The Politics of Knowledge: Area Studies and the Disciplines.* Edited by David L. Szanton. California: University of California Press. 1–33.

Walsh, Catherine. 2007. 'Shifting the Geopolitics of Critical Knowledge: Decolonial Thought and Cultural Studies "Others" in the Andes.' *Cultural Studies* 21, nos. 2–3: 224–39.

Walters, William, and Wendy Larner. 2002. 'The Political Rationality of "New Regionalism": Toward a Genealogy of the Region.' *Theory and Society* 31, no. 3: 391–432.

Events Attended

International Seminar of Reflection and Analysis on Andre Aubry's book *Planet Earth: Anti-Systemic Movements.* CIDESI-UNITIERRA, San Cristóbal de las Casas, Chiapas, México, 30–31 December 2009 and 1–2 January 2010.

Interviews Conducted

A: Leonor Aida Concha, REDGE Coordinator. 9 April 2008, REDGE offices in Mexico City.

B: Mari Carmen Martinez, REDGE and CODIMUJ. 9 April 2008, REDGE offices in Mexico City.

C: Alejandro Villamar, Member of RMALC, October 2008, Americas Social Forum, Ciudad de Guatemala.

In the workshop: 'Women Rights, and Anti-Capitalist/Anti-Patriarchal Resistance.' Summer 2008, Universidad de la Tierra/CIDESI, San Cristóbal de las Casas, Chiapas. The following activists are quoted in the paper:
A: Alma Padilla Garcia, Centro de Derechos Humanos de la Mujer Chiapaneca.
B: Gladys Alfaro, Coordinator, Centro de Investigacion-Accion de la Mujer Latinoamericana (CIAM).
C: Martha Figeroa, feminist lawyer and activist. Main prosecutor of Centro de Derechos Humanos Miguel Agustin Pro (Centro Pro) for the Acteal massacre.

12 Democratic Deficits and the Role of Civil Society in North America: The SPP and Beyond

JEFFREY AYRES AND LAURA MACDONALD

By August 2009, at the North American Leaders' Summit (NALS) in Guadalajara, Mexico, it was clear that the Security and Prosperity Partnership of North America (SPP) had died a quiet death. The 'Three Amigos Summit' had survived the transition from U.S. President George W. Bush to Barack Obama, with Obama meeting in Guadalajara with his counterparts Stephen Harper and Felipe Calderón, but the SPP had disappeared from their agenda. The only apparent reference to the SPP was the word 'process' in the last sentence of the summit declaration: 'We will continue to work through this North American Leaders' Summit process, *in an inclusive and transparent manner*, for the common benefit of the people of Mexico, Canada and the United States' (Joint Statement 2009; our emphasis). One telling indication of the loss of commitment to this process was the solemn declaration on the official U.S. government SPP website (www.spp.gov) that 'this website is an archive for SPP documents and will not be updated.' With this statement, a process that had begun four years earlier with high hopes of deepening North American integration through wide-ranging multisectoral regulatory harmonization seemed to grind to a halt.[1]

Civil society groups were jubilant about the SPP's demise and quickly claimed credit for stoking widespread unease about and criticism of the process, both of which had strengthened over its last year. Having begun as a fairly informal, ad hoc process for coordinating the priorities of participating governments under security and prosperity agendas, the SPP had quickly become a lightning rod for criticism as a result of perceptions that it was non-transparent and undemocratic. Groups involved in transnational collaboration against North American integration initiatives, such as the Council of Canadians (COC) and

Common Frontiers in Canada, Public Citizen and Global Exchange in the United States, and the *Red Mexicana ante el Libre Comercio* (RMALC) in Mexico, celebrated the end of the SPP process. Stuart Trew, the trade campaigner for the COC, declared that 'the NAFTA-plus agenda died at the latest North American Leader's summit … We killed it and we should be singing that from the rooftops' (Trew 2009). Meanwhile, the trinational Task Force on Renegotiating NAFTA, composed of progressive legislators from Canada, the United States, and Mexico, credited civil society group mobilizations and campaigns with helping defeat the SPP (Julian 2009).

However, the movement towards deepening continental cooperation received a surprising boost on 4 February 2011, when Prime Minister Harper and President Obama issued a joint declaration, 'Beyond the Border: A Shared Vision for Perimeter Security and Economic Competitiveness.[2] This 'Washington Declaration' (Sands 2011), issued following a meeting between the two leaders in Washington, established two new working groups: the Regulatory Cooperation Council (RCC) and the Beyond the Border Working Group (BBWG). These were separate initiatives, each with its own agenda, time frame, and consultation process. The RCC has purportedly been assigned the task of reducing the regulatory burden on Canada and the United States; the BBWG, of 'enhanc[ing] the security of the perimeter and streamlin[ing] border operations.'[3] The RCC and BBWG, after periods of 'consultation,' are to craft an action plan that will guide the two governments in their efforts to fulfil the declaration's goals. Both Clarkson and Golob in their chapters in this volume examine how these new efforts reflect continued asymmetries of power, a reaffirmation of 'double-bilateralism,' and contrasting preoccupations across the continent, with the new North American 'perimeter' distinctly leaving out Mexico and the wide array of U.S.–Mexico cross-border challenges.

We feel that the demise of the trilateral SPP and the emergence of the bilateral perimeter discussions also raise important questions about governance, democracy, and citizenship in the region. The measurable impact of civil society groups on discussions pertaining to North American integration or collaboration has always been slight, and the emergence of these new working groups around bilateral security and economic competitiveness demands that a conversation continue regarding the possible role for civil society in consultations on North American integration. It seems likely that civil society groups' portrayal of the process surrounding the SPP as non-transparent and undemocratic played some role in the demise of that process; but at the time of writing (July 2011), it is unclear to what extent input from civil society groups may influence the deliberations of the new perimeter working groups. We recognize that – as has been pointed out by Gilbert, Brodie, and Icaza elsewhere in this book – the failure of the SPP initiative by no means suggests that the basic neoliberal framework of security and prosperity via militarism and free trade has been eliminated from the regional agenda. In our view, the failed SPP represents an important case study for considering how North American regional integration remains plagued by a democratic deficit, in that the case invites consideration of the problems inherent in a mode of regional governance that lacks legitimacy, transparency, and consultation – a discussion that has become even more relevant in light of the new perimeter discussions.

The North American Free Trade Agreement's 'institutional vacuum' (Clarkson 2008) was well recognized even before the creation of the SPP. NAFTA exhibited a political model that eschewed democratic participation in favour of shallow, ineffective regional governance in the labour and environmental side agreements. The glaring exclusivity and secrecy that characterized SPP decision making, which was limited to small groups of business elites in consultation with bureaucracies in the respective countries, further inflamed legislative political opposition as well as civil society outrage over the sense of having become 'imaginary citizens' (Council of Canadians 2006) who had been deprived of the ability to provide input into deep integration discussions. So our primary goal in this chapter is to interrogate what the SPP's failure illustrates about the sources of and actors for change in the North American region, including concerns over democracy and citizenship. As discussed in the introduction to this volume, insights from the 'new regionalism' school and debates over the intersection between global governance and civil society will aid in our analysis.

First, the 'new regionalism' approach is useful insofar as it expands the parameters of analyses of regional integration beyond economic concerns to include a more pluralistic understanding of who the relevant actors are in regionalization and how these actors may undermine or enhance integration initiatives. In the case of North America, it is well known that business leaders allied with supportive legislators were the key promoters of continental integration beginning with the mid-1980s debates over CUSFTA (Langille 1987) and continuing through the negotiations of NAFTA and the SPP (CCCE 2004; Council on Foreign Relations 2005). But a major part of the story of North American integration has been the civil society opposition waged against it throughout more than two decades of contentious political activity, both national and transnational (Ayres and Macdonald 2009). In fact, there are a multitude of ideas about what North America – especially after NAFTA – actually 'means.' We are missing a significant part of the story of how North America has been constructed if we focus solely on increased trade and investment flows brought about by NAFTA to the exclusion of those visions of North America and transcontinental connections that civil society groups have developed through information exchange, conferences, speaking tours, and protest campaigns.

Moreover, while there is a vast literature about what we have called North American contentious politics, there have been fewer attempts to analyse the damage caused by the democratic deficit in North American regional governance. The rise and fall of the SPP thus raises important questions: Why have civil society groups outside of business circles not been able to participate more fully in discussions of deep integration? And how might more transparent and inclusionary processes of civil society engagement enhance the legitimacy of North American governance at a time when collaboration around issues of mutual concern by Canada, the United States, and Mexico is arguably needed? We recognize the dangers of idealizing 'civil society' actors as democratic forces. But we are interested in what Keck has called their potential for 'discursive representation' (2004, 45), which in our opinion would enhance the 'legitimacy game' (Van Rooy 2004) of North American governance discussions and initiatives. Civil society groups often lack the economic resources held by political and business actors, but they do promote ideas and norms and voice the concerns of their stakeholders, representing, as Keck points out, 'positions rather than populations, ideas rather than constituencies' (2004, 45).

In the first section of this chapter, we review the literature on global governance, democratic deficits, and the trend toward 'complex multilateralism' present in many forms of regional and global governance. In the second section, we assess how democratic deficits have manifested themselves across North America in the post-NAFTA era. We examine the role played by civil society groups around the NAFTA side agreements on labour and the environment, as well as the emergence of the SPP in the post-9/11 context, and examine the structures of representation that have or have not been produced. Based on secondary literature, government documents, parliamentary debates, and interviews with several senior Canadian government officials and civil society representatives, we examine the consultation mechanisms that have been created within the SPP process. We argue that the SPP's unique institutional architecture has created a fundamental inequity: elite-level business is represented in the process through the North American Competitiveness Council (NACC) established by the three governments; non-business civil society actors must make do with more limited, diffuse, and informal forms of consultation. Naturally, this institutional inequity has fuelled concerns by non-elite actors relating to the transparency, accountability, and democratic nature of the SPP process. Finally, we suggest that the 'legitimacy game' might be better played across North America if civil society participants were more fully included in discussions about the future of governance, economic integration, and cross-border collaboration in the region. Interestingly, there are signs that government bureaucrats assigned to the new working groups created for the discussions surrounding perimeter security and economic competitiveness have learned some lessons from the SPP's failed consultation process – a turn of events we consider in our conclusion.

Global Governance, Civil Society, and Democratic Deficits

Negotiations involving trade and investment rules and regulatory harmonization – and the resulting agreements and institutions – continue to be dogged by questions about transparency, legitimacy, and accountability (Scholte 2002; Koenig-Archibugi and Held 2004; Aaronson and Abouharb 2011). Essentially, what some see as the appropriate transnational functions of multilateral forums and regimes have with increased frequency clashed with what others see as the legitimate responsibilities of national democratic governments and the aspirations of their citizens. As discussed elsewhere in this volume (see the chapters by VanNijnatten and Craik and Brodie), the older 'club model' (Keohane and Nye 2002) of multilateral negotiations has been progressively delegitimized by a post–Cold War process of 'complex multilateralism' (O'Brien et al. 2000). International negotiations today are less likely to be dominated by a handful of powerful states; instead, they are often shaped by wide-ranging networks of civil society organizations, new information technologies, and the intrusion of social concerns into deliberations, as well as by rising states in the developing world, which demand a role in 'policy making' as opposed to the more traditional 'policy taking.'

The explosive growth in NGOs (Sikkink and Smith 2002) and their mobilization around international policies and new international institutions has paralleled ongoing shifts in power both *inside* states, from parliaments to the executive and to the bureaucracy, and *outside* states, as institutional power has diffused from the national to regional and supranational levels (Della Porta and Tarrow 2005, 1).

Arguably, the emergence of new political opportunities at the regional *and* international levels, including (but not limited to) the multiplying number of targets for activists in the newer trade and investment regimes, has encouraged innovation in NGO and civil society cross-border activism. The penchant for NGOs and civic groups to mobilize and collaborate across borders has been linked to the emergence of a multilevel political environment (Tarrow 2002; Sikkink 2005). Policy making is occurring at national, regional, and international levels, which has meant that new resources, leverage, and opportunities are emerging for activist networking, targeting, and challenges to elites, as the new policies and institutions become key points for claims making. The United Nations, the European Union, and the World Trade Organization have become focal points for transnational protest and networking, with NGOs targeting UN conferences, WTO ministerials, and EU policies (Gordenker and Weiss 1996; Clark, Friedman, and Hochstetler 1998; Imig and Tarrow 2001).

Some international forums have moved towards more consensual and inclusive modes of consultation and decision making. That said, democratic deficits remain a characteristic of many global and regional regimes. The concept of democratic deficit captures the sense shared by many publics around the world that they have lost control of their economic and political destinies and that processes of representation and democratic accountability have been undermined by global and regional integration pressures (Tanguay 2009). Core concerns that critics focus on when identifying democratic deficits within governance structures are 'representivity' (Van Rooy 2004), democratic accountability (Steffek and Ferreti 2009), and whether citizens beyond their elected elites have much opportunity to shape international debates and policy directions. How accountable are processes of global and regional governance to citizens' concerns and anxieties? How do elites work to ensure that 'input legitimacy' is taken as seriously as 'output legitimacy' (Scharpf 1999)? And perhaps more important, how has the exclusion of non-elite voices contributed to the current crisis of North American regionalism? As this chapter illustrates, North American elites from both the public and the private sector have, to their peril, downplayed issues of public diplomacy, legitimacy, and democracy; instead, they have developed a model of governance that lacks measures to generate accountability, participation, and public support.

North American Governance after NAFTA: The Emerging Legitimacy Gap

North American integration involved new modes of interaction between state and business elites. These modes were designed to reverse protectionist policies while attempting to finesse the lack of enthusiasm for liberalization among the citizens of the three countries. In many ways, the Canadian government's decision in the 1980s to pursue a bilateral free trade deal with the United States was the result of the reorganization of Canadian business under the ideological leadership of the Business Council on National Issues (BCNI). The privileged role of big business in the development of trade policy was institutionalized during the subsequent NAFTA negotiations; consultation mechanisms were established in the form of the International Trade Advisory Committee and Sectoral Advisory Groups on International Trade. These mechanisms, modelled on the U.S. trade policy system, were then copied by Mexico (Macdonald 2002b; Winham 1992).

These elite-led NAFTA negotiations sparked an early round of NGO cross-border strategizing and coalition building, modelled after the late-1980s mobilization against CUSFTA by nationalist and social activist coalitions in Canada. Civic groups in each of the three countries spearheaded national coalition building against the negotiations; they also reached out across borders to share strategies for opposing the deal (Massicotte 2003; Dreiling 1999). Mexican and Canadian groups found opportunities within the U.S. political system to target Congress and lobby against the accord; meanwhile, the negotiations provided a convenient focus for transnational mobilization and educational campaigns in the three NAFTA states. Thus, even though opportunities for formal consultation with non-elite actors were highly limited, by its very nature, the negotiation of a high-level, public international treaty created a prominent target for debate and contentious political activity both inside and outside formal political institutions. We argue that this bifurcation of forms of political representation between elite and non-elite groups entrenched political divisions regarding the North American project and created an insider/outsider dichotomy that would be difficult to overcome.

In the years following NAFTA's implementation, moreover, civil society groups continued to target NAFTA and exploit the newly emergent multilevel political opportunity structure. National actors and coalitions continued to target domestic political opportunities: the CTC lobbied the U.S. Congress against renewal of the presidential 'fast track' negotiating authority, while RMALC and the Zapatista Army of National Liberation exploited cracks emerging in the decades-long political hegemony held by the Institutional Revolutionary Party (PRI) to mobilize for reforms on behalf of constituencies threatened by NAFTA's neoliberal prescriptions. NAFTA also encouraged protests along the Mexico–U.S. border and stimulated broader sectoral collaboration among unions and women's and environmental groups in the three NAFTA states (Carr 1996; Cook 1997; Macdonald 2002a). Despite widespread scepticism about the side accords, civic groups from the three NAFTA states exploited regional political opportunities provided by the citizen petition mechanisms built into the NAFTA labour and environmental side accords to raise international awareness of labour and environmental abuses and to build solidarity around particular grievances in individual NAFTA states (Tollefson 2002; Stillerman 2003; Graubart 2008). Although these mechanisms lacked enforcement capacity, they did provide some openings for input and debate by non-elite actors, as well as opportunities to publicize the weaknesses of the three governments' records on labour and environmental issues. Nevertheless, even in Mexico, where civil society actors (including labour) had some hopes for the side accords, disenchantment was widespread by the time the SPP emerged.

The Architecture of the SPP: An Evolving Democratic Deficit

Whereas NAFTA seemed to some extent to produce the sorts of multilevel opportunity structures found elsewhere across regional and global governance schemes, the more recent SPP process appeared designed to limit and perhaps even reverse the minimal steps towards a more consultative system of North American governance. The SPP unfolded as an expansive initiative by the executive bodies of the three NAFTA states. Lacking the legislative backing given NAFTA, the SPP was designed to alleviate U.S. security concerns in the post-9/11 era regarding the U.S.–Canadian and U.S.–Mexican borders while pursuing a broad-based package of multisectoral regulatory harmonization. In particular, Canadian and Mexican officials promoted the SPP as a means to ensure that U.S. security concerns did not result in restricted access to the U.S. market – access that had been gained during the CUS-FTA and NAFTA talks. The SPP envisioned a space of 'market-oriented harmonization' with 'very little in the way of state role or infrastructure' imagined (Gilbert 2007).

Were the SPP's architects seeking to prevent the emergence of openings for citizen engagement, or to reduce traditional domestic political opportunities for civil society debate and leverage within political institutions, or both? In an era when other models of governance were being reshaped to meet the civil society demands of transparency and accountability, the SPP seemed designed to avoid the messy political confrontations and consultations attending the previous ten years of trade and investment summitry. Our research largely confirms the views of the critics: the SPP process gave business representatives disproportionate influence over the trilateral process, while non-elite views were largely excluded. It is important to emphasize that this lopsided consultation process was not inevitable but was the result of a series of forces: a dynamic of path dependency in which the lean institutional structure established under NAFTA tended to shut down opportunities for broadened consultation processes; the temporary transcendence of political forces committed to a narrow view of the integration process as market-driven; the 9/11 attacks, which led to the predominance of U.S. security concerns and attempts to link 'security' with 'prosperity'; and the polarization of views around North American integration, which led civil society actors to seek rejection or renegotiation of NAFTA, not inclusion in existing negotiations. In this context, non-elite actors were easily cast by governments as obstructionist, unconstructive, and ideological, while business was perceived as providing pragmatic and constructive advice. This dichotomous dynamic acted to foreclose alternative visions of the integration process.[4]

After the 9/11 terrorist attacks, rethinking of the North American relationship continued in elite circles, without substantive input from non-business civil society actors. One high-level report was published in April 2004 by the Canadian Council of Chief Executives (CCCE, formerly the BCNI, an important actor in the promotion of free trade with the United States in the 1980s). As discussed in the chapter by Brodie in this volume, the CCCE, a high-level business association comprising 150 leading Canadian businesses, had established the North American Security and Prosperity Initiative (NASPI) in 2003 to 'develop a strategy for shaping Canada's future within North America and beyond' (CCCE 2004, 1). The NASPI report highlighted Canada's continued heavy reliance on the U.S. economy; it also emphasized the need, in the light of emergence of 'fierce competitors' such as China, India, and Brazil, for 'developing a winning strategy in this competitive global environment' (ibid.). The NASPI report suggested that in this context, the Canadian strategy for managing its future on the North American continent should be based on the following five pillars: *'reinventing borders; regulatory efficiency; resource security; the North American defence alliance;* and *new institutions'* (ibid., 2; emphasis in original). Although new institutions were one of the NASPI's recommendations, the report distanced itself from the 'big idea' proposal, emphasizing that the 'goal of our strategy is not a single big agreement leading to big new supranational institutions' (ibid., 5).

The CCCE report may have inspired another prominent report – the Independent Task Force on North America, convened by the U.S.-based Council on Foreign Relations and chaired by John Manley, Pedro Aspe, and William Weld. Their report, 'Building a North American Community,' included ambitious recommendations such as 'the establishment by 2010 of a North American economic and security community, the boundaries of which would be defined by a common external tariff and an outer security perimeter' (Council on Foreign Relations 2005, xvii). North American governments, particularly the United States, were not ready to adopt the most ambitious elements of these proposals. However, the recognition of the need for action on the challenges being laid out by business did result in the SPP. A CCCE representative reflected on the 'juxtaposition of a pretty ambitious set of ideas, perhaps what was metaphorically called the Big Idea back then, [with] a set of 300-plus micro initiatives, a highly incremental program collected across departments of all three governments' (interview, Ottawa, May 2008).

Similarly, the NASPI document referred to a report prepared for the CCCE by former trade negotiator Michael Hart, which pointed out that Canada and the United States 'already work together through a vast network of formal and informal ties, and the key issue is where to strengthen this network' (CCCE 2004, 5). The CCCE report noted that continental initiatives such as a NAFTA Secretariat and consolidation or reform of the existing dispute settlement mechanisms were worth exploring, but 'given the rising tide of protectionist sentiment in the United States, significant expansion of the NAFTA or of NAFTA-based institutions seems unlikely in the short term' (ibid., 19). Hart's vision of an ambitious, far-reaching (but decentralized), informal, flexible, and low-key strategy was remarkably similar to the 'institutional lite' structure of what would emerge as the SPP. The council did recommend the development of strong networks among elected representatives in the three countries, as well as among business organizations,[5] and coordination with subnational governments. Notably lacking was any mention of the need to consult or engage with civil society actors beyond business, or indeed of the need to develop a strategy to convince the broader public of the merits of these proposals.

While there was a great deal of continuity between the recommendations of Canadian business and the eventual design of the SPP, there was also discontinuity. In particular, the main emphasis in the CCCE report was on bilateral Canada–U.S. relations, although it advocated a 'steady strengthening over time' of the trilateral North American partnership (ibid., 24). In contrast, the SPP's framework was formally trilateral, presumably because of the political difficulties in selling a purely bilateral approach in Washington, although it was not an approach that went far beyond the 'double-bilateralism' that characterized much of the North American relationship under NAFTA (Golob 1999; Pastor 2004). The SPP process was framed by the institutionalizing of annual leaders' summits, which would ensure high-level support and ongoing political attention to the process. The slogan that officials coined for the trilateral/bilateral process was 'three can talk, two can act' (interviews, Ottawa, May 2008).

Towards the end of the period 2001–4 there was a desire to continue the momentum built up in this process in order to counter pressure from Congress to implement programs such as what eventually became the Western Hemisphere Travel Initiative. The solution was to 'bump it up' to the level of ministers and leaders, above the bureaucratic level (interview, Ottawa, May 2008). As neo-institutionalists suggest, the institutions established in an earlier period tend to shape the choices available to policy makers at later stages, reflecting the dynamic captured by the term 'path dependency.' NAFTA's lack of high-level institutions as possible sites of contestation, debate, and discussion made the subsequent development of such institutions unlikely (see the discussion in the chapter by Golob).

The SPP's goal was thus not to create new commissions or organizations but to task existing organizations with the process. This would entail annual reporting on the issues to the leaders' summits, which would in effect push those issues higher up the list of bureaucrats' priorities. The decision to pursue the existing SPP institutional structure was also based on the perception that there was a lack of political will to adopt higher levels of institutionalization, because of sovereignty concerns in the three countries but also because there was a recognized likelihood of political protest against a more expansive initiative (interview, senior government official, Ottawa, January 2008).

The SPP's design was rather informal and ad hoc and went through several phases. Initially, after the Waco summit, governments had six months to consult with all government departments and develop a series of recommendations for governments regarding priorities on their bilateral and trilateral agendas (interview, Ottawa, May 2008). These priorities were then broken down into two areas, security and prosperity, although it became increasingly clear as time went on that the two overlapped. More than three hundred priorities were identified in the first report to the ministers (interview, 7 May 2008). Nine working groups were established under the prosperity agenda and ten under the security agenda,[6] and these working groups were charged with 'outreach with a variety of stakeholders within each country' (Beaudoin 2007). These stakeholders were defined on the U.S. government's website as located 'in the business sector, state and local governments, and non-government organizations' (White House 2005).

In line with Michael Hart's recommendation to the CCCE, the SPP working groups were merely an incremental phase in the further development (and limited trinationalization) of existing cross-border governmental relations, and the nature of the group varied across issue area. While some of these working groups were based on existing bilateral or trilateral groupings around certain long-standing policy issues, others were created at this time on a rather arbitrary basis (interview, Ottawa, May 2008).

At the second North American Leaders' Summit in Cancún in 2006, the incoming Canadian prime minister Stephen Harper suggested that the more than three hundred priorities be reduced to only five. His suggestion was accepted by the other two leaders (interview, Ottawa, May 2008).[7] Business leaders had expressed frustration with the unfocused nature of the three hundred priorities (interview, Ottawa, May 2008).

After this, the SPP took a more targeted and streamlined approach that incorporated the advice given by business. This constriction of the agenda for discussion may have reduced even further the opportunity for stakeholder consultation, since not all of these areas of renewed emphasis were subjects of working groups that, at least theoretically, could have carried out consultation on those topics.

The NACC: The Core of the Democratic Deficit

The ad hoc, technocratic, and decentralized nature of the SPP working groups made it difficult for them to carry out the functions assigned to them of outreach and consultation with a wide range of stakeholders. It seems likely that in some policy areas, such as the environment, where a greater tradition exists of consultation with non-business actors, more consultation occurred (VanNijnatten 2007, 675), while in many others, particularly in the area of security, broader consultation was non-existent. The fact that these consultations took place literally behind closed doors, without any public record, makes it difficult to evaluate this process. Perhaps more seriously, the process suffered from the more fundamental problem that non-business stakeholders appeared to be consulted, if at all, only on the technicalities of implementing the SPP agenda, and did not have any input into the broader design of the process. As well, as VanNijnatten notes regarding the issue of the environment, 'the lack of legislative scrutiny effectively closes off one potential avenue whereby environmental concerns might be raised and then integrated into SPP deliberations and programming' (ibid., 674).

While the SPP process was designed to bypass legislative scrutiny and operate below the public radar, it was probably the creation of the NACC that raised the most red flags and that did the most to ignite pre-existing concerns about public disempowerment associated with globalization. The NACC was created at the suggestion of Mexican president Vicente Fox, whose country's economy at that time was grappling with rising competition from the Asian economies. By this point, all three governments were headed by leaders from the political right, who accepted as given the idea of market-driven growth (ibid., 667).[8] The decision to create the NACC was in line with this neoliberal perspective, as well as with the decision at the North American Leaders' meeting in Cancún to narrow the range of priorities identified by bureaucrats to more strategic areas. The leaders asked the business leaders who had been invited to the Cancún meeting for strategic advice on the general direction of North America in a more competitive global environment. The composition of the NACC, in fact, varied by country. Harper chose ten leading CEOs (appointing d'Aquino from the CCCE as the leader of the Canadian secretariat); the Mexicans chose heads of business associations as well as CEOs; the United States designated individual companies as participants, often represented by vice-presidents responsible for Latin America (interviews, Ottawa, May

2008). Clearly, the NACC enjoyed a privileged position vis-à-vis other civil society actors, having been created and selected by governments, and having been invited make presentations directly to the leaders at meetings in Montebello and New Orleans. In contrast, other civil society leaders were excluded from these meetings.[9]

A CCCE representative noted that the process was partly shaped by an attempt to avoid the U.S. legislative process:

> Whoever advises the U.S. government, there is legislation that underpins it, and that legislation is passed by Congress. And the SPP and all the initiatives that had been suggested by us and by others would have required tremendous legislative change. And so, the thinking was, in order to achieve quick, short-term improvements along the border or on the regulatory front or in other areas, were there ways to come up with incremental initiatives that would require administrative change as opposed to legislative change? (interview, Ottawa, May 2008)

Government officials seemed to agree that there was a 'branding problem' with the SPP, as well as difficulties in articulating publicly the purpose of the process, especially in the context of a 'doubting public and media,' Democratic control of the U.S. Congress, traditional labour concerns about globalization, and NGO/civil society suspicion of U.S. intentions (interview, Ottawa, May 2008). One senior official also noted the problems inherent in explaining to the average person the esoteric details of issues such as food dye standards. Another official stated, regarding the question of consultation:

> There were consultations from the start with the usual stakeholders. We have always said that this is the responsibility of government departments responsible for specific issues. There is consultation on specific issues rather than the merits of SPP. We think that the merit is in the outcome ... If you want to influence the agenda, you have to be heard on the specific[s], rather than going too broad. (interview, Ottawa, May 2008)

Yet another senior official stated:

> Listening to the NACC members when I've had the privilege to do so, they're all talking about very practical things. They're concerned about the border, like Mr Ganong of Ganong Chocolates, his stuff gets held up by the Food and Drug Administration for months and he never gets an expla-

nation. Meanwhile, he's lost a contract. But they're not talking about metaphysical issues, they're talking about very practical things. And I think
that civil society thinks that there's this metaphysical conversation going
on and it's actually quite meat and potatoes and if they could deconstruct
their agenda into meat and potatoes, they would have all the access that
anybody has. (interview, Ottawa, May 2008)

This claim about the specifics and details of business input is at odds
with the claim that the NACC was created to give broad strategic advice
about the future of North American competitiveness.

A CCCE representative echoed the government representatives'
reflections about the practicality of business advice, contrasting it with
civil society's perceived obstructionism:

We don't, obviously, dictate outcomes. If we did, we'd be making much
more progress. But we can be constructive players in providing advice.
We know that when that advice is ... received, government has all sorts
of different avenues by which it can test the feasibility or the desirability
of taking action with other interest groups. There is not a body that meets
every year with the North American leaders to oppose the SPP because
why would you? (interview, Ottawa, May 2008)

The Failure of 'Integration by Stealth'

Despite official attempts to avoid public attention and debate, claims
multiplied that the SPP amounted to 'integration by stealth.' The last
couple of years prior to its demise witnessed the escalation of public
controversy around the process, particularly among right-wing groups
in the United States. Brian Bow and Arturo Santa Cruz posit that we
have seen a convergence of two forms of opposition to regionalism in
the United States: traditional interest-based opposition among groups
such as labour unions on the political left, and identity-based opposition on the political right. Notwithstanding their political differences
and lack of ties, both groups' critiques of the SPP focused strongly on
the exclusionary and secretive character of the process (Bow and Santa
Cruz 2009). The identity-based opponents of the SPP were fuelled by
long-standing xenophobic, isolationist, and paranoid strands in U.S.
political culture and alluded to high-level conspiracies. Prior to the
2008 elections, underdog Republican U.S. presidential candidate Ron
Paul charged on a CNN/YouTube debate: 'They're planning on [tak-

ing] millions of acres ... by eminent domain.' Furthermore, there was 'an unholy alliance of foreign consortiums and officials from several governments' promoting the idea. 'The ultimate goal,' he said, 'is not simply a superhighway, but an integrated North American Union – complete with a currency, a cross-national bureaucracy, and virtually borderless travel within the Union' (cited in Kovach 2007, 1).

At the same time, traditional civil society–based opponents of integration on the left across the region expressed concern or scepticism about the SPP, especially in the absence of extensive information about the outcomes of the SPP negotiations. With the lack of clear smoking guns, criticisms honed in on the secretive and exclusionary nature of the discussions and on the apparent privileging of business interests through the NACC. Government representatives claimed, to the contrary, that ample opportunities existed for consultations with a wide range of stakeholders through the multitude of working groups established in each country to support the broader process, and that extensive information was available to the public through the SPP website (www.spp-psp.gc.ca) (Beaudoin 2007, 8).

A Council of Canadians document denounced the undemocratic nature of the SPP process and called for the dissolution of the NACC:

> The SPP fails to address this fundamental democratic expectation because it was expressly conceived to circumvent democratic debate, oversight and ratification, by Parliament, and to exclude direct, transparent consultation with the public. Our leaders then took the extraordinary step of inviting powerful corporations to have a direct role in drafting government policies by creating the NACC, an organization with little interest in improving democracy on the continent. (Trew 2007)

Similarly, in her testimony before the Canadian Parliamentary Subcommittee on Trade, Canadian Labour Congress representative Teresa Healy challenged the initial designation of priorities for discussion and called for the abolition of the NACC; full public hearings and a vote in Parliament on the SPP; a review of the implications of further security cooperation with the United States for workers, especially immigrant workers; a review of processes of regulatory reform leading to hyperdevelopment of the tar sands and the downward harmonization of the tar sands; and an 'open, transparent, and accountable' process leading to a 'North American relationship built on democracy, human rights, and sovereignty' (Healy 2007).

Even some supporters of NAFTA and/or the SPP issued warnings about the dangers of the model of decision making that had been adopted. Chris Sands from the Hudson Institute contended that the SPP 'represented a much needed reform or update of the framework for economic integration' in North America. Nevertheless, he added, 'the SPP has been a failure in two important respects: its limited transparency has fueled conspiracy theories that hold that the SPP is a plot to reduce national sovereignty in each country; and it has failed to allay public concerns, mainly in the United States, that NAFTA has hurt U.S. prosperity more than it has helped – despite the ample economic data which provides evidence to the contrary' (Sands 2009; see also Anderson and Sands 2007).

Even American University professor Robert Pastor, who has passionately promoted North American integration and a North American community, argued similarly that North America had run into problems under the Bush administration partly because the benefits of integration 'have not been equitably shared with those who paid a price' (2008, 91). He argued that the Bush administration's 'incremental, quiet, business-based approach raised some legitimate concerns and provoked a nativist backlash. It was a mistake to allow CEOs to be the only outside advisers on deregulation and the harmonization of remaining regulations. Civil society and legislatures must be heard on these issues, which are less about business than about how to pursue environmental, labor, and health goals. More broadly, free trade is clearly not enough' (2008, 93).

In light of the growing evidence that NAFTA had failed to narrow the gap between living conditions in Mexico and those in the other two countries, reactions ranged from indifference to cynicism. Former NGO leader Carlos Heredia has stated:

The SPP was kind of a joke. No one paid attention to it except the bureaucrats who would come up and say we have something like 234 programs and agreements geared to facilitate everything from border facilitation to whatever, you name it. But it never got to be a brand name known by the population. At least people know about NAFTA. They can love it, they can hate it – nobody knew about the SPP but the bureaucrats in the three governments …

I'm not implying that it was some kind of secret conspiracy, I'm just saying it wasn't something that could provide enthusiasm for integration … It was designed in clandestinity, not because they wanted it like that, but because 99% of the population didn't hear about it. (interview, Mexico City, March 2010)

Mexico City–based critic Laura Carlsen, director of the Americas Program of the Centre for International Policy, similarly states:

In Mexico there's so much going on right now it's not even an issue. And there's so much disaffection and there's so much confusion. It was a big issue during the campaign of 2006 – the economic model – and the economic model should be an even a bigger issue now because it's failing more spectacularly than it was in 2006. But it's like people don't even know what's hit them, between the security statistics and struggling on a very individual basis to survive the crisis and the repression that's been released. And the opposition is struggling with the fraudulent elections of 2006 and not being able to do anything about it. There isn't much cohesion in Mexico right now to do anything for change. (interview, Mexico City, March 2010)

In light of widespread public concerns about the SPP's legitimacy, it is not surprising that it did not survive the end of the Bush administration. During his presidential campaign, Barack Obama expressed concerns about NAFTA, particularly the weakness of the labour and environmental side accords, and pledged not to participate in exclusionary and secretive international processes of the sort represented by the SPP. Opposition to NAFTA and the SPP among Obama's civil society supporters, particularly labour, and the success of grassroots campaigning by actors such as the Citizens' Trade Campaign, likely had a strong impact on his decision to quietly close down the SPP.

It is less clear whether civil society groups can affect the future shape of the North American region, especially when it comes to decision-making processes that might accompany efforts to deepen the Canada–U.S. relationship post-SPP. One response to the problem of selling the SPP to the public was to move away from an SPP 'brand' to a 'North American Leaders' Summit' brand – a move that became apparent during the New Orleans meeting. This move further distanced civil society groups from discussion of key concerns. Canadian officials have been quick to distinguish between the SPP and trilateral discussions through the NALS (interviews, Washington, May 2010). Yet as Sands again points out, the lack of standing working groups within the NALS provided even less opportunity than the SPP for citizen input (interview,

Washington, May 2010). And the fact that a summit scheduled for Canada in the summer of 2010 was never convened (purportedly because of difficulty finding a date because of Canada's role as host of the G8 and G20 meetings) raises further questions about the future of the region.

Conclusion: North America's Poor Record at the 'Legitimacy Game'

This saga of ongoing civil society opposition to elite frameworks of North American integration, and of citizens' groups' at least partial success in derailing those frameworks, reveals important lessons about the character of regionalization processes. First, as suggested in the 'new regionalisms' literature, theories of regional integration that ignore the role of non-state and non-business actors are clearly inadequate in explaining the nature and dynamics of regionalization. In the absence of public pronouncements or direct evidence about the causes of the SPP's demise, it is difficult to state definitively how important civil society actors were in this decision. These actors had little impact as long as neoliberal leaders from right-wing parties remained in power in all three countries. The election of a Democratic president in the United States, the region's hegemon, was undoubtedly a decisive factor in the SPP's fate. It seems likely, though, that civil society opposition played an important role in what was apparently the Obama administration's decision to cancel the SPP, in terms of direct influence within the Democratic Party and the shaping of broader public opinion in the United States.

Beyond empirical issues of the weight of civil society actors in regionalization processes, this case study raises both normative and pragmatic issues about democracy and citizenship in the North American region. As we indicated in the introduction to this volume, debates about trade and regulatory harmonization are not simply dry technical issues; they highlight important concerns about how citizens are, and see themselves to be, included in ongoing globalization processes. As Moore (2008, 300) has argued, while many students of global governance embrace the opportunity for cross-border cooperation and coordination promised by constructs such as NAFTA and the SPP, they may overlook 'historically grounded ... economic divisions and disparities' and fail to appreciate the impact of enduring power relationships between and across states. (Ayres [2004] has argued that despite considerable cross-border civil society interaction and cooperation in the wake of NAFTA's implementation, power relations under the accord remain essentially unchanged.) We would suggest further that, based on the record of the SPP process, the SPP's approach to regionalization reaffirmed the sorts of privileged political-economic relationships established under NAFTA. The SPP's demise suggests that this process was fundamentally flawed even in instrumentalist terms as a means of achieving its founders' goals of deeper continental integration. The privileging of big business actors over all others ultimately doomed it. More tinkering with the NAFTA formula is unlikely to solve this legitimacy deficit, however; and especially in light of the economic crisis that has struck the region, North American integration is likely stalled for the foreseeable future.

The increased inclusion of non-state actors in mechanisms of global governance is not primarily the result of global governors' democratic impulses; it also reflects their self-interested recognition that these actors bring alternative sources of information, as well as an attempt to legitimize international organizations in the eyes of an increasingly sceptical public. In the context of this chapter, government and business agreed that, based on past experience, civil society actors would not present practical solutions to concrete problems but would merely denounce the entire process. This reflected a tendency among political and business elites to question the democratic characteristics of civil society groups that have not been formally elected to positions of political influence. It is often assumed that output legitimacy – problem-solving effectiveness – is satisfied through the participation of elected officials and those appointed by them from the business sector to engage in international negotiations and policy making. We would argue that future discussions on North American issues should not be constrained by this limited view of governance beyond the state. Rather, we encourage greater consideration for the democratizing potential of wider civil society participation in regional governance processes.

Interestingly, as we noted at the beginning of our chapter, the new Beyond the Border and Regulatory Cooperation Council working groups established out of the February 2011 Perimeter Security and Economic Competitiveness Declaration do reflect evidence of what might be termed 'bureaucratic learning' on the part of those government officials who were burned by the SPP's demise. First, the new security perimeter proposal differs dramatically from the SPP in that it excludes completely Mexican economic and security concerns, reflecting a long-term Canadian goal of formally 'decoupling' the Americans' southern border policy from their northern border policy (Sands 2011), and perhaps as well the more difficult record of trilateral SPP security and regulatory discussions. At the same time, energy and regulatory concerns have been separated in the new perimeter discussions from contentious border privacy issues, with again the regulatory and border working groups having separate agendas and consultation processes (Canadian Labour Congress 2011). In fact, on this latter issue of consultation we find some noticeable changes from the non-transparent and bureaucratic workings of the SPP. In this regard, Chris Sands of the Hudson Institute issued a sharp comment to both governments immediately after the Washington Declaration: the two new working groups had failed to 'address the weakness of the doomed prior efforts, most notably of the Security and Prosperity Partnership ... by excluding Mexico and retaining the poor transparency, exclusively bureaucratic model, and exclusion of U.S. Congress and civil society groups' (ibid., 3).

Yet notably, the new working groups of government officials from selected Canadian and U.S. federal offices and departments seemed cognizant of the public relations fiasco of the SPP and of the need for a more transparent process for engaging stakeholders. Particularly notable have been the Canadian government's attempts to reach out to a broader array of civil society groups through both 'e-consultations' (which solicited more than one thousand comments to the BBWG as of early June 2011) and actual in-person meetings with civil society groups, during which officials have solicited questions and expressed a desire for transparency and accountability (to broader concerns). Such overtures were clearly absent from the SPP process, and while it is too early in the new perimeter discussions to gauge whether governments are serious at playing the 'legitimacy game' – some civil society groups are already characterizing these consultations as 'briefings' as opposed to give-and-take exchanges where the parameters of the perimeter discussions may be expanded to reflect broader stakeholder concerns – there is at least reason to believe that federal officials are taking more seriously if not the democratic credentials of civil society actors, then at least the potential public relations fiasco of ignoring once again the concerns of those actors.

In short, the SPP did not create a North American regional governance structure that would provide robust opportunities for civil society groups, and it is too soon to declare that the new perimeter security and economic competitiveness discussions represent a dramatic corrective to the democratic deficit in North American governance. While the targets for civic influence multiplied – from NAFTA negotiations, to the NAFTA labour and environmental side accords, to a new and expansive set of negotiations and political/business actors in the SPP process – non-business civil society groups did not gain new political leverage to advance their claims within the ongoing SPP negotiations. What we see continuing is twin processes of 'domestication and externalization' (Della Porta and Tarrow 2005) as frustrated social actors target – in vain – domestic institutions with complaints over the SPP experience, while other Canadian, U.S., and Mexican groups continue to connect and mobilize across borders to share strategies and publicize their opposition to neoliberal continental integration schemes. Tarrow (2005) has warned that the sort of complicated internationalism epitomized by the failed SPP process has unpredictable trajectories, 'creating arenas for conflict and cooperation that will not necessarily lead either to the triumph of global capitalism or to democratic outcomes' (2005, 28). Nevertheless, the tumultuous events of the past several years – the elections of Obama and the Harper Conservatives (with a majority); the crushing 2010 U.S. midterm election, during which the Democrats lost control over the House of Representatives; the eruption of the global financial crisis; the spiralling Mexican narco-insurgency with its explosion of killings; and the ever burgeoning debt crisis facing the United States – may break the path dependency that has been established in the North American region. Moreover, the spirit of trilateralism inherent in the imperfect SPP has evaporated, as pressures for greater bilateralism and an unbundling of regionalism become more prominent.

Notes

1 We found no similar statement or acknowledgment of the SPP's demise on the Canadian or Mexican foreign affairs websites. Canadian NDP trade critic Peter Julian suggests that it was the Obama administration that decided to pull the plug on the SPP initiative and that the Canadian government refrained from commenting for diplomatic reasons (interview, Ottawa, January 2010).
2 'Beyond the Border: A Shared Vision for Perimeter Security and Economic Competitiveness,' http://www.borderactionplan-plandactionfrontalier.gc.ca/psec-scep/declaration-declaration.aspx?lang=eng.
3 See http://www.BorderActionPlan.gc.ca and a powerpoint slide from the Government of Canada, 'Beyond the Border.'

4 Interviews to evaluate elite views of the development of the SPP process and the nature of consultation processes were carried out in January and May 2008 with senior officials from the main Canadian ministries responsible for the SPP process, and with the Canadian Council of Chief Executives (CCCE), formerly the Business Council on National Issues (BCNI). All government officials requested anonymity. Also, we have not identified the government ministries in which they were based because of the small number of individuals involved. Follow-up interviews with civil society actors occurred in January and February 2010, and with Mexican experts in March 2010.

5 The last recommendation of the report was for 'private sector engagement' in the form of the appointment of a 'private sector advisory group to support its new Cabinet Committee on Canada–United States Relations; (CCCE 2004, 29).

6 The nine prosperity working groups were as follows: e-commerce and ICT; energy; environment; financial services; food and agriculture; health; manufactured goods and sectoral and regional competitiveness; movement of goods; and transportation. The ten security working groups were as follows: traveller security; cargo security; border facilitation; aviation security; maritime security; law enforcement; intelligence cooperation; bio-protection; emergency management; and science and technology (http://www.psp-spp.gc.ca/overview/working_groups-en.aspx, accessed 6 March 2008).

7 The five identified priority areas were as follows: enhancing the global competitiveness of North America; safe food and products; sustainable energy and the environment; smart and secure borders; and emergency management and preparedness. The 'competitiveness' emphasis involved a commitment to implementing a 'regulatory cooperation framework' and an 'intellectual property action strategy,' developing an economic work plan to facilitate trade in specific sectors, and conducting an analysis of free trade agreements subsequent to NAFTA (Joint Statement 2007).

8 One senior government official noted that a 'quality of life' pillar was suggested but that it was difficult to 'grab onto': 'The Liberals have signed onto Kyoto, the Americans not, how do you really engage in it?' (interview, Ottawa, 2 May 2008). After that point, other priorities were identified that might be identified as fitting under 'quality of life,' such as food safety.

9 One senior official commented: 'The advice of the NACC was really important because it was created by the leaders – this advice is part of the equation and factored into decision making but in the context of advice from other actors. For example, food and product safety was identified

in Montebello as a major priority, it was never identified by the NACC'
(interview, Ottawa, May 2008).

References

Aaronson, Susan Ariel, and M. Rodwan Abouharb. 2011. 'Unexpected Bedfel-
lows: The GATT, the WTO, and *Some* Democratic Rights.' *International Studies Quarterly* 55: 379–408.

Anderson, Greg, and Christopher Sands. 2007. 'Negotiating North America:
The Security and Prosperity Partnership.' White Paper. Washington: Hud-
son Institute. http://hudson.org/files/pdf_upload/HudsonNegotiating-
NorthAmericaadvanceproof2.pdf.

Ayres, Jeffrey. 2004. 'Power Relations under NAFTA: Reassessing the Efficacy
of Contentious Transnationalism.' *Studies in Political Economy* 74 (Autumn
2004): 101–23.

Ayres, Jeffrey, and Laura Macdonald, eds. 2009. *Contentious Politics in North
America: National Protest and Transnational Collaboration under Continental
Integration.* Basingstoke: Palgrave Macmillan.

Beaudoin, Alain, Executive Director, Innovation Partnerships Branch, Department of Industry. 2007. Testimony before the Canadian Parliament, House
of Commons Standing Committee on International Trade. 10 May.

Bow, Brian, and Arturo Santa Cruz. 2009. 'From Interests to Identity? Opposition to North American Integration in the United States.' Paper presented to
the 2009 Annual Meeting of the American Political Science Association, 3–6
September, Toronto.

Canadian Council of Chief Executives. 2004. 'New Frontiers: Building a 21st
Century Canada–United States Partnership in North America.' April.
Ottawa.

Canadian Labour Congress. 2011. 'CLC Backgrounder on the Canada–United
States Declaration.' Ottawa.

Capling, Ann, and Kim Richard Nossal. 2009. 'The Contradictions of Regionalism in North America.' *Review of International Studies* 35, no. 1: 145–65.

Carr, Barry. 1996. 'Crossing Borders: Labor Internationalism in the Era of
NAFTA.' In *Neoliberalism Revisited: Economic Restructuring and Mexico's
Political Future.* Edited by Gerardo Otero. Boulder: Westview. 209–32.

Clark, Ann Marie, Elisabeth Friedman, and Kathryn Hochstetler. 1998. 'The
Sovereign Limits of Global Civil Society: A Comparison of NGO Participa-
tion in UN World Conferences on the Environment, Human Rights, and
Women.' *World Politics* 51, no. 1: 1–35.

Council of Canadians. 2006. 'Integrate This: Citizen's Guide to the Security and Prosperity Partnership.' http://www.canadians.org/integratethis/back-grounders/guide/corporate.html.

Council on Foreign Relations. 2005. 'Building a North American Community: Report of an Independent Task Force.' New York: Council on Foreign Relations.

Della Porta, Donatella, and Sidney Tarrow, eds. 2005. *Transnational Protest and Global Activism*. Lanham: Rowman and Littlefield.

Dreiling, Michael. 1999. 'Unionism in Transnational America: Divergent Practices and Contending Visions in Labor's Fight with NAFTA.' Paper presented at the Annual Meeting of the American Sociological Association, Chicago.

Foster, John. 2007. 'Beyond NAFTA: The Security and Prosperity Partnership,' Unpublished manuscript.

Gilbert, Emily. 2007. 'Leaky Borders and Solid Citizens: Governing Security, Prosperity, and Quality of Life in a North American Partnership.' *Antipode* 39, no. 1: 77–98.

Golob, Stephanie. 1999. *Crossing the Line: Sovereignty, Integration, and the Free Trade Decisions of Mexico and* Canada. PhD diss., Harvard University.

Gordenker, Leon, and Thomas Weiss. 1996. *NGOs, the UN, and Global Governance*. Boulder: Lynn Rienner.

Graubart, Jonathan. 2008. *Legalizing Transnational Activism: The Struggle to Gain Social Change from NAFTA's Citizen Petitions*. University Park: Penn State University Press.

Healy, Teresa. Senior Researcher, Canadian Labour Congress. 2007. Testimony before the Canadian Parliament House of Commons Standing Committee on International Trade, Ottawa, 3 May.

Imig, Doug, and Sidney Tarrow, eds. 2001. *Contentious Europeans: Protest and Politics in an Emerging Polity*. Lanham: Rowman and Littlefield.

Joint Statement, Prime Minister Harper, President Obama, and President Calderón. 2009. North American Leaders' Summit, Guadalajara, Mexico, 10 August 2009.

Julian, Peter. 2009. 'Task Force on Renegotiating NAFTA Encouraged by Quiet Demise of the SPP.' http://peterjulian.ndp.ca. Accessed 16 November 2011.

Keck, Margaret. 2004. 'Governance Regimes and the Politics of Discursive Representation.' In *Transnational Activism in Asia: Problems of Power and Democracy*. Edited by Nicola Piper and Anders Uhlin. London: Routledge. 43–60.

Keohane, Robert, and Joseph Nye. 2002. 'The Club Model of Multilateral Cooperation and Problems of Democratic Legitimacy.' In *Power and Governance in a Partially Globalized World*. Edited by Robert Keohane. New York: Routledge.

Koenig-Archibugi, Mathias, and David Held. 2004. 'Introduction.' In *Global Governance and Public Accountability.* Edited by David Held and Mathias Koenig-Archibugi. Chichester: Wiley-Blackwell. 1–7.

Kovach, Gretel C. 2007. 'Highway to Hell? Ron Paul's Worked Up about U.S. Sovereignty.' *Newsweek*, 1 December, 46.

Langille, David. 1987. 'The Business Council on National Issues and the Canadian State.' *Studies in Political Economy* 24: 41–85.

Macdonald, Laura. 2002a. 'Globalization and Social Movements: Comparing Women's Movements' Responses to NAFTA in Mexico, the U.S., and Canada.' *International Feminist Journal of Politics* 4, no. 2: 151–72.

– 2002b. 'Governance and State–Society Relations in Canada: The Challenges from Regional Integration.' In *Capacity for Choice: Canada in the New North America.* Edited by George Hoberg. Toronto: University of Toronto Press. 187–223.

Massicotte, Marie-Josée. 2003. 'Local Organizing and Global Struggles: Coalition Building for Social Justice in the Americas.' In *Global Civil Society and Its Limits.* Edited by Gordon Laxer and Sandra Halperin. Basingstoke: Palgrave. 105–25.

Moore, Phoebe. 2008. 'Global Governance: Lest We Forget!' *International Studies Review* 10: 294–302.

Pastor, Robert A. 'The Future of North America.' *Foreign Affairs.* 1 June 2008. Web. 23 Nov. 2011. http://www.foreignaffairs.com/articles/64451/robert-a-pastor/the-future-of-north-america. Last accessed November 2011.

– 2004. 'North America's Second Decade.' *Foreign Affairs* 83, no. 1 (January–February): 124–35.

O'Brien, Robert, Anne Marie Goetz, Jan Aart Scholte, and Marc Williams. 2000. *Contesting Global Governance: Multilateral Economic Institutions and Global Social Movements.* Cambridge: Cambridge University Press.

Sands, Christopher. 2011. *The Canada Gambit: Will It Revive North America?* Security and Foreign Affairs Briefing Paper. Washington: Hudson Institute. http://www.hudson.org/files/publications/Canada%20Gambit%20Web.pdf.

Scharpf, Fritz. 1999. *Governing in Europe: Effective and Democratic?* Oxford: Oxford University Press.

Scholte, Jan Aart. 2002. 'Civil Society and Democracy in Global Governance.' *Global Governance* 8: 281–304.

Sikkink, Kathryn. 2005. 'Patterns of Dynamic Multilevel Governance and the Insider–Outsider Coalition.' In *Transnational Protest and Global Activism.* Edited by Donatella Della Porta and Sidney Tarrow. Lanham: Rowman and Littlefield.

Sikkink, Kathryn, and Jackie Smith. 2002. 'Infrastructures for Change: Transnational Organizations, 1953–93.' In *Restructuring World Politics: Transnational Social Movements, Networks, and Norms.* Edited by Sanjeev Khagram, James V. Riker, and Kathryn Sikkink. Minneapolis: University of Minnesota Press.

Steffek, Jens, and Maria Paola Ferreti. 2009. 'Accountability or "Good Decisions"? The Competing Goals of Civil Society Participation in International Governance.' *Global Society* 23, no. 1: 37–57.

Stillerman, Joel. 2003. 'Transnational Activist Networks and the Emergence of Labor Internationalism in the NAFTA Countries.' *Social Science History* 27 no. 4: 577–601.

Tarrow, Sidney. 2005. *The New Transnational Activism.* Cambridge: Cambridge University Press.

– 2002. 'The New Transnational Contention: Social Movements and Institutions in Complex Internationalism.' Paper presented at the Annual Meeting of the American Political Science Association, Boston, 29 August–1 September.

Tollefson, Chris. 2002. 'Stormy Weather: The Recent History of the Citizen Submission Process of the North American Agreement on Environmental Cooperation.' In *Linking Trade, Environment, and Social Cohesion: NAFTA Experiences, Global Challenges.* Edited by John Kirton and Virginia Maclaren. Burlington: Ashgate.

Trew, Stuart. 2009. 'The SPP Is Dead, So Where's the Champagne?' *Canadian Perspectives* (Autumn): 5–6. http://www.canadians.org/publications/ CP/2009/autumn/SPP.pdf. Accessed 16 November 2011.

– 2007. '"More Power, Please": The North American Competitiveness Council's 2007 Report to SPP Leaders.' *IntegrateThis.ca.* 1 October.

VanNijnatten, Debora. 2007. 'The Security and Prosperity Agreement as an "Indicator Species" for the Emerging North American Environmental Regime.' *Politics and Policy* 35, no. 4: 664–82.

Van Rooy, Alison. 2004. *The Global Legitimacy Game: Civil Society, Globalization and Protest.* Houndmills: Palgrave Macmillan.

White House. 2005. 'Fact Sheet: Security and Prosperity Partnership of North America.' 23 March. http://www.whitehouse/gove on 6/3/2008. http://georgewbush-whitehouse.archives.gov/news/releases/2005/03/20050323-4.html. Accessed 16 November 2011.

Winham, Gilbert. 1992. *The Evolution of International Trade Agreements.* Toronto: University of Toronto Press.

Conclusion: Will North America Survive?

JANINE BRODIE

Introduction[1]

As the chapters in this volume attest, the future of North American regionalism is very much in question. This integration project was formally set in motion with the implementation of the NAFTA agreement in 1995. One among many different regional responses to the sea changes wrought by the acceleration of economic globalization in the late twentieth century, NAFTA rapidly consolidated the economies of Canada, Mexico, and the United States into the world's largest economic region. In the early 2000s the NAFTA zone surpassed the GDP of the twenty-five states comprising the European Union; although representing only 7% of the world's population, North America accounted for as much as 35% of the world's gross product before slipping into decline later in the decade (Clarkson 2008, 11, 27; Pastor 2010). Robert Pastor, a strong advocate of North Americanism, argues that the first five years of NAFTA were an unqualified success but that since 2001 it has been 'an unmitigated disaster' (2010, 1).

In the past decade, the North American project has been disrupted, redesigned, and sidelined, not the least by global terrorism and the resulting securitization of borders both to and within North America; increasing competition from emerging economies, particularly China; a global financial crisis that has dealt staggering blows to the American economy's public finances and consumer demand; and an alarming epidemic of drug war violence that threatens the very fabric of Mexican society and government (see the chapter by Cadena-Roa this volume). North American leaders attempted to revive and deepen continental integration in 2005 with the launch of the Security and Prosperity Partnership of North America (SPP); yet only four years later this NAFTA successor agreement was quietly abandoned by the leaders of all three NAFTA countries and disowned by the SPP's most fervent cheerleaders: continental corporate leaders and neoliberal policy networks. However short-lived, the design and uneven implementation of the SPP has significantly altered North American governance, leading Rosalba Icaza (in this volume) to caution us about jumping too quickly to the conclusion that it is a failed project. The SPP may indeed be dead, but its inscriptions on North American space surely have not disappeared (see the chapter by Gilbert in this volume; see also Brodie 2009). As this chapter outlines, the most appropriate question posed by contemporary developments may not be whether North America will survive, but rather, *what kind of North America will survive*? The announcement in early 2011 of negotiations between Canada and the United States to create an 'upper' North American security perimeter suggests that the continent is being progressively reconfigured as a security space.

Diagnoses

The distinguished contributors to this volume track numerous fault lines in the North American integration project from multiple vantage points and analytic commitments. Although some authors are more optimistic than others about whether the North American integration project can (or should) be revived, there is a broad consensus about two kinds of absences that have contributed to contemporary scepticism about its future – the absence of robust transnational institutions, and the absence of input and process legitimacy. North American regionalism has been consistently and deliberately advanced through what Ayres and Macdonald describe as a 'shallow governance' model (2006). In contrast to the elaborate and growing institutional moorings of the EU, North American governance has been advanced primarily through two partial trilateral agreements, NAFTA and the SPP. These agreements neither prescribed nor generated formal, transparent, or authoritative transnational institutions with the capacity to resolve conflicts among the three partner governments.[2] Nor did these agreements craft coherent continental responses to shared and emerging challenges such as climate change, illegal migration, transborder criminality, deindustrialization, uneven development, and growing income disparities within and between partner countries.

Instead, these nominally trilateral agreements have operated in an institutional vacuum (see Ayres and Macdonald in this volume), one that is maintained through periodic exchanges among networks of relatively low-level administrators with no formal or binding authority to consolidate and advance North American governance (see VanNijnatten and Craik in this volume). While NAFTA and the SPP promoted selected sectoral integration, many of the chapters in this volume underline that the absence of an institutional base is a critical factor in explaining 'the failure of continental governance to take root' in North America (see Clarkson in this volume). Without authoritative and transparent institutional foundations, the North American model has been consistently circumvented by dominant social actors, especially the corporate sector, and by the domestic politics of its dominant partner, the United States. As a result, the North American project has been repeatedly derailed by short-sighted national expediencies and unravelled by double-bilateralism (see Golob in this volume), stalemate, and inertia. The 2008 financial crisis, in particular, has turned the gaze of American governments inward in order to revive local economies and to respond to anxious electorates that associate continentalism and globalization with unemployment and economic uncertainty.

The contributors to this volume identify an absence of input and process legitimacy as the second set of factors that have clouded the future of North American regionalism. Wide networks of civil society actors throughout North America, among them nationalists, labour unions, indigenous organizations, feminists, libertarians, and fractions of the political right and left, have derided the North American project as a brazen manoeuvre by neoliberal politicians, their academic allies, and the corporate sector to achieve deep integration by stealth (see Healy in this volume). Both NAFTA and the SPP generated suspicion and resistance because the general public in all three partner countries was not invited into a broader public dialogue about the rationale for or the mechanisms to achieve North American integration; nor was it provided with meaningful avenues to address the many ways in which transnational governance has affected the rights and well-being of diverse populations (see Icaza and Ayres and Macdonald in this volume). Instead, NAFTA and the SPP were crafted behind closed doors by political executives and invisible policy networks and presented to the citizens of all three countries as *faits accomplis* regulatory changes, which purportedly would enhance competitiveness and the security and prosperity of the continent.

Both NAFTA and the SPP, as VanNijnatten and Craik argue in this volume, are textbook cases of the 'club model' of transgovernmental-ism, which is characterized by elitism and exclusive dialogue among the like-minded, who in this case were convinced of the efficacy of open markets, minimal government, and the veracity of neoclassical economics. Accordingly, corporate leaders and business-funded think tanks were accorded privileged access to region-making processes through, for example, the North American Competitiveness Coun-cil (NACC), thus blurring the line between state and non-state actors (see Allan and Vengroff in this volume). Critics of the project were dismissed and berated as 'conspiracy mongers' (Anderson and Sands 2009, A19), 'extremist nationalists' (d'Aquino 2005), and the 'doomsday choir' (d'Aquino 2007). This is not to say, however, that the proponents of continental integration were not acutely concerned about mount-ing public protests, which challenged the legitimacy of their project. In fact, the North American Competitiveness Council (NACC), the SPP'S executive-appointed corporate advisory group, warned North Ameri-ca's three leaders at their 2008 summit that 'unless we work together to turn about public misperceptions, other specific recommendations to improve North American competitiveness will become largely irrel-evant' (NACC 2008, 10). This lends credibility to VanNijnatten and Craik's assertion that 'legitimacy matters' and to Ayres and Macdon-ald's contention that 'regional governance fails if it lacks legitimacy, transparency and consultation' (in this volume).

Although each of the contributors to this volume focuses on the North American case, their analyses raise broader questions about the form and future of the 'new regionalism' itself. For example, can we assume that institutional thickness and input legitimacy are necessary for successful region building? What is the relationship between input and output legitimacy in transnational governance? Why do experi-ments in transnationalism fail, and how do these failures limit the range of future strategic responses? Focusing primarily on the short life and times of the SPP, the rest of this chapter argues first that the new region-alism is far more fluid and experimental than our theories perhaps con-cede. Second, the chapter demonstrates that even failed or abandoned experiments in transnational governance leave indelible imprints on political geographies and thereby establish new critical junctures and strategic dilemmas for national and transnational actors. The final sec-tion of this chapter outlines the ways in which North America's future continues to unfold.

New Regionalisms

In his comprehensive 2008 volume, *Does North America Exist?*, Stephen Clarkson argues that NAFTA gave birth to a 'new North America,' one that stretched from Guatemala to the Arctic, and, governed by a new economic constitution, albeit a partial one, stood confidently ready to compete with two other global growth poles, Europe and East Asia (2008, 4–5). This transformation from the 'old' North America of national norms, economic interdependencies, and bilateralism to a new global actor is an example of what is termed as 'the new regionalism,' one of the theoretical threads that connect many of the chapters in this volume. To draw the distinction more clearly between the old and the new, the old regionalism understands integration as a protracted if not evolutionary process propelled by endogenous factors such as economic interaction and common cultural and historical bonds. The old regionalism is associated with neofunctionalist approaches in international relations and, in particular, the work of Ernst Haas, who studied the European case in the 1960s. Haas argued that economic integration in one sector, such as in coal and steel, had 'spillover' effects, fuelling pressures to integrate other sectors and eventually to institutionalize political authority at the transnational level (1961).

Stephen Clarkson aptly observes that the foundations of the European Union took shape in another era when social democratic ideals and a strong state held sway (2008, 16). Nonetheless, we often find the unique European pathway to regionalization generalized as an incremental model of region making in which free trade or limited sectoral integration spills over in a domino sequence to a customs union, a common market, economic union, and, ultimately, political integration and transnational institutionalization (Hettne 2005, 546). In this old regionalism story (as well as some stories of the new regionalism), then, the end point of the integration process is envisioned as something resembling, or aspiring to, the institutional thickness of the EU (Larner and Walters 2002, 421). Equally important, the old regionalism prioritizes endogenous processes in its account of integration: the global economy is not factored in as a particularly relevant referent (ibid., 411).

The new regionalism literature, in contrast, presents transnational regionalization as a strategic response to the exogenous forces of globalization. It is a 'new' regionalism, not simply because this form of governance emerged only in recent decades, but also because it is fluid, variable, and not yet well understood. For example, analysts are divided on the question of whether the new regionalism is a response to globalization or merely a phase in the ongoing unfolding of globalization (Mittelman 1996; Larner and Walters 2002). Bob Jessop (2002), for one, argues that economic globalization has replaced the institutional and spatial matrices of the national state with a powerful triad of transnational economic regions: the EU, East Asia, and North America. Each of these is characterized by its own regional division of labour and new configurations of governance on local, national, and global scales (2002, 181–2; Brenner 2004). These powerful global actors characteristically fragment, transcend, and cross-cut national spaces, while their growing interpenetration has rendered the internal economies of each more fluid and unstable (Jessop 2002, 182).

Saskia Sassen (2007), in contrast, suggests that transnational institutionalism may only be bridging events in a more pervasive global transition from national to denationalized governance. She and others point to an emerging and advanced form of global governance, one that is characterized by overlapping international networks of regulators (Slaughter 2004; Craik and Dimento 2008; VanNijnatten and Craik in this volume), the privatization and proliferation of specialized types of authority, new geographies of power, and the denationalization of public policy (Sassen 2006, 1–4; 2007, 88–9). A good part of what we call globalization, Sassen contends, increasingly consists of 'an enormous variety of micro-processes,' generally advanced through the national state, which are 'far deeper and more radical' than changes set in motion by the reorganization of the international political economy (2006, 1; 2007, 88). This debate has important implications with respect to the question that animates the chapters in this book – the future of North America. It suggests that regional institutions are not especially critical if each of the three NAFTA countries denationalizes its policies to conform to broader international norms. Clarkson points to this conclusion when he argues (in this volume) that *global* rather than continental governance accounts for much of the trilateral regulatory harmonization that has been achieved in North America in recent decades.

Setting this debate aside for the moment, the new regionalism literature does concur on two fundamental points. First, regionalization is a strategic response to the global economy, which, as Larner and Walters importantly emphasize, is understood as a space of competition, investment, and trade flows that traverses national states (2002, 408). Second, the new regionalism, which typically has been invented through the discourses of exclusive clubs of region-building elites (Neumann 2003), is variable, reflexive, and conditional. As Jessop further explains, it is part of a new political economy of scale, one that

> does not involve a pregiven set of places, spaces or scales that are merely being reordered. Instead, new places are emerging, new spaces are being created, new scales of organization are being developed and new horizons of action are being imagined – all in the light of new forms of (understanding) competition and competitiveness ... The number of scales and temporalities of action that can be distinguished is immense but far fewer ever get explicitly institutionalized. (2002, 179–80)

These studies thus portray contemporary regionalization, not only in North America but globally, as far more provisional and experimental than our theories suggest. In many instances, regionalization has been an elite-driven strategy to reduce uncertainties or gain competitive advantage within the ever shifting parameters of the contemporary global economy (Larner and Walters 2002, 409). However, economic competitiveness is not the only motivation for national states to coalesce in transnational networks or to acquiesce to transnational rules and authority. Barry Buzan (1991), for example, argues that there are many different genres of the new regionalism, ranging from trading blocs to developmental regions to security regions. He defines the latter as a group of states whose primary security concerns link together sufficiently closely that they cannot consider their national security apart from one another (see also Hettne 2005, 553).

The early twenty-first century has brought new definitions of security that are more concerned with insulating selected cross-national spaces from 'collateral' impacts of globalization such as economic and environmental migration than with region building in the face of a common security threat – a practice often associated with Cold War politics. This contemporary trend – region building as a space of exclusion rather than a space of defence – is captured in the idea of a mobility regime. This concept has gained currency in recent years, in part as a reaction to the spatial imaginaries and claims of first-wave globalization thinking, which held that globalization had rapidly transformed a world of borders into a world of flows (Appaduri 2001). The unfolding of security politics of the twenty-first century has dampened these earlier unqualified representations, as reflected in a growing body of literature that now understands globalization as an amalgam of unstable and often contradictory polar tensions between mobility and immobility (Shamir

2005, 199), *de*-territorialization and *re*-territorialization (Adey 2006, 79; Lefebre 1991), and border dispersion and differentiation (Rumsford 2006, 157).

The idea of a mobility regime, which we will return to in an overview of the SPP later in the chapter, focuses precisely on the set of conditions and governing practices that selectively provide or deny classes of people and things with 'a license to move' (Shamir 2005, 201). Shamir, in particular, argues that a primary function of contemporary mobility regimes is to police the movement of people from the global South to the global North. He outlines three features that are characteristic of contemporary mobility regimes: they (1) separate privileged countries and regions from other regions of the world; (2) operate within the perimeters of privileged localities, countries, and economic and political blocs; and (3) depend on screening technologies and profiling (2005, 203–10). Through such practices, countries and regions in the North are built up as fortresses and systems of closure to prevent the mobility of people who are trapped in poverty or displaced by man-made and natural disasters and who seek a better life. In this new governing order, 'travelling for profit is encouraged; travelling for survival is condemned' (Bauman 2002, 84). Mobility thus is intricately tied to social justice in a global era.

In summary, the new regionalism literature begins with the premise that transnationalism is a response to, and exists in, a reflexive relationship with the complex and shifting parameters of globalization. However, as globalization continues to unfold in unanticipated ways, it is probably more accurate to talk about the new *regionalisms* than the new regionalism. Transnational regionalism entails many different experiments in governance, and, as with all experiments, some succeed, some succeed only partially, and some fail to achieve their projected objectives. It is an axiom of politics that innovations in governance, at whatever scale they are devised, do not always or even often materialize as they were initially imagined or planned. They encounter political and social terrains that already are deeply imprinted by asymmetries in power, and they run up against powerful residuals of previous orders that have embedded in them resilient knowledges, firm attachments to identity and place, and material interests that have a stake in the contours of change (Brodie 2013). Just as important, new governing strategies can be internally contradictory, producing complex patterns of cooperation, competition, fragmentation, intersection, and colonization (Dean 1999, 21–7). The yawning gap between aspiration and outcome, however, does not mean that policy experiments also fail to leave their mark on the political geographies upon which they have acted. To the contrary, they leave in their wake new problems begging for solutions, unanticipated strategic opportunities, reconfigured teams of winners and losers, and new points of no return.

As Emily Gilbert argues in this volume, there is no single narrative of regionalism: in fact, Jessop argues that there is a certain 'eccentricity' in the contemporary growth of cross-border regions (2002, 180). Exercises in regionalization such as NAFTA and the SPP are experimental and iterative – the successes, failures, and unintended outcomes created by one intervention inform the limits and opportunities of future strategic responses. I argue in the next section of this chapter that the SPP, which failed in its attempt to superimpose a mobility regime on top of NAFTA's continental economic geography, demonstrates the eccentricity and uncertainties of contemporary region building. The SPP ultimately failed to fully realize its vision of North America; nonetheless, it has changed the terrain of North America and transformed the calculus of North American integration. The SPP implemented a strategic trade-off that linked further continental economic integration to an American-inspired continental security regime; but this security agenda quickly displaced the economic and has been the predominant focus of North American integration in the wake of the 2008 economic crisis.

The SPP: Stepping Forward and Tumbling Backward

Presidents Vicente Fox and George W. Bush and Prime Minister Paul Martin launched the SPP in Waco, Texas, in March 2005. This NAFTA successor agreement was the product of a relentless campaign on the part of Canadian corporate leaders and their allies to achieve deeper continental economic integration in the aftermath of the 9/11 terrorist attacks. American borders were immediately closed on 11 September 2001, penalizing cross-border traffic and trade; very soon after, what had previously been celebrated as the world's longest undefended border and the world's largest trading zone was made progressively more costly and cumbersome as layers of security were imposed on the North American movement of goods and people. Jarred by this unanticipated disruption in North American supply chains, Canada's most prominent business organizations and business-friendly think tanks launched a flurry of conferences and research initiatives, all of them stressing the urgency of reinventing North American governance in the context of new global security threats as well as the challenges being posed by emerging economies (Brodie 2008).

All of the 'usual suspects' in Canada's robust neoliberal policy networks mobilized to link post-9/11 security anxieties with mounting obstacles to North American integration; but it was the Canadian Council of Chief Executives[3] (CCCE) that quickly assumed a leadership role in this revitalized continentalist campaign. Thomas d'Aquino, the CCCE's CEO and a gladiator in previous North American free trade wars, declared that fixing the Canada–U.S. relationship was the most urgent priority on Canada's political agenda (d'Aquino 2003). At the time, public opinion polls showed that only 1% of Canadians identified this relationship as their most important concern (Gutstein 2009, 14). Undeterred by such domestic indifference, the CCCE unveiled its North American Security and Prosperity Initiative (NASPI) in early 2003, which put flesh on the prevailing elite consensus that, in the post-9/11 era, 'North American economic and physical security are indivisible' (CCCE 2003, 1). NASPI's new vision for North America called for immediate joint action on five fronts: (1) a reinvented border, (2) regulatory harmonization, (3) continental energy and resource integration, (4) a reinvigorated military, and (5) a new North American institutional framework (ibid., 3–6). These core ideas were refined and expanded in the CCCE's 2004 discussion paper, 'New Frontiers,' which also telegraphed the eventual content of the SPP (CCCE 2004). The report of the Independent Task Force (ITF) on the Future of North America, 'Building a North American Community,' which was disseminated by the U.S. Council on Foreign Relations in 2004 and released several weeks after the Waco Summit, strongly endorsed the SPP. It also proposed using the SPP as a platform to create a new North American community by 2010 with a single market, a common external tariff, and an outer security perimeter (CFR 2005; CCCE 2005a). A preliminary draft of the ITF report was presented to the three NAFTA leaders a few weeks before the Waco Summit.

Although the 9/11 attacks bestowed a sense of urgency on this revisioning project, there had been growing recognition that NAFTA no longer adequately governed the continental economic spaces that it and the 1988 Canada–U.S. Free Trade Agreement (CUSFTA) had helped create. From Canada's perspective, NAFTA processes had failed to discipline the United States to abide by trade tribunal rulings; those same processes were also indifferent to non-tariff barriers to continental trade such as differing rules of origin and national regulatory regimes. The corporate community bemoaned in chorus that this 'tyranny of small differences' was undercutting the ability of North American entrepreneurs to compete effectively in continental and global markets. More broadly, NAFTA was providing less and less of a relative advantage in global markets because tariffs were progressively declining everywhere else (Stewart-Patterson 2007). CUSFTA and NAFTA had been configured as specific responses to a new international political economy, but this global economic system was rapidly changing as emerging economies such as China, Brazil, and India reconfigured patterns of economic growth, consumer demand, trade, and investment. According to the CCCE, North America needed a new agreement that would deepen and further entrench North American regionalism in the face of these shifting realities (ibid.). The month before the SPP was announced, John Castellani, President of the American Business Roundtable, expressed what had by then become the mantra of the North American corporate sector: 'The *North American Free Trade Agreement* (NAFTA) has brought real gains to people in all three countries over the past decade, but today we face daunting new challenges, including the relentless threat of international terrorism and the dramatic rise of developing economies such as China and India that are transforming global trade and investment … Our security interests and economic interests have become inextricably linked' (CCCE 2005b, 1).

The SPP thus was characterized by its framers as a necessary response to globalization and, building on NAFTA, as the next logical step in the consolidation of North America as a competitive region in the global economy. NAFTA, which had initially been sold as a trade deal, was now represented by proponents of continental integration as a 'lean document' and 'merely the first draft of an economic constitution for North America' (Pastor 2008, 125). However, the SPP advanced a very different model of continental governance than what had been set in place by NAFTA a decade earlier. The latter has been described as a form of 'supra-constitutionalism' (Clarkson 2004), and as 'new constitutionalism' and 'disciplinary neoliberalism' (Gill 1995). These terms highlight the ways in which economic globalization has been advanced through binding rules on trade and investment, which are enforced through NAFTA-like bilateral and multilateral trade agreements and international trade tribunals as well as through organizations such as the World Trade Organization (WTO). Such transnational regulatory regimes, it is argued, create new rights for global and regional capital operating within national spaces; they also discipline national governments to surrender a portion of their national sovereignty in order to comply with neoliberal orthodoxies; and they advance private sector norms and actors, not least through the adjudication of trade disputes (McBride 2006, 755).

Unlike NAFTA or its predecessor (CUSFTA), the SPP did not rest on formal treaties, binding rules, or juridical procedures enforced above the national state. Instead, it deployed trilateral executive–corporate collaboration, national policing and regulatory mechanisms, and 'soft law' (statements of principle, regulatory guidelines, and various micro-processes); in addition, it was largely implemented within the technical domain of national bureaucracies (Sassen 2006, 194; Lee and Campbell 2006; Campbell 2007). Though it shared the neoliberal aspirations of supra-constitutionalism, the SPP was the product of a hasty, expedient, and calculated bargain among region-building elites, who wedded Mexican and Canadian anxieties about diminished access to the American market with American preoccupations with national security and enhanced border surveillance in the wake of 9/11 (Brodie 2009). This elite-driven project thus welded together two very different sets of aspirations for the continent, two contradictory definitions of security, and two potentially conflicting governing rationalities and technologies. One, deferring to the expertise of neoclassical economics and corporate leaders, conflated the idea of security with free markets and open borders within North America; the other advanced a non-negotiable vision of national (American) security as the extension and securitization of borders to and within North America. The SPP, in other words, was merely one enactment of the contemporary global friction between the goals of economic liberalization and those of securitization.[4]

If the SPP's dual-track security and prosperity agendas had fatal design flaws, its framers certainly did not appreciate them at the time. On the plane ride home from Waco, for example, President Fox explained to the press on board: 'I would like you to understand the magnitude of what this [the SPP] means. It is transcendent; it's something that goes well beyond the relationship we have up to now' (Pickard 2005). D'Aquino similarly crowed that the 'comprehensive agenda laid out by the three leaders represents a quantum leap forward for the continent ... The new partnership agreement moves the North American agenda forward in a multitude of concrete and practical ways that add up to an ambitious vision for the future of our continent ... This agreement certainly represents big progress' (CCCE 2005c).

Stephanie Golob rightly observes (in this volume) that the SPP inaugural documents lacked bold pronouncements about North America as a new and vibrant geopolitical entity, although the ITF report (CFR 2005) and a few other North American policy networks, particularly the North American Forum (NAF n.d.) did experiment with various formulations of a North American community (Brodie 2008). The series of Leaders' Statements, issued after each annual summit, reflected a strategic and programmatic orientation with the goal of building selective continental regulatory spaces through trilateral cooperation. The 2005 inaugural leaders' communiqué, for example, explained that '*Our Partnership* ... is a *trilateral* effort to increase the security, prosperity, and quality of life of our citizens'; and in 2006 the leaders underlined that 'the success of *our countries* is enhanced by working *cooperatively*. This Partnership has increased *our institutional contacts* to respond to our vision of a stronger, more secure, and more prosperous region.' Again in 2007, North America's leaders continued to represent the SPP as a partnership among '*neighbours*' who '*share a commitment* to ensure North America remains a safe, secure and economically dynamic region, and a competitive player in global markets' (SPP 2005b, 2006, 2007b).

The SPP project, in other words, envisioned North America as a new geography of regulation, one that would identify and enhance legitimate flows of goods and people to and within the continent. A cursory reading of the SPP agreement reveals, above all else, a strategy to establish a North American mobility regime. The security agenda, for example, promised to 'further streamline the secure and efficient movement of legitimate, low risk traffic across our shared borders'; 'implement common border security and bioprotection strategies'; 'improve the legitimate flow of people and cargo at our shared borders'; 'reduce the costs of trade through the efficient movement of goods and people'; 'develop and implement a North American traveler strategy'; 'develop and implement a North American cargo security strategy'; 'develop and implement a strategy to enhance North American transportation and port security'; 'identify, develop, and deploy new technologies to advance our shared security goals and promote the legitimate flow of people and goods across our borders' ... the list goes on. The prosperity agenda aspired to 'ensure compatibility of regulations and standards and eliminat[e] redundant testing and certification requirements'; 'strengthen regulatory cooperation ... to minimize barriers'; 'lower the transaction costs of trade in goods'; 'increase competitiveness by exploring additional supply chains options'; and 'identify measures to facilitate further the movement of business persons within North America' (SPP 2005a, 1–5).

Public policies are generally assessed in terms of their outcomes, and to the degree that they achieve their expressed goals, they are considered to have 'output' as opposed to 'input' legitimacy. But regardless of whether new governing initiatives realize their programmatic goals, they transform the objects and spaces of regulation, often in unanticipated ways. Once heterogeneous landscapes are carved out and brought into conformity with new regimes of regulation, political rationalities, and intervention strategies (Frello 2008, 25–6; Fortier 2006, 315; Jessop 2002, 178). Put differently, regulatory spaces are both the sites and outcomes of governing strategies (Keil and Mahon 2009, 8-9): they are performed through governing discourses and regularized through the application of rules that are inscribed upon them (Walters 2004). The SPP's prosperity agenda, for example, sought to promote the mobility of goods within North America through regulatory harmonization, which strips products of their national markings, lubricates cross-national supply chains and selected sector integration, and levels frictions at diffuse border points. The security agenda committed the three NAFTA partners to adopt new definitions of insecurity, new surveillance technologies, and new configurations of North American borders. Characteristic of mobility regimes, the SPP sought to 'de-border' and then 're-border' North America without changing the formal territorial boundaries of its partner countries.

The chapters in this volume recount the many different regulatory changes that were quickly launched under the umbrella of the SPP as well as the uneven application of these diverse interventions. The prosperity agenda launched an ambitious strategy for regulatory harmonization, including a North American Regulatory Framework and a template of Common Regulatory Principles, both adopted at the 2007 Montebello Leaders' Summit. However, the general consensus is that progress on this file was too slow. In fact, many of the early supporters of the SPP later derided the agreement for its 'piddling efforts to move red tape' (Patterson 2007, B1) and 'sluggish' progress (d'Aquino 2009a). Others argue that recent steps towards North American regulatory harmonization in Canada may owe more to the 'Smart Regulation' policies launched by the Martin government in 2003 than to the SPP (Clarkson 2008, 445; Brodie 2009). For the past decade, both Canada and the United States have pursued regulatory guidelines that call for the elimination of uniquely national regulations, the promotion of voluntary codes and international product standards, and minimization of regulatory costs for business (Lee and Campbell 2006; Campbell 2007, 2008). This work is ongoing.

As Emily Gilbert's contribution to this volume details, the implementation of the SPP's security agenda was an entirely different story. The post-9/11 era has witnessed an explosion of security initiatives designed to regulate the mobility of things and people to and within North America – the Secure Border Initiative, a no-fly list, the Western Hemisphere Travel Initiative (WHTI), the Maritime Transport Security Clearance Program, VISIT (U.S. Visitor and Immigration Status Indicator Technology), the ShipRider Program, and the Customs Trade Partnership Against Terrorism are just a few. While the securitization of North America is not fully attributable to the SPP, it has surely authorized the concept of Fortress North America (Gilbert in this volume) and established the continent as a privileged space of mobility for those accorded a licence to move (Shamir 2005).

The most critical story to be told about the SPP, in fact, is that the security agenda quickly overpowered the prosperity agenda. By expediency as much as by planning, the SPP was configured as a strategic bargain, a trade-off, in which Canada and Mexico agreed to participate in securitization of North America in order to free up the movement of goods and people across its internal borders. What was not acknowledged or perhaps even fully recognized at the time was that the United States saw the SPP as on opportunity to push *its national security perimeter* to the edges of the continent (see Clarkson in this volume). Nevertheless, the contours of this new border were clearly outlined by Tom Ridge (the first Secretary of the U.S. Department of Homeland Security) and John Manley (then Canadian Deputy Prime Minister responsible for security) in 2003. The border of the future, they mused, 'is not simply a straight line between nations; it is a continuum that includes the airspace above it, the economic zones that surround it, the international ports of origin that serve it and the network of intelligence and law enforcement professionals who monitor and administer laws to protect it' (quoted in d'Aquino 2003, 34).

The staged implementation of this vision of a ubiquitous border intensified under the umbrella of the SPP. Security expertise, largely housed within the burgeoning Department of Homeland Security (DHS), colonized and subdued competing conceptions of economic security and open borders. The unhappy marriage of security and prosperity resulted in thicker and stickier borders within North America and has licensed the proliferation of security measures that act as non-tariff barriers on North American trade, effectively eroding the intent of both NAFTA and the SPP. The United States, in turn, selectively put the brakes on a variety of forms of mobility, citing security concerns. For example, the DHS curtailed a pilot border pre-clearance program at the Fort Erie–Buffalo border, and in 2007 the U.S. Department of Agriculture imposed an inspection fee on air, rail, and truck cargoes entering the United States (Ibbitson 2007, A21). This was an apparent response to the threat of bioterrorism. It is estimated that the inspection fee cost cross-border users $80 million its first year alone (Moens and Cust 2008, 13). Thus, in addition to making North American borders more cumbersome for trade, security also may be deployed as a non-tariff *barrier* to trade. Stockwell Day, a senior trade minister in the Harper cabinet at the time, elaborated on this point:

> One of the things I'm beginning to learn in trade matters is one of the tricks of the trade. You can get an industry ... [to] come forward to their government and say 'as a safety issue, or as a security issue, we need to demand this from Canadian products coming in.' Sometimes it can be a bona fide safety and security issue. A lot of times it's what we call a non-tariff barrier and they will use that. (quoted in Akin 2009a, A10)

Thus, by 2008 it was all too apparent to the SPP's promoters that their strategic compromise had backfired, and badly. The North American Competitiveness Council (NACC), Canada's major business-funded think tanks and lobbying organizations, the Canada–U.S. Project (see Healy in this volume), and Canada's Competition Policy Review Panel all urged the federal government to treat the thickening of borders as the most pressing priority on the contemporary North American agenda (Grady 2009, 48). Speaking at a meeting of the North American Forum in Washington in June 2008, Thomas d'Aquino of the CCCE summarized the core friction and frustration that had come to define the SPP experiment in regionalization: 'The central issue of North American competitiveness boils down to how we manage our borders, but these days, it seems every attempt to speed the secure flow of legitimate traffic runs into a brick wall' (2008a). As Stephen Clarkson explains, 'the new approach in which "security trumps trade" directly jeopardizes the previous decade's project of building an integrated North American market' (2008, 371; see also his chapter in this volume).

The short life of the SPP raises a number of important questions regarding the growing frictions in the international political economy among national security, global mobility, and economic liberalization. But it also begs the question of whether, over the span of a decade, the focus of the

North American governance project has shifted from economic integration to securitization. The essays by Clarkson, Gilbert, Cadena-Roa, Icaza, and others in this volume point to this transformation. Clearly this is also the conclusion of Christopher Sands of the U.S. Hudson Institute, who told an Ottawa audience in late 2008 that it is no longer possible for Canada to have independent security and intelligence policies, 'because we [the United States] need Canada to help protect ourselves,' and more pointedly, because 'homeland security is the gatekeeper with its finger on your jugular affecting your ability to move back and forth across the border, the market access upon which the Canadian economy depends' (quoted in Macleod 2008, A2). The announcement in early 2011 of negotiations to establish a Canada–U.S. continental security perimeter serves as further evidence that the SPP's failure to combine economic harmonization with security on a continental scale laid the foundations for the further securitization of the continent.

Thus the best laid plans of region building elites have brought the North American integration project full circle and perhaps even to a more vulnerable place than before the SPP bargain was initially conceived. In January 2009, amidst a growing financial catastrophe, d'Aquino told an exclusive audience that included Stephen Harper, Michael Ignatieff (then leader of the Official Opposition), and Dalton McGuinty (Premier of Ontario) that 'Canada is part of an economic universe that for the time being is without compass' (2009b). The CCCE's economic compass, which had steadily pointed due south for more than two decades, was now spinning in many directions.

Will North America Survive? Some Concluding Thoughts

In this chapter, I have stressed that transnational regionalism, in North America and globally, is irregular, fluid, and unfolding in unpredictable ways. It is also reflexive, reacting to changing environments, some of its own creation. Even nominal failures in governance irrevocably transform political geographies, establishing new premises for recalibrations of strategic advantage. Political actors then reflect on these transformed realities and respond to the new problems and opportunities that have emerged both inside and outside the new regime. These new conditions are emergent, which is to say that they would not have presented themselves to policy makers and stakeholders in the same way in absence of their previous strategic interventions. Reflexive actions also are not uniform, in that emergent properties create new opportunities for some and anomalous and compromising outcomes for others. In many ways, the questions of whether North America will survive – and, if it does, what *kind* of North America – will be settled through the reflexive actions of region-building elites and, in turn, the resistance of engaged publics. This is an open-ended process, but several reflexive postures have already gathered momentum in the wake of the SPP. Three dominate the contemporary North American landscape: sticky borders as levers, the invention of Upper North America, and voluntary convergence. These ideas constitute the foundations for the implementation of an 'upper' North American security perimeter.

The first reflexive posture, almost solely the prerogative of the United States, has been to use the thicker and stickier borders associated with the SPP's security agenda as a political lever to gain further concessions from its North American neighbours in areas often unrelated to security. The mere threat of thickening the border even further is a powerful political lever in continental relations. In 2008, for example, it was reported that the United States told the Canadian government that it would not address border frictions until Canada implemented more restrictive copyright protections as outlined in the SPP's Montebello Intellectual Property Action Plan adopted in 2007. In June 2008, Canada passed Bill C-61, which contained digital copyright provisions that are virtually identical to those prevailing in the United States (Campbell 2008, 129). The United States also has pressured Canada to release more information about its citizens to American security agencies, and by late 2009, Canada had entered into an enhanced data-sharing agreement with the United States.

Summing up this new leverage politics, Stewart Baker, Assistant Secretary of Homeland Security in the Bush administration, told an Ottawa audience in late 2008, 'we want to give you less access, but we want you to pay more, and by the way, we're standardizing this [with other visa-free countries] so that you're not so special anymore' (MacLeod 2008, A2). As the decade drew to a close, the Obama administration left little hope that the borders-as-levers strategy would be abandoned. In fact, Janet Napolitano, the newly appointed DHS Secretary, announced that the United States intended to treat its Canadian and Mexican borders equally, explaining that 'we shouldn't go light on one and heavy on the other' (quoted in Dark, Anderson and McLellan 2009, A17). These kinds of pronouncements send shivers down Ottawa's spine and are thus very effective in 'softening up' the negotiating environment between Canada and the United States. So it should perhaps come as no surprise that when the security perimeter negotiations were announced in early 2011, prominent American politicians, including former presidential candidate John McCain, ruminated rather loudly about the Canadian border being potentially more threatening to the United States than Mexico's border, arguing that Canada is a haven for terrorist groups.

A second reflexive strategy, which gained momentum among Canada's corporate elites and their policy networks in 2008, was the promotion of a new North American spatial imaginary, one that would erase Mexico from the prosperity map. This vision of an upper North American zone of economic integration constructs Mexico as a different place with different issues – so different, in fact, that any new initiatives beyond the SPP should be bilateral, involving only Canada and the United States. A series of policy papers and conference proceedings have made the case that the North American prosperity agenda has been 'mired in the complications of a three-way dialogue' (Sears 2009, 198; CUCUSP 2009; Healy in this volume) and that the 'deepening asymmetries among the countries are simply too vast ... A trilateral paradigm would hold back the natural and logical evolution of Canada–United States relations' (d'Aquino 2008c, 62). Accordingly, this vision of an upper North America holds that future policy initiatives should be guided by the principle – often repeated during the life of the SPP – that *'three can talk, two can do'* (d'Aquino 2008c, 61 emphasis his; NACC 2008, 12) or, as Fraser Institute researchers put it, 'three can talk, two can walk' (Moens and Cust 2008, 21).

This second reflexive strategy relies on discourses that construct Canada and the United States as essentially the same place and Mexico as foreign, alien, and 'out there,' not 'in here.' A 2009 op-ed in the *Globe and Mail* titled 'A Table for Two, Not Three,' written by John Manley, who assumed the leadership of the CCCE in January 2010, and Gordon Giffin, a former U.S. Ambassador to Canada, provides an instructive example of this new framing exercise. In it, Manley and Giffin assert that Canada and the United States have 'a unique bilateral relationship, a model international relations built over many decades based upon similar values and democratic institutions and common heritage.' They then point out the long history of military alliances between Canada and the United States and a series of economic partnerships such as CUSFTA and the Auto Pact. By contrast, they continue, 'the trilateral relationship began with NAFTA in 1994. It is an economic arrangement with none of the deep historical and other connotations of the Canada–

United States partnership.' They conclude that the 'concept of a North American Community' is 'a vision we continue to share ... But such a goal can be achieved only if Canada and the United States define a new and evolutionary template for our bilateral progress. It will take that anchor in the northern part of the continent to make continent wide progress possible' (2009, A13). The 2011 North American Security Perimeter negotiations involve only Canada and the United States.

This draws us to a third reflexive strategy, voluntary convergence. Although there is an emerging consensus that North America should be reimagined as a privileged northern zone of economic integration, there remains the recurring question of how to get the United States back to the bargaining table. Acutely aware that the SPP's security agenda has trumped its prosperity agenda, key business leaders and their policy networks now argue that, rather than focusing on irritants or formal bilateral negotiations, Canada should unilaterally adopt security and regulatory practices that converge with those of the United States (Toneguzzi 2009, F1; Dymond and Hart 2008). This was one important conclusion of a conference organized by the Canada–U.S. Project at Carleton University in December 2008 and the resulting report that was presented to Prime Minister Harper and Opposition Leader Ignatieff in January 2009 (Carleton University 2009; Macmillan 2009, 71, 75, 77; George 2009, 35). In effect, this third reflexive strategy of voluntary convergence recommends performing an upper North America without negotiating it into existence.

There is growing evidence that the federal government has begun to quietly deploy a voluntary convergence strategy in upper North American politics. In July 2009, for example, the Harper government quite unexpectedly declared that henceforth Canada would require visas for all Mexicans travelling to Canada, citing a recent rise in Mexican refugee claimants as its justification. Considering the significant costs to the Canadian economy owing to lost tourism dollars and the heavy toll exacted on Canada–Mexican relations, it is difficult to make sense of the introduction of visa controls (Simpson 2010, A13) – that is, until the United States' long-standing irritation with Canada's list of visa exemptions is factored into the equation. In contrast to the United States, Canada has not required visas for travellers from more than twenty countries, including Mexico, Hong Kong, and other members of the Commonwealth. Whatever the story about rampant and illegitimate refugee claimants, the visa requirement for Mexico appears to be an example of voluntary compliance. Also consistent with our earlier discussion of mobility regimes, Canada relaxed visa requirements for Mexican business leaders in early 2010.

Canada's reluctant approach to greenhouse gas emissions also can be read as an example of this third reflexive strategy. At the 2009 Copenhagen conference on climate change, Prime Minister Harper refused to commit Canada to reduction targets until the United States had unveiled its emission targets. The Harper government then adopted the same targets and, in early 2010, chastised the Quebec for aspiring to a more ambitious climate change strategy. Environment Minister Jim Prentice warned Quebec 'of the folly of attempting to go it alone in an integrated North American economy,' ignoring the fact that many American states also have more stringent environmental targets than those set by Washington (quoted in Ibbitson and Seguin 2010, A5). Days earlier, Jim Prentice had told a Calgary audience that 'Canada won't adopt cap and trade unless the US decides to go that route ... Our determination [is] to harmonize our climate policy with that of the United States ... We need to go even further in aligning our regulations' (quoted in Fekete 2010, E1). This melding of upper North American environmental policy contrasted with Mexico's more aggressive environmental ambitions under the leadership of President Calderon.

The 'Buy American' fiasco in the wake of the American stimulus package also rehearsed the leverage compliance scenario within a new upper North America. The January 2009 American Recovery and Reinvestment Act declared that for public works projects, only American-made iron, steel, and manufactured goods would be funded by the unprecedentedly huge recovery package. This precluded Canadian companies *and* American companies with supply chains in Canada from competing for lucrative state contracts. Canadian provincial and municipal procurement, which had been carved out of NAFTA, became the critical point of negotiation for achieving a Canadian exemption to the Recovery Act.[5] Thus, in August 2009, the Canadian government offered a quid quo pro to the United States. In return for access to the American stimulus package, Canadian provinces and municipalities would open their construction projects to American bidders for twenty months, until September 2011. Moreover, Canadian subnational governments also agreed to sign on to the WTO Agreement on Government Procurement, thereby permanently opening up this market to global bidders. The Obama administration, however, sat on this deal until February 2010, by which time over 90% of the stimulus contracts had already been signed.

These three reflexive strategies form the discursive foundations for the negotiation of a common security perimeter for upper North America, formally titled a 'Shared Vision for Perimeter Security and Economic Competitiveness,' which was formally announced by President Obama and Prime Minister Harper during the latter's visit to Washington in February 2011. Consistent with previous steps in the institutionalization of North American governance, these negotiations, staged behind closed doors, are being conducted by Canadian and American bureaucrats, with officials from the Department of Homeland Security predominating. The public has been provided with little information about the parameters of these negotiations, although shared policing both at and beyond North American borders, harmonized visa requirements, enhanced information sharing, cybercrime, and the development of biometric identifiers have been identified as initial discussion points.

At this point in our discussion, the renewed appeal of a North American security perimeter should be apparent. 'A unified and seamless system of North American defence' (CCCE 2008) presents itself as the only viable option to break down the SPP's legacy of thick borders. The possibility of a common security perimeter had been raised a few months before 9/11, but the idea was roundly rejected as an inconceivable surrender of national sovereignty (Potter 2009, A1). The SPP, although a failed experiment in regionalization, helped set in place what is, in effect, a de facto North American security perimeter. The current negotiations represent an institutionalization of this new political geography. However, the outcome of these negotiations may very well establish a regime of continental securitization that far exceeds the imagination of the early framers of the SPP. Ralph Nader, for example, suggests that 'once the U.S. government's national security scaffolding surrounds Canada', many policy matters will become 'national security' priorities. Canadian energy, water, the Canadian Arctic, anti-monopoly enforcement, and Canadian foreign investment policies could be subsumed under "national security" imperatives' (2011). The chapters in this book variously explore the question of whether North America will survive. But as negotiations in this new round of regionalization progress, the question of *what kind of North America* will survive seems a more appropriate and vexing issue for academics and citizens alike.

Notes

1 This research was supported by the Canada Research Chair program, in which I hold a Tier 1 Chair in Political Economy and Social Governance.
2 As is widely discussed, Chapter 11 of NAFTA provided authoritative and binding mechanisms for corporations to challenge and receive compensation from partner governments. See Clarkson (2008).
3 Previously called the Business Council on National Issues, the CCCE was founded in 1976. Identifying itself as Canada's premier business organization, it is composed of the chief executives of 150 leading corporations in Canada.
4 Securitization is understood here as a process in which things or people are named as threats and are made subject to various technologies of surveillance and coercion. See for example, http://www.apsu.edu/oconnort/GSS2010/GSS2010lect01a.htm.
5 The provinces did not provide much resistance to this requirement. In fact, reciprocal access to government procurement contracts was the starting point for a Canada–EU trade deal under negotiation. Moreover, a long list of Canadian business associations wrote an open letter to the premiers and territorial leaders urging them to open up their procurement contracts to foreign bidders.

References

Adey, Peter. 2006. 'If Mobility Is Everything Then It Is Nothing: Towards a Relational Politics of (Im)mobilities.' *Mobilities* 1, no. 1: 75–94.

Akin, David. 2009. 'Some U.S. Business May Block Trade: Day.' *Edmonton Journal*, 21 February, A10.

Anderson, Greg, and Christopher Sands. 2009. 'The Summit Pandemic.' *Edmonton Journal*, 8 August, A19.

Appadurai, Arjun. 2001. 'Grassroots Globalization and the Research Imagination.' In *Globalization*. Edited by Arjun Appadurai. Durham: Duke University Press.

Ayres, Jeffrey, and Laura Macdonald. 2006. 'Deep Integration and Shallow Governance: The Limits to Civil Society Engagement across North America.' *Policy and Society* 25, no. 3: 23–42.

Bauman, Zygmunt. 2002. *Society under Siege*. Cambridge: Polity.

Brenner, Neil. 2004. *New State Spaces: Urban Governance and the Rescaling of Statehood*. Oxford: Oxford University Press.

Brodie, Janine. 2013. 'Mobility Regimes: Reflections on the Short Life and Times of the Security and Prosperity Partnership of North America.' In *Mobilities, Knowledge, and Social Justice*. Edited by Suzan Ilcan. Montreal and Kingston: McGill–Queen's University Press.

– 2009. 'A Public Relations Disaster? The SPP and the Governance of North America.' *Revista Mexicana de Estudios Canadienses* 16: 15–33.

– 2008. 'Performing North America as Community.' In *Politics in North America: Redefining Continental Relations*. Edited by Yasmeen Abu-Laban, Radha Jhappan, and François Rocher. Peterborough: Broadview. 441–60.

Buzan, Barry. 1991. *People, States, and Fear: An Agenda for International Security Studies in the Post–Cold War Era*. New York: Harvester Wheatsheaf.

Campbell, Bruce. 2008. 'Harper and NAFTA-Plus.' In *The Harper Record*. Edited by Teresa Healy. Ottawa: Canadian Centre for Policy Alternatives, 123-137.

– 2007. 'Plan Is to Harmonize Regulations to Lower U.S. Levels.' *CCPA Monitor* 14, no. 5: 1, 6–9. http://www.policyalternatives.ca.

Canadian Council of Chief Executives (CCCE). 2008. 'From Common Sense to Bold Ambition: Moving Canada Forward on the Global Stage.' CCCE Submission to the Competition Policy Review Panel. http://www.ceocouncil.ca/publication/from-common-sense-to-bold-ambition-moving-canada-forward-on-the-global-stage. Accessed 22 November 2011.

– 2005a. 'Task Force Report Emphasizes Need for Urgent Action on North American Security and Prosperity.' http://www.ceocouncil.ca/news-item/task-force-report-emphasizes-need-for-urgent-action-on-north-american-security-and-prosperity-181. Accessed 22 November 2011.

– 2005b. 'Trilateral Security and Prosperity Will Boost Jobs and Investment, Say Canada's CEOs.' http://www.ceocouncil.ca/news-item/trilateral-security-and-prosperity-partnership-will-boost-jobs-and-investment-say-canadas-ceos-169. Accessed 22 November 2011.

– 2005c. 'North American Business Leaders Join Together to Support Strategic Initiative on Security and Prosperity.' http://www.ceocouncil.ca/news-item/north-american-business-leaders-join-together-to-support-strategic-initiative-on-security-and-prosperity-175. Accessed 22 November 2011.

– 2004. 'New Frontiers: Building a 21st Century Canada–United States Partnership in North America.' http://www.ceocouncil.ca/publication/new-frontiers-html-version. Accessed 22 November 2011.

– 2003. 'Security and Prosperity: Toward a New Canada–United States Partnership in North America.' http://www.ceocouncil.ca/publications/pdf/716af13644402901250657d4c418a12e/presentations_2003_01_01.pdf. Accessed 22 November 2011.

Carleton University Canada–U.S. Project (CUCUSP). 2009. *From Correct to Inspired: A Blueprint for Canada-U.S. Engagement.* http://www.canambusco. org/resources/ABluePrintforCanada-USEngagement.pdf. Accessed 22 November 2011.

Clarkson, Stephen. 2008. *Does North America Exist? Governing the Continent after NAFTA and 9/11.* Toronto: University of Toronto Press.

– 2004. 'Global Governance and the Semi-Peripheral State: The WTO and NAFTA as Canada's External Constitution.' In *Governing under Stress: Middle Powers and the Challenges of Globalization.* Edited by Marjorie Griffin Cohen and Stephen Clarkson. London: Zed.

Council on Foreign Relations (CFR). 2005. 'Building a North American Community: Independent Task Force Report no. 53.' Washington. http:// www.cfr.org/canada/building-north-american-community-report-inde-pendent-task-force-future-north-america/p8138. Accessed 22 November 2011.

Craik, Neil, and Joseph DiMento. 2008. 'Environmental Cooperation in the (Partially) Disaggregated State: Lessons from the Security and Prosperity Partnership of North America.' *Chicago Journal of International Law* 8, no. 2, 479–512.

d'Aquino, Thomas. 2009a. 'Enhancing the Canada–United States Partnership.' Testimony before the Standing Committee of Parliament on Foreign Affairs and International Development. 24 February. http://www.ceocouncil.ca/ publications/pdf/test_9b81a7ba7b50855be2232023a41d091c/Submission_ Standing_Committee_on_Foreign_Affairs_and_Intl_Dev_Feb_25_2009.pdf. Accessed 22 November 2011.

– 2009b. 'CEO Council Chief Executive Outlines Key Short Term and Long Term Priorities for Canada.' January 21. http://www.ceocouncil.ca/en/ view/?area_id=1&document_id=1305. Accessed 22 November 2011.

– 2008a 'Rekindling the Spirit of 1993: Forging a New Path Forward for North America.' Remarks to the North American Forum, Washington, 17 June. http://www.ceocouncil.ca/publication/ceo-council-chief-executive-calls-for-a-more-competitive-north-america-remarks-by-thomas-daquino-to-the-north-american-forum. Accessed 22 November 2011.

– 2008b. 'Seizing the Opportunities of Globalization.' *Policy Options,* June, 55–62. http://www.irpp.org/po/archive/jun08/daquino.pdf. Accessed 22 November 2011.

– 2007. 'Promoting a Better Understanding of the SPP.' http://www.ceocoun-cil.ca/publication/promoting-a-better-understanding-of-the-spp. Accessed 22 November 2011.

– 2005. 'A Stronger North America, A More Powerful Canada.' http://www.

ceocouncil.ca/publication/a-stronger-north-america-a-more-powerful-canada. Accessed 22 November 2011.

– 2003. 'Coaxing the Elephant: Can Canada Best Support Multilateralism by Cozying Up to the United States.' *Policy Options*, May. http://www.irpp.org/po/archive/may03/daquino.pdf. Accessed 22 November 2011.

Dark, Michael, Greg Anderson, and Anne McLellan. 2009. 'Place a Call to Mexico.' *Edmonton Journal*, 27 May, A17. http://www.americanstudies.ualberta.ca/nav01.cfm?nav01=83384. Accessed 22 November 2011.

Dean, Mitchell. 1999. *Governmentality: Power and Rule in Modern Society*. London: Sage.

Dymond, Bill, and Michael Hart. 2008. 'Navigating New Trade Routes: The Rise of Value Chains and Canadian Trade Policy.' Border Papers no. 259. March. Toronto: C.D. Howe Institute. http://www.cdhowe.org/pdf/commentary_259.pdf. Accessed 22 November 2011.

Fekete, Jason. 2010. 'Prentice Outlines Climate Change Policy.' *Edmonton Journal*, 2 February, E1.

Fortier, Anne-Marie. 2006. 'The Politics of Scaling, Timing, and Embodying: Rethinking the New Europe.' *Mobilities* 1, no. 3: 313–31.

Frello, Birgitta. 2008. 'Towards a Discursive Analysis of Movement: On the Making and Unmaking of Movement as an Object of Knowledge.' *Mobilities* 3, no. 1: 25–50.

George, Shirley-Ann. 2009. 'A New Canada–U.S. Border Vision.' Carleton University Canada–U.S. Border Project. Background Papers. In *From Correct to Inspired: A Blueprint for Canada-US Engagement*, 27–40. http://s3.amazonaws.com/zanran_storage/www.carleton.ca/ContentPages/8379237.pdf. Accessed 22 November 2011.

Gill, Stephen. 1995. 'Globalization, Market Civilization, and Disciplinary Neoliberalism.' *Millennium: Journal of International Studies* 23, no. 3: 399–423.

Grady, Patrick. 2009. 'A More Open and Secure Border for Trade, Investment, and People.' Carleton University Canada–U.S. Project. Background Papers. In *From Correct to Inspired: A Blueprint for Canada-US Engagement*, 41–8. http://s3.amazonaws.com/zanran_storage/www.carleton.ca/ContentPages/8379237.pdf. Accessed 22 November 2011.

Gutstein, Donald. 2009. *Not a Conspiracy Theory: How Business Propaganda Hijacks Democracy*. Toronto: Key Porter.

Haas, Ernst. 1961. 'International Integration: The European and the Universal Process.' *International Organization* 15, no. 3, 366–92.

Hettne, Bjorn. 2005. 'Beyond the "New" Regionalism.' *New Political Economy* 10, no. 4: 543–71.

Ibbitson, John. 2007. 'Say Goodbye to North America's Special Partnership.' *Globe and Mail*, 10 October, A21.

Ibbitson, John, and Rheal Seguin. 2010. 'As Charest Heats Up Battle over Climate Change, Tories Stand to Lose in Quebec.' *Globe and Mail*, 4 February, A1, A5.

Jessop, Bob. 2002. *The Future of the Capitalist State*. Cambridge: Polity.

Keil, Roger, and Rianne Mahon. 2009. 'Introduction.' In *Leviathan Undone? Towards a Political Economy of Scale*. Edited by Roger Keil and Rianne Mahon. Vancouver: UBC Press. 3–23.

Larner, Wendy, and William Walters. 2002. 'The Political Rationality of "New Regionalism:" Toward a Genealogy of Region.' *Theory and Society* 31: 391–432.

Lee, Marc, and Bruce Campbell. 2006. 'Putting Canadians at Risk.' Ottawa: Centre for Policy Alternatives. http://www.policyalternatives.ca/publications/reports/putting-canadians-risk. Accessed 22 November 2011.

Lefebre, Henri. [1974]1991. *The Production of Space*. Translated by Donald Nicholson-Smith. Oxford: Blackwell.

MacLeod, Ian. 2008. 'Free Ride into U.S. Is Over, Analyst says.' *Ottawa Journal*, 1 November, A1–A2.

Macmillan, Kathleen, 2009. 'A Canada-US Regulatory Accord.' Carleton University Canada–U.S. Project. Background Papers. In *From Correct to Inspired: A Blueprint for Canada-US Engagement*, 68-79 http://s3.amazonaws.com/zanran_storage/www.carleton.ca/ContentPages/8379237.pdf. Accessed 22 November 2011.

Manley, John, and Gordon Giffin. 2009. 'A Table for Two, Not Three.' *Globe and Mail*, 5 May, A13.

Mittelman, James. 1996. 'Rethinking the New Regionalism in the Context of Globalization.' *Global Governance* 2: 189–213.

McBride, Stephen. 2006. 'Reconfiguring Sovereignty: NAFTA Chapter 11 Dispute Settlement Procedures and the Issue of Public–Private Authority.' *Canadian Journal of Political Science* 39, no. 4: 755–77.

Moens, Alexander. 2010. 'Canada–U.S. Relations in 2010.' Backgrounder. Fraser Forum. 14–19 March. www.fraserinstitute.org/WorkArea/DownloadAsset.aspx?id=15723. Accessed 22 November 2011.

Moens, Alexander, and Michael Cust. 2008. 'Saving the North America Security and Prosperity Partnership: The Case for a North America Standards and Regulatory Area.' http://www.fraserinstitute.org/research-news/display.aspx?id=13414. Accessed 22 November 2011.

Nader, Ralph. 2011. 'Beware Deep Integration.' *Toronto Star*, 26 April. http://

www.thestar.com/Opinion/EditorialOpinion/article/980795. Accessed 22 November 2011.

Neumann, Iver. 2003. 'A Region-Building Approach.' In *Theories of New Regionalisms: A Palgrave Reader*. Edited by Fredrik Söderbaum and Timothy Shaw. Basingstoke: Palagrave Macmillan. 160–78.

North American Competitiveness Council (NACC). 2008. 'Meeting the Global Challenge: Private Sector Priorities for the Security and Prosperity Partnership of North America.' http://www.uschamber.com/reports/nacc-report-meeting-global-challenge. Accessed 22 November 2011.

– 2007. 'Building a Secure and Competitive North America: 2007 Report to Leaders.' August. http://www.uschamber.com/reports/building-secure-and-competitive-north-america-2007-report-leaders-north-american-competitive. Accessed 22 November 2011.

North American Forum (NAF). n.d. http://en.wikipedia.org/wiki/North_American_Forum. Accessed 22 November 2011.

Pastor, Robert. 2010. 'Should Canada, Mexico, and the United States Replace Two Dysfunctional Bilateral Relationships with a North American Community?' 14th Annual Distinguished Lecture in Political Science, Department of Political Science, University of Alberta, 15 March.

– 2008. 'The Future of North America; Replacing a Bad Neighbour Policy.' *Foreign Affairs* 87, no. 4: 85–90.

Patterson, Kelly. 2007. 'Continental Divide: All Eyes Are on Montebello.' *Ottawa Citizen*, 18 August, B1.

Pickard, Miguel. 2005. 'Trinational Elites Map North American Future.' http:// www.cipamericas.org/archives/1357. Accessed 22 November 2011.

Potter, Mitch. 2009. 'Canada Warms to Idea of Perimeter.' *Toronto Star*, 27 December, A1.

Rumsford, Chris. 2006. 'Theorizing Borders.' *European Journal of Social Theory* 9: 155–69.

Sassen, Saskia. 2007. 'Toward a Multiplication of Specialized Assemblages of Territory, Authority, and Rights.' *Parallax* 13, no. 1: 87–94.

– 2006. *Territory, Authority, Rights: From Medieval to Global Assemblages*. Princeton: Princeton University Press.

Sears, Robin. 2009. 'Overcoming the Obstacles to Community.' Carleton University Canada–U.S. Project. Background Papers. In *From Correct to Inspired: A Blueprint for Canada–U.S. Engagement*, 197–212. http://s3.amazonaws. com/zanran_storage/www.carleton.ca/ContentPages/8379237.pdf. Accessed 22 November 2011.

Security and Prosperity Partnership (SPP). 2009. 'Joint Statement by

North American Leaders.' http://news.gc.ca/web/article-eng.do?m=/ index&nid=472889. Accessed 22 November 2011.

– 2007a. 'Common Regulatory Principles and Inventory of Best Practices.' http://www.spp-psp.gc.ca/eic/site/spp-psp.nsf/eng/00094.html. Accessed 22 November 2011.

– 2007b. 'Statement by Ministers.' http://www.spp-psp.gc.ca/eic/site/spp-psp.nsf/eng/00046.html. Accessed 22 November 2011.

– 2006. 'Leaders' Joint Statement.' http://www.spp.gov/pdf/leaders_state-ment_2007_english.pdf. Accessed 22 November 2011.

– 2005a. Security and Prosperity Partnership of North America. http://www. spp-psp.gc.ca/eic/site/spp-psp.nsf/eng/home. Accessed 22 November 2011.

– 2005b 'Leaders' Statement: Security and Prosperity Partnership of North American Established.' http://www.spp-psp.gc.ca/eic/site/spp-psp.nsf/eng/00057.html. Accessed 22 November 2011.

Shamir, Ronen. 2005. 'Without Borders? Notes on Globalization as a Mobility Regime.' *Sociological Theory* 23, no. 2: 197–217.

Simpson, Jeffrey. 2010. 'While Mexicans Fume, Our Reputation and Revenues Take a Hit.' *Globe and Mail*, 2 February, A13.

Slaughter, Anne-Marie. 2004. *A New World Order*. Princeton: Princeton University Press.

Stewart-Patterson, David. 2007. 'North American Competitiveness Council Seeks to Strengthen Continental Prosperity.' http://www.ceocouncil.ca/publication/north-american-competitiveness-council-seeks-to-strengthen-continental-prosperity-article-by-david-stewart-patterson-in-fraser-forum. Accessed 22 November 2011.

Toneguzzi, Mario. 2009. 'FTA Benefits Being Offset, Beatty Says.' *Edmonton Journal*, 16 September, F1.

Walters, William. 2004. 'The Political Rationality of European Integration.' In *Global Governmentality: Governing International Spaces*. Edited by Wendy Larner and William Walters. London: Routledge. 155–73.

Index

Studies in Comparative Political Economy and Public Policy